Conquests & Consequences

D1602483

Conquests & Consequences

The American West from Frontier to Region

Carol L. Higham

University of North Carolina at Charlotte

William H. Katerberg

Calvin College

A CO-PUBLICATION OF

HARLAN DAVIDSON, INC.

773 Glenn Avenue
Wheeling, Illinois 60090
www.harlandavidson.com

THE BUFFALO BILL HISTORICAL CENTER

720 Sheridan Avenue
Cody, Wyoming 82414
www.bbhc.org

Visit us on the World Wide Web at www.harlandavidson.com

Library of Congress Cataloging-in-Publication Data

Higham, C. L.
  Conquests & consequences : the American West from frontier to region /
Carol L. Higham, William H. Katerberg.
    p. cm.
  Includes bibliographical references and index.
  ISBN 978-0-88295-270-3 (alk. paper)
  1. West (U.S.)—History. 2. West (U.S.)—Ethnic relations. 3. West (U.S.)—
Colonization. 4. Imperialism—Social aspects—West U.S.)—History. 5. Indians of
North America—West (U.S.)—History. 6. Acculturation—West (U.S.)—History.
7. Frontier and pioneer life—West (U.S.) 8. Frontier thesis. 9. West (U.S.)—
Historiography. 10. Regionalism—West (U.S.)—History. I. Katerberg,
William H. (William Henry), 1966- II. Title. III. Title: Conquests and consequences.
F591.H64 2009
978—dc22

                                                                    2009028089

Front cover art: *Judith Basin Encounter: When Charlie and Pablo had a Bad Day on the
Freeway,* George Gogas (b. 1929), acrylic on canvas, 32 x 59 inches, 1996
Back cover art: *Buffalo Bill–The Scout,* 1924, by Gertrude Vanderbilt Whitney (1875–
1942). Bronze, 149 inches; cast by Roman Bronze Works, N.Y. *Buffalo Bill Historical
Center, Wyoming. Gift of the artist. 3.58. BBHC photo by Sean Campbell.*
Cover design: Linda Gaio

Manufactured in the United States of America
11 10 09 1 2 3 MG

Contents

Photographs and Illustrations

Contents   ⅋   **vii**

Maps

Preface and Acknowledgments

Conquests and Consequences arose out of a group of discussions hosted at the Cody Institute for Western American Studies. Dr. Robert Pickering of the Buffalo Bill Historical Center (BBHC) invited teachers of Western American history from all types of institutions (large and small universities, West Coast, East Coast, Midwestern, Southern, private and tribal) to discuss what could be done to improve and aid the teaching of Western American history at the college level. Between barbecues and tours of the museum, we broke into intense discussion groups and made wish lists of what we would like: web pages, maps, oral history projects, research money, and, above all, an accessible, vibrant, and affordable survey textbook.

One afternoon we made an inventory of what we wanted in such a text, from practical matters such as size and list price to a *long* list of topics we wanted included. Several things had already become obvious. First, a text that covered all the topics suggested would be several volumes long and very expensive and therefore impractical. Second, we all realized why most western history texts suffer from too few illustrations and maps: the high cost of obtaining permission for publication. Finally, most textbooks already on the market lack cohesive narratives or clear, central themes: using a textbook that reads like a laundry list of facts and dates makes both teaching and learning difficult.

1902.—IRMA HOTEL.

The Irma Hotel, 1902. William "Buffalo Bill" Cody helped found Cody, Wyoming, in 1895. He built the hotel in 1902, naming it after his daughter. Luminaries such as Annie Oakley, Calamity Jane, and Frederic Remington stayed at the Irma. Buffalo Bill himself had a suite in the hotel, which visitors today can rent. *Buffalo Bill Historical Center, Cody, Wyoming; MS6.6.A.2.4.2.41*

As our group conversation continued at the Irma Hotel (opened by Buffalo Bill himself in 1902) later that night, we realized we could solve these problems. Instead of writing one long book that attempts, but could never succeed, to cover everything, we thought we could write a central text, one that introduces various issues associated with the U.S. West, outlines the history of the region, introduces key figures in that history, and sets out some of the major approaches to the study of that history. With a dynamic, relatively concise and highly affordable "core" survey text in place, we planned to complement and expand its scope with a series of smaller books that look at the American West from distinct perspectives: women, African Americans, religion, water, and the environment, to name but a few. These texts could be used with the main text or separately.

Then we—Carol and Will—jumped in (cowboy boots first, so to speak) and volunteered to write the survey text and edit the series of satellite texts. No one discouraged us. Just the opposite. Our colleagues who teach western history, Andrew J. Davidson, our publisher, and Bob Pickering of the BBHC actually encouraged us.

We immediately recognized the BBHC as a remarkable resource. With an archive and five separate museums (environmental, Buffalo Bill,

Western art, Plains Indians, and guns) under one roof, it could provide us with a wide range of interesting illustrations. Thanks to the BBHC's generosity and support, it is safe to say that *Conquests and Consequences* is the most lavishly illustrated Western history textbook to date.

Finally, we decided that this core text would address a central set of questions: How have diverse societies and empires shaped and reshaped the region over the centuries? In the American era, has the West been more of a colony or a region? When was the American West a colony? When exactly did it become a region? Is it today a national and international center of power in its own right? How does the concept of the frontier function in the West? *Instructors,* we designed this book as a launching pad for discussion and debate, both between you and your students and you and the text. Tell your students where you agree with us. Where you disagree, we hope you make a case for how wrong we are. *Students,* we want you to see what historians actually do: we argue—a lot. Behind these arguments, however, lie the critical analyses and interpretive perspectives that are essential to critical thinking, to thinking historically. Historians cannot do anything without evidence to study and are obliged to be accurate and faithful to the evidence. But historians also must decide where to begin and end their narratives, who the main characters are, what the essential issues, topics, and questions are and which ones we can safely leave out. In other words, we have to decide what *not* to include in every book, essay, classroom lecture, or assignment we prepare. When you write exams or papers, you must do the same. We trust that using this book in a course will leave you better informed about the history of the American West, but we also hope that it will encourage you to learn the habit and skills of thinking historically.

We could not even have begun this project without the visionary support of Dr. Robert Pickering and Dr. Robert Shimp of the BBHC and Andrew J. Davidson of Harlan Davidson, Inc. The staff at the BBHC's McCracken Research Library looked at our wish list and didn't bat an eye. Over the course of a week, they continuously brought out gem after gem with which to dazzle us. Dr. Kurt Graham, Ann Marie Donoghue, Meghan Peacock, Sean Campbell, Mary Robinson, Karling Abernathy, and Heidi Kennedy helped make this process easy. At Harlan Davidson, Inc., Linda Gaio helped us find images to supplement those from the BBHC. She also designed the book's cover. Our way west also was made easier by the historians on whose work we have built, whether or not we agree with them. The names of these scholars are listed in the suggested readings at the end of each chapter. Finally, readers of the second draft of the book confirmed for us that our approach was an appealing one and pressed us to fulfill its potential by filling in gaps and smoothing out rough passages.

It has been an exhilarating experience, both daunting and fun, to step out of our familiar areas of expertise and the relative privacy of the classroom and write a survey textbook. All errors of fact and foolhardy interpretations are, of course, of our own making and responsibility.

Carol L. Higham
William H. Katerberg

CHAPTER ONE

Introduction

I met a traveler from an antique land
Who said:—Two vast and trunkless legs of stone
Stand in the desert. Near them on the sand,
Half sunk, a shatter'd visage lies, whose frown
And wrinkled lip and sneer of cold command
Tell that its sculptor well those passions read
Which yet survive, stamp'd on these lifeless things,
The hand that mock'd them and the heart that fed.
And on the pedestal these words appear:
"My name is Ozymandias, king of kings:
Look on my works, ye mighty, and despair!"
Nothing beside remains: round the decay
Of that colossal wreck, boundless and bare,
The lone and level sands stretch far away.

—Percy Bysshe Shelley, "Ozymandias" (1818)

All empires fall. And this holds true for the empires of the American West. The first ones, regional Indian empires, fell nearly a thousand years ago. That of the Anasazi in the Southwest did in the 1300s, as did that of the mound builders of Cahokia, across the Mississippi River from modern-day St. Louis, in the late 1300s. So, too, will the American empire of our time. The Anasazi built canals, irrigation systems, towns and cities, highways, and magnificent ceremonial buildings, but their society eventually collapsed under the weight of geographic expansion, population growth, and drought. The people scattered, leaving a cultural legacy among the present-day Navajo and Hopi. The ruins of Chaco Canyon, in New Mexico, stand as a mute testimony both to the greatness of the Anasazi society and its fall. The mounds of Cahokia and other former cities of the mound-building societies in the Midwest and South are hardly recognizable today as evidence of empires lost. Most of them have partially eroded and lie under a blanket of grass and trees. Like the Anasazi, the mound builders grew beyond their resources, lost control of peoples they had subjugated, and eventually scattered. The Spanish, Mexican, Russian, French, and British peoples also built outposts and empires in the American West, leaving behind place names, ruins, people, and cultural trappings. What monuments will the people of the United States leave in the West? What legacies will survive them when their empire crumbles?

We Americans do not easily imagine ourselves or the United States disappearing into desert wastes or being succeeded someday by a stronger empire. But neither did the Anasazi nor the mound builders. For that matter, neither did the Spanish, Mexicans, French, Russians, nor British at the height of their influence. We Americans also generally do not think of the United States as an empire, except perhaps as an empire of freedom. But ask the Indians and Mexicans whose land Americans took if the United States is an empire. And haven't we done our best to try to conquer and remake nature with our monstrous dams, endless highways, and sprawling cities? We even try to tell wolves, bears, and buffalo where they can and cannot live.

A story from a 2007 issue of *High Country News* (a monthly magazine that examines social and ecological trends in the West) quotes Tom Wright, an archeologist from Phoenix, describing yet another lost Southwest Indian society. "The Hohokam kept extending their canal systems farther and farther from the [Salt River]," he explains. "You tend to find their sites under present-day Chandler [a suburb of Phoenix] or out in Goodyear. They kept increasing from the valley outward. The irrigation canals were the system that fed growth. Water was the lifeblood that flowed through these communities." Dig under the streets and parking lots of Phoenix and nearby towns, and not far beneath the surface you will find remnants of the Hohokam society. Wright sees irony and a warning in their story. "Now the lifeblood [of Phoenix] is traffic. The city grows along patterns of freeways. Water doesn't seem to count any more. We take it for granted. But whether people know it or not, like the Hohokams, we are an irrigation society living on imported water, and we're outstripping our resources. Sound familiar?"

It is important for us as Americans studying our past to see ourselves in this light, as merely one set of many peoples who have occupied the

West. We live with the ghosts, ruins, descendents, and heritages of societies past. It would be foolish pride to not see something of ourselves in their stories and not wonder: What has our history wrought and what will it bring? Indeed, with Native American communities in some parts of the West growing steadily in the twentieth century, and with the explosive growth of Chicano and Latino populations in recent decades, especially in the Southwest but also across the nation, we might wonder about the legacy of the American conquest. What will it mean in a couple of decades when brown people begin to outnumber white people in more and more parts of the West? Will such demographic changes matter little to the mainstream of U.S. culture? Will it signal the emergence of a new society or perhaps a successful reconquest of the region by past societies? And will it matter in 2050 whether the American West is a predominately brown, black, red, or white empire if the water runs out?

We are, obviously, still in the midst of creating our own history, so we cannot know the ultimate fate of the American empire. Will it fade slowly, like the European empires in the West in the seventeenth, eighteenth, and early nineteenth centuries and be succeeded and assimilated? Will it fail more suddenly and completely, like the empires of the Anasazi, Hohokam, and Cahokia? Or will it endure for a long time in some form, even if dramatically changed?

These questions—about empires of the past, the American West today, and the future of the region—point to the central themes in this brief history. How should we conceptualize that history? Any history book you read makes assumptions about the way the world works and what is important. No book is neutral or objective. The authors have to decide where to start and end the book, what people, topics, and issues to put at the center of the story, what to mention, and what to leave out. The choices we make as authors reflect our values and our views of how the world does and ought to work. In addition, no book is written in a historical vacuum. The issues that define our own time also shape what interests us as citizens and scholars when we study the past. And like all textbooks, this one is informed by the work of many generations of historians, and we cannot help but tell our story with them in mind. Some of their stories we reject and write against; others we use, build on, or subtly transform. The following sections of this chapter describe important interpretations of Western history and introduce the major themes in this book. Keep

Frederick Jackson Turner, 1906. *Courtesy of the Henry E. Huntington Library, San Marino, California*

these in mind as you read later chapters, but also take the time to read between the lines, to think about the assumptions that we make at different places in the book.

The point of doing this is not to assume bad faith on our part, any more than we would about the authors of other books. We have done our best to be careful, honest, and self-critical, but no authors are ever fully aware of how their personal views shape their writing. Different ways of seeing the past make reading different books about the same subject interesting. They are also what make history a dynamic field, spawning the arguments, controversies, and schools of thought that shape the historical profession.

Frontiers

The most influential historian of the American West has been Frederick Jackson Turner (1861–1932). Even though most of his work focused on Midwestern frontiers in the nineteenth century and Southern frontiers in

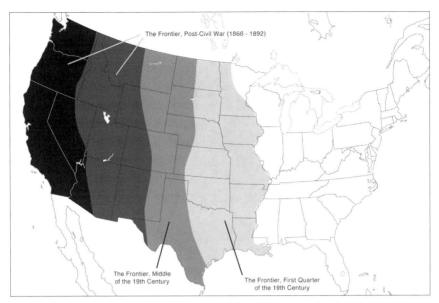

The Frontier, Post-Civil War (1866 - 1892)

The Frontier, Middle of the 19th Century

The Frontier, First Quarter of the 19th Century

A Visual Representation of Turner's Frontier Thesis. From *Two Mythic Wests*, by R. Douglas Francis, in *One West, Two Myths II*, ed. C. L. Higham and Robert Thacker (Calgary: University of Calgary Press, 2006). *Used by permission.*

the Colonial Period and Early Republic, he is remembered foremost for his work on the American West. His famous "frontier thesis" was the cornerstone of one of the first academic papers he presented to other scholars as a young historian, and it shaped how most historians, even most Americans, viewed the American West for the next hundred years.

Turner grew up in Wisconsin in the 1860s and 1870s. As a boy he caught glimpses of the frontier, from homesteading farmers to fur trappers. His father was a newspaper writer and passed on his gift for storytelling and explaining events to his son. When Turner went to graduate school to get his Ph.D. in history in the 1880s, he turned to his boyhood experiences and to the history of the frontier in his home region as a research topic.

In 1893, Turner went to Chicago to attend the meeting of the American Historical Association (AHA) and give a paper. The Columbian Exposition, a world fair, was being held in Chicago that same year to celebrate the 400TH anniversary of Christopher Columbus's "discovery" of the Americas. Also in town at the time was William "Buffalo Bill" Cody, another influential storyteller who was presenting his version of the his-

Buffalo Bill's Wild West, Historical Sketches & Programme, 1905. The program cover includes classic images of the mythic American West, but also "Rough Riders of the World" images from South America, Asia, Russia, and Europe, linking the frontier in the U.S. to imperial conquests in the wider world. *Buffalo Bill Historical Center, Cody, Wyoming; MS6.6.a1.12*

tory of the American West. In fact, Buffalo Bill invited the members of the AHA to his Wild West show, which included real cowboys and Indians who had personally fought in the recently concluded Indian wars of the 1870s and 1880s. Cody was a great showman and entertainer, but he, like the professional historians of the AHA, also considered himself an educator. His "living" version of Western American history—replete with gun-toting, trick-shooting cowboys and staged battles between cowboys, cavalry soldiers, and Indians—was certainly more vivid, and probably more influential than that of Turner, at least in the popular imagination.

Turner's paper, "The Significance of the Frontier in American History," did not receive a great deal of notice in Chicago in 1893. But Turner refined his "frontier thesis" in later papers and books and gave version after version of it over the course of many years in speeches to civic groups and academic audiences. In the process, he became an influential member of the AHA and a famous historian, moving from the University of Wisconsin to Harvard University in 1910.

Turner's frontier thesis is deceptively simple. He argued that in every generation of American history, from earliest times to the end of the nineteenth century, there had been a frontier. For as long as they had been on the continent, Americans had always enjoyed the opportunity to escape settled society and go to the wilderness to start a new life. For all sorts of reasons—a desire for adventure, for land of their own, for better land than they had, or to escape the law, debtors, or unwanted families—many did just that, leaving behind the familiar comforts of settled society and adapting to the primitive conditions of an often harsh, strange environment. "The wilderness masters the colonist. It finds him in a European dress, industries, tools, modes of travel, and thought," Turner said memorably. "It takes him from the railroad car and puts him in the birchbark canoe. It strips off the garments of civilization and arrays him in a hunting shirt and the moccasin. It puts him in the log cabin of the Cherokee and Iroquois and runs an Indian palisade around him. Before long he has gone to planting Indian corn and plowing with a sharp stick; he shouts the war cry and takes the scalp in orthodox Indian fashion." At first, then, the frontier changes the pioneers, forcing them to adapt. But, gradually, with their axes and plows, they transform the frontier, turning wilderness into farms, and then building towns and cities and a new society. Then, in the next generation, new pioneers head out to the next frontier, farther West, to do it again.

This cycle of returning to the primitive, transforming conditions of the frontier, and then building a new society out of the "wilderness," had defined U.S. history in Turner's view and, over the course of two centuries, had made its people less and less European and more and more American. On the frontier, Americans had to be pragmatic and inventive, giving up Old World ways and finding new ways to do things. "The result is that to the frontier the American intellect owes its striking characteristics," Turner explained. "That coarseness and strength combined with acuteness and inquisitiveness; that practical, inventive turn of mind, quick to find expedients . . . that restless, nervous energy; that dominant individualism, working for good and for evil, and withal that buoyancy and exuberance which comes with freedom—these are the traits of the frontier, or traits called out elsewhere because of the existence of the frontier." The frontier was the engine that made ethnically and culturally diverse Europeans into a new American people.

Ironically, Turner arrived at his powerful theory of American history at the very time he believed the frontier was ceasing to exist. He cited the national census of 1890 in his paper and noted that it proclaimed the end of a clear line between wilderness frontier and settled society in the American West. A concern, even a fear, about the future was implicit in Turner's frontier thesis, a fear shared by many Americans in the 1890s. If free land and the frontier had long been the source of the nation's wealth, its people's freedom, and the driving force in the creation of the American character, what did a future without a frontier hold? Was America doomed to decline, materially, morally, and politically? Such concerns led some Americans in Turner's time to advocate expansion overseas.

While no one can deny the influence that Turner's thesis had on the American mind, among scholars especially, it has many holes. It all but ignores Indians, Mexicans, Asians, and women. It is so focused on farming that it largely neglects the roles of mining, logging, oil, towns and cities, the railroads, big business, and the federal government in the development of the West. In addition, since it is more than one hundred years old, what good does Turner's thesis do a person who is trying to make sense of the history of the West in the twenty-first century?

While we can see Turner's story in books and TV shows like *Little House on the Prairie,* it was Buffalo Bill Cody's Wild West show that would define the TV and movie "Western." During the course of his

STRANGE PEOPLE FROM OUR NEW POSSESSIONS.

FAMILIES OF COSTA RICANS, SANDWICH ISLANDERS AND FILIPINOS.

We have delayed the publication of this historical narrative until the last possible moment, in hopes—which as we go to press we are gratified to be able to announce have been fully realized—that our special agent sent to Porto Rico and the Sandwich and the Philippine Islands would be able to secure the finest representatives of the strange and interesting aboriginals of the West Indies and the intermediate and remote Pacific isles, now grouped by the fate of war, the hand of progress and the conquering march of civilization under Old Glory's protecting folds.

These insular and oceanic chiefs and warriors, with their dark-eyed wives and wildly cunning children, uniquely and fascinatingly complete the ethnological scope of the Congress of Rough Riders of the World, which thus adds the last and greatest of living novelties and racial object lessons to keep step with the marvelous, potential and gigantic expansion of the nation ; the most stirring and romantic episodes in whose history it alone perpetuates, in both personality and heroic action. In semi-civilized and barbaric dress, ornaments and arms, these roamers of tropical jungles and surf-beaten volcanic shores will faithfully illustrate the martial, heathen and home peculiarities of their lives of intermingled feud, pastimes and superstitions ; introducing extraordinary feats of strength and skill with primitive weapons, singular and sinuous dances, supple gymnastics, pagan ceremonies and peculiar sports, such as comparatively but few Christian eyes have ever seen.

Paradoxical, too, as it would naturally appear in connection with people born and raised under such insular conditions, there will be found among them horsemen fully meriting the high compliment of a place in COLONEL CODY's Congress of Rough Riders of the World ; equestrians full of nerve and dash and sure of seat, even if their accoutrements seem outlandish and their methods surprisingly grotesque to continental riders and audiences. Elsewhere they will receive and everywhere certainly secure, the wider recognition their fine physical characteristics and novel accomplishments so well deserve. Meantime, COL. CODY begs now to, for the first time, cordially introduce them to his and their future fellow-countrymen.

Strange People from Our New Possessions. Taken from a Buffalo Bill Cody Wild West show program, in 1899 or 1900. The image and text illustrate Cody's racial thought and his goal of using his show to educate his audiences, and they reveal the connection he made between U.S. expansion across the frontier West and expansion overseas in the late 1800s and early 1900s. *Buffalo Bill Historical Center, Cody, Wyoming; MS6.6.A.2.2.2.63* long and illustrious life, William F. Cody was a buffalo hunter, army scout, and hunting guide, but he was foremost a showman. The writers of dime novels had made him a legend as early as the 1870s. In 1883 he created his first Wild West Show, holding rodeo-style events and featuring trick shooting and riding and staged battles with real Indians, including Sitting Bull, the famous Sioux chief, for a time in 1885. Out of Buffalo Bill's Wild West Show evolved the "Western," one of the most popular film and television genres of the twentieth century and today. It's hard for us to think of the West without images of John Wayne, Clint Eastwood, or Kevin Costner and TV shows like *Gunsmoke, Bonanza,* or HBO's *Deadwood* leaping to mind. This is the West won from Indians and Mexicans, the West of "last stands" by Texans at the Alamo and by General Custer and the Seventh Cavalry at the Little Big Horn River, the West of wagon trains attacked by "savages," and the West of cattle drives, saloons, brothels, rustlers, and shootouts: the West people around the world know and love as "Wild." Cody connected the American conquest of its Western frontier to European imperialism, staging scenes of European conquests and battles in Asia and Africa in his show. In 1899 and the early years of the twentieth century he began to incorporate Filipinos and other people from America's "New Possessions" into his show, after the United States had conquered and colonized the Philippines and a variety of small island chains in the Pacific Ocean. It is not only scholars who see the settlement of the frontier West as a story of imperial conquest. Cody and many other Americans at the time did so too.

Together, the stories of Frederick Jackson Turner and Buffalo Bill Cody have shaped the popular mythology and history of the American nation, though most have forgotten Cody's eager embrace of overseas empire and imperialist adventure. More than Turner's thesis, the idea of the "Wild West" acknowledges the Indians, but it treats all Indian peoples as primitive, even savage, and as defeated peoples fated to disappear as "Americans" (read white people) conquered the frontier and settled the land. When news reporters depict presidents like Ronald Reagan (who played cowboys in films before he became president in 1981) as acting like cowboys or sheriffs, taking on the enemies of the United States, they are drawing on the idea that America remains a nation defined by its frontier era: Americans are rough, raw, a little uncivilized, freedom loving, individualistic, inventive, and always ready for a fight.

Imperialism lies at the heart of a second scholarly way of defining frontiers. In a book that compares the American frontier to frontiers in South Africa and Canada, Howard Lamar and Leonard Thompson defined frontiers as "zones of interaction" between indigenous people living in a territory and intruders. Frontiers are not wildernesses, but peopled. A frontier "opens," Lamar and Thompson argued, the moment the intruders arrive and encounter the native peoples of a territory. The encounter often begins peacefully, if the native peoples do not perceive an immediate threat to their safety. The two groups often engage in trade and many times the intruders send missionaries into the natives' villages. Conflict invariably begins when the native peoples recognize the newcomers as a threat to them and their way of life—because the latter bring disease, try to take control of the land and other resources, or try to conquer or enslave the native peoples. A frontier "closes" when one group or the other asserts control over the territory.

In all three territories analyzed in Lamar and Thompson's book, the frontiers closed at the end of the nineteenth century, when Indian groups surrendered to American and Canadian forces, signed treaties, and agreed to live on reservations, and, in the case of South Africa, when the British finally conquered native groups such as the Zulu. The outcomes varied significantly. The Indians of North America had all but died out by the end of the nineteenth century and did not at the time constitute a significant source of labor. In contrast, white South Africans segregated the black population of the nation and implemented a racially based system known as Apartheid, with black South Africans remaining the majority of the population and a repressed, cheap labor force for most of the twentieth century. Like Turner's frontier thesis, it is not clear how that of Lamar and Thompson helps us to interpret the American West since the closing of the frontier. It does, however, remind us to pay careful attention to the legacies of the conquest of the region, among them the descendents of conquered peoples in the twentieth century, and to the fact that opening the West for white Americans required closing it to other peoples.

Lamar and Thompson's work influenced students such as Patricia Limerick, a member of a new generation of historians of the American West who rose to prominence in the 1980s and became known as the New Western Historians. Limerick and her colleagues attacked Turner's frontier thesis and instead said that the story of the American West is one of "invasion, conquest, colonization, exploitation, development, [and] expansion of the world market." They emphasized the place of women, racial minorities, urban development and other topics neglected by Turner. They especially wanted to move beyond frontiers and think about the West in ways that would connect the legacies and processes of the so-called frontier era to the twentieth century. In so doing, these scholars echoed "metropolitan" themes that historians in Canada had been emphasizing for decades.

Empires and Metropolises

In the revolution that created the United States, rebellious Americans rejected and pushed out the British Empire. The Loyalists, who rejected the revolution and kept faith with Britain, helped to found Canada. The symbolic difference between rebels and Loyalists underscores the Canadian version of the history of the North American West: the "metropolitan" thesis. While the frontier thesis stresses leaving the Old World (settled society) behind and rejecting its inherited ways of doing things, the metropolitan thesis speaks to the enduring influence of Old World institutions, values, and methods on the frontier.

When they looked at the history of Canada during the Colonial Era, from the 1600s to the 1800s, historians like Harold Innis and J. M. S. Careless saw the influence of powerful political, economic, and cultural institutions. Political leaders and businessmen in the capital cities of Old World empires such as France and Britain—metropolitan centers—controlled the colonies. Innis used the fur trade as an example, showing how banks, investors, government officials, and European merchants ultimately determined the prices commanded by North American furs, both at the trading post and in European markets. To be sure, frontier technologies such as birch-bark canoes and York boats made a difference and Indians and colonial French fur traders sometimes had a strong bargaining position. Nevertheless, in the long run, the greater financial, military, and industrial resources of France gave it control of the frontier—over what Innis and Careless referred to as the "periphery." From this point of view, the frontier is not the center of the story, but a side note on the edge of empire. After Great Britain defeated France in North America in the French and Indian War (1754–63), the territory of New France (which includes much of present-day Canada) became British territory. Now, instead of Paris controlling the frontier periphery of Canada, London did so. Later on, as colonial society evolved in the nineteenth century and Canada became more independent of Great Britain, Canadian cities like Montreal, Ottawa, and Toronto controlled the Western and Northern frontiers of Canada. Along with this military, political, and economic control came cultural and intellectual influence.

Canadian historians thus have tended to emphasize the enduring influence of Old World ways on the frontier. Indeed, in the twentieth century, they have shown how metropolitan centers in the United States have influenced Canada—the political and economic power coming from the United States (New York, Chicago, Washington, D.C., and Los Angeles) and bringing American cultural influence with it in the form of television shows, films, popular music, books (including textbooks), newspapers, and magazines.

What might the history of the American West look like if we applied the metropolitan thesis to it? Now the emphasis would be on the influence

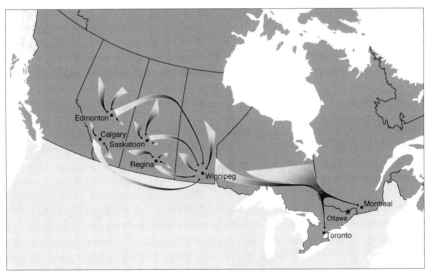

A Visual Representation of the Theory of Metropolitanism. The map shows the links between peripheral regions in the Canadian West and its regional metropolitan centers and the links between those cities and larger metropolitan centers in eastern Canada. From *Two Mythic Wests*, by R. Douglas Francis, in *One West, Two Myths II,* ed. C. L. Higham and Robert Thacker (Calgary: University of Calgary Press, 2006). *Used by permission.*

that politicians, administrators, and army officials in Washington, D.C., had over the frontier. We would examine how the American military and settlers conquered the region, taking control of it from Indian nations and Mexico. We would highlight the power of investors, corporations, banks, and railroads based in big Eastern and Midwestern cities like New York and Chicago over the course of events in the West. We would look at the West as something like a "colony" of the eastern United States. Instead of Turner's ideas about the frontier as the driving force behind the creation of a new society, we would emphasize what the West inherited from the societies that dispatched settlers, businesses, and laborers to the region. In short, we would turn the frontier thesis upside down, looking at the influence of Great Britain, France, and Spain on the American colonies and Mexico, followed by the influence of the Northeast, Midwest, and South on the American West. We would not have to throw out Turner's ideas completely, but instead of focusing on the frontier on its own, we would focus on how the West's relationship with the larger United States and wider world did much to define it. In examining the twentieth century, we would stress how the West evolved from a sort of colony to a power center in its own right, one with metropolitan centers that exercised influence in the United States as well as around the world. New Western Historians such as Richard White, William Cronon, and William Robins have emphasized these kinds of themes. For example, in a book entitled *Nature's Metropolis,* Cronon showed how railroads, manufacturers, and retailers in Chicago profoundly shaped, even controlled, the economic development of the West during the late nineteenth century.

In this book, we follow and adapt aspects of both the frontier and the metropolitan approaches. From the frontier thesis, we take Turner's insights into how people adapt their cultural traditions and lifeways to new environmental and social situations when coming into a place that they, at least, consider a frontier. Part of that adaptation, as Lamar and Thompson emphasize, is a response to the native peoples who already live in the region and call it home. This encounter between intruders and indigenous peoples, however mutual or violent, changes both. Nevertheless, as metropolitan theorists insist, we argue that in the long run major centers of political, economic, and cultural influence outside the frontier exercise a powerful, even dominant, influence over it and over the ways of life of both native peoples and frontier settlers. The frontier, then, is not a place to escape from Old Worlds, but a place where invaders transplant and adapt Old World ways as they encounter the indigenous peoples already living there.

Regions and Regionalism

The New Western Historians used metropolitan ideas and emphasized conquest and racial conflict in the books and essays they wrote and the classes they taught in the 1980s and 1990s, but they also called attention to what they called "place." Another problem with Turner's frontier thesis, they said, was that he focused too narrowly on the frontier as the "process" through which a supposedly unsettled wilderness became a new American society. As a result, he neglected to look closely at the West as a "place" in its own right, one that existed before and after his frontier era. To be fair, in his later writings Turner did analyze what he called "sectionalism," or regionalism, but these writings did not have the same influence as did his frontier thesis. How does it help us to think of the West as a place, or a region, and look at its history from that perspective?

First, one must define *region*. There are several ways to do so. A distinct geography or climate can constitute a region. So too can a particular type of economy. Finally, common cultures, social institutions, and forms of government can define regions. The term *regionalism* refers to people's sense of identity as residents of the same place and to efforts to promote their collective interest. Does the West as a whole fall into any of these definitions of region?

To address this question, we might also pause to ponder the physical boundaries of the American West. In 1992 in an essay in *Montana: The Magazine of Western History,* historian Walter Nugent reported that when asked to define the geographical boundaries of the American West, news reporters, historians, and other Western writers gave very different answers. Some said that the West starts at the Mississippi River and includes everything to the Pacific Coast. Others disagreed, arguing that California and coastal areas of Oregon and Washington are not really part of the West because their climates are too different and their residents too urbane and politically liberal to qualify as Western. The Great Plains, the Southwest, and the Mountain West constitute the true West, this second group contended. Along these lines, an important historian of the West named Walter Prescott Webb argued in *Harper's Magazine* in 1957 that aridity (the lack of rain and other readily available sources of fresh water west of the 100th meridian) defines the region. This point of view helps to explain the massive dam-building projects in the twentieth-century West, as state and federal governments sought to provide fresh water to farmers and cities. By contrast, the Pacific Northwest gets enough water to be considered a coniferous rainforest. Aridity may define Las Vegas, Phoenix, and L.A., but not Seattle and Portland. We have the same kind of problem if we ask what kind of economy the West as a region has. The obvious response is: "When, exactly, and where?"

This book considers the American West as the entire continental United States west of the Mississippi River. It does not include Hawaii and Alaska, except in off-hand comparisons, even though these states have histories with obvious "frontier" and "metropolitan" themes that parallel those of the trans-Mississippi West. We are aware that one can question the concept of "one West," and we acknowledge the histories of the diverse subregions in the larger West (and parallels beyond the borders of the United States). In a survey history textbook, especially a concise one such as this, dividing the West into ever-smaller units is not practical. While there are always going to be exceptions, the themes we apply to the study of Western history are by design broad and thought-provoking, meant to give readers a handle on an otherwise unwieldy mixed bag of facts, dates, names, and events. We hope students will view the West as regional whole, pay attention to geographic, social, and cultural diversity within the larger region, and keep in mind the interaction of the West with the rest of the nation, the world, and the forces we have come to call globalization. After all, the West is not an isolated place but a borderland region, one with close ties especially to northern Mexico and western Canada.

Borderlands

Thinking about the American West as a "borderland" tied to Mexico and Canada offers another way to view the region, most obviously in relation to the Mexican border. Much of the so-called American West was for two hundred years part of the Spanish empire and then part of Mexico, right up until the conclusion of the American War with Mexico in 1848. With the stroke of a pen on a treaty, the substantial "Hispanic" or Mexican population (but still not the Indian population) instantly became U.S. citizens, a part of the "American" people. In the years and decades that followed, not unlike today, the border remained porous, with Mexicans, Mexican Americans, and Indians moving back and forth across it, often living as if it did not exist. In the twentieth century (and continuing today) migrant laborers from Mexico played an integral role in the economy of the American West, along with "Latinos" from Central and South America. Factories, shopping, and tourism in northern Mexico remain important to the U.S. economy. In the next few decades, people of Mexican/Latino descent will eclipse whites to become the largest population group in the many parts of the American West.

From this point of view, the history of New Spain and Spanish culture are an essential part of American history, every bit as important as the history of the colonies of Great Britain on the Atlantic seaboard and the (westward) expansion of Anglo-American culture. In terms of the history of the region, then, we might equally well think of the West as the "North," which is the viewpoint of all of those who lived in New Spain and currently live in Mexico and Central America. A stirring and critically acclaimed film made in the 1980s about migrant workers from Guatemala living in Los Angeles was entitled *El Norte,* a term used by the residents of New Spain for hundreds of years to refer to their far north *frontera.* Mexicans, Mexican Americans, and other Spanish-speaking people are hardly newcomers to the American West. They are longtime citizens and residents, some of whose families owned large *ranchos* and lived prosperous lives for many generations before suddenly finding themselves in the "American West" and watching without recourse as their new "fellow Americans" squatted on and otherwise took their land. This perspective on the West is not a new one. One of Frederick Jackson Turner's first students in the 1890s, Herbert Eugene Bolton, created the field of Spanish borderlands studies, teaching at the University of California at Berkeley for many years and directing the Bancroft Library at Berkeley, with its important collections in sources on the region. Bolton and later borderlands scholars such as John Francis Bannon and Gloria Anzaldúa have strongly disagreed with Turner's vision of an Americanizing frontier and instead have emphasized the ongoing, evolving, and diverse Spanish-Mexican influence in the region.

Thinking in terms of borderlands leads in other directions as well. During much of the history of the American West, the Canadian border to the north did not exist. When, in this book, we discuss the French and English empires in the West, the fur trade, and the history of Indian peoples in the centuries and millennia before the arrival of Europeans, the story crosses freely back and forth across the present-day U.S.-Canadian border. Many of the themes explored here also can be used to study the history of the Canadian West during both the frontier era and the twentieth century. In recent years, a number of films set in the American West have been shot north of the border in Canada. So, practically speaking, if there is any such thing as "one West" (a unified region), it probably includes parts of Canada and Mexico. This book also looks at the influence of migrants from eastern parts of the United States on the West. A good example is the effect of the arrival in the West of many thousands of displaced and desperate Southerners in the mid-twentieth century, during the Great Depression, Dust Bowl, and World War II. The West is a distinct region, but it has never been autonomous. Both its borders and who had the authority to draw them have changed over time and often been disputed.

The West and the World

Finally, we need to view the American West as part of the larger Pacific Rim. Indeed, Asian immigrants have shaped the history of the region since the California Gold Rush of the late 1840s and 1850s. In addition, American trade with China, Japan, and other Asian nations, as well as wars with Japan and in Korea and Vietnam, were important to the evolution of the American West. Americans studying their history usually look to the Atlantic Ocean and to the long relationship between the United States and the nations of Europe. But from the viewpoint of the American West, we also need to cast an eye on the Pacific. Today, more than 6 million people of Asian descent live in the West and more than 12 million in the United States as a whole. That is about 4 percent of the national population, a proportion that will rise to 9 percent by 2050 if projected trends continue. Beyond people, trade and investment increasingly tie the United States to the markets of Asia. For Asians, the "West" has been an eastern frontier. This example also is a good reminder that the American conquest and settlement of the West was part of a larger process of globalization, one that people have come to recognize only recently but began more than 150 years ago when the first Chinese came to the West looking for gold.

Conclusion: Old Issues, New Answers?

As the beginning of this chapter suggests, one of the issues we will consider in this book is the environment. For example, just like every one of the many groups of people who lived in the West before them, Americans have tried to overcome the lack of sufficient amounts of water. For a while, they thought they had the problem solved. However, just as the supposedly conquered native peoples did not fade away but are still in the West and demanding their rights, so, too, has the problem of water (a problem, at least, from the viewpoint of capitalist economic development and unchecked population growth), come back again and again, nature refusing to bend to the will of Anglo-American pioneers and their descendents.

None of the issues we raise are abstract ones, merely the "stuff" of history. On the contrary, the history of the American West remains a tangible part of the day-to-day lives of all the people who live in the region, whether it is the place of Indians and people of Mexican and Latino descent, the question of who should have access to water, the state of the economy, or the relationship of the region to the nation and the world. As much as the region and its residents have changed in the past, they will continue to do so in the future. This does not mean that there are ready, easy lessons to learn from the West of the past. It is more the case that gaining a historical perspective on the region will make some contemporary problems seem more familiar, perhaps helping us to make better sense of them and, at the same time, making the region seem a stranger, more diverse, and even more interesting place than most people today realize.

❧ Suggested Readings ∞

Careless, J. M. S. *Frontier and Metropolis: Regions, Cities, and Identities in Canada before 1914.* Toronto: University of Toronto Press, 1989.

Cronon, William. *Nature's Metropolis: Chicago and the Great West.* New York: W. W. Norton & Company, 1991.

Deloria, Philip, and Neal Salisbury, eds. *A Companion to American Indian History.* Malden, MA: Blackwell Publishing, 2002.

Deverell, William, ed. *A Companion to the American West.* Malden, MA: Blackwell Publishing, 2004.

Etulain, Richard, ed. *Writing Western History: Essays on Major Western Historians.* Albuquerque: University of New Mexico Press, 1991.

Higham, Carol, and Robert Thacker, eds. *One West, Two Myths: Volume II: Essays on Comparison.* Calgary, Alberta: University of Calgary Press, 2007.

Klein, Kerwin Lee. *Frontiers of Historical Imagination: Narrating the European Conquest of Native America, 1890–1990.* Berkeley: University of California Press, 1997.

Lamar, Howard, ed. *The New Encyclopedia of the American West.* New Haven: Yale University Press, 1998.

Lamar, Howard, and Leonard Thompson, eds., *The Frontier in History: North America and Southern Africa Compared.* New Haven: Yale University Press, 1981.

Limerick, Patricia Nelson. *The Legacy of Conquest: The Unbroken Past of the American West.* New York: Norton, 1987. Reissued by Norton with a new preface in 2006.

Limerick, Patricia Nelson, Clyde A. Milner II, and Charles Rankin, eds. *Trails: Toward a New Western History.* Lawrence: University Press of Kansas, 1991.

Masumoto, Valerie, and Blake Allmendinger, eds. *Over the Edge: Remapping the American West.* Berkeley: University of California Press, 1999.

Milner II, Clyde A., Carol A. O'Connor, and Martha A. Sandweiss, eds. *The Oxford History of the American West.* New York: Oxford University Press, 1994.

Nugent, Walter. *Into the West: The Story of Its People.* New York: Knopf, 1999.

Robbins, William G. *Colony & Empire: The Capitalist Transformation of the American West.* Lawrence: University Press of Kansas, 1994.

Robinson, Forrest G., ed. *The New Western History: The Territory Ahead.* Tucson: University of Arizona Press, 1998.

Turner, Frederick Jackson. *Rereading Frederick Jackson Turner: "The Significance of the Frontier in American History" and Other Essays.* New Haven: Yale University Press, 1998.

White, Richard. *"It's Your Misfortune and None of My Own": A New History of the American West.* Norman: University of Oklahoma Press, 1991.

Some of these books are broad histories with extensive bibliographies. In addition to the books listed as suggested readings in later chapters, these can be consulted generally for more readings on topics covering the range of material.

CHAPTER TWO

The First West: Native Peoples

Try to imagine the West as the first European and American explorers, pioneers, prospectors, and settlers did. Before you lies a land teeming with resources: minerals to be mined, soil to be tilled, timber to be harvested, rivers to be harnessed, animals to be hunted—and people. Make no mistake, the intruders, especially the first Europeans to arrive in the region, saw the native peoples as a resource—potential trading partners, potential laborers (slave or free), and, for some, potential converts to one or another form of Christianity. But whatever their motivations, both Europeans and the Americans who followed them into the West saw the native peoples as part of the environment, closer to the animals that populated the landscape than to themselves.

What the Europeans and Americans never imagined was that the indigenous peoples they encountered employed hundreds of different languages, economies, and social and political structures. Nor could they have known of the vast trading networks, systems of alliances, or variety of agriculture that the Indians already had in place.

This chapter begins the story of the West by taking a look at the peoples who inhabited it before the arrival of the Europeans and the Americans. In particular, it discusses these indigenous groups during the 1300s and 1400s, just before Christopher Columbus "discovered" a world new to Europe. In this pre-Columbian period, six main cultural groups inhabited the North American continent west of the Mississippi River: Indian peoples of the Great Plains, the Southwest, the Great Basin, the Columbia Plateau, California, and the Northwest Coast. About some groups, such as the Southwest, we know quite a bit. About others, like the Plains Indians, we know comparatively little. Strangely, our knowledge of all these groups has less to do with their accomplishments, or the artifacts they left behind, and more to do with the urban development of the West. In those places where large nineteenth- and twentieth-century cities and populations sprang up, and construction crews unearthed archeological evidence, we know a good deal more about the pre-Columbian native peoples who once lived in them. The converse is true in places where the land has remained agricultural or been left undisturbed.

The Great Plains

In the center of what is now the continental United States, just west of the Mississippi River valley, lies the Great Plains. A semi-arid region, the Great Plains consists of vast expanses of grasslands parted by a relatively small number of rivers. While the land might appear barren to the untrained eye, the seas of grass actually cover some of the richest soil in the world. Plains Indian groups inhabited this large swath of land covering western Minnesota, Iowa, and parts of Missouri, North and South Dakota, Nebraska, Kansas, Oklahoma, and northern Texas, with some overlap into eastern Colorado, Wyoming, and Montana. With limited means of transportation—the Spanish did not introduce the horse to the region until the sixteenth century—the majority of the Plains peoples stuck to the edges of the grasslands, sometimes following the tributaries of rivers into the interior to hunt. The Dakota (one group of people known as the Sioux), the Arapaho, the Blackfeet, and the Mandan are all considered Plains Indians though, other, smaller groups existed. The Plains Indians were the last group within the continental United States to encounter an imperial presence and the first western group to suffer directly from Indian policies forged more than a thousand miles away in Washington, D.C., when the United States government forced eastern tribes into the Plains Indians' territories.

This map shows the geographical location of the six major cultural groups who inhabited the West in pre-Columbian North America.

It is an image of Plains Indians that comes to the minds of most people when they think of Indians of the West: a stoic male warrior wearing an elaborate headdress, atop a horse and holding a staff or a rifle. This is the type of image made famous by the artists Frederic Remington and Charles M. Russell. But that imagery represents a (highly stylized) portrait of the nineteenth century, not the Pre-Columbian period, meaning the 1,000 or so years before Columbus arrived in the Western Hemisphere. With neither the horse nor the gun, Plains Indians used dogs to help them move their belongings from camp to camp, and bows and arrows as weapons and hunting tools. Although they relied on hunting, Plains Indians also engaged in agriculture, growing maize, squash, beans, and other crops to supplement their diet of bison (buffalo), deer, and other hoofed mammals.

The Plains Indians lived in three general locales, which shaped their respective economies and societies, all of which mixed hunting with loose forms of agriculture. Those located on the eastern edge of the grasslands grew corn but undertook periodic buffalo hunts. Because they practiced agriculture, they were relatively settled, living in earth lodges near their cornfields. This stability created an elaborate social organization, with a clan system based on family groupings. The peoples of the eastern Plains were matrilocal, meaning that when a couple got married, they moved into the village or house of the wife's mother, who was the head of household. Women also served as the heads of clan. The clans controlled politics and religion but fostered the creation of men's organizations, such as those focused on warfare or the curing of meat, which involved a ceremony of religious significance. Those who lived in the marshes of the northern lake areas relied heavily on the cultivation of wild rice, using corn, which they grew themselves or traded for, as a supplement. These groups drew their protein primarily from deer rather than buffalo. Finally, those on the western edges of the grasslands hunted buffalo and pronghorns and engaged in trade with the eastern groups to obtain agricultural staples. These peoples were more nomadic, joining up in large groups during the summer hunts but separating into smaller, extended family units during the winter months. In general, these groups' continuous pursuit of migratory game shaped their economies and their technology. It also shaped their gender relations, as men and older boys tended to leave camp to hunt while women and girls stayed in camp to plant, oversee, and harvest crops. This pattern created distinct gender roles, with warfare and hunting generally male preserves.

Anthropologists consider all pre-Columbian Plains Indians semi-nomadic because they routinely moved between a winter and a summer camp, as opposed to truly nomadic peoples who follow herds and never set up permanent or even semi-permanent living quarters. Because Plains Indians practiced agriculture, the summer camps were more or less stationary. Because they moved between seasons, Plains Indians developed mobile housing in the form of *tipis,* (tents made out of buffalo hides stretched around poles that easily collapsed for transport).

Plains Indian nations or tribes lived in small groups of less than a hundred persons comprising several generations. The economic demands (food, materials for housing) of living on the Plains limited the size of villages. Their political structure featured a council made up of representatives of different concerns within the tribe: a war chief, a chief in charge of food (planning and storage), and others. The tribes traded with other villages within their band as well as with other tribes for foodstuffs, such as dried corn, and useful items like buffalo robes, arrowheads, and tools. Most of the pre-Columbian Great Plains groups produced enough food to have developed storage systems. Competition over trade and resources led to warfare between groups. Some groups had fortified sites with ditches to prevent attack. On the Great Plains and across the first West, trade played an important role in supplying basic needs. Archaeologists have found items from across North America in Plains Indian archaeological sites, from copper discs to seashells to potsherds from the Southwest, attesting to the wide reach of the pre-Columbian trading networks.

During the 1400s and 1500s, migration from other regions led to explosive population growth. This growth led to larger villages, which in turn led to larger political units. As the population grew and diversified, their religion diversified. Some groups maintained small altars in their homes with medicine bundles to promote harmony and a connection to ancestors. Some groups created large public ceremonial sites where they practiced ceremonies like the Sun Dance, a summer ritual of worship and manhood.

The Southwest

Compared to those of the Plains, the Indians of the Southwest lived in a relatively poor environment. With little rainfall, the high deserts, mesas, canyons, and mountain ranges of the region were harsh environments in which to survive. Yet not only did the Southwest groups survive, but they developed unique methods to use the environment to their advantage, allowing them to expand and diversify their societies over the course of some six thousand years before the arrival of the Spanish. Although anthropologists and ethnologists categorize them as one group, the Southwest peoples comprised several different groups who resided across present-day west Texas, New Mexico, and Arizona. Archaeological evidence from the region shows that various pre-Columbian groups had developed agriculture at least two thousand years before Columbus made landfall in the Caribbean. And more than one thousand years before that moment of first contact in the early 1500s, groups in the Southwest produced their own distinct pottery and had established trading networks.

Arizona cliff dwellers. This nineteenth-century German drawing depicts cliff dwellers in the Southwest. Note the sheep herders and the ruins of the marketplace/kiva in the foreground. *Buffalo Bill Historical Center, Cody, Wyoming; 51.51.296*

"Guarding the Cornfields" by Seth Eastman. This nineteenth-century drawing illustrates how some western Indian groups planted and protected their corn crops. Note that women provide the labor in this picture. *Buffalo Bill Historical Center, Cody, Wyoming; Vincent Mercaldo Collection, VM0001*

Two major cultures, the Anasazi and the Hohokam, dominated the Southwest from 1100 through the 1300s. Anasazi had absorbed a previous group known as the Mogollon in 900 A.D., just as a third set of peoples, the Hohokam, moved into the region from Mexico. We do not know what they called themselves, but the word *Anasazi* means "old one" in Dene, the language of the Navajo. The Anasazi lived in the Four Corners region of the Southwest, the spot where the states of Utah, Colorado, Arizona, and New Mexico meet at right angles. Living in deep canyons, the Anasazi built multistory apartment-like dwellings, often tucked up against the faces of cliffs, mesas, or ravines, for protection from enemies as well as from the flash floods that can quickly turn dry riverbeds and valleys into violent torrents. These compounds, shaped like a D, were self-contained units, encompassing separate spaces for living, storage, religious practice, and trash receptacles. Every community contained a great kiva, or round house, in which to conduct religious ceremonies. Their religion revolved around rain and fostering community. They divided their society into classes, with a small group at the top who oversaw the collection of taxes, the distribution of water, and trade and religious practices. Around these D-shaped compounds, they practiced dry farming, which consists of planting seeds deeply into the hard, parched soil to take advantage of the torrential rains that periodically flood the canyons and flow through the area. In other words, they planted seeds deeply enough so that they would retain water from the violent floods but not wash away in them. Additionally, they had elaborate defense systems, consisting of lookout posts and fire towers. Warning fires set in these positions could be seen from anywhere in the valley.

The Anasazi introduced a vast trading system to the Southwest, one that would continue long after their demise and impress the Europeans who eventually arrived in the region. Locally they traded in perishable goods, like food, between their own bands and villages or with those of the Hohokam. Long-distance trade items included pottery, weavings, turquoise, and other artisanal goods. Archaeologists have found Anasazi goods as far south as Central America and as far north as the Northwest Pacific Coast. Trade, both with local and far-flung groups, served several purposes beyond the acquisition of desired goods. Contact with other groups within and outside of the region provided exposure to other languages and information and stimulated the rise of a class of skilled artists. Anthropologists point out that this suggests a stability of economy. In other words, if you have to spend most of your time looking for or producing food, you have little or no time to produce art or develop elaborate religious rituals or support a class of people solely devoted to religion. If, however, a society can stabilize food production, thereby reducing the number of people involved in it, it allows other fields to develop. Stable food production also allows for larger groups of people to live together in one place. Despite a difficult environment, the accepted number for the major Anasazi settlement at Chaco Canyon is 15,000 spread over 75 towns and villages.

At some point around the 1300s, the Anasazi disappeared, died off, or joined other groups. (The fate of the Anasazi represents one of the most active debates in current archaeology.) Parts of their culture and civilization still exist in that of modern-day Pueblo peoples. Some people believe that the Anasazi did not disappear but became the Pueblo Indians. Others believe that disease or other Indian groups wiped out the Anasazi. Still

Tipis on the Plains. A nineteenth-century photograph of an Arapaho tipi, representative of Great Plains housing. *Buffalo Bill Historical Center, Cody Wyoming; Vincent Mercaldo Collection, P.17.1867*

others believe they simply moved on during a time of environmental strife such as an extended drought.

The Pueblo Indians were village dwellers with a steady and stable population supported by farming. They, too, lived in apartment-style housing tucked into mesa and canyon walls. They grew corn, beans, squash, and cotton, which they wove into cloth and used to trade with other groups. Unlike other groups who practiced agriculture at the time, Pueblo men farmed and the women supported them in these efforts.

Like the Anasazi, the Hohokam are believed to be the ancestors of modern groups. Originally raiders who migrated up into the Southwest from Mexico, the Hohokam settled in the southern parts of present-day New Mexico and Arizona. Though they resided in the desert, they tamed it through the use of elaborate irrigation canals, eventually building a system that spanned hundreds of miles to bring water to their fields. Unlike the Anasazi, the Hohokam resided in platform mounds similar to large ones found in Mexico. Just like those of the Anasazi and Pueblo,

Hohokam housing served many purposes, with separate spaces devoted to religious practice, security, socializing, and storage. While raising food-stuffs, including corn and squash, they also grew cotton, which they wove into blankets for trade. The Hohokam are the ancestors of the Akimel O'odham (Pima) and the Tohono O'odham (Papagos.) One of their settlements, Snaketown, near present-day Phoenix, probably had 300 to 600 residents and was occupied for close to 1,200 years. Because the Hohokam and their descendants produced surplus food supplies, they too engaged in elaborate trade both with local and distant tribes. They also suffered a decline around 1300, when a period of drought settled on the region. Most archaeologists believed the Hohokam dispersed and joined other tribes.

The period around 1300 represents a time of chaos and dramatic shifts in the Southwest region. As the Anasazi and Hohokam struggled with environmental issues, two other groups moved into the Southwest: the Navajo and the Apache. As far as archaeologists are able to determine, the Navajo appear to be Athapaskan, meaning their language is related to that of tribes and nations in western Canada and Alaska. The Navajo arrived in the Southwest initially as raiders who preyed on other groups for food and supplies. Their arrival during a time of environmental strife may have led to more warfare within the region, as groups competed for very limited resources. The Navajo were quick, however, to adapt to the environment and adopt successful methods of farming. The men continued to hunt antelope and other hoofed animals while the women cultivated crops. The Navajo became particularly successful producing corn and weaving distinctive items for trade—not the wool blankets and rugs they produce today, but baskets. Much later, when the Spanish introduced sheep to the region, the Navajo quickly learned to keep flocks, becoming adept at using wool and woolen products as trade resources.

The Apache appear to have moved into the Southwest from the Great Basin, after intertribal warfare drove them out of that region. They also adapted to the strains of life in the desert, but in a different way than the Navajos. Rather than taking up agriculture themselves, they pursued hunting and gathering while conducting raids on their more sedentary neighbors to obtain food and other necessary supplies. They did not engage in trade, per se; they took what they needed, thereby developing skills that would come in handy later when dealing with the Europeans.

Groups in the Southwest illustrate a diversity of economic, social, and political forms. Despite the harsh and inhospitable climate, by the 1500s, Southwest Indians had created vibrant and distinct societies.

The Great Basin

In the pre-Columbian period, the peoples of the Great Basin might have been the only truly nomadic groups in the western United States. Covering a large area from western Wyoming through Nevada, Utah, and the eastern, desert parts of California, the Great Basin was home to the Paiutes, Utes, Shoshone, and Bannock. Living in a dry, hardscrabble region, one of high deserts and mountains with few rivers and little rain, Great Basin peoples followed the herds of antelope or buffalo on their seasonal migrations, making them highly mobile. This cyclical travel and reliance on hunting shaped both the peoples' lifestyles and technology.

In the spring, Great Basin men hunted groundhogs and ground squirrels while women gathered seeds and plants for food and medicinal uses. They supplemented their diets with ground nuts, like piñons, which they often stored in underground containers along their migratory routes to help sustain them when game became scarce. Harvesting piñons usually came at the end of the fall, right before winter set in, with the women using large poles of their making to knock the full piñons to the ground.

In the summer and fall, men hunted pronghorns and rabbits by driving them into enclosures, the antelope into box canyons or corrals, the rabbits into netting spread across a wide area. Once they had cornered the frightened animals, the people killed only as many of them as they needed and released the others. Even children participated in rabbit drives. Where possible, Great Basin peoples fished, adding that rich source of protein to their diet. Because of the unforgiving environment, peoples of the region tended to live in very small groups of fifty or less. They also lived a much less elaborate lifestyle than their neighbors in the Southwest or the Plains, with fewer material possessions. Because their high degree of mobility limited their food supply, they relied heavily on regional trade to supplement the food their environment provided. Great Basin peoples tended to trade items readily available to them, such as rabbit skins, for goods they needed, such as grains and beans.

Living in high deserts and mountain ranges posed special challenges to the survival of Great Basin peoples. These they met by developing unique technologies: snowshoes, for example, helped them traverse deep snow-drifts in the mountains. Their housing units varied depending on which subregion they inhabited. In some areas they built tipis, which, as mentioned, were easy to collapse and highly portable. In others, they turned to willow or brush huts that they could build quickly and not think twice about abandoning when it came time to follow the herds. In the southern subregion, the Paiutes developed a form of irrigation to help them support the growth of wild plants. While this did not technically constitute agriculture, it did demonstrate a degree of control over the environment.

The nearly constant mobility of the Great Basin peoples not only shaped their relationships, but what we know about them today. Though they tended to travel in small bands, they maintained extensive interrelations. People intermarried between bands, creating blood ties and other familial relationships. They also traded between bands for desired items and jointly used land, meaning that, at times, different bands felt comfortable hunting in the same area. This practice, however, created overlapping territories, which in times of environmental strife might spark tensions. And though we know something about their methods of trade, hunting, and land use, their high level of mobility led to few concentrated archaeological sites, so we have few artifacts to tell us about their religious practices, familial relationships, or how they chose their leaders. Because they did not settle in permanent villages, their trash and debris—which help archaeologists and ethnohistorians tease out the histories of pre-Columbian peoples—lies spread out over a vast, relatively underdeveloped, territory. We may learn more about the Great Basin peoples in the coming century, but at this point our knowledge remains limited.

The Columbia Plateau

The Indian groups of the Columbia Plateau inhabited present-day Idaho, eastern Washington, and eastern Oregon in an area lying roughly between the Cascade and Rocky mountains. The landscape consists of wide river valleys and lush forests, with foothills slopping up to craggy mountain peaks. The Columbia Plateau Indians included the Salish, Coeur d'Alene, Kalispel, and Spokane groups. The Plateau peoples were semi-nomadic, with winter camps on the plateaus and summer camps in the river valleys, where fishing was abundant. They relied on fish, game, and roots for their food. Archaeological evidence shows that they harvested fish, rather than simply catching them. To do so, they built platforms over places on the river through which the salmon had to swim upstream to spawn. Using dip-nets, the Plateau peoples collected large quantities of salmon. After eating some of the fish fresh, these Indians would dry the rest of it for consumption in the winter, when food stores might otherwise be low. At the end of the fishing season, they would move up onto the plateaus above the rivers, where game was more abundant. They did not farm or practice agriculture, which in turn limited their population.

Like other groups, their means of survival shaped their technology. Columbia Plateau peoples built large canoes and houses. A typical canoe, carved out of a tree trunk, was twenty-two feet long, almost twice as long as a modern fiberglass canoe. Sometimes they built multifamily long houses that could measure up to 70 feet in length by 20 feet in width. At other times, they built pit houses that measured fifteen feet (roughly the length of an average single dormitory room) to thirty feet in diameter. Called pit houses because the floor rested a few feet below the surface, this style allowed for some natural insulation. Evidence suggests food was prepared in a communal village cookhouse rather than by individual families in their housing units. This practice points to a stratification of society that designated some people as food preparers and others as hunters or gatherers. The villages also had designated places for food storage, both natural caves and hidden underground caches. Storing food allowed them to guard against starvation in lean years, suggesting a stability of food production that produced a surplus. So even though they moved seasonally, they knew stores of food awaited their return and resettlement.

Their semi-nomadic lifestyle between the rivers and the plateaus shaped their practices and their community structures. They did not collect large amounts of material goods. Even though they typically moved between only two primary locales, the more material goods they possessed, the more they would have to move or store. Though they believed in a form of equal rights, they did recognize people's different strengths. Consequently, they chose leaders for their abilities, and positions were not inherited. Each village represented a political unit based loosely on family units but evidence shows that people could move between villages and units. Columbia Plateau peoples built kinship relations between bands through marriage and trade. Like the Great Basin peoples, these peoples cross-utilized resources, allowing multiple groups to use resources at one time rather than fencing off territories for one group. Therefore, kinship ties, while important, were not the ultimate definers of status or relationships. Despite this seemingly egalitarian form of politics, little political integration existed between bands or villages.

Despite the lack of political integration between villages, Columbia Plateau peoples possessed a well-developed set of religious beliefs and practices that were uniform across the region. They focused on the life-cycle: birth, puberty, marriage, death. At various points in a member's life, he would follow a vision quest, a period when the individual is left alone to come in contact with other forces, such as spirits, nature, and the future. They practiced seasonal celebrations, also tied to the natural cycle. Perhaps most important, they had shamans, individuals responsible for controlling and communicating with the spirit world. The fact that they had a class of people devoted to this pursuit suggests that their food sources and economy were stable enough to support social stratification.

California

The Indians who inhabited present-day California lived in a wealthy environment compared to peoples in the Southwest or Great Basin. On the coast, California Indians had ready, and relatively easy, access to a rich marine life that afforded them a wide variety of fresh seafood. Those in the interior lived among a wide abundance of plants that yielded nuts and fruits without cultivation, as well as forests full of prey animals. For these people, hunting and gathering was so easy that, unlike other hunting and gathering groups, the California Indians were able to develop permanent settlements and relatively large communities with complex social systems in the pre-Columbian period.

Although the Chumash and Modoc, like other California groups, relied on their rich environment for survival, they had established agriculture, but only of tobacco, which they used in curing and religious ceremonies. Women gathered acorns, pine nuts, berries, and other plant products, some of which they processed into other forms, such as bread. The men hunted deer and other small mammals, or fished. Because they

California Indians and their summer huts. One example of what California Indians'
housing looked like. *Buffalo Bill Historical Center, Cody, Wyoming; Vincent Mercaldo
Collection, VM0002*

were able to create a supply and surplus of goods, they developed extensive
trading networks within the region. Shells and other items traveled from
the coast to the inland regions; berries and hides traveled from the interior
to the coast.

Beyond the ability to trade, other aspects of California life suggest a
stable economy. Coastal peoples produced large plank boats with which
they were able to navigate the seas and capture marine life, including large
fish, for their sustenance. The coastal groups also produced soapstone
trade goods and objects. Additionally, a wide diversity of languages and
housing styles sprung up between northern California and the communities to the south. Northern California Indians lived in plank houses,
which looked amazingly like European homes to the Europeans. Those
in central California lived in pit houses. The Southern California Indians
lived in domed grass houses, replete with porches and shaded areas. As in

the case of the Southwestern groups, a diversity of housing styles was a response to the environment.

Though the California peoples represented different ethnic groups, they shared languages and cultures across the region and a complex political system. Mainly patrilineal, California peoples used marriage to build ties between groups. Some groups, such as the Pomo and Miwoc, formed confederacies, or large political groups used to dominate a territory. Most of the groups organized themselves in village communities, consisting of several families. A leader or chief acted on authority of the village. In many regions, a central town existed with several smaller subordinate towns. Their chiefs met in council in the central town, where food and goods were stored centrally. Chiefs gained power through material goods, which defined status. Material wealth remained somewhat static and inherited, meaning that status would be inherited as well.

This focus on wealth led to a stratified society. At the top were the chiefs, who either inherited their positions or, in some cases, accrued enough wealth to gain power, authority, and respect. A chief managed the food and goods, distributing them within the village or affiliated villages. This power released the chief from other duties. Next in line for power were the shamans, who controlled religious rites. Though these roles were open to all with talent, they often went to those with wealth and status. Below the shamans were the councilors and managers. They served as consensus builders who tried to generate support for the chief's actions. Specialists represented the next tier. These people included tax collectors and skilled artisans, like basketmakers. At the bottom were commoners, who paid taxes to the specialists and the elite class. Beneath them lay the lowest class, possibly made up of slaves or people who could not pay taxes. Though California peoples resided in smaller groups than did their counterparts in the Southwest, their stable environment also supported social stratification.

The Northwest Coast

Overlapping with the California Indians territorially were the Northwest Coast peoples, groups that lived in present-day northern California and coastal Oregon and Washington. (Their territory also extended into British Columbia, but we will limit our discussion to the current continental

United States.) They include the Haidas, Makah, Kwakiutls, and Tlingit. Like the California Indians to the south, the Northwest Coast groups relied heavily on marine life, sustaining themselves through fishing and the hunting of sea mammals. They built their villages near the coast and their environment shaped their technology.

Northwest Coast Indians were premier woodworkers who built large wooden boats (45 feet by 6 feet), large wooden houses (65 feet by 35 feet, roughly the size of a double-wide trailer home) and huge totem poles that served to illustrate family and clan histories. We know more about Northwest Coast peoples than other pre-Columbian groups thanks to an important natural disaster. Just before 1492, a landslide buried the village of Ozette, on the coast of Washington state. The archaeologists who excavated that site learned a great deal about Northwest cultures, economies, and politics.

Northwest Coast societies revolved around the ocean and the rivers. Some groups lived on the coast, whereas others lived upriver. In either case, a reliance on salmon and other large fish shaped their culture and their economies. Though they did not develop agriculture, they created a stable enough society to build permanent villages and conduct trade with other groups. And though their means of survival, fishing, was labor intensive, they still managed to create art and other high-quality goods for trade.

Typically, a village of Northwest Coast peoples survived by fishing for salmon, hunting deer, and collecting local edible plants. Because the winters were somewhat harsh, they spent much of the spring and summer months creating food stores. This they accomplished by drying large amounts of fish. Men caught the fish, women cleaned them, and everyone worked together to dry the fish on racks throughout the warm months. Because they fished for a wide variety of species, both freshwater and saltwater, they developed a variety of hooks and fishing techniques. To fish in the ocean, they made seafaring boats, which some groups, like the Makah and the Quinault, also used to hunt sea lions and whales.

Archaeological evidence shows that Northwest Coast peoples produced tools made from stone, bone, antlers, and shell. Additionally, evidence suggests they had made steel tools before the arrival of Europeans. Some scholars theorize that the steel, which is not native to that part of the country, came from wrecked Asian junks. In any case, the Northwest Coast peoples created steel knives and *adzes* (tools that shape wood), aiding them in the production of their housing, boats, and totem poles. The Northwest Coast environment consisted of beaches, steep rock cliffs, and forests of huge trees, which the Northwest Coast peoples learned to fell and turn into houses, boats, and elaborate carvings. In addition to the sophisticated wood-working tools, they also produced intricate weavings, using a variety of materials including dog hair, the wool from wild goats, and reeds.

Thanks to the relative economic stability of their food supply, Northwest Coast peoples became a socially stratified society. Three classes existed: high-status elites, commoners, and slaves. High-status individuals often were the political leaders, though family and kinship groups represented the political unit within these societies. Slaves were those people captured in raids, purchased, or the offspring of a high-status man and a slave woman. Slaves had no chance to elevate their status.

Class, kinship, and wealth defined one's status within the society. Northwest Coast societies based their social structure on the process of accumulating and dispersing wealth. In other words, the more you had, the more you could give away, thereby putting the receivers in your debt and raising your own status. The legitimization of class centered on the potlatch ceremony. Potlatching occurred when a person changed status in some way: birth, puberty, marriage, death. The family hosting the potlatch previously had accumulated gifts, including food and trading goods, which they presented or gave away to attending members of the ceremony. By accepting the gift, the guests acknowledged and accepted the change in status.

Though they maintained a certain economic stability, all was not quiet on the Northwest Coast. Two issues suggest constant change and strife within the region: language and warfare. Linguists have found that Northwest Coast peoples spoke both a variety of languages and a variety of dialects of those languages. This linguistic diversity suggests that, historically, various groups moved through this region as they traveled to other parts of the Americas. It also means that new groups arrived and stayed in the area, while others moved on, leaving behind linguistic traces. A diversity of language also suggests and supports the physical evidence of trade between far-flung groups. Finally, language patterns demonstrate which groups maintained regular contact through trade or warfare.

Archaeological evidence indicates that two types of warfare dominated the region. Large-scale warfare erupted periodically between Northwest

Coast societies, as groups sought to increase or redefine their territories. Evidence also suggests small-scale periodic raids from one village or society to another. These raids functioned as a way to gain foodstuffs, items, or slaves without trading for them. Therefore, the Northwest Coast peoples were not strangers to warfare or unprepared to wage it when the Europeans arrived in their land.

Warfare and trade goods also represent the existence of another phenomenon: trade. There is material evidence of trade, like the finding of buffalo robes and other items not native to the region, and linguistic evidence of trade, such as the record of several surviving trading languages. The fact that Northwest Coast societies were able to create luxury goods for themselves, such as elaborate carvings, also suggests that they enjoyed an excess of items with which they could conduct trade with other groups within and outside of their region. Archaeologists have found shells and carvings from the Northwest Coast in the interior of the continent, suggesting that trade circles extended far beyond tribal and even regional areas.

Similarities

As demonstrated above, the six groups that inhabited what became the Western United States before the arrival of the Spanish in North America were a diverse group of nations, bands, and tribes. Europeans often glossed over these differences in hopes of simplifying the process of conquest and expansion. Yet they also often missed outright the similarities between the six groups. Despite a wide range of economies, political structures, and languages, the six groups of the pre-Columbian West shared many things.

Their environment shaped their societies and their technologies. Some remained hunters and gatherers, while others developed permanent cities and agriculture. But across the six groups, all developed their own forms of architecture, art forms (including pottery and weaving), food supply, and weaponry. These surplus items became important resources for the trading networks that crisscrossed North America.

At this point, you may be asking yourself why we keep bringing up trade. It is because trade between the pre-Columbian Indian groups of the West tells us several important things. First, you cannot trade if you do not have goods to trade. In other words, any society needs a surplus, or at least a stable, supply of food in order that some members might have the time to make works of art or items for trade. Second, trade is not just about goods and food; it is also about language, information, and kinship. Groups that interact through trade either learn each other's language or create trading dialects (also called pidgins). Inevitably, trading partners exchange information about their home regions. They also exchanged humans, both as slaves and as marriage partners, to forge ties of kinship, which cements trading alliances. Most groups found marriage partners outside their immediate family group, extending their connections to other peoples. (As we all know, people are likely to do business with people they know and like, and it certainly does not hurt your loyalty to a business if a relative happens to run or own it.) Conversely, trade often took place away from villages or outside of residences. Certain central locations, like Sault-Ste. Marie in Michigan, became clearinghouses where multiple groups met to trade. In Pueblo villages, people conducted trade outside town walls for security. Such places represent only the first step on a long road. Most exotic trade items, buffalo robes and seashells for example, passed through multiple hands and regions. While neighbors might trade goods, some of those goods would be passed on through the system.

Trade plays an important role in the development of the American West. The Europeans who arrived with lofty ideas of conquest hoped to be able to piggyback onto trading systems already in place. This would be far easier than creating new trading systems—especially considering that the Europeans often spoke no Indian languages and had only a limited knowledge of the land. The Spanish and the French utilized native trading systems and looked to them for a variety of resources. Trading systems also tended to dictate where Spanish, French, English, and American settlements sprang up, and they defined economic and political territories, which brings us to our next similarity: warfare.

Native North America was constantly in flux well before the arrival of the Europeans. As the rather brief overview of life in the West before 1492 demonstrates, groups moved and changed territories. The Apaches drifted into the Southwest area. The Plains Indians made incursions onto the grasslands from the West and the East. A variety of groups passed through the territories of the Northwest Coast peoples. As different people moved into a particular area, competition for resources increased. Two principal ways evolved as a means to settle these conflicts: warfare and alliance building, both practiced widely before Europeans arrived. Many groups, such as the Navajo and the Sioux, had extensive experience in both the art of warfare and negotiation before the Europeans made their way into their homelands. Therefore, the assumptions of previous scholars that Indians either attacked the Europeans they encountered because they seemed like a threat or ran away at the sight of them is false and oversimplified. As Europeans made their way into the various regions of native North America, they met Indians who demanded respect, accountability, and negotiation. But thanks to other factors (namely disease and environmental stress), this was not always possible.

Finally, all of the native groups of the West had developed cosmologies that explained how the world had begun and their people came to be. Europeans often saw these creation stories as childish tales because the narrative differed from the creation story of the Judeo-Christian tradition. Elementally, however, the Indians' creation stories differed little from the first part of Genesis, describing how the world came to be, how it came to be populated, defining gender roles, and setting up the local environment. Like all peoples, the six major groups were curious about how they came to be and their purpose in life.

Change Wrought by Europeans

In the chapters that follow, we will look closely at the three major European groups who entered the American West. First, though, we need to discuss three major changes that the Europeans brought to the Indians soon after, and in some cases even before, first contact: disease, livestock, and other non-native, non-human stowaways. These elements radically reshaped Indian populations and cultures in ways only recently understood. These changes, in turn, rebounded back on the Europeans in ways they never could have foreseen. The "Columbian Exchange," as it has been called, was an unpredictable two-way street that reshaped not only Western but world history.

From the minute Columbus, or any other European explorer or traveler, stepped onto American soil, be it North, Central, or South America, he left behind pathogens that would spread like wildfire across the continent. At the turn of the sixteenth century, Europeans lived in crowded cities that were cesspools of disease. Europeans who entered adulthood had necessarily survived various waves of so-called childhood diseases. Smallpox, bubonic plague, typhus, yellow fever, measles, the mumps, colds, and the flu crisscrossed Europe on a regular basis, exposing Europeans to a host of pathogens. Those European who crossed the Atlantic bore with them immunity to those diseases, but also the bacteria and viruses that might thrive in new hosts, or victims. Therefore, from the moment Europeans exchanged words with a native person, they possibly had transmitted disease, unwittingly, but with often deadly consequences.

For the peoples of the Americas, the Atlantic Ocean had served as a barrier for thousands of years. Native Americans had therefore been so isolated from most of the diseases that had plagued Europe, Africa, the Middle East, and Asia that they, unlike the intruders, had virtually no natural or acquired immunity to those same diseases. Additionally, some biologists and anthropologists now believe that genetic data points to a more limited genetic diversity amongst Indians, which further limited their ability to fight off new diseases. Soon after first contact, or the first time an Indian group met a European group, the Indians suddenly came down with smallpox and other epidemic diseases. Unsure how to deal with these illnesses, Indians, especially those in the western United States, often crowded around the ill persons in hopes of supporting them. Unintentionally, they provided the perfect situation for the disease to spread: close contact. Though Europeans had figured out issues of quarantine and limiting contact, they still did not understand incubation. This fact means that when a disease struck a city, people often fled to the countryside to avoid it but simply ended up spreading it farther. The various sicknesses brought by the Europeans devastated the Indian populations of western North America.

Scholars disagree on the exact numbers, but estimates of death rates range from 50 to 90 percent of any given Indian population. We do know that explorers who arrived in a given area soon after first contact often found empty villages, unburied corpses, and empty fields, suggesting a recent catastrophe. In any given society, the first to die from epidemic disease were the very young and the very old. For many native societies, this death pattern undid their system of growth and development. Survivors found themselves adrift. They had lost their past (and in some cases their histories) and their future in one fell swoop. In addition, many survivors suffered from guilt and a strong desire to join their families in the

Vasco Núñez de Balboa (1475–1519), Spanish explorer. Balboa ordering Indians to be torn to pieces by dogs. Copper engraving, 16th century. *Courtesy New York Public Library, Mid-Manhattan Picture Collection #807963*

afterlife. Suicide rates appear to have been high amongst those who made it through the first wave of disease. Those survivors, though, remained vulnerable to other diseases as well as to attacks from groups unaffected by disease. Therefore, the diseases brought to the West by Europeans also destabilized relationships between Indian nations, as traditionally strong groups weakened by disease became targets for other groups. Many times when one group attacked the remnants of another, the aggressors quickly picked up the disease and spread it anew. Finally, trade inevitably spread disease, just as it spread language and customs.

In the initial contact between Indians and Europeans, Europeans also left behind other agents of change: non-native animals and plants. Europeans brought with them pigs, sheep, cattle, horses, and dogs—large war dogs bred to hunt and maim other animals, including humans, and quite unlike the native dogs. The pigs, sheep, and cattle they brought as portable food. The dogs they brought as a weapon. Europeans left behind individuals of all the domesticated species, to lighten the load on the return crossing and to make room for any riches they might want to tote back to Europe. Pigs, cattle, sheep, and horses imparted new diseases to native animals, trampled and ate Indians' crops, and multiplied—rapidly. The Indians did, however, adopt livestock as valuable resources. The Navajo, as mentioned, became sheepherders. The Apache, Comanche, and Sioux became expert equestrians, adapting their entire lifestyles around the horse (this is what we mean when we speak of the "horse culture"). One man's trash became another man's cultural revolution. However, the Indians' adoption of livestock also destabilized the political and economic landscape. Those who became herders were able to produce a steadier supply of food and surpluses for trade, which increased their economic power. Those who adopted the horse became stronger militarily, often at the expense of agriculture and other stabilizing forces. In short, the arrival of the Europeans, well before formal colonization, dramatically changed the human and animal landscape of the West.

Europeans also brought non-human stowaways to North America. Norwegian grey rats, the fleas riding on them, and crabgrass and dandelions all presented challenges to the peoples of North America. The rats spread rapidly and ate food supplies. Larger than native species of rats, the newcomers did more damage as their colonies grew and they devoured more food. Additionally, the fleas they carried bore diseases, such as the bubonic plague. Obviously, the fleas spread disease even in those places where no European peoples were present or had ever visited. Finally, Europeans inadvertently brought the seeds of crabgrass and dandelions on their clothes and trading items. As these plants took seed, they spread, threatening native crops and plants. This development led to new agricultural challenges for the Indians.

The Numbers Game

You may have noticed that when discussing certain Indian groups we mentioned a population number for some but not all. As mentioned above, disease hit the Indian population of the West hard. The problem is that we do not know how hard it actually hit, or precisely which disease hit which group—or when. Because disease was an unintentional exchange, its spread was uncontrolled and not easily or regularly documented. All we know for certain is that disease hit wherever Europeans landed. This fact means that the coastal groups (such as the California and Northwest Coast peoples) and those in the direct path of Europeans (the Southwest who encountered the Spanish as the latter moved north from Mexico) often experienced disease before more-isolated groups such as the Plains Indians. Additionally, people on trading routes passed along disease as well as goods and information. This, coupled with the other radical changes wrought by the early interactions with Europeans and the animals and plants they introduced to the ecosystem, makes it difficult to know the full extent of the changes Europeans wrought on the Indians who inhabited North America before 1492—especially since no one knows a great deal about the latter peoples in the first place. Unfortunately, population estimates were still questionable more than 350 years later, which tells us something about who was, and who was not, writing the history of the United States and from whose perspective.

In 1939, anthropologist Alfred Kroeber believed that at the time of Columbus there probably had been only 8 million Indians in the whole Western Hemisphere, including North, Central, and South America. He based his work on the estimates made by anthropologist James Mooney of the Bureau of Ethnology, who declared in 1910 that only 1,150,000 Indians lived north of Mexico at "the coming of the white man." As you will see in the next few chapters, Mooney's phrase "coming of the white man" is rather vague, as Indians and Europeans came into contact over a period of 350 years. Additionally, Mooney believed that only slightly more than 400,000 Indians lived within the United States proper in 1492 (being compiled in 1910, this number excludes Alaska and Hawaii). While we may never know exactly how many Indians inhabited North America before the arrival of the Europeans, trying to answer that question helps us better understand historical and archaeological methods as well as how politics infuses the questions we ask and the answers we give.

Historically, several factors influenced the numbers. European explorers and the initial colonists commented (in their journals or reports back to their sponsors) on the number of Indians they had seen or encountered in North America. Some Europeans willfully overreported the number of Indians for two reasons. First, for those interested in the Indians as slaves or workers, more was definitely better. Second, those who successfully fought and conquered Indian groups probably raised the numbers to highlight their prowess and superiority. Under other circumstances, Europeans underestimated the number of Indians in any one place. They assumed the groups were nomadic and therefore covered large amounts of territory, accounting for the constant sightings of Indians. Since they did not interact with all the Indians they encountered, Europeans assumed they were seeing the same groups over and over, instead of realizing that they might be seeing different tribes, nations, or even villages. Additionally, some European observers purposely underreported the number of Indians they had seen in order to present the land as largely unoccupied and therefore available for European settlement. Finally, until recently, it was devilishly hard to figure out the number of Indians in the Americas before European conquest and settlement because those same populations had already been reduced, some drastically so, by disease spread at and soon after first contact. Remember, thanks to regular contact between one Indian group and another, disease continued to spread after the very first Europeans reboarded their boats. So the initial accounts and numbers are, to say the least, problematic.

Other factors preclude historians and anthropologists from accurately counting Indians in the pre-Columbian period. Even before the arrival of the Europeans, different native nations moved or regrouped (think of the Apache and the Navajo.) This fact makes it hard, based purely on archaeological evidence, to tell when a group died out or which ones migrated or joined another group. Think about the Anasazi. We know they were under environmental stress but did they simply die out, move to another region, or join up with other groups—or all three? Additionally, after disease strikes other factors take a toll on a given population. Weaker groups are more likely to suffer attack and lose military engagements, further reducing their populations. They are also more likely to have their women and young children taken captive in raids. These problems, coupled with lower fertility rates in the wake of certain diseases also serve to retard population growth. All of these factors hinder answering the question: how many Indians resided in North America before the Europeans settled it or arrived?

By 1850, when the U.S. government released its estimate of 350,000 to 500,000 Indians living west of the Mississippi, dramatic new factors were coming into play. In the 1850s, with the California Gold Rush and overland migration to Oregon, and especially in the 1860s, with the passage of the Homestead Act and the completion of the transcontinental railroad, American settlement west of the Mississippi began to boom. Portraying the Indian population as small and well on its way to extinction presented the expansion of the United States as ordained and inevitable—the "Manifest Destiny" about which you are always reading in U.S. history texts.

The low population estimates of 1900 had yet another effect. In the late nineteenth century, archaeologists, anthropologists and ethnographers assumed that the majority of Indians in the pre-Columbian period were nomadic. When they began to find large villages, burial mounds, and significant structures, these scholars assumed these structures must have belonged to Indians killed off in the not-so-distant past by the present-day groups. They failed to recognize that societies are fluid and that one capable of building a large temple mound in 1490 might eventually be weakened by outside events like climatic change, disease, or warfare. Remember also that what archaeologists find shapes archaeology. Archaeologists and others discovered much of the evidence of monumental pre-Columbian Indian architecture and living sites in the nineteenth and twentieth centuries, this as towns and cities in the West went up or expanded.

In recent years, scholars have been able to use new methodologies to estimate population numbers. These include counting all the references to Indian populations in the accounts of early European explorers. (As an excellent example, try counting and then locating the living sites of all the groups mentioned by the Spaniard Cabeza de Vaca in his journal of 1527.) Other scholars, like Henry Dobyns, an anthropologist, have done environmental surveys and calculated how many people such an environment might have been able to support based on the lifestyles of the Indians studied. Additionally, over the last thirty years further archaeological discoveries have yielded ruins and artifacts that suggest larger populations in certain areas than previously assumed. On this basis, Dobyns set the number of indigenous peoples as high as 18 million in 1491 in what is now the continental United States. Some argue that all of the Americas was home to more than 100 million indigenous people. In 2004, the Smithsonian Institution declared the number of indigenous people in North America to have been 2,359,350. They based this precise figure on ethnographic and archaeological evidence as well as by adding up all the known and estimated tribal sizes. Of course, the population of North America did not spread evenly across the continent. Coastal areas like California and the Northwest Coast would have supported larger populations than drier interior areas like the Great Basin. According to this report, the populations of Western regions in 1492 would have been roughly as follows: Northwest Coast, 144,000; California, 216,000; Southwest, 495,000; Great Basin, 38,000; Columbia Plateau, 87,000 and the Great Plains, 234,000—for a total of 1,215,000. This recent estimate is larger than Mooney's estimate for all of North America (north of Mexico), though still lower than estimates by Dobyns and others who use population projection techniques. Now compare these numbers with the numbers from 1900 for the United States as a whole (based on tribal records and censuses for the Indian population): the Bureau of Indian Affairs (BIA) listed 270,000; the U.S. Census listed 240,000; and scholars today estimate as many as 510,000. And these sets of numbers are considered middle-of-the-road estimates, demonstrating just how complex this problem can be, especially when people of mixed-race ancestry are factored in. In addition, according to Mooney, in 1900 there were a little more than 100,000 indigenous peoples in Canada and about 30,000 in Alaska. This was the nadir, the low point, of the indigenous populations of North America. From this time, they began to rise, doing so steadily, especially since the middle decades of the twentieth century. In 2000, the U.S. Census counted 2,476,000 people who reported a single race of American Indian, and a total of 4,119,000 that also includes people of multiple-race ancestry. In turn, the Canadian census of 2001 counted 565,000 people of singular indigenous ancestry and 754,000 with multiple ancestries, for a total of 1,320,000. Even now, the best that census takers and demographers can do is to come up with rough numbers, as it is often difficult to decide who is a person of indigenous descent and who is a mixed-race person with significant indigenous ancestry. Perhaps most important, in recent decades Native American peoples in the United States and First Nations peoples in Canada have been able to determine for themselves who are members of their communities.

Politically charged, the debate about numbers continues, and it continues to shape other debates as well. For our purposes, even a good estimate of the number of Indians is important, for it shapes how we view the experience of the Europeans and Americans who came to the West later. The obstacles the intruders faced and the rewards they reaped were directly related to the Indians. As you will see in the next three chapters, some European groups used the Indians and their trading and political systems to their advantage. Others found themselves repeatedly stymied by Indians who, for a variety of reasons, refused to bend to the will of others.

∽ Suggested Readings ∾

Bonvillain, Nancy. *Native Nations.* New York: Prentice Hall, 2001.

Dickason, Olive. *Canada's First Nations.* Norman: University of Oklahoma Press, 2002.

Fisher, Robin. *Contact and Conflict.* Vancouver: University of British Columbia Press,1990.

Jennings, Francis. *The Founders of America: From the Earliest Migrations to the Present.* New York: W. W. Norton, 1993.

Josephy, Alvin Jr., ed. *America in 1492: The World of the Indian Peoples before the Arrival of Columbus.* New York: Vintage Books, 1993.

Kehoe, Alice. *North American Indians: A Comprehensive Account.* New York: Prentice-Hall 1992.

Kicza, John E. *The Peoples and Civilizations of the Americas before Contact.* Washington, D.C.: American Historical Association, 1998.

Mann, Charles C. *1491: New Revelations of the Americas before Columbus.* New York: Knopf, 2005.

Waldman, Carl. *The Atlas of the North American Indian,* Revised edition. New York: Checkmark Books, 2000.

CHAPTER THREE

West is North:
The Spanish Empire

As the Indians of North America continued to reshape their societies through warfare and trade, a new player appeared on the horizon. The arrival of the Spanish changed the lives of the Indians and the Spanish forever. Both sides entered into the new relationship with preconceptions about how the world worked. In the case of the Spanish, the previous 500 years of their history set them up to view the Indians and the Americas as a reward for service to God.

The first white people whom the Indians of the American West encountered came from the Iberian Peninsula, a part of Europe in which history had departed in substantive ways from that of the rest of the continent. What chiefly separated the history of the Iberian peoples from that of other Europeans was the conquest of Spain by Muslims from northern Africa (Arabs or Berbers known loosely as Moors) who sought to spread their Islamic faith. The Muslim domination of the peninsula, which began in A.D. 711, prompted an almost constant state of warfare to oust the Muslim intruders. In each Christian state of Spain, the wars bolstered the role of the king as the military leader of the *Reconquista,* the term generally used to refer to the centuries of struggle to regain Spain from the Muslims. Following a tradition used by the Moorish invaders, Christian fighters surrendered one-fifth of the spoils of their conquests to the monarch—a custom that granted further power and wealth to the monarchy and set the stage for future practices in the Americas.

Efforts to resist the aggressors and reconquer the motherland molded Spanish culture during the Middle Ages, the military campaigns to expel the Muslims turning into a way of life that accentuated the warrior hallmarks of valor, tenacity, and survival at any cost—traits embraced by the *conquistadores* (conquerors) whatever their social station. Through time, moreover, the Reconquista assumed the aura of a religious crusade. This crusade mentality prompted the Crown to bestow the role of ally on the Catholic Church, and the preachings of the Church on behalf of the war rendered numerous social and political privileges to the clergy. In turn, the Catholic Church gained power as a political institution, becoming an active part of the government.

The constant warfare and disruption of the Reconquista also encouraged the raising of sheep and cattle in agrarian regions of Spain as people found that livestock brought higher and quicker profits than did their crops. Unlike crops, herds of animals could be moved quickly out of harm's way during warfare. Cattle ranching flourished after the Reconquista. Some lords raised breeds of cattle that became widely known for the quality of their beef and hides. Seasonally, *vaqueros* (cowboys) drove the stock cross-country from the northern summer grazing lands to winter in southern pastures. The vaqueros developed a distinctive dress and equipment, as well as cattle-ranching traditions and practices such as the *rodeo* (round-up), which were later transplanted to parts of the "New World" that came under Spain's dominance, including, of course, the American West. The Reconquista changed Spain religiously, politically and economically. These changes influenced Spain's relationship to the peoples of the Americas.

Historians sometimes speak of a "watershed," a certain year or event in a people's history that triggers rapid and overwhelming changes, leading either to great advancements or disastrous declines. For Spain, 1492 was a watershed that propelled the modest nation on the fringe of Western Europe into one of the dominant powers not only of the known world, but also in the soon-to-be-discovered New World.

In 1491, Spanish armies finally took the last step in the long march of the Reconquista when they ousted the last of the Moors from Granada, the southern tip of Spain. Now Spain had freed itself from the Muslims and reclaimed the land for Christ. The next year, Queen Isabella gave her consent to an Italian mariner named Christopher Columbus to sail under the flag of Spain in a westerly course to the East Indies. Columbus did not set off to find new lands and new people. He left Spain to find a quicker route to Asia, the better to capitalize on trade with China, Japan, and India. Therefore, Columbus's principal motivation to undertake his first trans-Atlantic voyage (he would make a total of four before he died) was economic and political gain. He also saw it as a mission in the tradition of the Spanish Reconquista: a Christian journey to the wilderness, a crusade, and a challenge. If successful, he would achieve great things for Spain and Latin Christendom.

From the port of Palos in southern Spain, Columbus, in command of three small sailing ships, steered toward the Canary Islands, already claimed and colonized by the Spaniards after the brutal conquest and enslavement of the islands' native peoples. After reprovisioning in the Canaries, the crews headed west into seas never before sailed by Europeans. On October 12, 1492, after little more than a month at sea, Columbus sighted land. He had not reached Asia, as he had assumed; rather he came ashore on the modern-day Bahamas. He named the first island on which he stepped San Salvador (Holy Savior). Arriving home in March 1493, Columbus announced his finds, including the "discovery" of the new peoples, the "Indians," ripe for conversion or "restoration" to Christianity. To the devout Catholics of Spain, these people seemed to be a gift from God, rewarding them for having expelled the Muslims and reconverting (as the Spanish saw it) many of the residents of southern Spain to Catholicism.

Following Columbus's grand find, Spain proceeded to transform the "New World," as the Europeans had dubbed it, into colonies that would provide the Spaniards with the elusive riches they had hoped to reap by finding a shortcut to Asia. They were determined to wield their new-found confidence and power. Now a new wave of consquistadores, who in many ways resembled those who had reconquered the peninsula from the Muslims, took the initiative for the acquisition and subordination of new dominions. Characteristics of the traditional conquistador—courage and tenacity, but also callousness, a propensity toward violence, religious zeal, and a desire for riches and glory—thus typified those who led the conquest of the New World.

God, Gold, and Glory

Historians often sum up the goals of the Spanish Empire as "God, gold, and glory." This aphorism, while catchy, fails to describe adequately what the Spanish hoped to accomplish in their American colonies. Spain was a devoutly Catholic country. As mentioned, the protracted struggle of the Reconquista had molded and solidified Spain's Catholic identity and evangelical zeal. Having recently expelled the Muslims, whom the Spanish deemed "infidels" because they had rejected Christianity, Spanish theologians and rulers truly believed God had chosen them to fulfill God's wish and Spain's destiny. Columbus's "discovery" of Hispaniola and Central America (remember, he did not actually discover North America), coming within a year of the end of the Reconquista, provided a whole New World of peoples whom the Spanish might "save" by bringing them to Christianity. In the theologians' minds, the Spanish Empire needed to convert the Indians—the "God." They also recognized that if the Spanish could not convert the Indians, they could at least enslave them, turning them into an economic resource. King Ferdinand and Queen Isabella funded Columbus on a second voyage for just that reason. But the royal couple also had economic goals in mind—the "gold." Originally, Columbus had hoped that by sailing west he might find a faster passage to India, with its gold, silver, spices, and other valuable trading commodities. With the knowledge of a faster route, Spain could achieve "glory" by dominating world trade and thereby the known world, meaning, Europe. While Columbus failed in his original goal, he accidentally found other resources, including Indians.

Spain wasted little time launching future explorations and colonizing the Caribbean and Mexico, in the expectation that they would unearth large quantities of gold, silver, and other valuable resources. In this sense, the Caribbean was a huge disappointment to the Spanish. They found little gold on the islands, though they did find many heathens, people unexposed to Christianity, waiting, they believed, to be brought to God—as in the Europeans' God. Those who refused the Spanish offer of Christianity became slaves.

After the experience in the Caribbean, the Spanish refocused their goals farther west. Mexico, as it turned out, held much gold and silver, as well as people to enslave to help extract the riches. Taking Mexico, how-

This etching shows Christopher Columbus being greeted by native people upon his landing on the island of Hispaniola. In the background, soldiers plant a cross and native women flee from the arriving sailors. *Library of Congress, LC-USZ62-8390*

ever, required the conquest of a sophisticated and powerful empire, that of the Aztecs centered in what is now Mexico City. The Aztec were a warrior people unafraid to fight (once they figured out who the strange-looking Spaniards were and what it is they actually wanted of them), and the Aztec empire had resources and a political and economic structure in place. The Aztecs had conquered other groups within present-day Mexico. Their empire controlled trade and centralized the government of the area. This fact allowed the Spanish to gain a large amount of territory by conquering one group and its institutions. With the Spanish conquest of the Aztec Empire in 1519–21 (led by the ruthless conquistador Hernán Cortés but aided greatly by the diseases the Spanish had unwittingly transferred to the indigenous people), the foundation of the Spanish Empire in North America had been laid.

Three Branches of the Spanish Empire

The history and the goals of the Spanish shaped the structure of their empire, which in turn molded the development of their American colonies and influenced those lands well after the Spanish lost control of them. Despite the great distances involved (from Spain to Mexico, northern New Spain and most of Central and South America) and a wide variety of populations (Aztecs, Incans, and Navajo, to name but a few), the Spanish Empire was well organized, with three distinct branches of bureaucracy: the Council of the Indies, the *Audiencia* (a royal court of justice with some administrative duties), and the Catholic Church. Each branch had its own role, though considerable overlap existed between their responsibilities. This overlap caused problems, for both the Spanish and the Indians they ruled, particularly in northern New Spain, what is now the Southwest of the United States. The conflicts, inherent within the structure of the Spanish bureaucracy, shaped the Spanish experience in the West, or rather, the far northern *frontera* (frontier) of New Spain.

The Council of the Indies represented the main administrative arm of the bureaucracy. Its responsibilities included drafting laws that governed the colonies, influencing appointments to bureaucratic positions, such as governors and tax collectors, and reviewing administrations and officials. In addition to these duties, it acted as the court of highest appeal for legal matters and held the power to approve papal bulls, which are agreements or laws

Spanish North America. This map illustrates the breadth of the Spanish empire in
North America through 1800.

issued by the Catholic Church through the Pope. Though the Council of the
Indies gave itself the right to approve papal bulls, on the whole it was a rub-
ber-stamp process of simply putting the Spanish approval on Catholic law,
another sign of how intertwined were the Church and the state.

    The Audiencia represented the second branch. It acted as the judicial
arm of the government, though it also served as a legislative consultant,
meaning it offered legal advice to the Council but did not create or pass
laws itself. The Audiencia also oversaw the collection of the royal revenues. Remember, Spain was a monarchy and all taxes as well as the "royal
fifth" established during the Reconquista, one-fifth of the spoils of any
finds of gold or silver, ultimately went to the Crown. The Audiencia also
nominated people to serve as minor officials in the civil and ecclesiastical

(meaning Church-related) services. Thus, the Audiencia would nominate a person as a colonial governor or tax-collector but the Council of the Indies might veto the nomination or suggest someone else. The Crown also made the Audiencia responsible for the welfare of the Indians, whom the Crown perceived as its responsibility. In that capacity, the Crown allotted land grants, called *encomiendas,* to Spanish settlers in New Spain. These encomiendas included not only the land but the Indians who lived on it. In this way, the Spanish simply saw the Indians as part of the land granted to colonists for development. While the landowner required the Indians to work the encomienda, the Crown and the Audiencia expected the landowner to feed and clothe the laborers and not to abuse them. This institution created a paternalistic relationship between the Spanish and the Indians, one that later groups of Spanish would recreate, both formally and informally, across Spain's North American holdings.

The Catholic Church represented the third arm of the colonial government, which the Crown considered under its control. It played an important role in the creation of policy and in the treatment of the Indians. Naturally, this arm of the Spanish empire bore inherent conflicts of interest. It is important to remember that in the sixteenth century, the papacy, meaning the Pope, and the Roman Catholic Church often ruled like a nation-state, influencing other governments and making treaties and sweeping pronouncements. The Catholic Church's large role in Spanish and other European societies often led to conflicts. Monarchs at this time believed their power came directly from God, meaning they ruled by "Divine Right." Nevertheless, the Pope also claimed his power came directly from God. Thus, both the Pope and the monarchs believed they had divine power. If they disagreed, through whom was God really speaking, the Spanish king in Madrid or the Pope in Rome?

The Church wielded a certain amount of power in the Spanish Empire. The Pope sanctioned the exploration and colonization of the Americas under an agreement of 1493, which mandated that the Spanish would convert the Indians before doing anything else. The Crown required the conquistadors to introduce the ideas of Christianity, but it sent priests along with the soldiers to sustain that conversion.

On the ground in the Spanish empire, the Church consisted of two different groups: secular priests and sacred orders. Secular priests were individual priests who went to northern New Spain to work with the

Spanish population that settled there. The Audiencia appointed the secular priests individually, but the Catholic Church oversaw their activities. Secular priests in New Spain could own personal property, in some cases massive amounts of land. The sacred orders were the holy orders of priests: Dominicans, Augustinians, Franciscans, and Jesuits. They came to convert and comfort the Indians and *mestizos* (the offspring of Spanish men and Indian women). The Audiencia appointed these priests as an order, meaning that the Spanish asked the Franciscans or the Jesuits to dispatch priests to a specific region. Individual priests within these orders could not own property or land grants but the orders to which they belonged could, eventually making some of them powerful in regional politics. The Franciscans and Jesuits, to name two, amassed a great amount of land and power in what became the West.

The Missions

The practice of conducting missionary activity among the Muslim occupiers had been used in Spain during the Reconquista, which evolved into the system found in northern New Spain by the 1580s. Indeed, the Spanish empire used the mission system as one of the main institutions to secure the frontier in northern New Spain. Missions became outposts of

Pueblo of Santa Ana. An early nineteenth-century engraving of the pueblo of Santa Ana in New Mexico. Note the chapel and the burros, two Spanish imports. *Courtesy, The Newberry Library*

the empire but also created communities of mestizos and converted and unconverted Indians as well as trading centers. In the Americas, the mission system was preceded by a debate over whether or not the Indians were human. In 1511, Bartolomé de Las Casas, a former colonist who became a priest and a founder of a utopian mission, asked his fellow Christians of the Indians, "Are these not men? Have they not rational souls?" With these questions, Las Casas set off both a debate and an institution within the Spanish empire. Prior to their realization that a whole New World existed, Europeans had created a biblically based timeline that explained the presence of Africans and Asians. American Indians did not fit into this model. For a hundred years, the Spanish debated whether the Indians had souls and were therefore human. This debate concerned rather big stakes. If the Indians were not human, then this fact released the Spanish and other Europeans from their duty to convert them. After all, only human beings had souls and one needed a soul in order to be saved. If the Indians were not human, it also absolved all the explorers and conquistadors who had committed crimes against them. Yet if they were human, then the empire must convert them, protect them, and treat them as fellow Christians. In this case, any crimes committed against the Indians would endanger the souls of the explorers and conquistadors. For sixteenth-century Catholics, not knowing the answers to these questions complicated considerably the mission to the New World.

In 1513, a group of theologians wrote up the *Requerimiento* inviting the Indians to become Christians or, if they chose not to, suffer the consequences: enslavement or death. Read in Spanish to the Indians when the Spanish approached them, the Requerimiento naturally had little effect. Since the majority of Indians did not speak Spanish, and even those who could at this time had only a loose command of the language, virtually none of them understood the concepts being promulgated in the Requerimiento or acted on them. Their response, or lack thereof, allowed the Spanish invaders to interpret it however they chose: either the Indians had silently agreed to become conquered nations of the Spanish Empire and convert to Christianity, or they had refused Spain's generous offer and must be punished.

The methodology changed in 1537, when the Pope issued the *Bull Sublimis Deus,* which declared, "Indians are truly men capable of understanding the catholic faith." Initially, in order to achieve their goal of conversion, the missionaries used force. At first, priests traveled with expeditions and converted Indians they encountered along the way. Then, Spanish sacred orders began to set up Christian communities based on Thomas More's work *Utopia* (1516). More advocated several tenets for a Christian community: communal property, a six-hour workday, the giving up of luxury goods, the election of family magistrates, and dividing the fruits of labor equally among the workers. The founders of the mission system hoped to teach the Indians agriculture, ignoring the traditional agriculture the Indians already employed. In theory, the mission system quelled Indian insurgency by feeding them and keeping them close by the mission, and by making them useful to the colonial government without enslaving them. Eventually, after 1573, the Spanish government moved to this form of "friendly persuasion," especially in northern New Spain.

Since the "padres," or fathers, in the mission came from the sacred orders, they were ecclesiastical priests. The Council of the Indies had, as mentioned, sent them to the Americas to help convert and protect the Indians. This was their sole mission. The priests who worked with the Indians followed a plan based on their limited, and often paternalistic, understanding of the Indians, all of whom the priests viewed as one homogenous group. First, they would "dazzle" the Indians with gifts: beads, bells, colorful clothing, and sacred images. The exchange of gifts worked well because of certain cultural similarities between the Indians and the newcomers. Southwestern Indian groups believed giving a gift obligated the receiver to the giver. Europeans believed gift giving demonstrated the receiver's power over the giver, the gift a form of tribute. They did not always agree, however, on what constituted a gift, and this disparity created tension. For example, Pueblo women considered sex a gift, but many Spanish men saw sex as a way to dishonor or dominate native women. Understandably, these different interpretations often led to conflict.

After the exchange of gifts, the friars would then settle in urban areas and expect the Indians to build a house and church for them, which the Indians often did out of obligation. In the beginning, the friars focused on converting the leaders and their children. They sought to remove children from the undue influence of their parents to achieve the mission of conversion. Additionally, the missions often drew on multiple groups of

An early Spanish illustration of the "Heathen Seris," an Indian people who came to the Jesuit missions near the modern Arizona-Mexico border in the early nineteenth century. *Courtesy, The Newberry Library*

Indians for their population. This created a multicultural society in which, for example, Pimas, Hopis, and members of different Indian groups lived side by side within the mission.

While they tried to reshape the various Indian cultures, the priests also tried to learn as much as they could about these groups. Spanish priests became expert linguists and ethnographers, unintentionally recording Indian languages and cultures for posterity. They taught the mission Indians Spanish, thereby providing the various groups with a new common language they could use to communicate among themselves. Finally, the padres also attempted to protect the Indians from less scrupulous Spaniards. They took their role as protectors of the Indians as seriously as their time and culture would permit. The padres fought to keep squatters and land grabbers from taking over Indian land, and they often intervened in conflicts between colonists and Indians.

And several conflicts sprung up within the Spanish government when the ecclesiastical priests refused to follow rulings against the Indians, the priests claiming their first responsibility was to the Pope. Indeed, the missionaries served two masters: the Pope had granted them power, but the Spanish government fiscally and militarily supported their work in the missions of New Spain. Additionally, the government built *presidios,* or garrisoned forts, nearby or within mission compounds to protect the padres and their charges from "hostile" Indian groups. They represented another frontier institution with roots in the Reconquista. The Spanish government not only paid for the costs of building these forts, but it paid the salaries of the soldiers and for all the services and supplies they needed. Individuals provided monetary gifts to support the work of the Church, but the Church expected Indians who worked within the walls of the missions to be self-supporting. In the end, the Spanish empire did not intend for the missions to last for hundreds of years as they did. The government and the Church had hoped that the converts would soon take over the missions and use them to create Catholic communities, becoming active participants in the empire.

So why, you may ask, did so many Indians join the missions? Individuals did so for many different but mostly practical reasons. Under certain conditions, what historians and sociologists call "pull factors," Indians went to the missions to gain better food, material goods, and a level of stability not otherwise available to them. Additionally, some Indians believed that the priests acted like powerful witches who could control the elements and shape the future. Others entered the missions due to so-called "push factors," to get relief from famine or drought or seek shelter from their traditional enemies or some new group of raiders who had recently moved into the area. Finally, some Indians went to the missions out of curiosity and a desire to learn new things, absorbing and adapting what they wished to from the priests' lessons. Some groups simply added the Virgin Mary and the Catholic saints to their own cosmology. The Gabrielino of California believed that a woman named Chukit gave birth to the "Son of God" after lightning impregnated her, a belief they simply transferred to the Virgin Mary. Some Indians became true converts. Others practiced Christianity when in the missions and their own religion when outside of them. One of the main problems with the mission system was the transitory nature of the population. Few Indians in northern New Spain stayed at the missions for their entire lives. Because the Indians moved in and out of the missions as it served them, several other informal processes occurred. Those who left took components of Spanish culture, practices, mores, and language with them.

Missions became centers of trade, between the Spanish and different Indian groups, and between the mission Indians and the non-mission Indians. The missions also became targets for retaliation by groups who did not join them. Towns sprang up around some of the missions, but they were not peopled by converts. In reality, mestizos and non-Indians populated these towns, which served to stabilize the frontier of northern New Spain, just not in the way the Spanish had intended.

After the Reconquista, the Spanish had employed the *municipio* or township to establish and secure new territories within Spain. This system, too, they imported to their American colonies, and it became the local form of political organization there. As the Spanish gained new territory, they legally required the Indians and colonists to be attached to a municipio. The Spanish called this a *congregacion,* and it effectively provided social control as well as centralizing trade and tax collection.

Cabildos, or town councils, ran the townships. They consisted of six to twelve local men from influential families. In the early days of the Spanish colonies, these were *encomenderos,* or local Spaniards with aristocratic pretensions. A *corregidor,* or government-appointed official, ran the town council, creating a link between the centralized government and the local authorities. The town councils also worked with the provincial governor, appointed by the Audencia with the approval of the Council of the Indies. While the Spanish did not allow Indians to serve on cabildos, in New Mexico and California they were granted their own cabildos as a way of co-opting them into the Spanish system.

Northern New Spain

What we consider the American Southwest, meaning west Texas, New Mexico, Arizona, and California, the Spanish considered "northern New Spain." When they looked to the "frontier," they faced northward. After they conquered the powerful Aztec Empire that had controlled the majority of Mexican Indian groups, the Spanish moved northward expecting to find other Indian empires to overtake. Instead, they found small, disparate groups with no large, central organization. Much as their experiences with the Reconquista and Columbus's grand find had shaped Spain's approach to colonizing the New World, so did their experience with the Aztec shape its expectations in trying to colonize the frontier, the northern frontier, of New Spain.

The Spanish began their conquest of Mexico in 1519 when Hernán Cortés marched into what is now Mexico City. Cortés represented a new breed of conquistador. Too young to have participated in the Reconquista, Cortés spent his early adulthood in Hispaniola and Cuba. By the time he headed to Mexico, the Spanish empire had written laws regulating exploration and the treatment of the Indians. Whereas Columbus had headed out for the unknown to prove his worth to the royals, Cortés headed out to establish himself politically and financially. He sought to gain political power through conquest and riches that would help him maintain that power. Cortés still paid service to the religious aspect of the mission, writing King Charles V that "I came by order of Your Majesty to protect their lives as well as their property and to teach them they were to adore but one God, who is in the heavens, Creator and Maker of all things. . . ," yet he focused much more on accruing riches.

When Cortés encountered the Aztec in 1519, he found a civilization that very much resembled European civilizations. To European eyes, the Aztec, based in their beautiful capital city of Tenochtitlán, possessed several of the hallmarks of civilization. They had monumental structures, power and control over conquered, tribute-paying states, a large and powerful religious institution that appeared to organize public life, a socially stratified society replete with peasants, a middle class, rulers, a monarchy, and, most important, riches including exotic animals, gold, and silver. The Aztec built alliances and conquered other cultures to build and maintain their empire, and they had created elaborate trading systems to help support their lavish lifestyle. Their system appeared to be a "barbaric" mirror of the one from which Cortés and his men emerged. And though there were important differences between the political organization of the Spanish and Aztec empires, the latter was a pyramid-like set up, with a few powerful people in control and lots of poor people at the bottom. Indeed, the Aztec class structure made the conquest of Mexico seem like an easy proposition for Cortés. Once he had the emperor, Monteczuma, out of the way, Cortés simply planned to insert Spanish officials in the place of Aztec administrators, the Catholic Church in place of the indigenous religion, and then begin reaping, for himself and Spain, the benefits of conquest. As Cortés bragged to the King, "It is certain, that, if they served God with the same faith, and fervour, and diligence, they would surely work miracles." Unfortunately, for Cortés and his men, the conquest of Mexico proved to be a long and brutal struggle that spanned several years and took the lives of many Spaniards. This conquest, however, paled in comparison to the task that lay before the Spanish who wished to conquer northern New Spain.

During the first half of the sixteenth century, though, the Spanish showed little interest in settling the northern *frontera* of New Spain. Instead, they had hoped to find other groups like the wealthy Aztec whom they might conquer then enslave and redirect their resources toward Spain. Besides, other parts of the Spanish Empire, like Central and South America, possessed better land for colonization and more obvious resources. Consequently, in the first half of the sixteenth century, except for the members of a few random *entradas* (expeditions), the Indians of the Southwest had little or no contact with the Spanish and, therefore, did not learn much about them.

The earliest European account of part of what would become northern New Spain came from Alvar Núñez Cabeza de Vaca, a member of an ill-fated mission that landed initially in Florida in 1528. After becoming stranded from their ships and losing their commander, Cabeza de Vaca and his fellow castaways, including an African slave named Estevanico, improvised, killing their mounts and using their hides to make five small boats, which they hoped to sail back to Cuba. Instead they blew west across the Gulf of Mexico, crashing on the coast of Texas, where they began an overland trek in search of Mexico. On this journey they encountered numerous Indian groups, some of whom were friendly, one of whom enslaved the Spaniards, perhaps a nice turn of fate as far as Estevanico was concerned. Cabeza de Vaca and his men had several exciting adventures, including, at one point, posing as medicine men and "healing" sick Indians with their curative cross. Eventually, they broke free of their captors and traveled through West Texas, finally reaching Mexico eight years later, but full of claims that the Indians of the area they had traversed held great riches. Cabeza de Vaca wrote, "Throughout all this land where there are mountains, we saw great evidence of gold and antimony, iron, copper, and other metals." This news inspired other entradas into the northern frontier from 1539 to 1543: one north from Mexico City into present-day Arizona and New Mexico led by Francisco Vásquez de Coronado, during which the party saw the Grand Canyon and Estevanico was killed by the Zunis; one led by Hernándo De Soto, credited with "discovering" the Mississippi River, in which his men buried him on their return trip from what is now the Southeastern United States; one led by Coronado and Martín de Alarcón to New Mexico; and a sailing voyage led by Juan Rodríguez Cabrillo and Bartolmé Ferrer, who traveled north along the coast of Alta California. All of these parties searched in vain for the Seven Cities of Cíbola and other vast riches and opportunities described by Cabeza de Vaca.

According to legend, the Seven Cities of Cíbola (a term meaning buffalo that the Spanish had heard the Zunis use and now applied as a place-name to the pueblos of the Zuni) were clustered together amidst high mounds of gold, silver, and other treasures. It is possible that early explorers had seen quartz in the cliff walls of the housing units of the Pueblos glinting in the desert sun. Instead of piles of riches, what the Spanish found instead were the Pueblo Indians, who were at first hospitable but soon tired of their greedy and obnoxious guests. Coronado's and De Soto's expeditions treated the Pueblo Indians as if they were their own personal convenience stores. They demanded food and supplies from the Indians to keep their missions going. The Pueblo, in an attempt to rid themselves of the Spanish and in a moment of great cultural understanding, assigned an Indian, called the Turk, to lead the Spanish on to Cíbola. Of course, there was no Cíbola and the Turk led Coronado all the way to Kansas in hopes of abandoning his party out there on the prairies where they would die of starvation. Supposedly, Coronado, upon learning of this trick, killed the Turk and retraced their route back to Pueblo territory. Whether this story is true or not, the physical evidence and Coronado's records do show he moved up the Rio Grande valley and kept going, supposedly on information that Cíbola was just ahead in the next village. In short, the Indians remained skeptical of the Spanish intentions and annoyed by their constant intrusions.

As we saw in Chapter Two, the Southwest Indians included groups who made their livelihood in different ways: farming, hunting, raiding, trading, and certain combinations thereof. Additionally, they had created trading networks that linked them to each other as well as to groups outside the region. But their loose alliances and trading networks by no means resembled that which the Spanish had encountered in Mexico. Nor did they have gold or elaborate stores of goods that the Spanish valued highly. Finally, there was no overarching, dominant group. They had not consolidated power in urban areas, something that had made it easier for the Spanish to conquer the empires of the Aztec and the Maya. The Spanish had assumed that the conquest of northern New Spain would be relatively simple: locate the seat of Indian empires, lop off the heads of state, and take control of both the government and the distribution of resources. As mentioned, they truly believed they would find large stores of gold, silver, and other riches, as well as large populations whom they could enslave. Instead they found numerous disparate groups, spread over a large area, with few resources that they coveted.

The Spanish, therefore, did not begin colonizing northern New Spain until the 1580s. They took possession of New Mexico in 1598, establishing the capital at Santa Fé with the help of Indian labor. But taking possession of and controlling a territory are two different things. Northern New Spain quickly became a drain on the Royal Treasury, as the expenses soon exceeded revenues. The frontier settlements grew slowly, with only about 3,000 Spanish inhabiting the area during the seventeenth century. Until the last part of that century, the Spanish built no presidios in northern New Spain. Part of this stems from the fact that until that time, there appeared to be little threat to the frontier regions of New Spain from the other European powers. Where they could, the Spanish relied on the labor of the Indians, instead of that of settlers or soldiers, to establish a colony. As the Spanish marched toward northern New Spain, they employed strategies they had learned on their march from the Yucatán to what is now Mexico City, using Indian allies to conquer other groups of Indians and, in some cases, using friendly Indians as colonists. To hold the frontier they dispatched missionaries and soldiers.

Additionally, the Southwest Indians engaged in a different type of warfare than had the Aztec, Mayan, or the Spanish. They tended either to move away from intruders, hiding in the hills or mountains, or practice retaliatory, guerilla raids. In Mexico, the Spanish encountered a united front and siege warfare, wherein both the Aztec and the Maya had hunkered down in their towns to defend themselves. In contrast, Spanish soldiers often arrived in various places in northern New Spain only to find empty villages, the Indians hiding elsewhere (a strategy certain groups used to deal with other groups who raided them.) At other times the Indians raided and re-raided the Spanish as they tried to move north, picking away at the long trains of people, goods, and animals, taking what they wanted when they wanted it. This process made bringing supplies up from Mexico City and other large towns in the interior to northern New Spain both slow and expensive. Nonetheless, the Spanish needed to import as many items as they could in order to try to colonize the North.

Though they did not find large amounts of processed gold and silver on the northern frontier, they did find deposits of raw silver and other minerals that could be mined. Since the Indians had not already created any mines, the Spanish had to build them. In Mexico, not only had the Indians created mines but they had long ago learned to work as skilled miners. The Spanish quickly discovered that the Indians of northern New Spain made lousy slaves who had absolutely no experience in mining. Those Indians they tried to enslave for other purposes tended to die of exhaustion or run away to rejoin their tribes. This situation forced the Spanish to begin importing African slaves to fill the void in 1601.

Because northern New Spain did not hold the traditional riches associated with the other American colonies, the Spanish ran into a problem with their own people. The colonial army required Spanish soldiers to supply themselves with a horse, a uniform, and a weapon. An individual, therefore, invested a good deal of his own money to join the army, based on the belief that he would earn back his investment and a whole lot more through his share of the plunder his unit would garner in the New World. In a tradition that went back to the Reconquista, a certain amount of that plunder (one-fifth) went to the King, and some went to the leader of the expedition, but the rest, up to three-fifths, went to individual soldiers.

When riches did not appear in northern New Spain, the rate of desertion rose. Other soldiers chose to supplement their pay by capturing and enslaving Indians, as they appeared to be the only resource available.

The Spanish government tried to solve this problem by bringing in colonists and granting them encomiendas. But many of the colonists assumed these land grants would function like those in Mexico and Central America, wherein the grantees often took over existing Indian farms and mines and the colonists themselves did little work. Again, this was not the situation in the colonial settlements of northern New Spain. Eventually, the government stopped granting encomiendas to settlers and began granting them *haciendas* and *estancias,* which were grazing rights for cattle or sheep. This move represented an attempt to work with the reality of the environment and adapt to it. The Spanish finally understood that the land would not make for a quick gain and encouraged the colonists to develop revenue-producing industries such as ranching. But the Church quickly became dominant in these matters, as the missionary orders owned a great deal of land and controlled many of the haciendas and estancias. This fact limited the amount of land available to average settlers, making the prospect of a move to a province of northern New Spain even less attractive. Colonists expected the missions and the Indians to supply them with food and other goods, an assumption that quickly created tension between the Indians and the colonists, many of whom eventually fled the colony rather than stay out their land grant. If the Spanish had relied chiefly on colonists to secure the region, they soon would have lost control of northern New Spain.

The Pueblo Revolt

On a hot August morning in 1680, after nearly a hundred years of occupation, the Pueblo peoples of northern New Spain revolted against the Spanish. In many ways the odds were in favor of the Pueblo peoples. Only about three thousand Spanish, including administrators, colonists, priests, and a few soldiers, lived in northern New Spain. No formal presidios or barracks of soldiers existed. The Spanish occupiers, while mainly clustered around Santa Fé, were spread out across the territory, making them vulnerable to attack. By the end of August, the Pueblos had killed more than four hundred Spaniards and destroyed farms and settlements.

The rebels also killed twenty-one of the twenty-three Spanish missionaries living among them. Now the majority of the Spanish occupants of New Mexico lay dead or were on their way south to El Paso, where the surviving Spanish and some loyal Pueblos set up a government in exile. For thirteen years, the Pueblo Indians of New Mexico succeeded in keeping the Spanish out of their territory. In addition to being a turning point in Southwest Indian–Spanish relations, the Pueblo Revolt demonstrates many of the issues that crippled the northern territory.

Primarily, the Pueblo Revolt was about the Indians rejecting the Spanish: their occupation of the land, their culture, and their labor demands. Over the course of the 1600s, northern New Spain became a colony of conflicts. The Church and the State spent much of their time arguing about who would control the Indian population and how. The Church claimed responsibility for the Indians' souls and threatened excommunication to any Spaniard who interfered. The State claimed authority over the Indians' labor and the products thereof, levying large taxes and tributes on the Indian populations. Now add settlers who felt trapped in a less-productive colony (as compared to the Spanish ones farther south) and treated the Indians as slaves and whipping boys. Then layer on top of the situation a clergy who abused their Indian and mestizo charges, told them their traditional beliefs were silly superstitions, and attempted to change all levels of the Pueblo social fabric. All of this equals a colony under stress and, perhaps, on the verge of self-destruction.

Outside forces added to the internal stress. In the mid-1600s, waves of famine wracked northern New Spain. These famines made paying taxes and tributes almost impossible for the Indian population. At the same time, the Apaches began raiding more often, destroying what few resources the Pueblos had left. Famine, church-state conflict, and oppression pressed the Pueblo peoples against the wall. In the 1650s and 1675, groups of Pueblo Indians attempted to revolt against the Spanish. The Spanish responded brutally. In one case, they cut off the foot of all the males in the village involved. Such a response hardly fostered respect or friendship on the part of the Indians.

Thus, conditions were horrible in the colony on multiple levels. Though the Spanish tended to portray the Revolt as an aberration, in reality it represented the culmination of growing anger amongst the Pueblo and other Indian peoples, and this anger led them to work together in a way unimagined by the Spanish. To organize a revolt that encompasses the length of New Mexico, some seventeen thousand Pueblos speaking six different languages and spread across twenty-four nations had to communicate with each other, put differences aside, and rebel simultaneously.

Those who participated in the Revolt also demonstrated the affect the Spanish had on the region. One of the leaders of the Pueblo Revolt was a shaman named Popé, whom the Spanish had whipped and humiliated in one of their crackdowns. Popé is a controversial historical figure. New Mexico erected a statue to him in Washington, D.C., based on his role as the leader of the Pueblo Revolt. Nevertheless, some historians dispute his role in the Revolt. In addition, his status as a mestizo complicates the story even further. What does it tell us, ask some historians, if someone who was part-Indian, part-Spanish led an Indian revolt? At the very least, it tells us a lot about acculturation within this part of the Spanish Empire. Popé had ties, both biological and cultural, to both sides of the conflict. He served as a shaman for a Pueblo area, and he had spent some time in a mission. While he might have served as a bridge or culture broker between the two cultures, partially because of Spanish racial attitudes, he ended up as a revolutionary leader for the Pueblo Indians and their allies.

The Spanish believed strongly in biology as destiny, as did most Europeans at the time. They also adopted a belief that environment shaped societies. Thus, in their American colonies people made keen social distinctions between the Spanish-born (*Peninsulares*) and those born in the colonies. Unlike later groups, they differentiated between people of "pure" Indian blood and those who were "part" Spanish, as if Spanish blood were somehow different and better. This does not mean, however, that the Spanish necessarily granted more rights to mestizos than they did to Indians, at least not in this period. They treated mestizos similarly to Indians, while expressing the belief that they might be easier to convert because of their Spanish blood. Though Popé was part Spanish, he did not receive any special favors from the Spanish government. If anything, the Spanish viewed him with more suspicion. As a product of both cultures, he knew the Spaniards' weaknesses and the Pueblos' strengths.

The planning of the Revolt demonstrates the level of biculturalism attained by the participating Pueblo Indians and the mestizos. First, they cut off the capital, effectively isolating the Spanish from the central authorities. Second, they sent messengers into the capital explaining that

Pueblo Indian. A nineteenth-century photograph of Alejandro Padilla, of Isleta Pueblo, wearing an outfit of combined Indian and Spanish origin. *Courtesy, The Newberry Library*

the Indians were in charge and that they had posted guards to keep the Spanish from escaping or going for help. Finally, they timed the attack between supply caravans. These caravans came every three years from Mexico. The Indians and the mestizos knew enough to strike right before the next caravan arrived, meaning that all sorts of important supplies, like ammunition, would be low. Thus, while the Spanish may not have learned much about how to survive in New Mexico, the Indians and mestizos had certainly learned a lot about how the Spanish functioned.

It took the Spanish the better part of thirteen years to reclaim the New Mexico colony. They did so for reasons that had little to do with revenge. In the mid-1690s, reports came back to Mexico City that the French were trading guns within the former colony. Not wanting to see one of their major European competitors, the French, gain access to their territory, the Spanish mounted an expedition and retook it.

Nonetheless, the Spanish had learned some important lessons. After the Revolt, the Spanish co-opted the Indian and mestizo populations. They made local chiefs and headmen responsible for tax collection. The Crown disbursed land grants directly to Indian groups, merely putting a Spanish imprint on what the Indians already considered their own land. This act, however, made the Indians *part* of the colony instead a *possession* of it. Now the Spanish administrators were much less likely to dictate the terms of labor, limiting mission work to certain areas based on the needs of the local Indians. Mestizos became active members of the bureaucracy, serving as petit bureaucrats and local magistrates. Finally, the Spanish built presidios and staffed them with garrisons of soldiers to protect the missions on the farthest frontier from incursions from other European powers. The Spanish and then the Mexicans controlled the vast Southwest until the American War with Mexico in 1848. In the intervening 150 years, the Indians had become accustomed to dealing with or ignoring an outside power in their midst. When the Americans arrived, expecting the Indians to move out of their way, it was a shock for both sides. The Indians had no intention of bowing before the Americans, as they had long since stopped doing for the Spanish. But the Americans had no intention of treating the Indians of the Southwest as citizens.

The Texas Empire

Ironically, the Pueblo Revolt led to an expansion of northern New Spain to the east. As survivors of the Revolt flooded into El Paso, a sleepy frontier town, it became apparent that many were going to wait out the Revolt there. As El Paso grew, so did interest in colonizing Texas.

Explorers, including Cabeza de Vaca, had mapped and explored Texas before its settlement. The authorities, when confronted with the large expanses of land, the varied populations of Indians, and the lack of easily accessible resources to plunder, always saw it as too expensive to settle. When the empire had problems convincing colonists to stay in New Mexico, the government figured Texas would be worse. All that changed after the Pueblo Revolt, when the survivors escaped to El Paso.

The Spanish first settled El Paso in the 1650s as an important trading post between the Spanish and the various Indian groups that migrated through West Texas, many of whom traded with Plains Indians for valuable buffalo hides. In exchange for these hides, the Spanish traded metal, cloth, and horses. The horse trade defined this period, as groups like the Apache and the Comanche began to restructure their societies around horses. The increased mobility allowed these groups to expand their territories and dominate other groups. Thus, the Spanish, while maintaining a minimal presence in Texas, proved to be a great influence on the Indians in the area.

In 1680, survivors from Santa Fé ended up in El Paso. They brought with them Indian allies, who were also fleeing the Pueblos. Though the refugees hoped to return to New Mexico, it soon became apparent that El Paso was to be the de facto capital of New Mexico for the exiles. The presence of the Indian allies led the Catholic Church to establish a mission there to serve the Indians. Between the mission and the Spanish exiles, El Paso grew into a gateway for future Spanish settlement of Texas. El Paso continued to grow after the first attempt at reconquest of New Mexico failed in 1682 and more settlers arrived. Yet the Spanish still held back from building colonies throughout Texas because they were afraid of losing money in Texas as they had in New Mexico.

The French forced their hand. In 1685, René Robert Cavelier, Sieur de La Salle began exploration in present-day Texas. La Salle was a seasoned explorer. In 1683, he followed the Mississippi River from its northern point down into the Gulf of Mexico. He believed it actually emptied just east of New Spain, but such a mistake was typical of this period. Armed with that information, he went to the King of France and proposed a new trip: to establish a colony at the mouth of the Mississippi, so that France could invade New Spain.

La Salle's expedition represents several common themes in this period. First, as France and Spain feuded over issues in Europe, these feuds spilled over into their colonies. France would be more than happy to relieve Spain of some of its colonies in North America and vice versa. Second, European rulers based their decisions about new territories not on the territories themselves, but on the value of those territories to others. In other words, Spain may have considered Texas theirs, but they made no move to colonize it until the French did. Finally, part of La Salle's argument to the King of France revolved around the assumption that Indian allies would help overthrow the Spanish. European groups usually assumed that the Indians would side with them over their European rivals. So, to achieve these goals, La Salle set off for the mouth of the Mississippi, approaching it from the Gulf rather than from upstream.

Almost immediately, he ran into trouble. Spain and France settled their differences two weeks after he left. The King of France, therefore, was not that interested in invading Spanish territory. La Salle persevered. Next, he could not find the mouth of the Mississippi, which appeared to be hidden by various barrier islands. Remember, he came at the mouth from the sea this time instead of overland. With no accurate maps available, it is

A typical home on the Texas *frontera*. *From* "Mexicans in San Antonio, Texas, 1887" *series, E. K. Sturdevant, photographer, Daughters of the Republic of Texas Library.*

understandable that this task proved difficult. Eventually, frustrated by his lack of success, La Salle constructed a fort, which he named Fort St. Louis after the King, 400 miles west of the actual mouth of the Mississippi. He then set off to find the mouth, covering a large swath of Texas. In the meantime, the Spanish became aware of his expedition and his purpose.

The Spanish did not want to lose Texas even though they did not control it or use it. They were concerned that a French presence in the Gulf of Mexico would threaten their shipping and lead to the invasion of northern New Spain. The Spanish colonial government sent a group of soldiers in search of La Salle. In an ironic twist of history, the search for La Salle, whose colony Fort St. Louis failed, led to the Spanish settlement of Texas. As the Spanish searched for La Salle, they established colonies, settlements and relations with the Indians to try to secure the area for themselves. Ultimately, the Spanish sent four expeditions between 1685 and 1689 in search of La Salle.

These expeditions established a military presence along with a religious one. Each of the expeditions included both a military commander and a priest to better assess the needs of the Indians. One such priest felt the Caddo Indians wanted missions and begged Mexico City to supply them. As would happen in other parts of the Spanish empire, the military created presidios to protect the supply lines that ran from El Paso to east Texas. These supply lines provided necessary trading items to keep the missions and settlements going. The Spanish established their first mission in Texas at San Francisco de los Tejas in 1690. In a reactive fashion, they built the mission to Christianize the Indians and stabilize the frontier so that the French, who were establishing trading posts and sending in priests of their own, would not succeed. In 1691, the Spanish government granted Texas its own governor, making it an official part of the Spanish empire. By 1692, the mission at San Francisco de los Tejas had already failed, the missionaries burying the bells and cannons and fleeing.

Growth in Texas remained stagnant for the next 20 years. The Spanish continued to expand northern Mexico and built a series of presidios along the present-day border between Texas and Mexico. In the end, this line of presidios strengthened settlement in East Texas, providing a more secure frontier off which the Spanish could build East Texas. East Texas did not seem so isolated when a chain of presidios and trading spots existed in West Texas as opposed to New Mexico. As interest in East

Texas grew, the Spanish founded San Antonio in 1718, again as a way of forestalling the French, who really just wanted trade with the Indians, not control of the territory.

San Antonio became a significant settlement. It replaced El Paso as an important launching pad for settlement into East Texas. Remember: settlers to East Texas during the Spanish empire came from Mexico or New Mexico, so San Antonio would be a convenient place to begin their settlement. Many of the soldiers mustering out of the presidios settled there. Additionally, many of the new settlers around San Antonio started cattle ranches, introducing a new industry to Texas. The Indians proved less happy with this development. During the 1700s, the Spanish had several conflicts with the Apaches, who proved formidable enemies. The Comanche also sought to drive the Spanish out of Central Texas. By the 1740s, Spain considered shutting down the missions in Texas, again. In addition to expense and threats from Indians, there were few to no converts. Despite this, they approved a plan to expand missions in East Texas. These new missions failed as well. In the end, while the missions failed, small communities of Spaniards, mestizos, and a small number of converted Indians held on, finally holding Texas for Spain.

The California Empire

If Spain thought the conquest of the diverse societies of northern New Spain had been a struggle, the conquest of California proved even more difficult. As we saw in Chapter Two, California Indians were quite diverse—with more than 300 dialects spoken, a myriad of small political units and populations, and a high population density. It was not like the Aztec Empire, with one central government, nor were there large settlements, as in the Southwest.

It took Spain almost two hundred years to invade California, thanks in part to the problems encountered in the Southwest and elsewhere in their vast empire and a reluctance to spend the money it would take to establish missions there. In 1542, Juan Rodriguez Cabrillo landed in California. Sent to find the mythical Northwest Passage, a supposed sea route across the North American continent to Asia, he found California instead. As he sailed up the coast, he kept his eyes open for potential ports for Spanish ships. After landing several times, he thought he had found the next Mexico: a land teeming with resources ripe for the taking.

California also became attractive as an outpost to help the Spanish control the Pacific. With an active trade in the Philippines and growing threats from British and Dutch traders, the Council of the Indies considered establishing missions and forts in California around 1608. But as New Mexico and other colonies continued to drain resources, expansion into California was halted.

The Spanish did not return to Alta California until 1769, when they needed to establish a barrier between their main northern prize, Mexico, and the Russians, who were moving into northern California and Alaska, and the British, who controlled present-day Oregon, Washington, and British Columbia. California proved to be a lucrative if daunting colony. The California colony constantly teetered on the brink of failure as the Spanish struggled to control the Indian population, establish Spanish forms of agriculture, and secure the frontier. By this period, the mission system served as a means to hold the frontier. Military officers were sent with missionaries on their "sacred expedition" to help control and establish the frontier. Military officer Gaspar de Portolá and Father Junípero Serra went to establish both a presidio and a mission. The Spanish authorities had joined these two institutions after the Pueblo Revolt to try to quell future uprisings. Together, Portolá and Serra founded 21 missions in California.

In order to consolidate their power over the Indians, the Spanish had reconfigured their model of conquest. Missions now served the purpose of controlling the Indians as well as introducing them to Christianity. Under the *reducción,* missions gathered several native villages into one mission for education and conversion. The Indians were not able to leave, unlike in New Mexico, where there was a transitory population. Tied to the missions were the presidios. The missions provided the garrisoned troops with food, native labor, and, in some cases, native women. Finally, they established a *República de Indios,* or Republic of Indians, to provide civil order. These were cabildos run by Christian Indians to enforce order on the local community. Many scholars credit this institution with limiting the number of revolts within California. Still, the Indians did not exactly embrace this system. Just like in the Southwest, several revolts occurred. As early as 1775, Indians rose up and destroyed missions, including those at San Diego and Santa Barbara.

The California missions achieved a higher level of success, meaning they attracted more converts than did their counterparts in other areas of northern New Spain. With close to 300,000 Indians within the present boundaries of California, the padres worked in an area with a high population density. This fact meant that an established mission had access to many more people to convert than did those in the less-populated colony of New Mexico. What's more, the Spanish were the only game in town. No other European empire had established trade or relations with the Indians in California. And while it's not possible to determine how many Indians truly converted, we know for certain that as more Indians came to live within or nearby the mission walls, their mortality rate increased. As one Franciscan reported, "They live well free but as soon as we reduce them to a Christian and community life . . . they fatten, sicken, and die." The enclosed quarters increased the rate of disease as well as infant mortality. Disease reduced the Indian population by one-third over 50 years. Despite this, the mission population continued to increase, with slightly less than 10 percent of the Indian population living within missions in 1821, the last year of Spanish rule.

Spanish-Indian Interactions

Think about what you might know about the Spanish. Do you envision conquistadors riding into villages, killing people as they went? Do you think of atrocities committed under the Spanish flag with priests blessing each action as they proceeded? If this is what comes to mind, then you are imagining what historians call the Black Legend, or *la leyenda negra,* started and perpetuated by the English during the sixteenth century. English translators and compilers of Spanish explorations tweaked the reports to portray the Spanish as cruel, vicious, and inhumane. Two impetuses drove this presentation. First, the English coveted and fought for some Spanish territories and the wealth they generated. Second, as England became a Protestant nation, the English sought to critique Spain, a Roman Catholic one, for how it used religion to conquer and destroy other peoples. As with all insulting accusations, the Black Legend took on a life of its own, even influencing views of Hispanics today.

Contrary to this popular belief, the Spanish were no worse or better in their treatment of Indians than were the British. Typically, the Spanish incorporated Indians into their communities (more so than did the British or the French, albeit at a lower status), and often intermarried with them. We also need to keep historical context in mind. Europe as a whole was still adjusting to the idea that the Indians of the New World even existed—and that they might truly be human beings. Much of early Spanish law affecting Indians revolved around efforts to convert them and confusion about their humanity.

Because of the debate over the status of the Indians and the promise to convert them, the Spanish Crown and the Council of the Indies passed numerous laws intended to protect the Indians. We need to examine these laws in two ways. First, the intent of the law demonstrates how society wrestled with the issue of these other peoples. Second, enforcement demonstrates how serious the government was about the law. It also shows, as you will see, whether the people affected by the law felt it would treat them fairly.

The King and Queen considered the Indians under Crown Protection, meaning that they were responsible for the Indians' welfare. (This paternalistic relationship became a precursor for the trusteeship used by the United States nearly four hundred years later.) By 1512, King Ferdinand passed a law stating, "No Indian shall be whipped or beaten or called 'dog' or any other name unless it be his proper name." As odd as this law may sound to us today, it tells us significant things: it attempts to ban the mistreatment of Indians, and it tries to regulate a certain level of respect of native beliefs and names. And evidence shows that a significant number of Spaniards were convicted of mistreatment of Indians. Around the same time, native courts were established throughout the colonies, wherein Indians could bring complaints against Spaniards. Again, we do not know how evenly enforced the law was, but we do know that quite a few Indians filed cases in the courts, suggesting they expected fair treatment.

But, as we know all too well, just because there are laws on the books does not mean that people will obey them or not find loopholes in them. Two Spanish laws demonstrate this point. In 1512, the Council of Indies passed the Cannibal Law. It declared that any group that practiced cannibalism clearly lacked souls and, therefore, was ineligible for conversion. As mentioned, the Spanish figured they could ethically enslave those who refused conversion. The law did not outline how one was to determine whether or not an Indian was cannibalistic, creating an easy out for conquistadors who encountered recalcitrant Indians. Similarly, a law passed in 1542 banning the enslavement of Indians also contained loopholes. Treasonous Indians, even converts, could be enslaved, which increased the number of Indians accused of treason as well as the number of mock trials for Indians. The purpose behind these laws was to display a desire, probably a genuine one on the part of the Crown and the Council, to try to protect the Indians from unscrupulous Spaniards. In short, they did try to fulfill their Christian duty.

As the Spanish moved northward into northern New Spain, they became aware of how vast the country was and how little support they would receive from their own colonists. Over the course of their time on the northern frontier of New Spain, the Spanish came to use the Indians as allies, administrators, and in other capacities, giving them a distinct role in the empire. As they moved northward, the Spanish brought with them Indians from Mexico as colonists and soldiers. They consistently used different groups of Indians as allies against other groups. And after a series of Indian-led revolts in the late seventeenth century, the Spanish grafted their bureaucratic hierarchy onto Indian tribal hierarchies, using chiefs and other high-ranking officials as administrators and tax collectors within the Spanish Empire, much as they had been used in their respective tribal governments. This cooptation of Indians into the empire created problems for Europeans who came to the American West later with the expectation of being able to treat Indians solely as chattel.

The Spanish also treated Indians and their relationship to the land differently than did the other European groups who followed. Remember the encomiendas: they granted colonists land *and* labor. The Spanish viewed the Indians as part of the land, an active part of the environment. That said, the Spanish did not view the Indians as they did pronghorns or deer. They also argued the Indians owned the land because they occupied it. It is through this logic that the Spanish eventually granted certain tribes encomiendas, haciendas, and estancias of their own. These land grants meant that the various groups, such as the Hopis and Navajos, possessed actual pieces of paper that granted them control over their land—something that would be very important to the British and later the Americans.

But what, you may ask, did the Indians think of the Spanish? From the period of the first explorations, the Indians realized that the Spanish were a whole lot of trouble. Early explorers expected supplies and support from the Indians, constantly hassling them to tell them where they might find gold and other riches. They left their livestock loose to graze on or trample Indians crops. They also introduced epidemic diseases that took the lives of an untold number of persons. Things did not improve once a colony was established.

The Spanish introduced a tax system that required money and labor from the Indians. Suddenly, the Spanish expected the Indians to help them build roads, houses and tend crops and livestock—all this in exchange for the right to live where they had always lived. Resentment quickly built among the various Indian groups. Beginning in the 1600s, revolts began to explode across northern New Spain, and Spanish officials brutally quelled most of these uprisings. Such punishment did little to endear the Spanish to the Indians. As the missions cracked down and tried to stamp out native beliefs, these beliefs simply went underground, as did a growing resentment of the Spanish. When this resentment finally boiled over in the Pueblo Revolt of 1680, the Indians "burned the images, temples, crosses, rosaries, and things of divine worship, committing such atrocities as killing priests, Spaniards, women and children."

The Indians eventually gained another ally in their hatred of the Spanish, the mestizos. Ignored and not officially recognized by the Spanish, most mestizos lived between two cultures, finding the various Indian groups more welcoming than the Spanish. Originally, even the missions would not welcome the growing mestizo population, as their purpose was to convert the Indians, not mestizos. This isolation from the Spanish and an alliance with the Indians led to a strong and dangerous (for the Europeans, that is) alliance between the mestizos and the Pueblo Indians.

Effects of the Spanish Empire

The Spanish Empire and its interactions with the Indians of the Southwest set the stage for future incursions and conflicts. When Mexico won its independence from Spain in a decade long revolution between 1810 and 1821, Mexican-born (*criollo*) Spaniards, mestizos, and Indians fought against the peninsulares and Spain. But Mexico continued to struggle to protect and control its northern frontier provinces, like Spain before it. Indian groups such as the Apaches and Utes continued to raid frontier settlements, while other groups traded with them or sought protection under them. Mexican independence led to another change, for in the 1820s, in the interests of economic development, the new Mexican government would open its northern provinces to trade with American merchants and even settlement by Americans (in Texas).

By the time Americans began arriving in significant numbers in the 1820s and 1830s, the Indians of the Southwest had experienced almost three hundred years of contact with the Spanish Empire and Mexico. And that contact had changed all the peoples involved. The Spanish co-opted some Indian groups by including them in the process of empire: using headmen and chiefs as tax collectors, or letting mestizos serve in the bureaucracy. The Spanish came to rely on Indian labor and goods to keep the empire going. They granted the Indians limited land rights to convince them to become allies. These land rights complicated matters for later empires, as the Indians actually had pieces of paper that granted them ownership of the land. Additionally, the Indians had become accustomed to being incorporated, though not as equals, into the empire.

The Indians adapted to the Spanish. Many became bilingual and bicultural. As more Indians spoke Spanish, they found themselves able to communicate effectively among all the different indigenous groups in the region. This fact created intertribal ties that Americans often discounted or ignored years later. As the Spanish and Indian populations intermarried, a whole new borderlands and regional culture emerged, one that would shape the nation of Mexico.

∽ Suggested Readings ∾

Calvert, Robert A., Arnoldo De León, and Gregg Cantrell. *The History of Texas,* 4th Ed. Wheeling, IL: Harlan Davidson, Inc., 2007.

Campbell, Randolph B. *Gone to Texas: A History of the Lone Star State.* New York: Oxford University Press, 2003.

Hackel, Stephen. *Children of Coyote, Missionaries of Saint Francis: Indian-Spanish Relations in Colonial California.* Chapel Hill: University of North Carolina Press, 2005.

Jackson, Robert H. and Edward Castillo. *Indians, Franciscans, and Spanish Colonization: The Impact of the Mission System on California Indians.* Albuquerque: University of New Mexico Press, 1995.

Knaut, Andrew. *The Pueblo Revolt of 1680: Conquest and Resistance in Seventeenth-Century New Mexico.* Norman: University of Oklahoma Press, 1995.

Krieger, Alex. *We Came Naked and Barefoot: The Journey of Cabeza de Vaca across North America.* Austin: University of Texas Press, 2002.

Thomas, Hugh. *Conquest: Montezuma, Cortes, and the Fall of Old Mexico.* New York: Simon and Schuster, 1993.

Thomas, Hugh. *Rivers of Gold: The Rise of the Spanish Empire, from Columbus to Magellan.* New York: Random House, 2003.

Pagden, Anthony. *Lords of All the World: Ideologies of Empire in Spain, Britain and France c. 1500–c. 1800.* New Haven: Yale University Press, 1995.

Reséndez, Andrés. *A Land So Strange: The Epic Journey of Cabeza de Vaca.* New York: Basic Books, 2007.

Weber, David. *The Spanish Frontier in North America.* New Haven: Yale University, 1992.

CHAPTER FOUR

West is South: The French Empire

Traditionally, American historians have treated the French Empire in North America as a footnote, despite its lasting effect on place names—Illinois, St. Louis, Louisiana, and the Tetons to name but a few. Nevertheless, in Western and American Indian history, the French played a critical role. They controlled slightly more land than the Spanish did in what became the United States and far more than the British did. The French method of colonization and control of its colonies differed radically from those of the other European colonizers. Additionally, the French presence drove decisions made by both the Spanish and the English, who viewed the French as competition for land, resources, and trade. Finally, through their trade and contact with the Indians west of the Mississippi and west of the Rockies, it was the French who introduced a large number of Indian nations to European languages, cultures, social mores, and economic ideas.

Territory

With relatively few Frenchmen, the French controlled more territory in colonial North America than either the Spanish or the British. By the early 1700s, French territory ran from the Atlantic Ocean to the Rocky Mountains in what is now Canada and the Northwest United States, with a center core that stretched down the Mississippi River valley and across the Missouri River valley. Beyond that large region, French traders and trappers also fanned out through Spanish and English territories, trying to undermine those nations' trade with the Indians. French traders, trappers, and missionaries drew some of the first maps of the western half of North America. They explored and mapped the Missouri River, parts of the Rocky Mountains, and the Columbia River valley, among other important geographical features of the West.

In 1534, Jacques Cartier arrived in Northeastern North America, shortly after the Spanish had landed in the Southeast. When the French arrived, the Spanish represented their only European competition on the continent. Cartier and other early explorers attempted to settle colonies along the St. Lawrence River in present-day Canada. The Spanish and French both sought to milk North America for its riches to help support wars and political tussles back in Europe. Where the Spanish focused on mines and settlers, the French concentrated on the fur trade. Like early settlements in Northern New Spain, the early French colonies failed.

Eventually, however, the French managed to use a small number of colonies to secure a huge swath of territory. The French employed two types of colonies. In the East, along the Gulf of Mexico and up the Mississippi River and over to the Appalachian Mountains, they created forts and trading centers, importing colonists who farmed and traded with the Indians. These colonies established a boundary between French territory and what would become British territory, such as Fort Toulouse in present-day Alabama, or between French and Spanish territory, such as Natchitoches on the Red River in present-day Texas. Into the Gulf Coast region, the French brought colonists and African slaves, who built small plantations on which they grew staple crops like corn and beans to trade with the Indians for deer and beaver skins. Why staple crops? The French discovered that the Indians could do more hunting and processing of furs and skins if they did not have to farm. In addition to manufactured goods like kettles and axe heads, the French in the Southeast traded food, which eventually made the Indians largely dependent on the French, something the Spanish and the British, who did not trade in food at first, were slow to notice.

The French developed a different sort of colony on the western and northern frontiers, where there was less pressure from other European groups. There they established trading posts, often at the confluence of Indian trading paths or in spots where Indian groups traditionally traded. Unlike the Spanish in their southeastern colonies, the French did not import colonists into the West: the western territory was a place in which to conduct trade. Though parts of the western territory rubbed against Spanish territory to the south (present-day Texas, New Mexico, and Colorado) and British territory on the West Coast of North America (Oregon, Washington, and Mississippi), the French relied on their trading and political relationships with the Indians to secure their North American territory.

The French wanted to create outposts of control with which to irritate their European rivals: the Spanish and the British. First, the French established settlements, including a plantation system, in present-day Louisiana, to control trade coming down the Mississippi River and also to keep an eye on the Spanish trade out of Mexico and the British trade in the southern Appalachians. Then the French established forts and settlements in today's Quebec to keep an eye on the British. Yet the vast majority of French territory in the West remained only nominally under their control, a form of control that was mainly economic.

Structure

The French had one basic reason for coming to North America: trade. Originally, an informal system of trade sprung up between French fishermen, who came to the northern coast of North America for cod, and the coastal Indians. Remember that various Indian societies had already established lucrative trading systems that crisscrossed North America. Once the French realized this system existed, they insinuated themselves into it. To be exact, the French wanted to join the lucrative fur trade in beaver pelts and deerskins that flowed out of North America. This fur trade became more formal with the establishment of trading posts in the Northeast in 1600, just before the British arrived in the same area. These post often consisted of no more than a wooden building built at a crossroads where trade among Indians already occurred. Many trading posts were located near or on rivers, to facilitate the transportation of goods. Major ones included Rivière du Loup (Wolf River) along the St. Lawrence River, Trois-Riviéres (Three Rivers) in Quebec, and Miramichi (Clans of the Micmac) off the

A fur trader and his wares. This nineteenth-century photograph illustrates the reality of the fur trade. *Library and Archives Canada/C-001229, 1947-009 NPC*

Gulf of St. Lawrence. How lucrative was the fur trade? In 1602, a beaver skin cost two knives in trade with the Indians. By 1610, it cost 15–20 knives, still a good bargain. Beaver pelts and deerskins were extremely important in Europe from the sixteenth century through the mid-eighteenth century. By this time, Europeans had hunted the beaver and deer population in Europe to near extinction. While people from peasants to kings wore leather clothing, hence the need for deerskins, beaver pelts were a luxury item, initially at least. In Europe, with long rainy and snowy winters, waterproof and warm were two qualities that people demanded in their clothing; beaver pelts, when felted, produced a material that was both.

Early explorers discovered that many Indian groups not only hunted beaver but also processed them in a way that made felting easier. Felting is the process whereby fibers are wetted and rubbed until they bond with one another. It creates a fabric that lacks stitches or holes, places where water or wind can penetrate.

In Europe, the Russians controlled the felting market, and European trappers had long sent most beaver pelts harvested in Europe to Russia for felting. The Russians used mercury to break or dissolve the guard hairs on the beaver pelt. Many of the hatters contracted mercury poisoning, which quickly causes insanity (hence a possible source of the phrase "mad as a hatter"). Pelts harvested by Indians quickly interrupted the Russian monopoly on felting. Two types of pelts came out of North America: coat and parchment. Coat pelts were the most prized, because the Indians processed them by wearing them. Indians wore beaver pelts with the fur facing in, a practice that eventually wore off the guard hairs. Therefore, these pelts were already partially processed, making them very valuable to Europeans who wanted to cut out the Russians. Parchment pelts were unprocessed pelts brought directly to the trading post; these still had to be sent to Russia for felting.

Instead of trying to create a bureaucracy in North America and import their own methods of administrating a large territory, as had the Spanish, the French chose to layer their own goals on top of the Indian systems of trade and governance already in place. They took advantage of the elaborate and long-standing trading networks the Indians had created and maintained for many years. The French did, as mentioned, establish forts and some outposts staffed with French administrators to help them maintain the frontier against the British in the East and the Spanish in the Southwest. But the majority of French personnel consisted of two groups: *coureurs de bois* (runners of the woods), and *voyageurs* (travelers). Coureurs de bois, often referred to as "traders" by the English, were individuals who engaged in the fur trade without the official oversight of the French government. Voyageurs, or trappers, were second-generation coureurs de bois who operated with licenses, or the express consent of the French government. Coureurs de bois arranged trade between Indian groups and helped the Indians bring their goods (meaning furs) to the French outposts. Voyageurs lived with the Indians and helped facilitate trade and the economic and political issues that shaped or affected trade. For instance, voyageurs worked to create peace treaties and trade alliances between groups to keep trade flowing over certain areas. They sought out new territory by making alliances and friends with new groups of Indians. Both coureurs de bois and voyageurs came as single men, often in financial debt to the government for the cost of their passage. They tended to be illiterate but had decided to go to New France for lack of other options. The majority of them stayed in New France, intermarrying with Indian groups and producing a viable and active population of *Métis* (persons who were half-French and half-Indian.) The French government, while encouraging the efforts of the voyageurs and coureurs de bois, did not support them through subsidies or protection. Once one of these men headed off downriver with a group of Indians, he was on his own to get himself and his goods back to the French outposts. This system put the Frenchmen at the mercy of the Indians. To survive, they needed to create blood ties and build the loyalty of the Indians by participating directly in their customs, culture, warfare, and economies.

Two important processes happen when different groups of people suddenly interact with one another: acculturation and assimilation. The French acculturated, meaning they adopted the cultural practices of the Indians both consciously and unconsciously. Acculturation tends to occur subtly, over time, and is a two-way street. As the French acculturated to

These canoes were typical modes of transportation for Indians and fur traders in New France. *Buffalo Bill Historical Center, Cody, Wyoming;* Harper's Weekly *June 20th 1874, Vincent Mercaldo Collection, VM0003*

the Indians, the Indians, in turn, acculturated to the French, learning to speak French and gaining an understanding of French ideas and trading practices. Assimilation represents a forced change, usually one brought about by a dominant force or society. Of the European groups discussed so far, the Spanish practiced assimilation in their American empire. They did their best to force the Indians to adopt their language, religion, and culture. Nonetheless, acculturation and assimilation usually coexist. The Franciscans in New Spain tried hard to assimilate some Indians into the Catholic Church. After the Pueblo Revolt of 1680, the Spanish adopted local political structures when reorganizing Northern New Spain, thereby switching to acculturation. The French, on the other hand, focused more on acculturation from the start.

The voyageurs became as much a part of the local cultures as they could. The French government allowed, even encouraged, intermarriage, which usually meant living as husband and wife according to local, Indian custom, known as *mariages à la façon du pays* (in the manner of the country). This practice provided voyageurs the opportunity to learn Indian languages, customs, and the political landscape, knowledge they then exploited to facilitate trade. More important, intermarriage created blood ties between the voyageurs and the various groups of Indians with whom they wished to trade. Blood ties were very important in Indian cultures, as mentioned in Chapter Two. By learning the local politics, the voyageurs learned to take advantage of political opportunities. For example, voyageurs and administrators worked hard in the Southeast, meaning present-day Louisiana, Alabama, and Mississippi, to create peace treaties and alliances between Indian groups. The French understood that war slowed economic development and progress, so they withheld trade from groups who would not lay down their arms and interact peacefully. Essentially they were using trade embargos to keep trade flowing. If the Cherokee wanted to trade with the French, they needed to make peace with the Choctaw and the Chickasaw.

The French provided the Indians with enticing trade options, more so than their European rivals: the Spanish, the British, and eventually the Americans. The French attempted, though not always successfully, to trade items that the Indians wanted. When they traded durable goods, such as kettles and axes, they understood that at a certain point these items would saturate the market, and the French would need to introduce new products. Because of their close relations with the Indians, they understood that in most Indian societies within their territory, women conducted trade. And since women also processed most of the fur and pelts, it was very important to keep them happy. Therefore, the French brought to the table items such as fabric and cooking utensils that they knew would help and appeal to women. Because the voyageurs lived within Indian communities, they knew firsthand what people would want and need. This relationship underlay the decision of the French to trade to the Indians an important item that the Spanish and British would not: guns.

Guns became an extremely important trading item. Believing considerably in their technological superiority, the Spanish and the British feared that introducing guns to the Indians would shift negatively the balance of power. The French did not feel this way. They wanted the Indians to be as efficient hunters as possible, and guns helped achieve that goal. And, as they were not organic trading items, guns made the Indians more economically dependent on the French. In other words, bullets and musket balls could not be manufactured out of the natural resources available to the Indians. Therefore, once a culture adopted the gun, they needed a constant supply of things they could not make for themselves, like gunpowder, minié balls, and other supplies necessary to use and maintain that weapon. Dependency, however, went both ways: just as the French became dependent on the fur trade, the Indians became dependent on guns.

The ability to kill more animals more efficiently meant that some Indian groups depleted the natural resources around them. Put simply, they overhunted. The Micmacs of eastern Canada represent one such case in point. The Micmacs acquired guns from the French in order to increase their production of beaver pelts. But guns helped them wipe out the beaver in their territory. This depletion created not just economic problems, but religious and cultural ones as well.

Micmac society had traditionally been a hunting one, centered on a reverence of the beaver and other animals of their territory and an understanding that the continued welfare of society rested on proper respect for and usage of these natural resources. Guns threw this philosophy and practice out of balance. Furthermore, the French coupled the introduction of guns with the introduction of Christianity. The Micmac viewed Christianity as a new and powerful ideology, seeing it as somehow related to the superior technology of the gun. So, just as the gun undid the ecological balance, Christianity and its perceived power destabilized the religious and cultural balance. As the Micmac became more involved in trade on European terms, they abandoned their beliefs and tools in favor of those of the white man, including their belief that the Micmac played a role in the preservation of the ecosystem. Eventually, the beaver ceased to exist within Micmac territory, as did their traditional religion and their culture.

Guns also destabilized the political landscape. When they first received guns, many Indians in French territory valued the ammunition so highly that they did not use the weapons in warfare except as a means for scaring the other side. Often one group in a conflict possessed guns and the other side did not. This changed the traditional balance of power. For example, the French traded guns with the Creek, Chickasaw, and Natchez in the mid-1500s. This exchange led to the rise to power and dominance of all three groups in the Southeast.

One must keep in mind, however, that the guns available at the time were not the ones you see in films depicting this period, but muskets that were heavy (up to ten pounds) and unwieldy (up to six feet long), making running through the forest with one of them awkward to say the least. On top of that, these weapons were inaccurate and had a nasty tendency to "backfire" into the faces of their users. Arrows and other weapons, which had evolved over centuries for use in the forest, were far lighter and easier to use. Slowly, however, guns became more dominant in warfare, which wrought unexpected changes on the Indians' social and political landscapes.

Guns possessed more killing and destructive power, but bows and arrows were stealthier and took far less time to "reload." Guns killed more people than did arrows, but not for the reasons you might think. Arrow wounds tend to be clean: in one side, out the other. They can be cauterized and tend not to result in broken bones, which can become infected. An arrow wound in a major organ or artery can, of course, be fatal, but the majority of arrows go through flesh. A musket ball, on the other hand, creates a ragged, tearing wound. And musket balls shatter bones, leaving bone fragments that often become infected. People hit with a musket ball tend not to die on the battlefield, but sometime later of infection.

The higher death rate reshaped many Indian societies by changing the gender ratio. Most Indian warfare solely involved men, so when the use of guns resulted in a higher death toll, an increasing number of women were left without husbands and partners. The dearth of men created a new problem for Indian societies. Women produced children who represented the future of the tribe. Fewer husbands meant fewer children. Additionally, women processed most of the hides, oversaw agriculture, and controlled trade. However, women who had to worry about protecting themselves and their children had a lot less time to process hides or produce food. In short, Indian societies had to restructure their cultures in response to the changes caused by guns.

The higher death tolls increased the rate among Indian groups of kidnapping and adopting of both men and women. To put it bluntly, new bodies replaced those killed in battle. Both male and female captives benefited from this change. Prior to the introduction of the gun, war captives, particularly men, were tortured and killed to restore honor. After the introduction of the gun, Indian societies were more likely to adopt the men captured in raids or battle. The increased rate of capture and adoption also destabilized societies and led to more raiding, as stronger tribes began to take more captives from weaker ones—which inevitably led to more warfare.

In general, trade with the French changed Indian cultures in the North, much as conquest by the Spanish had in the South. The Blackfeet, in what is now Montana, illustrate this process. As this group began to trade with the French, the pressure on the Indians to produce more beaver pelts increased. Since women processed the beaver pelts after the men killed the animals, women became more highly prized within Blackfeet society. Bride prices increased and a new item became the bride price

Red River Cart. An alternative method for transporting furs used by the Métis, this cart was named after the Red River in Manitoba, a fur-trading hub. *Buffalo Bill Historical Center, Cody, Wyoming; Vincent Mercaldo Collection, VM0004*

standard: the horse. To marry a woman who could process many beaver pelts, a man had to come up with several horses to give her father. The groom typically obtained the horses by taking them from other tribes. But other tribes protected their horses fiercely, which meant that many young men got themselves killed on horse raids. As increased warfare killed young men in increasing numbers, the gender ratios in the tribe became uneven, with women outnumbering men. This situation gave women serious economic value. The more wives a man had, the more beaver pelts he could hope to process and the more trade items he could hope to obtain. This cycle led to polygamy among the Blackfeet, a cultural change not encouraged or suggested by the French but nonetheless caused by their trade.

The French empire differed from the Spanish empire. After the failure of early colonies, the French focused on trade. To succeed in this goal, they melded themselves into the existing economies and cultural systems already built and maintained by the Indians. The French started out dependent on the Indians but eventually leveled the relationship with the implementation of the gun trade. By intermarrying with the Indians, the French became intertwined with Indian societies and their goals. Yet they remained enmeshed in European conflicts and ideas. Because of this duality, the French also followed the Spanish into the world of conversion.

Missions

Like the Spanish, the French believed part of their role in North America involved bringing Christianity to the Indians. A Catholic nation, France's history and relationship with the Church differed radically from that of Spain. One hundred years after the Spanish expelled the Muslims from Western Europe, the new threat to Catholicism seemingly came from within. France verged on a religious war between the Catholics and the new Protestants, called Huguenots. Additionally, the role of a monarch or king had evolved in the ensuing one hundred years. Now, in addition to believing they ruled by divine right, kings perceived themselves as absolutists with the power to unify the kingdom, just as God had the power to regulate the Universe. The King of France saw himself as God's representative on earth, thus shutting the Pope out of the equation of power. Thus, unlike the Spanish, who incorporated the Church into their empire's bureaucracy, the French government allowed and encouraged the Church but did not incorporate it into the state to the same degree.

Father Marquette descending the Mississippi, 1673, by O.E. Berninghaus. *The New York Public Library Picture Collection #808237u*

The French King granted the missionaries the right to work in New France, but he did not support them in their work financially. That duty fell to individuals and companies that sought to explore and reap the resources of New France. The King offered potential investors in New France a trade-off: you can have the rights to the resources you find, if you help Christianize the Indians. In other words, he outsourced the need to Christianize the Indians, putting the cost and onus on entrepreneurs and explorers. Whereas the Spanish empire absorbed the cost of missions as the price of doing business, the French cut expenses by making individuals and groups of investors, called companies, pay for the tab. The Duc de Ventador, an individual, and the Compagnie du Saint-Sacrament, a mercantile company, both paid to bring individual missionaries and religious orders to New France. This act essentially freed the French government from that expense, allowing it to focus more on developing the economic aspects of the colonies.

The story of Samuel de Champlain illustrates this process. Champlain was an explorer, cartographer, and entrepreneur who wanted to settle New France and reap the benefits of the land. Unlike Columbus, who petitioned the King and Queen of Spain for money, Champlain raised his own money but did petition the King of France for permission to explore present-day eastern Canada. In that petition, he laid out four goals. First, he planned to introduce the Indians to the Catholic faith. Then, he planned to claim the land and resources of the land for the King

New France, 1750. This map shows the territory of New France circa 1750 as
well as the land that France ceded to Great Britain in 1713: the area around
Hudson Bay, the east coast of Canada, and Newfoundland. (France ceded the
rest of Canada to Great Britain after the French and Indian War, 1975–63,
and sold Louisiana to the United States in 1803.) Note the size of the territory
France controlled in the mid-eighteenth century in what would become the
continental United States as compared to that controlled respectively by Spain
and Great Britain at the time. Also note that New France included major
waterways and ports that served as highways into the interior of North
America: the St. Lawrence River, which begins in Lake Ontario, the
Mississippi River, which ends in the Gulf of Mexico, and the Ohio and
Tennessee rivers.

of France. Additionally, he wanted to find a water route to Asia through the region, the famed Northwest Passage. Finally, he wanted to establish colonies to help settle the area for France. He summed it up to the King: "to teach these peoples, along with the knowledge of God, the glory and triumphs of your Majesty, so that with the French speech they may also acquire a French heart and spirit." To do all this, he created the Company of 100 Associates that raised the money he needed to cover the costs of ships and crew and take four Recollet priests with him.

Recollet priests were associated with the Franciscan order of priests in Spain, which administered more than 500 missions in New Spain at the time. Therefore, the French believed the Recollets would have a better understanding of the Indians. They began arriving in 1618 with papal permission. The Recollets encountered several problems. First, they supported settlement in the colony, seeing that as one way to introduce the Indians to Catholicism. Champlain founded several settlements, all of which failed due to the harsh conditions and the lack of support from the French government. His focus on settlements was at odds with the King's focus on trade. Additionally, the Recollets firmly believed that the Indians were degraded and possibly incapable of becoming Catholics and quickly dismissed them as unworthy of conversion. The Recollets left New France in 1624 and the French replaced them with another order who would wield much greater influence among the Indians: the Jesuits.

The Jesuits in New France differed significantly from the Franciscans already at work in New Spain. The Jesuits defined themselves as a group at war with the rise of Protestantism, not with infidels. By the turn of the seventeenth century, the Catholic Church viewed the rise of Protestantism as a more serious threat than that posed by infidels. In the eyes of the Catholic Church, infidels rejected Christianity but Protestants *misinterpreted* it, a movement that, left unchecked, might usurp the authority of the Catholic Church. Jesuits were committed to maintaining the unity of the Catholic Church. To do that, they vowed to serve as warriors for the preservation of the Church, beliefs that shaped their work with the Indians of North America.

The Jesuits viewed the Indians as raw material for conversion; the missionaries' goal was to secure the Indians' souls for the Catholic Church before Protestant groups could do so. As far as the Jesuits were concerned, conversion and alliance went hand in hand. The Jesuits were more open to integrating popular forms of religion, and they were more comfortable with letting the Indians practice a syncretic (melded) form of Catholicism than Franciscans or Protestants. For example, the Jesuits worked with the Huron, a group who lived along present-day Lake Huron. They were a sizeable group, numbering about 2,000–3,000 people in 1615. A confederacy of smaller tribes, they served an important go-between role with the Algonkin and the Montagnais. Hurons who attended Mass but also spoke to the Great Spirit did not bother the Jesuits. Additionally, the Jesuits were cultural rationalists. They believed that even minor similarities between cultures suggested greater ones. For example, Jesuits believed firmly that one must suffer for one's faith. One of their greatest heroes was Jean de Brebeuf whom the Iroquois flailed or "flayed" and roasted alive. Iroquois, Huron, and other Northeastern Indians also believed that sufferance represented the achievement of manhood. The two ideas dovetailed, as both groups viewed suffering as a means to greater status, whether in society or in the hereafter.

The Jesuits advocated living with the Indians to understand better their cultures in order to convert them. The "black robes," as the Northeastern Indians called them, paddled canoes with the Indians, ate their food, slept in their houses, and hunted with them. Once embedded in a tribe, the Jesuits resented the intrusion of the traders, whom they blamed for introducing immoral ideas to the Indians. They accused the traders of everything from fornicating with Indians to swearing in front of them. The traders saw the Jesuits as disrupting the trade they had worked so hard to establish, by distracting the Indians from hunting and processing furs with their lessons and preachings.

If you were a French missionary in New France, here is a snapshot of what your life might look like. A sponsor like Ventador or Champlain would pay to sail you to New France. You would arrive in New France and be taken by traders or trappers, or in rare cases, by a French administrator, to a trading post and left there. Now you were on your own. It was your responsibility to find a group of Indians who would agree to take you in with them, support you, and let you set up a residence in or nearby their village. You were expected to adopt their lifestyle: eat their food, sleep in their houses, paddle canoes with them. The Jesuits believed this was the only way for missionaries to learn several important things. First, they needed to become fluent in the specific language. Second, they needed to understand the culture of the tribe in order to see the similarities and the overlaps that might make conversion possible. Thanks to this process and the massive reports these missionaries sent back to their superiors in France, we know a lot about native groups in French territory during the 1500s and 1600s. Since French Catholic missions spread beyond French territory, with missionaries crossing the Rocky Mountains and establishing missions in Idaho, Washington, and Oregon, they influenced a wide variety of groups well before other Europeans even made contact with them.

While the French government provided little support for the Jesuits and the missions, it also expected little in return. The French did not use missions to secure their territory or frontier as the Spanish had. That role belonged to the traders and trappers. Instead, the French government expected the missionaries to do no harm to established trading relationships. In fact, there are several points during the history of New France when the French government withdrew missionaries and banned them from the territories because they had disrupted trading relations.

The missionaries in New France differed in other ways from their counterparts in the Southwest. Unlike in New Spain, where missionaries tended to be priests, several female orders worked in New France. This movement aided conversion efforts, particularly in the eastern part of New France. Many of the native groups in those areas were matriarchal, employing clan mother systems. This meant that women played a more dominant role in decision making within the tribe and within the lives of sons. While clashes did erupt between the Jesuits and Iroquois women in particular, the presence of French women religious did encourage the conversion of Indian women. These converts, in turn, used their influence to convince other members of their tribes to convert.

On the surface, it appears that the Spanish and the French shared a desire to convert as many Indians as they could, but the similarities end there. Whereas the Crown and the state sponsored missions in New Spain, in New France, individuals paid for the missions. The Spanish used missions to secure the frontier and assimilate the Indians. The French expected missionaries to insinuate themselves into Indian societies and acculturate to those societies. The Spanish used missions as trading centers. The French warned missionaries not to disrupt trade. These different attitudes toward conversion influenced different attitudes toward the Indians.

Indian Relations

As in New Spain, in New France the intruders' interaction with Indians shaped native groups' ideas about how trade and relations would work with all Europeans. Because of their reduced bureaucracy and emphasis on trade, the French interacted with the Indians as partners, though not as equals. The Indians provided the intruders not just pelts but also knowledge of and access to trading systems. This factor gave the former power in the relationship. The French needed the Indians, especially in the beginning, more than the reverse. Any good economist will tell you that people respond to incentives. Until the introduction of firearms as a trading item, French-Indian trade favored the Indians. The French so desired trade with the Indians that even Champlain sought to develop trading ties. At one point, he went on raids with the Montagnais and Algonkin, allies of the Huron, against the Iroquois, winning respect when he and four other Frenchmen used their muskets to kill several Iroquois and defeat them. Furs and pelts were commonplace for the Indians but in great demand among the French. It was guns and the Indians' dependence on the French for them that evened out the relationship.

From the writings of priests, explorers, and officers, it is clear that the French felt much of the same ethnocentricity toward the Indians as the Spanish. They felt that their religion was the superior vision and that they had a superior ability to think abstractly. French writers decried the lack of hierarchy and bureaucracy within Indian systems of governance. Champlain complained, "the freedom of the children in these countries, is so great, they prove so incapable of government and discipline . . . we must despair of their conversion without the conversion of their parents." But even as they criticized the Indians, the French remained focused on their main goal: trade. They wanted to make sure that their ideas did not disrupt the fur trade that proved more lucrative than almost any other trade.

Despite their feeling of superiority, the French interacted so closely with Indians that they wound up changing Indian societies in significant ways. The French, for example, intermarried with the Indians and even encouraged the practice. To the modern eye, this suggests a conflict. How could the French have seen the Indians as inferior if they married them? First, remember that in Europe during the time most marriages were arranged for economic or social reasons. Marriages between French traders and Indian women followed the same pattern. Through intermarriage, the traders gained an entry into the trading systems and the Indians gained access to European goods. Second, equality within marriage represents a twentieth-century concept. Most European nation-states in the seventeenth and eighteenth centuries viewed women as property. French men, like their European counterparts, did not consider women as their equals. Marriage or sexual relations with Indian women represented a means to an economic end and a form of dominance, not necessarily a love match.

The Jesuits influenced French perceptions of the image of the Indian. In their attempt to understand better the Indians whom they wanted to convert, the Jesuits became keen observers of them. The picture they produced of Indians was a multilayered one. Though the Jesuits saw the Indians as inferior, they did not think they were without merit. Jesuit accounts comment on the Indians' focus on family issues, their sense of humor, and their strong sense of loyalty, even while complaining about their lack of "proper" religion, their lack of respect for the Jesuits, and their different sexual mores. The Jesuits' relationship with Indian women underscores the double-edged sword of their observations. Jesuit priests recognized the importance of the matrilineal aspects of various Indian societies. In doing so, they structured their conversion efforts around introducing the image and importance of the Virgin Mary. This suggested an exchange: one powerful mother figure for another. When Huron women, in particular, rejected Catholicism, the priests' descriptions of them in their journals and reports became much harsher, describing them as "unlovable," "overbearing," "rough and wild," and "scornful." Now the missionaries railed against the amount of influence and freedom Huron women had within their societies.

Jesuits and other authors at this time helped to create the image of the "noble savage." The French conceived of Indians as wild and free; in French *l'homme sauvage* means "wild man." They saw them as free of hierarchy, of institutions such as the Church and the state, and of regulation. Nonetheless, they believed the Indians were rational men who would eventually see the logic and clarity of Christianity and come to embrace it. Champlain declared to the King, "by no means so savage but that in time and through intercourse with civilization they be refined." Unlike the Spanish, who saw it as an either-or proposition (convert or else), the French saw Indians as peoples in need of being led to Christianity. These two factors, trade and conversion, also shaped how the French treated the Métis, the offspring of French fathers and Indian mothers. Unlike the Spanish, who viewed the mestizos with suspicion, fearing they might harbor split loyalties, the French viewed the Métis as bridges between both cultures. Again, they did not treat the Métis as equals but they did value them as facilitators in trade and conversion, seeing them as the physical embodiment of the change from one society and system to another.

ເ໐ Suggested Readings ເ໐

Blackburn, Carole. *Harvest of Souls: The Jesuit Missions and Colonialism in North America, 1632–1650.* Montreal: McGill-Queen's University Press, 2000.

Calloway, Colin, ed. *The World Turned Upside Down: Indian Voices from Early America.* Boston: St. Martin's Press, 1994.

Hafen, LeRoy. *French Fur Traders and Voyageurs in the American West.* Lincoln: University of Nebraska, 1997.

Lewis, Henry. *The Robidoux Chronicles: Ethnohistory of the French-American Fur Trade.* Victoria: Trafford Publishing, 2004.

Nute, Grace Lee. *The Voyageur.* St. Paul: Minnesota Historical Society Press, 1987.

Podruchny, Carolyn. *Making the Voyageur World: Travelers and Traders in the North American Fur Trade.* Toronto: University of Toronto, 2006.

Sleeper-Smith, Susan. *Indian Women and French Men: Rethinking Cultural Encounter In the Western Great Lakes.* Amherst: University of Massachusetts Press, 2001.

Usner, Daniel. *Indians, Settlers and Slaves in a Frontier Exchange Economy.* Williamsburg: Institute of Early American History and Culture, 1992.

Van Kirk, Sylvia. *Many Tender Ties: Women in Fur Trade Society, 1670–1870.* Norman: University of Oklahoma Press, 1983.

White, Richard. *The Middle Ground: Indians, Empires, and Republics in the Great Lakes Region, 1650–1815.* New York: Cambridge University Press, 1991.

CHAPTER FIVE

The English Empire: Turner's First West

In 1620, the English arrived in Plymouth and Charlestown (Charleston) to begin a permanent incursion into North America. Preceded by the Spanish by a hundred years and the French by seventy-five, the English were the latecomers to the imperial struggle for the continent. They settled along the Atlantic Coast, spreading north and south from what became Massachusetts and south from what became Virginia. In the North, they immediately ran into the Iroquois Confederacy, which controlled most of western New York State, and the French, who controlled present-day Maine and large parts of the Ohio River valley. In the South, they encountered Powhatan's Confederacy in Virginia, and the Spanish, who controlled parts of Georgia and Florida. The Iroquois, the French, Powhatan, and the Spanish resented the English intrusion. As the English colonies grew west toward the Appalachian Mountains, which they viewed as an obstacle to expansion, they found the French well established as traders with the Cherokee, Creek, and other Indian nations. France also possessed a strong outpost in Louisiana, further complicating English expansion. Until the early 1700s, the English remained hemmed in by these other empires and frustrated by native confederacies. Internal politics, economic crises, and other issues complicated their attempts at expansion. Despite all this, American historians portray the English as the creators of the concept of the West, often at the expense of the Spanish and French empires and always at the expense of native societies and empires that came before them.

Land and Trade

There were two distinct parts to the British Empire in North America, a fact often left out of U.S. history textbooks. There were the Northern colonies, including Massachusetts and its Puritan founders, and there were the Southern colonies, including Jamestown, Virginia, and Charleston, South Carolina. Grade school history taught most of us that the Puritans came to America to escape religious persecution in Europe. That is true

Iroquois village life in the eastern woodlands as depicted by John White. Note the crops and how much the Indian village resembles an English village of the same period, with a central square surrounded by houses. *Library of Congress, LC-USZ62-52444*

up to a point, but focusing too tightly on religious persecution hides the basic reason for their move to Massachusetts: land. The Puritans wanted and needed land to found their own "Zion in the wilderness," a place where *they* would have *total* control over religious observation. (Again, grade school history taught us that the Puritans stood for religious toleration—but that only applied to them.) And when they looked to what they deemed "New England," they perceived the land as empty and theirs for the taking because the Indians living on it had not tamed it and were not using it in the manner that the Christian God deemed proper. In this, they referred to Genesis 1:28, "Be fruitful and multiply, and fill the earth and *subdue* it; and have *dominion* over the fish of the sea and over the birds of the air and over every living thing that moves upon the earth." Puritans built farms and towns, as well as churches, displacing Indians and spending very little time worrying about it. This attitude toward nature directly influenced the Puritans', as well as other Englishmen's, relationship with the Indians.

Soon, other people from England and other parts of Europe moved into the northern colonies looking for land to farm and develop. Strict tax and inheritance laws prevented these people from obtaining land of their own in England. England, Germany, and other European countries all suffered land crises during this period, for wealthy nobles and landlords, including the Catholic and Anglican churches, were the primary landholders. In addition, only the first-born son could inherit his father's land, a patrilineal system that left second and third sons largely out of luck. Finally, the growing (and increasingly wealthy) merchant class often found it impossible to buy into land controlled by noblemen, and poor people stood no chance of gaining land. Why was land so important? Land was the basis of both economic and political power: no land, no power. The realization that North America contained a large amount of "undeveloped" land attracted many people to settle it. By 1700, the Puritans had already become the minority in New England.

In the southern colonies, land was also important, but so was the establishment of trade with the Indians. Trade drew the British to the southeastern Atlantic Seaboard of North America. Landed gentry (people one of several steps below the monarchy who owned land in perpetuity through inheritance) and entrepreneurs looking to establish trading companies helped found Britain's southern colonies. Initially, they began by raiding Spanish and French ships for resources taken from their American colonies. Then, they decided to cut out the middle man and begin their own trading relationships with the Indians, from whom they gained deer skins, beaver pelts, and tobacco. Tobacco use caught on quickly in England and the rest of Europe, where people happily chewed, smoked and "snuffed" tobacco as it became all the rage. Soon the English were cultivating tobacco for trade with Europe and with the Indians. Just as the French grew food for the Indians to increase their hunting time, the British soon grew tobacco for them for the same reason. If the Indians did not need to cultivate tobacco, then they could spend more time hunting and processing pelts.

Unlike the French, the British attempted to take total control of and regulate trade. They licensed traders and required them to renew their licenses regularly in colonial capitals. This stipulation meant that traders had to leave the field on a regular basis and return to the urban centers of British colonies, breaking up, or at least suspending, their relationships with the Indians. The British government also taxed the traders. Finally, the colonial governments negotiated trade and treaties with the Indian groups, not the traders, essentially shutting the traders out of the process. This process left British traders with very little say in the trading policy, as well as the vulnerable targets of Indian frustrations over broken treaties or trade agreements.

In general, the British wanted land on which to settle colonists who would, in turn, produce export commodities—staple crops and cash crops—needed or wanted in Great Britain or other parts of the British Empire. In the North, these colonists built small family farms and grew staple crops (crops with a steady demand that one can eat, like wheat, or use to make products, like flax.) In the South, colonists built colonial plantations that grew cash crops (crops for export or sale only, like tobacco.) Keep in mind that a colonial plantation was nothing like a nineteenth-century antebellum one in the "Old South." A "plantation" in the colonial period simply meant a farm owned by a family that used indentured servants and/or a few slaves to cultivate a crop for market only. Most everybody on the plantation lived in the same house, the help typically making up three or so people outside of the family.

Whether in the North or the South, the English defined unoccupied land quite simply: either you possessed legal title to the land or you did not. In other words, you needed a piece of paper to claim the land as yours. (Of course, the Americans would inherit this idea from the British.) Moreover, this concept of free land served the purposes of the British. The Indians in the Northeast and Southeast did not have pieces of paper for their land, only oral traditions about their homelands. And even though the Indians cultivated the land, the English did not consider their forms of cultivation sufficient evidence of good "use" of it. In what became the United States, the English seemed to ignore the idea of the right to use land without owning it individually (usufruct). In Canada, policymakers applied this common British legal concept to the Indians and other groups. Because the British focused much of their colonial development around land use versus trade and riches, their colonial structure differed from that of the French and the British.

Structure

The structure of the British Empire in North America resembles that of the Spanish far more than that of the French. First, it had a centralized government in London: it was the King and Parliament that granted colonies. Thus, though people like William Penn, the Quaker founder of Pennsylvania, could dictate the tone of settlement and social conduct in a given colony, the granting of land and the regulation of the colonists remained grounded in London. Taxes, land grants, the appointment of colonial governors, and all other major economic and political decisions came directly from the King and Parliament. Like Spain's, Britain's far-flung central authority created many problems for the colonial governments and for the colonists, including the raising of tensions between local governments and colonists and between colonists and local Indians.

Unlike settlers in northern New Spain, British colonists, both in the North and the South, attempted to push the boundaries of their respective colonies westward to escape the nagging oversight of the British colonial government and maintain economic growth. Colonists constantly chafed under taxation and other policies of the British government and sought to alleviate the pressure by moving beyond its control. Some who did so were famous, like Thomas Merton, who created a radical colony in what is now New Hampshire that promoted religious and sexual freedom. He established it just outside of the bounds of Massachusetts to sidestep the control of the Puritan fathers and the colonial government (one in the same at the time.) Other groups were less famous but no less important, like the residents of Deerfield, Massachusetts, and those of western Virginia. These two communities best represent, through their relationships with the British and neighboring Indian groups, some of the frontier and colonial tensions created by the structure of the British government in its American colonies.

British colonists in Massachusetts and Virginia subdivided their land among all their sons, a practice that made for increasingly smaller properties with each generation, leading to smaller and therefore less successful farms. Additionally, many indentured servants were to receive land at the end of their tenure, but as colonial communities grew, less and less land was available in the established parts of the colonies. In need of free land and unhappy with their local governing bodies, British colonists looked west. In the case of both Deerfield and western Virginia, colonists founded their town on the edge of the colony, the frontier so to speak, to escape British oversight, improve trade with Indians, and gain land.

By moving to the frontier, however, settlers in Deerfield, western Virginia, and other fringe communities became caught up in international politics and Indian relations. To the east lay the British colonial government and its overbearing taxes and regulations. To the west lay the various Indian nations, including powerful confederacies who resented the intrusion of the settlers. In these cases, the two communities paid high taxes to the central colonial government, monies the settlers hoped the colonial government would spend on security (protection against the Indians) and internal improvements (the building of roads back to the main markets.) But since they existed on the periphery, neither community was represented by its colonial government and the colonial representatives in London had little or no knowledge of the townspeople's existence, much less their needs. Parliament, the King, and the colonial governor, with little regard or input from residents of the frontier, directed the movement of resources, including troops, around the colonies. Both Deerfield and western Virginia fell victim to constant Indian attacks, set off by the various Indian groups' perception that the English settlers were encroaching on their lands, which, in fact, they were. Additionally, the frontier colonists lacked reliable means to get their goods (edible goods in the North, tobacco in the South) from their farms to the markets in the eastern part of the colonies and, from there, back to Europe. Harassed by Indians and crushed by transportation costs and taxation, both groups demanded and fought for better representation and some attention from the East.

On February 28, 1704, Indians and their French allies attacked Deerfield, killing more than 40 people, capturing many more, and burning much of the town to the ground. More of the captive residents of Deerfield died on the forced march north, back to the Indian settlements, some having succumbed to the cold and others killed for offering resistance.

Sadly, for colonists living in Deerfield, western Virginia, and a number of other frontier communities, the Indians often solved the problem, wiping out entire settlements over the issue of intrusion into Indian lands. Nonetheless, the fights that these and other communities waged with the British power structure ended up shaping the structure of the United States government, which granted much more representation to the individual states than the British government ever had. Indeed, the founding fathers attempted to guarantee that their new nation would not be saddled with a regional core of control: whether or not they succeeded is something to ask yourself as you read the rest of this book.

Indian Relations

The British viewed and dealt with Indians differently than had the Spanish or the French. In fact, the British viewed themselves as superior to the other European powers in the way they handled the Indians. Two factors influenced the relationships the British forged with the various Indian nations they encountered. First, unlike either the French or the Spanish, the British had previous experience as a colonizer, in Ireland, and they applied the lessons and ideas learned there to the Indians of North America. During their occupation of Ireland, the British considered the Irish uncivilized peoples, seeing them as tribal, primitive, and brutal. As had the Irish, the Indians occupied a key resource, land, which the British felt they underused and wished to dole out to British colonists. The Protestant British, not unlike the Catholic Spanish whom they detested, thought God would reward them for taking land away from the heathens in North America, who were not using it properly, and would make that same land "productive."

And, as mentioned, the British had two types of colonies in North America. Based on their different priorities, colonists in the North and the South viewed and treated the Indians differently. Northern colonists primarily wanted land. Thus, they saw Indians at worst as a threat and at best as a hindrance. The southern colonists wanted land, too, but they were quite eager to trade with the Indians. Therefore, in the southern colonies, British settlers viewed the Indians a bit more as the Spanish and the French did: as a resource for trading goods.

For those who administered the northern colonies, coloring the Indians as a standing threat served several purposes. It helped them control their own colonists by threatening them with the wild Indians who surrounded them. It also allowed the British to pursue policies of extermination and warfare. The British, much more than the Spanish or the French, executed war against various Indian tribes. The fact that they brought a standing army with them, a tool that neither the Spanish nor French arrived with, helped the British pursue and design this policy.

In the southern colonies, the British initially viewed the Indians as a resource, since one of the first items traded in the South was Indian slaves. Because of the nature of this early trade, the British established trade with the southern Indians through intimidation and violence, a policy that encouraged one Indian group to raid another for slaves, leading to more intertribal warfare. One key to the British means of success in the Southeast was to keep the Indians there destabilized, off balance so that the British could make incursions into their territory. A look at a map of the growth of the southeastern colonies demonstrates that this policy worked very well. Destabilizing the Indians of the Southeast also upset the carefully built balance of the French and Spanish trading networks and alliances. This policy eventually forced the French and the Spanish to spend a great deal of time and money quelling Indian revolts and wars. Soon the British had driven the Spanish out of Georgia and parts of Florida.

Thanks to the early Indian slave trade and the ensuing policies, the Indians saw the British as a decent but highly problematic source of goods. Like the other European intruders, the British perceived themselves as superior to the Indians. They treated the Indians not as trading partners but as people with whom they traded. The British tended to choose the trading items, the trading locations, and the method of trade, a great departure from the Indians' experiences with the French. The British refused to trade guns with the Indians, fearing they would use them against the British. Often, they tried to trade inferior goods, broken guns for example, to the Indians, who rejected them. They also built trading relationships by encouraging warfare. The British often required one Indian group to attack another, as a test of loyalty, before trading with them. This tactic demonstrates the (intentionally) temporary nature of their relationship with the Indians. By encouraging intertribal warfare, the British hoped to clear out groups to make more land available for settlement. Though early British settlement stopped at the Blue Ridge and then the Appalachian mountains, the British maps of the respective colonies almost always extended their western boundary line to the Mississippi River, signaling their intent from day one to spread that far west.

In both the northern and southern colonies, British colonists and officials felt the Indians should assimilate, as some Irish had done in Ireland, or get out of the way of a superior civilization. The British made a few attempts to assimilate the Indians into British society, all of which failed. In the North, the Puritans set up praying villages. Peopled by Indian converts to Protestant Christianity, one of the main tenets of "civilization" for the British, these villages often comprised members of various Indian groups, many of whom had "converted" only after the ravages of disease or warfare had left them refugees. In the villages, white ministers and lay Indian ministers taught the Indians how to be British, including what sort of house in which to reside, what clothes to wear, and what to name their children. The British modeled the praying villages on traditional English and Puritan villages, except they segregated the Indian residents from the white population. Only "praying" Indians lived in these villages, a fact that made them prime targets of aggression from both sides: English colonists, seeking revenge on any Indians they could find after an attack or raid on their village, often attacked "praying Indians"; local tribes seeking revenge against the English during times of war often figured the praying Indians, who dressed and behaved like the English, were "English" enough. While aware of tribal distinctions, the British tended to ignore them when war broke out. During the Pequot War (1637), British settlers attacked and destroyed praying villages even though no Pequots resided in them. Unfortunately, praying villages also regularly suffered outbreaks of fatal diseases, the towns unintentionally becoming death camps for many New England Indians.

In the southern colonies, the British attempted to educate the children of Indian leaders by offering them an education in British towns. Some Indian leaders embraced this opportunity, not because they saw their own system as inferior but because they believed if their children understood the British, they could better deal with them. Like those Indians in the praying villages in New England, though, many students sent to live among the British succumbed to disease. These deaths understandably made Indian leaders less inclined to send their best and brightest to study with the British.

The policy of assimilation underscores the British predilection for ethnocentricity. All human groups are ethnocentric, meaning that they believe their ethnicity or religion is superior to that of all others. The British thought they were superior to the French, the Spanish, as well as the Iroquois, the Pequot, and Delaware. In turn, each of these groups felt the same way toward each other and the British. In this light, the British defined assimilation and being British in very narrow terms: in order to qualify one had to be a Protestant Christian, speak English, live in certain types of houses, farm in a particular manner, and behave like the British. The British banned colonial officials from marrying Indians and other non-British, a prohibition that effectively made assimilation difficult. Whereas the Spanish looked the other way at intermarriage, eventually they incorporated mestizos into the empire, and the French encouraged it as a way of forming kinship ties, the British banned it outright. This limited the types of interactions and ties that they could create with the Indians. Even if the British saw the Indians as beneath them ethnically and socially, they still found them useful politically.

And the British did engage with the Indians politically. In the North, in the late 1600s, they created the Covenant Chain, a series of agreements between themselves and the Iroquois to work together but not as formal allies. The Chain was created by an agreement between the governor of the colony of New York, who faced constant threats from the French and hostile Indian groups. Under its terms, if a tribe within the Iroquois Confederacy, which included the Mohawk, Seneca, Oneida, Onondaga, Cayuga, and Tuscarora, viewed the British as friends, then they would defend British settlements against attacks by the French and Indian tribes outside the Confederacy. Nevertheless, there was another side to this type of allegiance. If the Iroquois wished to attack one of

Colonel Henry Bouquet of the British Army in council with Indian tribesmembers in present-day Ohio in 1764. Note that the Indians are speaking and the British are taking notes. *Library of Congress, LC-USZ62-104*

their enemies, for example the Huron, they expected the British to join them in the campaign. Finally, if a tribe within the Iroquois Confederacy remained neutral in a particular conflict, they would decide whether to allow the British safe passage through their territory to reach the French or other enemies. The Chain, therefore, functioned in two ways: it allowed groups within the Iroquois Confederacy to maintain a sense of autonomy while still helping the British secure the frontier.

The Chain worked for both the Iroquois and the British because it supported each group's perceptions about its own internal politics. The Iroquois viewed the Chain as an extension of theri own Confederacy, which was essentially a group of autonomous peoples who combined their efforts for mutual defense, but only when it benefited all of the groups. The British viewed the Chain differently. They thought of it as a hierarchy with the colony of New York at the top and the Iroquois subordinate to it. Interestingly, the British of New York also viewed the colony of New England as subordinate to them, because that colony relied upon New

York to secure the border. At the bottom of the structure, underneath the Iroquois and New England, lay all the dependent nations who relied on the Iroquois for protection.

Like the Spanish and the French, the British had a complicated relationship with the various Indian nations they encountered. While viewing the Indians as inferior, the British realized they needed them politically and economically. The British frequently used the Indians as allies, soldiers, and pawns in order to control their territory. And like their predecessors, the British needed the Indians' resources, the land, pelts, and other resources they controlled.

The British Legacy

Even though the British never crossed the Mississippi River, they, more than the Spanish and the French, set the stage and tone of American westward expansion and mythmaking. Immediately after the American Revolution in 1776, the new United States government continued many of the policies of the British. It retained the Office of Indian Affairs, which was responsible for all negotiations and regulation of trade with Indian nations. Unlike the French and later the Spanish, the United States government came to rely on a centralized system of dealing with the Indians. Instead of letting every state negotiate with individual tribes, only the federal government possessed that right. The Constitution even stated that outright, banning states from negotiations. This centralization allowed the federal government to send the military against the Indians, though at various points the states dispatched their own militias against the Indians as well.

The young United States also continued the British policy of seeing the Indians primarily as a hindrance and a menace. One of the first acts of the new government as the states began to expand westward was the policy of Indian removal. In the 1830s, the United States government removed the Five Civilized Tribes: (Cherokee, Choctaw, Chickasaw, Creek, and Seminole) from the Southeast. Sadly, the whites referred to them as the "Five Civilized Tribes" because they appeared to have adopted white ways, including, in the case of the Cherokee, writing a constitution to support their government. While imitation may be the highest form of flattery, it is also the biggest political threat. Though the details differ from locale to locale, the overall policy repeated that of the British government: terminate land claims on whatever pretense seemed convenient, then force the Indians to relocate beyond the current boundaries of the government. In removing these groups of Indians, the United States government violated treaties between these Indians and the British, thereby violating treaties between the British and the United States government as well. Yet the justification rang true to that of the British. In the eyes of the Americans, the Indians failed to use the land properly and had no title to it. Indian political organizations like the Iroquois Confederacy and the Cherokee Constitution represented a threat to the newfound sovereignty and security of the United States. Rather than try to incorporate the Indians, some Americans posited, perhaps they should just get them out of the way. The Indians had no issue with this part of the position; they did not want to be incorporated into the United States. They saw themselves as superior sovereign nations free from the control of various European empires; it was the Americans, they felt, who needed to find another place to live.

Beyond the policy of removal, and contradictorally, the Americans extended the policy of assimilation. While legally the Indians were considered citizens of "separate nations," socially they were seen as different. Euro-Americans within the United States expected Indians who agreed to removal to become part of the United States. In the 1820s, the United States Congress created the "Civilization Fund" for the purpose of helping the Indians become Americans by Christianizing them and civilizing them to the standards of the United States.

The British Empire also influenced patterns of land use in the new republic. The British had routinely looked the other way when colonists ignored treaty lines and squatted on Indian land, and the Americans saw no reason to stop this practice. Instead, they encouraged it, allowing settlers to go beyond the boundaries of the United States and squat all over what eventually became the continental United States. Tennessee, Kentucky, Oregon, Washington, to name a few, were states founded essentially by illegal settlers, violating treaties and agreements between the United States government and other European governments and/or Indian nations. The claiming of land trumped the rule of law and treaty preservation whatever the cost.

Perhaps most important for the study of the West is how the British legacy influenced early American historians' view of the West and how it was settled. Early historians such as Frederick Jackson Turner viewed the West only from the vantage point of the East—that of the British colonists who became Americans. They downgraded or simply ignored the points of view of the Spanish, who, after all reached the West first, and the French. Viewing the growth of the West purely from the East allowed for a linear development, a grandiosity of creation that would not have been sustainable by looking at the settlement of the West in the messy, whirlpool manner in which it actually happened.

Frederick Jackson Turner and the Frontier

In 1893, at the annual meeting of the then fledgling American Historical Association, Frederick Jackson Turner, an assistant professor from the University of Wisconsin, declared the American frontier (by which he meant the United States frontier) closed. With this statement, Turner single-handedly created the field of "Western American history" and set off important, though sometimes tedious, debates about the following questions: What is a frontier? Does its frontier experience make the United States unique? Where, exactly, is the West? Does the West exist if there is no longer a frontier? Turner's declaration also spawned years of criticism, as later historians pointed out the holes in Turner's thesis. Where, they ask, are women and Indians? Is the West a place or a process? Was settling the frontier in the United States always an east-to-west movement? Some historians have declared Turner's Frontier Thesis dead. Yet it remains part of the popular definition of the West, as demonstrated by a 2007 *New York Times* article on the midterm U.S. elections, which misused Turner's thesis to explain why Western states would be more likely to vote for a female candidate for president—arguing that the West was the region in which the nation had traditionally tried out new political ideas and practices.

Why, you may ask, are we considering Turner's frontier thesis in a chapter about the British in North America? Don't we already know all we need to know about Turner from the introduction to this book? Simply put, no. Turner based his thesis on the accumulation of land. So while we have considered how historians have used Turner's ideas, now we need to consider how Turner used the history of the British and American settlement of the East Coast of the United States to formulate his ideas about frontiers in the West.

Turner sums up his thesis neatly in his original essay, "The Significance of the Frontier in American history":

> The existence of an area of free land, its continuous recession, and the advance of American settlement westward, explain American development.

The thesis has three distinct points in support of what made the "American experience" unique, or at least important. Turner identified three waves of settlement that moved from east to west. The first wave began when British settlement spread beyond the "fall line and tidewater regions" and into the Ohio River valley in the North and the Blue Ridge Mountains and North Carolina Piedmont in the South. These developments took place in the one hundred years before the American Revolution, halted only briefly by the Proclamation Line of 1763. This line, drawn by the British at the conclusion of the French and Indian War in a vain attempt to appease Indian fears of being overrun by British settlers, ran down the spine of the Appalachian Mountains. It barred British colonists from crossing west and the Indians from crossing east. In reality, both groups crossed back and forth as they pleased.

This first wave continued after the American Revolution, as Americans settled Tennessee, Kentucky, and Ohio. By the 1820s, Turner stated, the "settled areas included Ohio, southern Indiana, and Illinois, southeastern Missouri, and about one-half of Louisiana." This settlement therefore pushed the line of the frontier west to the Great Lakes Region and beyond the Mississippi River, at which point the second wave of settlement began.

The second wave moved much quicker than the first. By the 1860s, the frontier had leap-frogged the Rocky Mountains and drew near the Pacific Coast. The Plains states (Kansas, Nebraska, and Indian Territory, now known as Oklahoma) represented the last line of settlement. After 1880, the third and final stage of the process filled the open land in the coastal West and the upper Great Plains (North Dakota, South Dakota.) Thus according to Turner, in 1893 no more open land existed and settlement in the U.S. West had effectively closed the frontier. Two questions leap to mind: How did he define *open land*? And how did he define *settlement*?

One problematic thing about interpreting Turner's thesis is that he based much of it on census records. He looked at how much land was still "open" or "free" for settlement versus how much was under cultivation or otherwise developed. Though he mentioned the Indians at various points throughout the essay, he treated all of their remaining land as open to settlement, just as the British and the United States government always had. By using census records, Turner restricted the definition of free land to that as described and counted by the government. We do not know how he would have treated ownership of land within the former Spanish territories because he seems to restrict his definition of the West to areas north of that. (He did mention Texas twice, but no other part of the current Southwest.) For Turner and the United States government, free land was that which was not under cultivation or development and therefore untaxed. He could not define settled land as that owned by U.S. citizens because citizenship was not a requirement to own land. Indeed, European immigrants, whom Turner did recognize as an important catalyst to the closing of the frontier, settled much western land without becoming U.S. citizens.

"Settlement," for Turner, did not just mean cultivation of the land, for he identified specific stages in the transition from frontier to settlement. Turner saw this transition as more of a process than a sudden event. It began with what he called the Indian Trader's Frontier, which he attributed first to the French and English and then to the Americans. Ranchers replaced these traders as the catalyst on the frontier. Farmers eventually replaced ranchers in the process. It is at this point that settlement occurred.

Literature and other forms of popular culture also captured these stages. James Fennimore Cooper replicated them in his Leatherstocking Tales about eighteenth-century New York. These stories glorify the conflict between frontiersmen, settlers, and Indians, illustrating the shifting stages about which Turner wrote. Many Westerns replicate the stages as well, including *The Virginian,* a 1902 novel made into four film versions (1914, 1923, 1929, 1946), a TV series (1962–71) and a TV movie (2000), and the films *My Darling Clementine* (1946) and *Shane* (1953). Larry McMurtry's Pulitzer-Prize winning novel (1986) and TV miniseries, *Lonesome Dove,* illustrates marvelously the passing of the ranching frontier (and its culture and economy) and its replacement with the farming frontier (and its culture and economy). In the above examples, the heroes embody Turner's concept of an American: one changed by the frontier.

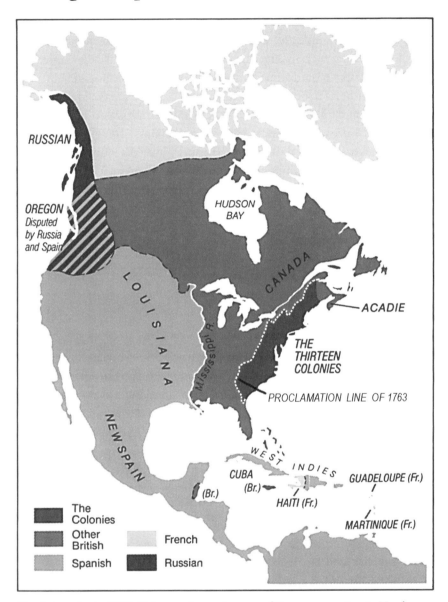

North America in 1763. This map shows the state of European empires in North America at the close of the French and Indian War.

Turner's stages emerged from his reliance on the early Southwest frontier of the United States for his evidence. By the "Southwest," Turner referred not to Arizona, New Mexico, California, and Texas, but to the early development of what was southwest from the vantage point of the original thirteen British colonies, meaning Mississippi, Alabama, and Louisiana. His examples all come from these states, with none coming from what today we consider the West. Thus, one of Turner's greatest points in his essay regards how American democracy developed.

For its time, Turner's thesis expressed radical ideas. He was one of the first scholars to argue that American history was not simply an extension of European history. He also complained forcefully that too much American history writing, at the time, focused around the issue of slavery, ignoring other important factors that shaped the development of the United States. Finally, by recognizing the importance of the West and its frontier(s), he turned historians west, exhorting them to look in their own backyards to see the development of democracy in America. So, whether or not one agrees with Turner, his thesis, warts and all, kick-started Western American history and the debates that continue to shape it.

Turner and the European Empires

As the godfather of Western American history, Turner shaped how historians conceived the field. We spent three chapters on the European empires not only because they introduced European lifestyles and politics to the Indians and helped create the West but also because they were important to how Turner conceptualized both the frontier and the West. For Turner, the three major European empires showed some important similarities. First, they all had a frontier. These frontiers required the development of structures and institutions to maintain and secure them. Second, they all interacted with the Indians, economically, politically, militarily, and, to greater or lesser degrees, socially. Third, all three empires came to North America for economic reasons, which led to the stages identified by Turner: trader, rancher, and farmer.

Recent historical studies have focused on the major differences between the three European empires, specifically how each one defined and established its frontiers, which tells us a great deal about the empires themselves. The Spanish employed missions and presidios; the French used traders, trappers and intermarriage; the British used warfare and settlements. The way each colonizer tried to control its frontiers shaped how each empire related to the Indians. The Spanish eventually accepted the mestizo population into their bureaucracy; the French intermarried with and created alliances with Indian groups; the British focused much more on warfare and removal. Yet even as historians gripe about how Turner missed the nuances of these various frontiers, many of them are studying frontiers because of Turner. Whether Turner's thesis is correct or not, it is an unavoidable legacy within Western history, and the debates about this legacy continue to shape the West and how we view it.

☙ Suggested Readings ❧

Aquila, Richard. *The Iroquois Restoration: Iroquois Diplomacy on the Colonial Frontier, 1701–1754.* Lincoln: University of Nebraska, 1983.

Crane, Verner. *The Southern Frontier, 1670–1732.* New York: W. W. North and Company, 1981.

Etulain, Richard. *Does the Frontier Experience Make American Exceptional?* New York: Bedford/St. Martin's, 1999.

Lepore, Jill. *The Name of War: King Philip's War and the Origins of American Identity.* New York: Alfred A. Knopf, 1998.

Martin, Joel. *Sacred Revolt: The Muskogees' Struggle for a New World.* Boston: Beacon Press, 1991.

Milling, Chapman. *Red Carolinians.* Chapel Hill: University of North Carolina, 1940.

Nash, Gary. *Red, White and Black: The Peoples of North America.* New York: Prentice Hall, 2005. Fifth edition.

Slotkin, Richard. *Regeneration Through Violence: The Mythology of the American Frontier, 1600–1800.* Middleton, CT: Wesleyan University Press, 1973.

Taylor, Alan. *The Divided Ground: Indians, Settlers, and the Northern Borderland of The American Revolution.* New York: Vintage Books, 2007.

Turner, Frederick Jackson. "The Significance of the Frontier in American History." *Report of the American Historical Association,* 1893: 199–277.

CHAPTER SIX

Growing Pains

In 1804, Meriwether Lewis and William Clark stood on the bluffs of the Missouri River looking west. Tasked by President Thomas Jefferson with mapping the immense and newly acquired Louisiana Purchase, they set off at the head of the "Corps of Discovery" to find a water passage from St. Louis to the Pacific Ocean, as well as unknown Indian tribes, animals, plants, geographical features, and resources that might prove valuable to the United States. They were to go where no man, or at least no white American man, had gone before. Picture them standing on the coast at Fort Clatsop, admiring the Pacific Ocean. Now add two others to that picture, standing on either side of Lewis and Clark: Toussaint Charbonneau and Sacajawea. Charbonneau was a Frenchman who had traded and trapped throughout many parts of the West, and Sacajawea was his Shoshoni wife. Unlike Lewis and Clark, they knew much about the region that Lewis and Clark had just "explored."

It is important to view the exploration of the West through a different lens than the one that suggests Lewis and Clark topped a list of "firsts." Jefferson had long been interested in the West, well before the Louisiana Purchase of 1803. In 1792, he proposed that the American Philosophical Society send an expedition West, following the Missouri River all the way to the Pacific. The society declined but the idea had been born. Jefferson knew that the French and various Indian groups already had extensive knowledge about the Louisiana Purchase territory. Their extensive trade and use of the resources of the region were the very things that had convinced him that the land was valuable. Additionally, Jefferson was highly curious about the indigenous peoples of the West. He wanted a better understanding of the Indian groups' cultures, religions, societies, economies, and political structures, for he believed this information would make it easier for the United States to acculturate the Indians of the region to American society.

Jefferson dispatched Lewis and Clark west for two basic reasons: to confirm the value of the land and to discover any potential problems with it. In short, Jefferson wanted the United States's new purchase appraised. All three men hoped the expedition would find a quick passage across the continent. They already knew the land held vast herds of animals, large groups of Indians, and many rivers. Beyond that, they did not know a great deal about what other resources or problems lay beyond St. Louis. Only in this way did the "discovery" of the new American West proceed.

Exploration and Settlement: The Flood Begins

The way each successive group has reimagined the landscape played an important role in Western American history. Where one group saw a Great American Desert, others saw fertile farmland. Where one group saw dense old-growth forests, others saw timber resources. Where one group saw a sparkling river, others saw gold. The pattern continues to this day. This constant reconstruction of the landscape began with the different Indian groups whenever they changed territories, and it continued with the Europeans and then the Americans. Therefore, *exploration* does not mean finding things that no one else has found; lt simply means discovering different aspects of a place that serve one's purpose.

This process happened with the territory known as the Louisiana Purchase, comprising land from much of present-day Louisiana, including the vital port city of New Orleans, and all or portions of 14 other current U.S. states. When the French controlled this vast territory, they saw it in terms of two resources: fur-bearing animals (beaver and deer) and Indian trade economies. As we saw in Chapter Four, the French structured their empire around these resources and utilized them as best they could. Eventually, the size of this territory and the European pressures on it led the French to relinquish it to the Americans for strategic reasons.

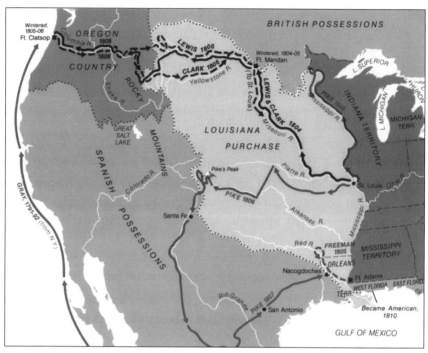

The Louisiana Purchase and Explorations of the Far West

In the late 1700s, frontier pressures forced the French to re-evaluate their control of that large North American territory. As a result of the conclusion of the French and Indian War in 1763, the Spanish possessed Louisiana, which meant they controlled the mouth of the Mississippi River, thereby overseeing, and taxing if they wished, all of the many staple crops, trade items, and natural resources that came downriver from the interior of the continent. At the time, the Mississippi River acted as a giant (waterborne) interstate highway. Once goods made it to the terminal market in New Orleans, merchants distributed them to ports all over the nation and the world. Whoever controlled the mouth of the Mississippi, meaning the Port of New Orleans, controlled the economic lifeblood of the middle of the continent. This fact made New Orleans an important prize for European powers, and one that Americans now wished to gain. In 1800, Napoleon, the ruler of France, retook New Orleans from the Spanish by means of a secretly concluded treaty. Now Jefferson saw his chance to get American hands on the important port city. The President threatened to side with Britain against France in current conflicts unless France sold the United States New Orleans. Embroiled in wars in Europe and still trying to regain French control of the valuable sugar-producing colony of Saint Domingue (now Haiti) after a bloody rebellion there, a preoccupied Napoleon ultimately agreed to sell the United States not just New Orleans but the entire Louisiana Territory for $15 million.

With one swipe of the pen, the physical size of the United States doubled. Within the new territory lay vast amounts of potential farmland, hundreds of different Indian nations, and a dying fur trade just waiting to be revitalized. The Purchase also ended European influence and conflict in a large part of the West, though not in the entire region.

The Purchase fired the imagination of the American people. Had God ordained Americans, because of their faith and republican values, to take all the land to the Pacific? Like the Spanish had long ago looked at Columbus's find, Americans on the East Coast saw Louisiana as God's reward for their good works. It appeared to be validation of the Puritan belief that civilized Christian people should subdue the land and make it productive. Finally, the Louisiana Purchase raised the issue of territorial governance. How would the United States government, based on the eastern edge of the continent, manage such a huge swath of territory lying so far away? How would that same government oversee the flow of its citizens into this new land?

Enter Lewis and Clark—and Clark's manservant York, a black slave who had little choice about joining the expedition. Jefferson hired Meriwether Lewis, his private secretary, and William Clark, an old army companion of Lewis, to lead a small group of regular servicemen and volunteers that composed the Corps of Discovery charged with exploring the Louisiana Purchase. The President wanted Lewis and Clark to extend the fur trade west and gain advanced knowledge of the peoples and geography of the region. As mentioned, Jefferson had wanted the West explored since 1792, and he had begun negotiations with Lewis and Clark even before having finished his negotiations with France. The Corps of Discovery launched from St. Louis in 1804. The men traveled in heavy, unwieldy canoes laden with supplies: mathematical instruments, camping equipment, clothing, arms, medicine, a library (including a four-volume dictionary and a copy of Linnaeus for categorizing plants) and gifts for

Indians (including pocket mirrors, sewing needles, silk ribbons, knives, and tomahawks that doubled as pipes.) The Corps spent the winter near present-day Fargo, North Dakota, on the Missouri River with the Mandan and Minnatree Indian nations, without whom the men of the Corps would not have survived. Over the course of that winter, two significant things happened. First, Lewis and Clark learned a lot about what lay upriver from the Mandan and the Minnatree, who traded extensively up and down the Missouri. Second, they added three people to their crew: a French trapper, Toussaint Charbonneau, one of his Shoshoni wives, Sacajawea, and their infant son, Jean Baptiste Charbonneau, whom she bore in February 1805. This couple represented the previous imagining of the Louisiana Purchase. Charbonneau, who spoke French and Indian languages but little English, had been a trader and trapper up and down the Missouri and beyond. Sacajawea was a Shoshoni, from present-day Idaho, who had been captured by the Hidatsa, married off to or bought by Charbonneau, and now lived among the Mandan. Of all the members of the Corps, only she had crossed the Rockies. Her knowledge and language skills would prove invaluable to the success—and the very survival—of the Lewis and Clark expedition.

During the following summer, the expedition portaged through the Rocky Mountains, meaning they had to carry their heavy canoes filled with all their supplies and trade goods over mountainous terrain to get from one river to another. Once on the western slope of the Rockies, they went down the Clearwater, Snake, and Columbia rivers to the Pacific Coast. By this point, they realized there was not a continuous river passage all the way across the northern part of the territory, as they had hoped. On what is now the Oregon coast, they established Fort Clatsop, on the banks of the Columbia River, to solidify their control of the territory, even though the British and the French still maintained a presence on the Pacific Coast. After winter broke, they headed home. Near the headwaters of the Missouri River, not far from present-day Yellowstone Park, they split into two groups, one led by Lewis and the other by Clark, in order to map a greater amount of territory. The Corps reconvened on the Missouri in August 1806 in present-day North Dakota and then paddled downriver back to St. Louis.

Unbeknownst to the Corps, two things were happening back East. Jefferson had given up hope of ever seeing Lewis and Clark again. He assumed, because of the lack of communication and their failure to return in what he considered a timely manner, that they had been lost or killed. This assumption demonstrates how little Thomas Jefferson and other Americans understood about the vastness of the territory they had recently bought. Also, unhappy over having lost New Orleans and the Americans having taken over the vast western territory, the Spanish sent at least four expeditions from Santa Fé to stop Lewis and Clark. Though some historians believe that one Spanish party came within fifty miles of Lewis and Clark, the two expeditions never crossed paths. Nonetheless, the Spanish effort illustrates the imperial tensions still lingering in the West. Now that the Americans controlled the Louisiana Purchase territory, they shared such a long border with the Spanish.

Lewis and Clark provided a description of the land that encouraged U.S. development and settlement. As with all explorers, they provided some misinformation based on their objective. They misunderstood, for example, some of the roles of Indians (they viewed Indian women as abused and felt Indian traders were greedy because they haggled over prices) and the course of some of the rivers they traveled. They did not see or understand the potential of the Great Plains as productive farmland, but nor did many of the people who followed them. They did, however, report on the vast herds of animals that roamed the Plains, that some groups of Indians were dying off (thanks to European diseases, which they did not realize), and on the forests, rivers, and other natural resources that would attract settlers and entrepreneurs to the West. Remember that Lewis and Clark took a northern route across the Louisiana Purchase. Therefore, they never saw the central Great Plains or the northern parts of the Southwest, like present-day Oklahoma and Northern Texas. The picture there was, of course, much different, with its large mestizo, Spanish, and Indian populations living in towns, ranches, and farms.

In short, their exploration set off a flood of migration—some of which was voluntary, some of which was not—from the East to parts of the new West. During the 1820s, the Cherokee Nation, one of the Indian nations that whites considered to be the Five Civilized Tribes, suddenly found themselves at odds with the State of Georgia. (Their national territory touched the boundaries of the states of Georgia, Tennessee, North Carolina, and South Carolina.) The surrounding white population appeared to resent their literacy and well-developed farms. The Cherokee, in an effort to establish their nationality on par with that of the United States, ratified their own Constitution, which the State of Georgia viewed as an infringement on its government. Georgia perceived and defined Cherokee territory as state territory and attempted to regulate the Cherokee, passing laws that affected them.

The Cherokee saw themselves as a separate, sovereign nation, as evidenced by their new Constitution, the treaties they had signed with the British and the new United States, and the United States' own Constitution. After Georgia passed several laws that challenged their sovereignty, the Cherokee sought redress in the courts. In 1831, they sued the State of Georgia (*Cherokee Nation* v. *State of Georgia*) in the Supreme Court. The Supreme Court accepted the case because the Constitution charges that body with overseeing cases in which a *foreign nation* sues an American state or entity. The Supreme Court sided against the Cherokee, deeming them a "domestic dependent nation." In 1832, an American named Samuel Austin Worcester, who worked as a missionary in Cherokee territory, sued after the Georgia militia arrested him within Cherokee territory for violating a law that Georgia had passed prohibiting whites from living in Cherokee territory. He claimed Georgia violated his rights when they enforced their laws outside of their state boundaries. In *Worcester* v. *Georgia*, the Supreme Court sided against Georgia and with Worcester, now defining the Cherokee as a "distinct society."

At this point, the United States government stepped in. It forcibly removed the Cherokee in 1838 (some of whom had already agreed to removal before the deadline to avoid such a conflict) to what whites considered the most worthless land of the Louisiana Purchase: Arkansas, Oklahoma, and Kansas. First, the government rounded up the remaining Cherokee and placed them in stockades. Then, the military escorted the Cherokee families as they walked from Tennessee, Georgia, and North Carolina to Indian Territory over the course of a year. Neither the state governments nor the federal government compensated the Cherokee for the land, livestock, and possessions they left behind, which was taken by whites before the Cherokee owners were even out of sight. The military escorting the Cherokee failed to provide adequate food or shelter during the several-month journey. Historians believe between 4,000 and 8,000 Cherokee died on what became know as the Trail of Tears. This number does not include those who died while in the stockades or those the militia hunted down and killed in the North Carolina, Tennessee, and Georgia mountains. Soon after the Trail of Tears, in 1839, the United States government forcibly moved the Choctaw, Chickasaw, Creek, and the Seminole from the Southeast in a similar manner.

These forced migrants brought change to the West. In many ways, the Cherokee were the first "American" migrants to the region. Many of the tribes' members had intermarried with Scots-Irish immigrants who had come across the Appalachian Mountains to escape taxes and regulation under the British. Many were literate, in Cherokee as well as in English. They left behind prosperous farms and businesses in Georgia, Tennessee, and North Carolina, which they hoped somehow to rekindle in the new territories into which the federal government had forced them. In their letters back to relatives in the East, the Cherokees, whites who had intermarried with them, missionaries, and others who accompanied them commented on the rich resources available to them in Oklahoma and the other territories. These communications with people in the East eventually encouraged others, both Cherokees and Americans, to move west into the so-called Indian Territory. Nevertheless, the relocated Indians also lamented those resources they left behind. This pattern of riches and rags, gain and loss, followed most migrants west.

In Indian Territory, the Cherokee and the other removed tribes encountered Western Indians who bore little resemblance to them, culturally or otherwise. Colonel E. C. Boudinot, a leader of the Cherokee and a Civil War hero, described the Plains Indians in 1873 as "the savage Indians." The Western Indians who inhabited Oklahoma, Arkansas, northern Texas, and southern Kansas were mainly Plains Indians who had adopted the horse culture when the Spanish introduced the horse to North America. This transition meant that though they still practiced some agriculture, the Plains Indians focused most of their energies on hunting buffalo and other game on horseback and, because of their high mobility, warfare. Extensive warfare had existed between the various tribal groups, especially on the Great Plains, for many years before the arrival in Indian Territory of the Southeastern transplants. The Plains Indians during this period were semi-nomadic, moving their tipis between winter camps and summer hunting zones. The transplanted Southeastern Indians lived in houses, read books, and kept accounts.

This engraving shows the early nineteenth-century conception of the Great Plains as the Great American Desert. *Buffalo Bill Historical Center, Cody, Wyoming; 51.51.135*

They looked like whites to the Plains Indians, who looked like savages to the Cherokee and their Southeastern brethren. The clash of cultures brought changes to the territory, including intertribal warfare between the Cherokee and the Comanche in 1838.

This fact raises the question: If the Five Civilized Tribes and the Plains Indians were so different, why did the United States government put them together? The answer lies in how the United States government viewed what became known as Indian Territory. In 1806, Lt. Zebulon Pike was dispatched west to explore the Central and Southern Great Plains, which, upon his return, he deemed unsuitable for farming. Stephen H. Long, who led a journey of scientific discovery west in 1819, reiterated that determination. Upon his return to the East, Long dubbed the Great Plains "the Great American Desert." And the Great American Desert, the explorers reported, was unlike other parts of the United States. It got less than 20 inches of rainfall per year. It lacked large trees. The summers were long and very hot, and the winters were very windy and especially cold. Few of the plants that grew there were green. Additionally, prairie grasses, which looked dry and brittle, covered most of the land. Thanks to the descriptions of Pike and Long, government officials theorized that since the land probably was unsuitable for farming, it might serve as the perfect place for the federal government to send the remaining Indians, whom Americans believed did not farm and, thanks in part to Lewis and Clark's report, were dying out anyway.

In 1838, the same year that the United States government sent the Cherokee and other tribes to the Great Plains at the point of a gun, John C. Fremont, a major general in the U.S. Army's corps of topographical engineers dispatched to explore the territory between the Missouri River and the northern frontier, challenged the idea of the Great American Desert. He argued that cattle could graze on the prairies grass, making it perfect for ranching. After surveying what is now the Great Basin region of Nevada and Utah in 1845, he saw that region as a true desert and the Great Plains as a prairie. It would not be until the development and importation onto the Plains of a plow with a metal share (the blade that cuts the soil) that white settlers realized that some of the richest soil in the world lay beneath the seas of prairie grass.

Despite the United States government's misinformed opinions of the Five Civilized Tribes and the Plains Indians, the two groups were very different. The Cherokee and the other Southeastern tribes brought black slaves with them to the West. By the 1830s, the debate over slavery had begun to heat up in the United States, but only in abstract terms. But by the time the Civil War began in 1861, the Cherokee and other groups had moved slaves into the West, as had some white groups. Additionally, the Five Civilized Tribes immediately began to try to develop their new land in the same fashion as they had done in the East. In 1839, one year after Removal, the Cherokee had adopted a new constitution, a new political system, opened schools, and begun printing a bilingual newspaper, all without reimbursement or financial help from the U.S. government. They put up buildings and fences, they dammed streams, and they established roads and schools and other institutions that reshaped the environment and interrupted traditional Great Plains life.

Even as the Cherokee and the other Civilized Tribes were fighting their forced migration west, another immigration movement began to build steam. In 1834, the American Board of Commissioners for Foreign Missions (ABCFM), a Presbyterian-Congregationalist group founded in Massachusetts, petitioned the United States government for permission to establish Protestant missions among the Indians in Oregon territory. The missionaries sought to achieve two goals: make the Indians into Protestants and bring Protestant settlers into the area. Bringing settlers to the area would secure the territory for the United States (through the time-honored tradition of squatting) and, in the missionaries' minds, expose the Indians to farming. Congress granted the missionaries the permission they sought, even though the territory did not belong solely to the United States. In 1818, the United States and Great Britain had agreed to control the Oregon territory jointly, an agreement that did not necessarily mean authorizing settlement. Additionally, French Catholic priests entered the territory in 1838, working among the Indians to convert them to Catholicism. None of these facts deterred Jason Lee (who left his wife, Ann, in New England), Marcus Whitman, Henry Harmon Spaulding and their wives, Narcissa Whitman and Eliza Spaulding.

The desire of the missionaries, who came from New England and upstate New York, to work in Oregon stemmed directly from an incident involving Lewis and Clark. According to stories, sometime around 1830 (or before, depending on the source), two Nez Perce arrived in St. Louis looking for a copy of the "Book of Heaven," meaning the Bible, shown to them by Lewis and Clark. Some versions of the tale state that

This picture provides a more realistic portrayal of pioneers and Indians. Note the lack of women in the picture. *Buffalo Bill Historical Center, Cody, Wyoming; 51.51.162*

the men came east after their tribe suffered from an outbreak of a devastating disease. Others claim they had come all the way to St. Louis out of a burning desire to seek Christ. Whatever the reason, the story spread in the nascent Protestant missionary movement in New England and New York, and it inspired missionaries to begin planning to go to Nez Perce territory. Whatever the truth about the Indians' visit, the Lees, Whitmans, and Spauldings took it as an open invitation. After traveling by riverboat, horse, and wagon from the Ohio River valley, they arrived in the Willamette Valley in 1836; they set up missions to the Cayuse and Nez Perce. Several problems, however, impeded their progress in converting these Indians to Protestant Christianity and American ways.

First, the group of the five missionaries broke into three factions, as all of the missionaries wanted to run the missions but none of them wanted to work directly with the Indians. By 1837, Marcus Whitman headed back on horseback to the East Coast to recruit American settlers for the valley. He and the others believed that if Christian (read Protestant) Americans surrounded the Indians, they would influence the Indians positively and lead to a faster rate of conversion, a typical belief at this time. While Whitman headed east, small pox and other diseases broke out among the Indians, who blamed the missionaries for their plight. Additionally, tensions rose between the French Catholic missionaries and the newcomers, as each group tried to convince the Indians that theirs was the only way to salvation. Over the next eleven years, Whitman filled the valley with migrants who established farms and disrupted the agricultural traditions of the Indians, disease reduced the Indian populations, the Protestant missionaries fought amongst themselves and with the Catholic missionaries, and national tensions rose between the Americans and the British, who viewed the growing number of American settlers in Oregon as squatters.

Caught in the middle of all these tensions, the Cayuse and Nez Perce had had enough, decrying the missionaries for the diseases and disruptions. In 1847, two leaders of the Cayuse, Tilaukait and Tamsuky, called upon Marcus Whitman at his house. They and their allies then killed fourteen of the missionaries and the migrants. The Cayuse and Nez Perce captured the survivors and ransomed them to the Hudson's Bay Company for blankets and other supplies. Dubbed the "Whitman Massacre" by Henry Harmon Spaulding, the one missionary who survived it, the event quickly became an international incident. (Spaulding survived because the ABCFM had recalled him in 1846 for unbecoming behavior. Supposedly, he whipped Indians who failed to convert to Christianity.) Spaulding blamed the French Catholic missionaries for the bloodshed, claiming they had directed the Indians to kill the Protestant migrants and missionaries. His accusations suggested several things. They made the French look like a fading empire who grasped for control, and it made the Indians look malleable. They also implied an international conspiracy, which led the U.S. government to threaten to send a garrison of men to quell the Cayuse and Nez Perce. This plan went nowhere until the British threatened to send troops from Fort Vancouver to settle the region down, an act which forced the Americans to send a garrison of soldiers to secure the land as American soil and protect the remaining settlers. This move effectively grabbed Oregon and Washington for the United States. (The conflict with Britain over the Oregon territory was solved officially in the Oregon Treaty, signed with Great Britain in 1846, establishing the international border at the 49th parallel line. The United States did not want to risk war with Britain while in a war with Mexico.)

The Whitman Massacre set the pattern for other land grabs and raised important issues that would arise in other settlement areas. The United States would look the other way or tacitly allow whites to settle in the area, deny knowledge of them, and then use any attempt by the true owners of the land (usually Indians but sometimes other empires) to evict the American squatters as grounds for sending in soldiers, effectively taking the land for the white settlers. Yet few accounts from the time grant the Cayuse and the Nez Perce the right to feel anger at the missionaries for bringing settlers and disease to their land. Perhaps more important, Henry Spaulding kept the massacre in the public eye for as long as he could, portraying Marcus Whitman and the other missionaries as martyrs for the cause of American westward expansion. He even proposed that statues of Whitman be made for all western state capitols in order to commemorate the "fact" that Whitman had saved the West for America, a gesture that illustrates well the idea of Manifest Destiny. Many Americans came to believe that God intended them to have all the land between the Mississippi and the Pacific Ocean because they, unlike any previous residents, would use it as the Almighty intended. A journalist named John L. O'Sullivan first called this belief "Manifest Destiny." In a 1845 newspaper article he argued that the United States should annex Mexico. The idea has its roots in the Puritan belief that they had inherited the mantle of the ancient Israelites. Just as God had promised the Israelites the land of Canaan, so too had God promised the Puritans New England. Just as God blessed the Israelites for following him faithfully, so the Puritans believed, he would bless them if they served as a godly example with their "city on a hill" in New England. This belief justified the various wars against the Indians led by the Puritans and their descendents.

During the American Revolution, this sense of God-given destiny took on an additional political component. Leaders believed that America's Providential mission provided a shining example of freedom to the world. They believed God would bless them with land for providing this example. Manifest Destiny became a form of religious and political idealism, but it also justified harnessing the land and violently expelling its current inhabitants. While not all Americans believed in it, certain groups (politicians, missionaries, Mormons) used it to justify their expansion of power. These beliefs elevated expansion and settlement to a religious and political mission and demonized opposition to that settlement as anti-progress, anti-American, and even un-Christian.

Just as the Federal government was removing the Five Civilized Tribes and the Whitmans and their followers were heading to Oregon, another group began their movement west: the Mormons, or, as they call themselves, the Church of Latter-Day Saints (LDS). From the beginning, the LDS sparked controversy. In the 1820s in upstate New York, the founder of the church, Joseph Smith, claimed that an angel named Moroni had led him to find golden plates that chronicled a struggle between two groups that had previously inhabited the Americas. The translation of these plates became the *Book of Mormon* and the main doctrine of the church. Many of Smith's contemporaries found the discovery, translation, and eventual disappearance of the golden plates patently unbelievable—though, one could argue, no more so than burning bushes or an immaculate conception.

The *Book of Mormon* incorporates an account of "God's dealings with the ancient inhabitants of the Americas," making the LDS a uniquely American religion; still, just as Christianity has it roots in Judaism, Latter-Day Saints' beliefs and holy scriptures evolved out of Christianity. By the 1840s, Latter-Day Saints advocated "the new and everlasting covenant of celestial marriage," also known as plural marriage or polygamy, for certain

Brigham Young became president of the Quorum of the Twelve Apostles after Joseph Smith's death in 1844. He realized that Illinois no longer provided a safe haven for the LDS and orchestrated the move to Utah. In 1846, he convinced 500 young men to serve in the Mexican-American War, helping to pay for the trek to Utah and proving LDS loyalty to the United States. The first territorial governor and superintendent of Indian affairs in Utah, the federal government removed him just before the Utah War of 1857–58. *Library of Congress, LC-USZ62-50029*

male members. This new belief split the Church of Latter-Day Saints as it excluded some men from the practice. More important for their relations with the United States government, their practice of polygamy aggravated non-Saints, whom Mormons call "gentiles." From the beginning, the "gentile" American neighbors of Mormons found the beliefs of the new group startling and threatening, leading to almost constant persecution of Mormons throughout the nineteenth century.

Trying to find a place to live and practice their religion in peace, Smith and his followers continually moved west: Ohio, then Missouri and Illinois, and eventually, Utah. In the 1830s, they thought they had found sanctuary in Missouri and Illinois, but they were wrong. In 1838, the governor of Missouri sent militiamen against Mormon settlements, killing 18 Latter-Day Saints, and driving more than 15,000 members of the church out of the state. From Missouri, they moved to Nauvoo in Illinois. Their respite did not last long. In 1844, locals killed Joseph Smith and his brother Hyrum while the two were in "protective custody." Illinois revoked Nauvoo's charter in 1845, forcing its residents to leave. In 1846, mobs torched the LDS temple in Nauvoo, forcing the last of the residents to flee.

They reconvened in Winter Quarters, Nebraska, where their new leader, Brigham Young, began to organize a mass migration outside of

U.S. territory to what became Utah in Mexican territory. Born in rural New England, Young became a Mormon at the age of 31 and rose quickly to become an advisor to Smith. Between 1847 and 1860, Young moved several thousand LDS members west to Salt Lake City. The majority of these migrants pushed large handcarts bearing all their possessions the 1,300 miles from Winter Quarters to Salt Lake City, guided by several companies. One reason Young chose the site for Salt Lake City was the backdrop of the Wasatch Range, which seemed to shield the migrants from the outside world—namely the United States. In search of their own Zion, a place where they could control their destiny, the migrants quickly built Salt Lake City.

Like other immigrants to the West, the Latter-Day Saints both left the United States and maintained ties to it. Mexico actually owned the land to which they moved, but Mexico had its hands full trying to repel American squatters all over its far northern provinces. With the outbreak of the Mexican-American War in 1846, the move to Utah became much easier for the Mormons. Latter-Day Saints settled towns and farms, set their own laws and sent word and support back to those followers who wanted to come west. They wisely contributed the Mormon Battalion, made up of Latter-Day Saints soldiers, to the United States government's efforts in the Mexican-American War. This move made them appear patriotic and loyal while helping to break Mexico's control over the territory they now occupied. Many Latter-Day Saints remained fiercely loyal to the United States and the Constitution, which they believed protected their right to practice their religion as they chose. They had less success breaking the ties of the Paiute and Ute Indians who occupied the territory to their homelands. Brigham Young instituted an "open hand, mailed fist" Indian policy: feed the Indians when possible (to make them dependent), but attack them whenever necessary. It should be pointed out that this policy was similar to that of the Spanish and the United States. Tensions remained high between the Indians and the Mormons well into the twentieth century.

As it had on the Cherokee, the U.S. government forced change on the Latter-Day Saints. In 1857, President Buchanan sent troops against the "rebellious Mormons" based on the government's belief that they were creating a theocracy, or a colony based on religious beliefs, in Utah. (This move seems ironic since the Puritans helped found the United States as a religious colony.) Remember, after the Mexican-American War, Utah became a U.S. territory and fell under federal jurisdiction. This fact initially failed to concern the Latter-Day Saints, as they thought the Constitution protected their religious rights. In any case, federal troops marched toward Utah to set them straight.

As in Oregon, events in Utah converged to shape the outcome of the standoff. Even as the federal troops headed west, an incident known as the Mountain Meadows Massacre occurred in southwest Utah. In August 1857, a wagon train of gentiles on their way to California was attacked and massacred. The incident remains highly controversial, for different parties ascribe to differing accounts of it. Initially, the government of Utah blamed Indians for the attack and claimed they forced Mormons to participate. Eventually, the Indians claimed the reverse happened. In any case, a cover-up ensued. In the end, the federal government tried and executed John D. Lee, the Indian Agent in the territory and a Mormon close to Brigham Young, for his role in the massacre twenty years after the fact. In the short term, however, the incident overwhelmed the federal authorities, who took it as evidence of just how un-American the Latter-Day Saints had become.

Meanwhile, in what has become known as the Utah War, Brigham Young ordered that federal troops be stopped by cutting off their supplies. Latter-Day Saints burned two major trading posts and disrupted supply trains. Young also planned to destroy Salt Lake City and lead a mass exodus south if the troops could not be stopped. Eventually, negotiations began and federal troops marched through an empty Salt Lake City to establish a federal fort, Fort Floyd. Later that year, in a concession, Young gave up his position as governor of the territory. By 1862, polygamy had been outlawed and the fort had been abandoned, thanks to the Civil War. The Latter-Day Saints refused to give up polygamy, however, and the Utah territory remained in limbo into the 1890s, as federal officials and politicians refused to consider welcoming into the federal union a state whose predominant residents officially embraced and surreptitiously practiced polygamy.

We have considered three groups of westering immigrants: the Five Civilized Tribes who went west involuntarily, the Mormons who went west involuntarily but gained control of new lands, and the Whitmans and their followers went west willingly. These three groups shared some things. They all moved to areas that were new and unexplored to them. They all invaded the territories of Western Indian groups and, to varying degrees, had to deal with them. Finally, all three struggled to establish new communities.

Shortly after the dispute over the Oregon Territory and just after Cherokee Removal, the United States engaged in its first war outside of its borders. The pretext was the annexation by the United States of Texas, which originally was part of northern New Spain and then of Mexico, which had won its independence from Spain in 1821. In the early 1830s, in an attempt to secure its northern state of Tejas from land-grabbing Americans, the Mexican government invited settlers from the United States to apply for *colonias* or colonies. Several men, the most prominent of whom was Stephen F. Austin, agreed to become agents for colonization, known as *empresarios.* In exchange for large amounts of land for themselves, the empresarios agreed to take hundreds of settlers, who would swear allegiance to the government of Mexico and promise to convert to Catholicism, into designated lands or colonies in Texas. In the ideal, the immigrants would also establish farms and ranches, thereby helping to settle the region from the Indians and, officials in Mexico City hoped, serve as a bulwark against American squatters settling illegally in Mexican territory. But only a few years later the population of Texas had begun to swell with Americans who had no intention of becoming loyal citizens of Mexico and rose in rebellion against Antonio López de Santa Anna, the president of Mexico and commanding general of the nation's army. At this point, the population of the newly declared Republic of Texas included Anglos, Tejanos, Indians, and blacks, both free and enslaved. In 1837, the United States recognized the sovereignty of the Republic of Texas. Mexico, on the other hand, did not and threatened to reclaim Texas, sending several occupying forces north from Mexico City. In 1845, the United States annexed Texas into the Union, as the Texans had requested. Mexico was outraged that the United States had annexed such a large part of what it still considered its sovereign territory and clashes on both sides of the Rio Grande soon led to war. At the end of the War with Mexico (1846–48), also known as the Mexican-American War, the United States had conquered from Mexico all of present-day Texas, New Mexico, Arizona, and California. While adding massive amounts of territory to the United States, the conflict also created new problems to the issues of settlement of the West.

All of the newly won Mexican territories formerly had belonged to the Spanish. This change affected two important populations: Spanish/Mexican citizens and Indians. Despite granting all the Mexican citizens U.S. citizenship upon taking control of the region, many Mexican Americans lost their land through squatting and schemes by incoming Americans. In keeping with its Indian policy at the time, the federal government did not grant Indians in the new territories U.S. citizenship. But much to the surprise of the government, it discovered that the Spanish had given the Indians land grants (*encomiendas, rancherias,* etc.) These grants meant that the Indians possessed pieces of paper, legal titles to their land, unlike the Indians in any other part of what was quickly becoming the United States. So what makes this important? Let's go back and review English land policy with the Indians.

Remember: the English demanded to see legal title designating the land as legally owned if they were to respect property rights. If one could not produce a title and did not appear to be "using" the land in a manner deemed acceptable by the British, then the British declared said land as "free" or "open" for settlement, meaning that any British citizen who promised to "improve" the land could now settle on it. To improve the land meant to cultivate it, to use it to produce something valuable to the British Empire. When the British signed treaties with the Indians, this process gave the tribes de facto rights to their land. In the Peace of Paris, the treaty that officially ended the War for Independence in 1783, the British gave the United States all its lands east of the Mississippi River but required the new nation to recognize Great Britain's former agreements with the Indians. While the Americans rarely recognized the former agreements as promised, they were quick to extend the British idea that only a paper title in hand granted a person official ownership of his or her land. This system worked well when it came to taking the land of the Plains Indians and those groups living in the Northwest, who had no such pieces of paper in their possession, but the Indians of the newly won Southwest presented a new problem.

The Southwestern nations possessed land grants from the King of Spain designating the land as theirs. Like anyone who had land in the former Spanish colonies they had some form of grant allocating the land to them. The United States could not, then, simply reject the validity of those land grants because they were much like those held by the other settlers in the area, including Anglos. Such a move would disenfranchise Anglo land-owners along with Hispanic and Indian landowners. Therefore, the vast new territories of the Southwest did not come without strings attached.

From the journey of Lewis and Clark until the end of the War with Mexico, the United States grew threefold as it acquired everything west of the Mississippi River, which incorporated new geographies, new environments, and vast new populations into the United States. It also brought about new conflicts with old empires. Finally, it led to new issues and new solutions for the United States government.

Patterns of Statehood

As Americans ventured into newly won territories, Turner's pattern of settlement seemingly unfolded. Traders moved into these "unclaimed" lands, followed by those who could exploit the resources, such as trappers, miners, and lumberjacks. On the heels of these men came settlers who took up ranching and eventually farming. The case studies of Oregon and Texas fit this pattern, but only in a limited way. Turner's thesis gives credit only to Americans, ignoring two important groups: Indians and previous European explorers and settlers.

Turner notwithstanding, both Indians and previously arrived Euro-peans obviously played important roles in developing the West. Both the English and French wanted Oregon because of the trading networks built there by the Indians and the natural resources available, timber to name but one. Turner did not make it clear in his thesis whether by *traders* and *miners* he meant only those in or from the United States. In the case of Oregon, the traders who "discovered" the region for American interests were French and British. Their success in the area attracted American trading companies, which, in turn, attracted settlers. Applying Turner's thesis to the settlement of Oregon raises an interesting and important question. Did Turner define the frontier as a uniquely American experience, or did he simply use the United States for his examples, implying that one could apply his thesis to any frontier?

The case of Texas presents the same question from a different angle. The Spanish province of Tejas, while not one of their more successful ones, was an established colony for nearly two hundred years before United States citizens began to move into it. Though some historians argue that

Deadwood Dick's Cabin. Richard W. Clarke, a.k.a. Deadwood Dick, stands in front
of his basic cabin, typical of early land improvements. You can visit this cabin today
in Cody, Wyoming. *Buffalo Bill Historical Center, Cody, Wyoming, Vincent Mercaldo
Collection, P.71.182*

Texans "settled" Texas, many Spanish, Mexican, and Tejano farmers,
ranchers, and businessmen might disagree with them. While East Texas
had remained relatively underdeveloped, South Texas and other regions of
the vast territory were as settled as many parts of the American Southeast
at the time of U.S. annexation. So how did Texas, New Mexico, Arizona,
and California suddenly become the *American* frontier?

Extending the line of the frontier after having obtained more land
was an issue that the United States government had dealt with before
in limited form. Soon after the United States achieved its independence
from Great Britain, the United States government passed land ordinances
in 1784 and 1785 to try to govern the formerly British land along the
Ohio River. The Ordinance of 1784 divided the land between the Ohio

River and the Mississippi into ten separate states. Yet it failed to explain how the government would distribute the land or how the territory would be settled. The Ordinance of 1785 addressed these issues. It decreed that government surveyors would divide the territories into six-square-mile townships. In turn, each township would be subdivided into one-square mile sections, each equaling 640 acres. Each of these sections would be numbered. The government retained one section in each township for veterans of the American Revolution and for a school. The rest of the sections were to be sold at public auction for a minimum of $1 per acre. While Indians and settlers already occupied some of this land, soon the majority of it was settled and became states.

The founding fathers created a unique system for the birth of states. They wanted to avoid the colonial system of the British that created two tiers of regions: provinces, which had representation in government, and colonies, which either had no or less representation. Therefore, in the Northwest Ordinance of 1787—which covered the territories that became present-day Ohio, Illinois, Indiana, Michigan, and Wisconsin—the U.S. Congress set out the process of achieving statehood very clearly. When an area became a territory, Congress would appoint a territorial governor. Once there were 60,000 adults in a territory—*adults* was often interpreted to mean qualified voters, or white male property owners—the territory could draft its own state constitution and submit it to Congress for consideration and, hopefully, approval. Then the state could apply for admission to the Union, which Congress grants after a vote. While this process sounds very specific, it leaves many vague spaces of interpretation. Who is an adult? Can Congress reject a state's application? What needs to be covered in the constitution of the would-be state? All of these questions were posed again and again as what we consider the Midwestern and then Western states tried to and did become part of the Union.

By the turn of the nineteenth century, Thomas Jefferson, who seemed to have had land on his mind a great deal, foresaw a time when other territories might join the United States and felt that there should be a plan to govern those areas-in-waiting. In particular, he formulated a plan that would consider populations, boundaries, a system of land sale, and the creation of townships, with one parcel reserved for education. His vision came to fruition in the Land Ordinance of 1796, in which the government laid out precisely the process by which a territory would become a state.

Typical survey and subdivision of land into a township. This diagram represents Northwest Ordinance surveying of land. This grid would be placed over land to subdivide it for settlement. From *The Land of Promise: Dakota: How to Go and What to Do When You Get There* by the Chicago, Milwaukee, and St. Paul Railway Company. Rare book collection. *Buffalo Bill Historical Center, Cody, Wyoming; RBF.655. C44.1882, p.14*

First the governor of a territory would authorize a census. If the territory had enough residents (meaning white ones) to qualify for admission, the governor next called a constitutional congress charged with writing a state constitution, which not only outlined the rights for the citizens of that state but also designated who would qualify as a voter. It is important to remember there was no federal standard (until the Voting Rights Act of 1965) for who could vote. In the states formed from the original 13 colonies, only white male property owners could vote. In 1796, Tennessee became the first state to join the Union that did not require property ownership to vote. One still had to be a white adult male to vote, but dropping the property-ownership requirement was a radical move for its time. It also greatly increased the population of the state, as people moved into Tennessee, many simply in order to gain the franchise. After the constitutional congress within the territory presented a constitution to the governor, the population of the territory would ratify the constitution and hold elections for state offices. Then, the United States Congress would pass the new state's constitution, creating a new state.

Important differences existed between states and territories. When a territory was organized, the president appointed a govenor and three judges, who established and administered basic laws. After its population reached 5,000, a territory elected a legislature and sent a non-voting delegate to Congress. Once it became a state, it took on the same status as the original 13 states and sent voting members to the U.S. House of Representatives and Senate. States could also decide how to appoint or elect state officials, judges, and police. For the Indians statehood meant that the federal government would take over Indian-white relations from the territorial governor, often sending U.S. Army troops in to do the negotiating, which usually led to treaties in which the Indians ceded much of their land to the U.S. government. Then, upon any pretense of breaking said treaties, such as defending their remaining land from white squatters, the U.S. government would claim the Indians had "broken" the terms of the treaty and deem them as "hostile," which meant it sent the U.S. Army back into Indian country to fight and/or remove the Indians of the new state.

Turner portrayed the settling of the United States as an east-to-west process, a solemn march to the Pacific Ocean, interrupted occasionally by Indian wars and other setbacks. In reality, those territories with good ocean ports or river access or that had the most valuable resources attracted settlers and were settled before those in the center of the nation. Missouri (1821), Iowa (1846), Minnesota (1858), California (1850) and Oregon (1859) all became states before the central Great Plains states of Nebraska (1864), Colorado (1876), and North Dakota, South Dakota, and Montana (all in 1889). Missouri, Iowa, and Minnesota bordered long stretches of the Mississippi River. This geographical fact meant that goods and resources could easily be shipped from those territories to ready markets. This economic feasibility made the efforts of settlers successful and in turn attracted more settlers. The Gold Rush of 1848–49 attracted not just gold miners but also settlers and business people to California, very quickly increasing the population of that territory to a level suitable for statehood. Less than ten years after the Whitman Massacre, as settlers poured in through the ports of Oregon and Washington and from across the Oregon Trail, virtually ignoring the center of the nation as they traversed it in covered wagons drawn by horses or oxen, Oregon had a population that qualified it for application for statehood.

Manifest Destiny and the World

If you opened a newspaper during the early to mid nineteenth century, the debates dominating the headlines would center on the concept of *Manifest Destiny*. The term was coined by a journalist in the 1840s, but the concept was familiar by the turn of the century. It grew out of various interpretations of the national purpose. The majority of Americans believed that the area west of the Mississippi should belong to them because they had created a democratic, Christian nation out of whole cloth in the East. Now debates raged over how far the United States could or should extend the concept of Manifest Destiny and how to convince other populations, (namely those whom the concept and believers in the concept would displace) that the Manifest Destiny of the United States was inevitable. Congress and reformers (including missionaries, educators, and philanthropists) debated what they termed the "Indian Problem," whether the remaining "free" Indians of the American West were fading away before the superior American society or should be integrated into it. Few voices suggested that Indian nations should remain separate, sovereign nations or that they deserved the individual freedoms enjoyed by citizens of the United States. (Not until 1925 did the United States government see fit to grant U.S. citizenship to Indians.) The same issues arose immediately after the War with Mexico. The United States suddenly encompassed a large territory formerly governed by Mexico. Overnight, many thousands of Mexican citizens abruptly became U.S. citizens. Yet these people did not fit the assumed standards of American society; they were Spanish-speaking, Catholic, and often mestizo, not Anglo-Protestants. The question was: will they assimilate or should we just ignore them and import American culture into the regions in which they are currently the majority population?

By the 1890s, Americans (at least white Americans) were not satisfied with simply controlling the continental United States. They hungrily looked at Hawaii and Alaska, as well as the Philippines and other foreign lands. The U.S. government and speculators began to seek resources, strategic military positions overseas, and further proof that Providence continued to smile on them.

☙ Suggested Readings ❧

Ambrose, Stephen. *Undaunted Courage: Meriwether Lewis, Thomas Jefferson, and the Opening of the American West.* New York: Simon and Schuster, 2002.

Arrington, Leonard, and Davis Britton. *The Mormon Experience: A History of the Latter-Day Saints.* New York: Knopf, 1979.

Campbell, Randolph B. *Gone to Texas: A History of the Lone Star State.* New York: Oxford University Press, 2003.

Conley, Robert. *The Cherokee Nation.* Albuquerque: University of New Mexico Press, 2008.

Goetzman, William. *New Lands, New Men: America and the Second Great Age of Discovery.* New York: Viking, 1986.

Higham, C. L. *Noble, Wretched and Redeemable: Protestant Missionaries to the Indians in Canada and the United States.* Albuquerque: University of New Mexico Press, 2000.

Howe, Daniel Walker. *What Hath God Wrought: The Transformation of America, 1815–1848.* New York: Oxford University Press, 2007.

Jeffrey, Julie Roy. *Converting the West: A Biography of Narcissa Whitman.* Norman: University of Oklahoma, 1991.

Kerstetter, Todd. *God's Country, Uncle Sam's Land: Faith and Conflict in the American West.* Urbana: University of Illinois Press, 2006.

Perdue, Theda, and Michael Green. *Cherokee Nation and the Trail of Tears.* New York: Viking, 2007.

Unruh, John. *The Plains Across: The Overland Emigrants and the Trans-Mississippi West, 1840–1860.* Champaign-Urbana: University of Illinois Press, 1993.

CHAPTER SEVEN

Putting Down Roots

In the 1950s, the Canadian historian J. M. S. Careless wrote an article entitled "Frontierism, Metropolitanism and Canadian History," in which he attempted to explain the growth and development of the Canadian West. He stated right off the bat that a "dynamic" frontier had shaped the Canadian West, just as Turner had maintained about the United States. While stating that Turner's thesis may be correct for the United States, Careless, in pondering Canada's westward expansion, embraced and expanded on what is known as the "Laurentian interpretation." This theory suggested that the St. Lawrence River provided the basis and center for the development of Canada. Some refer to this as the East's affect on the West, yet Careless pushed this notion one step further by combining it with the idea of "metropolitanism." This idea, you may remember from Chapter One, focused on the development of the West around metropolitan areas. In short form, the West only grows in significance and develops in response to the needs of the East and the major cities thereof. A forest might stand for centuries, but it only becomes "important" as a source of "timber" when an expanding city in the East needs wood products. Careless argued that the West grew around the needs of metropolitan centers, and that those areas beyond the reach of the centers failed to grow. Some historians refer to Careless as the Canadian Turner.

As in the case of Turner, though, it is important to look at how Careless built his theory. Besides looking at the theories of previous historians,

Careless looked to Europe and its influence on the history of Canada. Without London and its need for certain resources, there could not have been a developed West. That said, Careless saw metropolitan centers rising and falling in succession. Over time, Ottawa replaced London and Calgary replaced Ottawa as the center driving western development in Canada. The views of Canadian historians of Careless's generation, just like those of Turner's, represented a certain kind of training. They saw Canada as part of the British colonial system and a participant in the imperialist mission of Great Britain. Whereas American historians like Turner, who ignored the Spanish and French empires, often baulked at admitting any ties to Europe, Canadian historians, at least at this time, sought to see how Europe aided and abetted in the creation of Canada and, in particular, western Canada. For Careless and others of his cadre, Canadian civilization is an extension of European civilization. In recent years, more historians have examined how the United States West does or does not fit the metropolitan theory. For many historians, though, this means accepting the idea that the United States *colonized* the West.

Colonialism, Imperialism, and the West

So what, exactly, do *colonialism* and *imperialism* mean? Colonialism is the invasion by the people of one nation into part or all of another nation or land, dominating the indigenous peoples and ultimately enslaving or assimilating them into their transplanted culture and society. That done, the colonizer sends a proportion of its own nationals to live in the dominated region, or colony, to help it produce marketable goods or extract the land's natural resources for export. The colonizing nation extends to its colonists its laws, but not the full freedoms or rights of citizenship, and generally uses the colony as it pleases for economic, political, or strategic reasons. J. A. Hobson, an English economist and critic of colonialism and imperialism, sums it up best: "Colonialism . . . may be considered a genuine expansion of nationality, a territorial engagement of the stock, language and institutions of the nation." In other words, a nation extends its culture and institutions beyond its national boundaries. From our previous examples, Great Britain was one colonizer of North America.

Imperialism is different. In imperialism, a small number of the dominant nation's citizens—often businesspersons—moves into a foreign land but continues to live within the confines of their own nation's laws, institutions, and cultural norms. These expatriates (expats) end up running the other country as a privileged minority, overriding local institutions but not extending the laws or institutions of their home country to the native inhabitants. As Hobson describes it, "their [the natives of the infiltrated country] political and economic structure of society is wholly alien from that of the mother country." Nineteenth-century imperialism occurred when industrialized countries (England, France, and the United States, to name a few) dominated non-industrial countries to gain access to their markets and raw materials. Some theorists believe that overproduction of goods led to the need to create new markets. New markets, in turn, led to a need for more raw materials to make the goods, so a never-ending cycle ensued.

Historians and other theorists have proposed other ideas. Joseph Schumpeter, a German economist whose theory of imperialism emerged immediately after World War I, argued that European countries, and by extension the United States, needed to dominate others to feel superior and strong. Such domination also served as a safety valve for internal conflicts within the dominating countries. When citizens of the dominating country complained about economic or political conditions, two things happened: the government compared their situation favorably with that of the colonized people, or they shipped the complainers to the colonies. The colonies, therefore, provided a safety valve for the mother country.

Imperialism and colonialism also went hand in hand with the rise of nationalism in Europe and the United States during the nineteenth century. Not unlike previous Spanish, French and English empires in the sixteenth and seventeenth century, these nations felt they had a *duty* to expand and bring their civilization to the rest of the world. They were the missionaries of national beliefs. In other words, God must have made them great and powerful nations so that they would spread their superior civilizations. Nationalism and Manifest Destiny have an ugly step-sister: racism. Many Europeans and Americans felt that their ability to dominate other peoples or even other societies demonstrated their cultural superiority. And the anthropological theories and scientific thinking of the nineteenth century supported these assumptions, positing that richer peoples, meaning white Europeans, were *naturally* superior to people who were at this time in history materially poorer, meaning Africans and indigenous Americans, north and south. Now so-called reformers argued that Africans were predestined to toil at manual labor and that the American Indians were predestined to fade away before the march of "progress." Such arguments—self-serving interpretations of Charles Darwin's ideas—seemed simply to confirm what Americans and Europeans already believed: they were better than everyone else. However, this rampant ethnocentricity eventually led to horrific conflicts between the different imperialist nation-states themselves, as they ran out of weaker places to dominate and began to eye one another.

So far, we have discussed three North American empires, those of Spain, France, and Great Britain. They shared several elements that made them colonial empires. Each one of them expanded for political and economic reasons. Each found justifications for this expansion that masked the real reasons, or at least confounded them. Spain had a land crisis and needed gold to support the incessant religious wars it waged in Europe, conflicts that exhausted the Spanish treasury of silver and gold as fast as its galleons could bring it over from the Americas. Providence, they believed, continued to favor them, and no less than the Pope blessed their mission of conversion. France and England followed suit, though with their own twists on the Providence angle. The second driving cause of expansion was resource development. The Spanish, who managed to spend themselves near bankruptcy, sought increasingly more gold and silver and kept expanding their boundaries to find more. The French needed more pelts and stretched their empire farther and farther west to find them. The British wanted land for the production of staple crops, and when they populated all the open land they could, they claimed a genuine need for more land.

Additionally, all three European colonizers of North America defined all the land around them as free and available, maybe not for settlement, but certainly for ownership. The Spanish provided land grants to the Indians, settlers, and missions to help establish and keep the land as part of the Spanish Empire. The French created trading posts and alliances with Indian groups to mark the land as theirs. The British built forts and farms to do the same. All of these institutions helped the respective European empires extend their governance over new territory. Administrators in Europe—not those in the colonies—made the majority of decisions about these three empires. The Council of the Indies in Spain, Parliament in Britain, and the King in France, all made policy decisions that affected the colonies without any say of the colonists.

Finally, all of the colonies served as safety valves for their founding European empires. They became places where problem peoples (like the Puritans) could go or be banished. The colonies relieved social and economic pressures, such as land crises, but they also created new problems, like mixed populations, tensions between European empires in North America that ended up sparking wars in Europe, and huge investments of time and money to oversee and regulate huge trans-Atlantic empires.

But the nineteenth-century American West was a wholly different proposition. A region settled by individuals who had come to it for their own reasons, the American West did not fit into the colonial model. Or did it? At least two institutions point to some aspects of metropolitanism and colonialism in the American West: the Homestead Act and the railroads. Additionally, the ranching industry and its hero, the cowboy, also relied on metropolitan institutions and relationships to survive. When you finish this chapter, ask yourself: Was the nineteenth-century American West merely a colony of the Eastern United States?

The Homestead Act

In 1862 the United States Congress passed a unique piece of legislation, the Homestead Act, to apportion the millions of acres of Western land that the federal government claimed as its sovereign possession. (The various western Indian nations felt differently about that assumption.) Based on the Ordinance of 1785, which Congress designed to survey and sell off unclaimed land to settlers after the American Revolution, the Homestead Act of 1862 sought to sell land directly to the population. After the Louisiana Purchase and the land grab that ensued after the War with Mexico, the federal government released land in parcels to private land companies. Similar to the Spanish system of colonias, these land companies recruited settlers, laid out a town platte or plan as designated in the Ordinance of 1785, often named the fledgling town, then transported settlers to the spot. In contrast, the Homestead Act sold land directly to individual settlers, allowing *them* to select the land they wished to settle and, with luck, someday own.

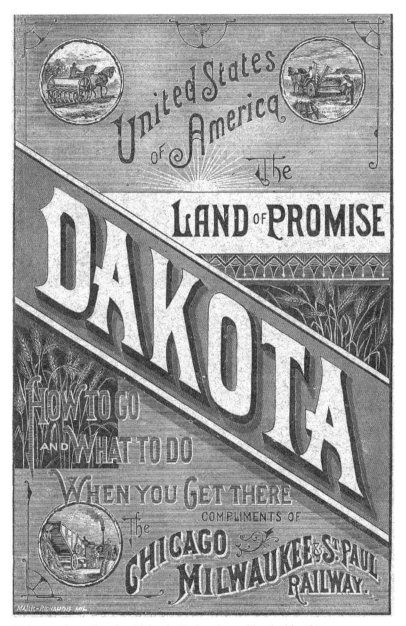

Title page for railroad guidebook. Railroads used books like this one to attract settlers and visitors to the West. From *The Land of Promise: Dakota: How to Go and What to Do When You Get There* by the Chicago, Milwaukee, and St. Paul Railway Company. Rare book collection. *Buffalo Bill Historical Center, Cody, Wyoming; RB.F.655.C44.1882 Title Page*

A sweeping piece of legislation, probably unrivaled by any other power at this time (though later imitated by Canada in its West), the Homestead Act illustrates Turner's contention that democracy worked better when there was a frontier to keep it active. The Homestead Act also demonstrates how greatly people in the East misunderstood the environment of the Great Plains and other parts of the West. Under the terms of the Act, any citizen or perspective citizen could claim any surveyed but unclaimed piece of public land. Unlike in other nations in which only citizens could own land, the Homestead Act opened up the West to foreign-born residents who *intended* to become citizens. Nothing in the Act required those who obtained land through it to become U.S. citizens and many who used the Homestead Act to gain land never became citizens. This fact led to an unusually high number of foreign-born landowners in some states such as the Dakotas and Minnesota. By 1870, three out of ten settlers and half of the men over the age of twenty-one born in Utah, Arizona, Nevada, Idaho, and California were foreign-born. Unintentionally, the act ended up changing the idea of what civilizing the territory meant because so many of the so-called civilizers did not represent mainstream, native-born America.

As mentioned, the Homestead Act defined free land as that surveyed but unclaimed, just as Turner would later. This definition meant that any land that the United States government had surveyed after claiming it from another nation or other entity was "open" for settlement. How the government defined *unclaimed* becomes more problematic. When Congress passed the first Homestead Act in 1862, unclaimed land meant all that obtained through the Louisiana Purchase, the War with Mexico, and through extinguished land titles from Indian groups. By the end of the nineteenth century, it came to mean land that the United States government considered underutilized by Indians and others.

Just because land was surveyed did not mean it was clearly marked. If you think about modern surveying techniques, you see a line of stakes with orange flags delineating property lines. Often, surveyed land simply meant that which someone in Washington, D.C., had surveyed on a map. Using geographic landmarks, the surveying teams would lay out the plots for the homesteaders and land companies. Once on the site, an individual homesteader with a survey in hand found it virtually impossible to tell what was surveyed and unclaimed versus what was claimed, say by the Indians or another nation, or not yet surveyed. There were no fences or other clear boundaries between Indian lands, Canadian lands, and unclaimed surveyed lands. Because land companies originally claimed large tracts of land, it was much easier for them to use surveys (also because this was their business). By 1862, Indian nations had ceded only one-third of the lands west of the Mississippi to the United States government. Generally, however, American settlers and pioneers interpreted any land as unclaimed if they did not see a homestead on it. This concept naturally led to lots of squatting on Indian lands. As settlers built sod houses and fences, Indian nations became increasingly hostile when these people happened to settle on their land. Most of the early-nineteenth-century treaties between Indian nations and the U.S. government guaranteed boundaries in perpetuity for Indian lands in return for a reduction of their original size. However, when the United States government refused to enforce these treaties, by ignoring the fact that whites were squatting on Indian land, the Indians often handled the situation on their own. The government typically interpreted these moves as hostile actions that violated the treaties, thereby legitimating the squatters' claims. In other words, in the American West, squatting paid off; while not legal, it often became legitimate. Understandably, the logic behind this legal gamesmanship left the Indians feeling betrayed, bewildered, and angry.

Why did the United States government support, or at least not remove, squatters? Just like the British or, for that matter, the Spanish, the United States government thought its citizens used the land properly while the Indians did not. It believed Western Indian nations, in particular the Plains Indians, were nomadic peoples—constantly on the move to follow the herds of buffalo—who held no attachment to the land they roamed. They ignored Indian agricultural developments because they did not resemble traditional American farms; the Indians' crops were overseen by women, were not fenced in, and were allowed to grow without heavy tending. To the Americans, if the land appeared to be unproductive, it was unclaimed.

Many historians point to Jeffersonian agrarianism—the belief that individual farmers who work their own land provide the basis for a democratic republic—as the impetus for westward expansion and homesteading. They point to the Louisiana Purchase to demonstrate that Jefferson believed that all Americans should have the right to own and work their own land. Many missionaries and other reformers believed that turning Western Indians (meaning those of the Plains, Southwest, and Columbia Plateau) into farmers would turn them into Jeffersonian agrarians who would whole-heartedly accept American political and social values. But a blanket acceptance of Jeffersonian agrarianism ignores other traditions that had supported the same idea—the British, French, and Spanish had also encouraged Indian ownership and production of land—as well as the high failure rate of individual farmers. Finally, a firm belief in this unique relationship between a citizen and the land makes it easier to justify the displacement of Indian, Hispanic, and other landowners who wanted to pursue different methods of land use.

The United States government expected settlers to succeed quickly under the Homestead Act. Each land grant executed under it gave the settler 160 acres, roughly the size of successful family farms east of the Mississippi. To gain title to the land, the "homesteader" had to live on the land for five years. During that time, the Act required him to make improvements on that land, meaning build a house or farm on it and, ideally, plant crops. At the end of the trial period, the homesteader paid a fee to register the land and claim the title to it. On the face of it, this policy implies that the settlers were getting land for free. One of the great myths about the United States West is that anyone could go there and make their fortune: land for the taking. In reality, even without having to buy land to homestead, settlers needed access to capital to improve the land. Many an immigrant or settler arrived in the West without the money for tools or seeds or the skills necessary to build a farm or household from the ground up.

The lack of capital kept many people out of the land rush and settlement in the West. Under the first part of the Homestead Act, one could indeed receive 160 acres without a cent for a down payment, but without a title to the land one could not borrow against it to buy the tools and seeds necessary to develop or improve it. Later revisions of the Homestead Act remedied this problem: if one wanted to own his land outright after six months, so that he might borrow against it, he could pay $1.25 an acre, or $200, for it. While this may sound cheap by twenty-first-century standards, the amount represented more than most people's annual income. And if a homesteader shelled out $200 for the land, he now had 200 fewer dollars with which to purchase equipment and supplies.

Though the homesteader could now borrow against the land, such a move greatly increased the chances that he would find himself over his head in debt and lose the land to the lender, which is exactly what happened in many cases.

Land speculators were quick to figure out how they stood to profit from this clause in the Homestead Act. Take George Stewart in Paonia, Colorado. He owned a local mine and employed several hundred miners. He offered to stake his employees money to buy their own homesteads, with the catch that they had to sign the title over to him until they paid off the debt in full. Few managed to do so, and Stewart quickly gained what became a large and successful cattle ranch, which supported him after the mine went bust. The miners, landless and jobless, moved on if they could, or wound up working for Stewart on the ranch. The intention of the Homestead Act was to distribute land, but also to put it directly in the hands of individuals. Yet, despite what the Declaration of Independence assures us, not all individuals are created equal and some gained considerable land and power under the act while others watched their dreams wash away with floodwaters or dry up during drought and blow away.

Other problems arose out of the Homestead Act. The government sold millions of acres of good agricultural land to land speculators and gave it to railroad companies (to subsidize railroad construction), effectively blocking agricultural development across large parts of the West. In some areas, government surveyors ignored previous land claims and grants, particularly in the states formerly owned by Spain. Hispanic landowners—some of whose families had owned the land, from small farming plots to huge ranches that covered many square miles—found their land listed as unclaimed, despite land grants and paperwork deeding them the land. Many outraged Hispanic landowners, who, keep in mind, were U.S. citizens as of the end of the War with Mexico, took their cases to court only to have white judges side with whites who had moved onto the land under the auspices of the Homestead Act or just squatted on it and refused to leave. Additionally, people quickly discovered that 160 acres in the semi-arid West was too small a plot to support a family, much less produce a crop to sell elsewhere. In areas with an average rainfall of 20 inches or less, many traditional crops from the Eastern United States did not fare well. Even after immigrants introduced such crops as turkey red (a drought-resistant wheat that can grow under extreme weather conditions), western migrants still needed more than 160 acres of land and a

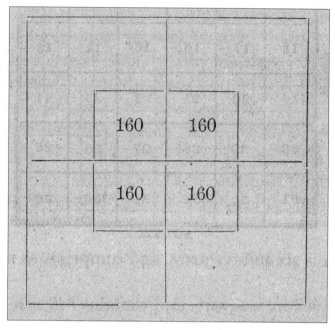

Diagram of timber culture. This diagram, from a railroad guide, illustrates a basic plot for the Timber Culture Act. From *The Land of Promise: Dakota: How to Go and What to Do When You Get There* by the Chicago, Milwaukee, and St. Paul Railway Company. *Rare book collection. Buffalo Bill Historical Center, Cody Wyoming; RB.F.655.C44.1882, p. 13*

regular source of water to succeed as farmers. Eventually, Congress revised the provision to make the grants 640 acres. When that, too, failed to alleviate all of the problems of would-be western farmers, Congress passed the Timber Culture Act in 1873. Designed to help ranchers, it allowed homesteaders to apply for an additional 160 acres, which also became their property once they planted forty acres of trees on it. When that requirement proved too onerous, Congress reduced the quota to ten acres of trees. In short, the Homestead Act opened the door to but did not guarantee success.

Despite its cons, the Homestead Act also had some important pros. Later versions of it allowed women to homestead, a change that granted freedom to many women by giving them the chance to create their own wealth through property ownership. Although the act had intended to help families homestead more acreage, many women successfully used provisions of it to gain a measure of security. In addition to allowing people who intended to become citizens to homestead without requiring citizenship, the act did not mention race, an unusual point for the time. In other words, the Homestead Act allowed African Americans, Hispanics, and Asians to try their luck at homesteading and, hopefully, end up with land of their own.

One group that took advantage of the lack of racial bias in the Homestead Act was the Exodusters. Named after the Biblical journey and the trip to the Great Plains (*Exodus* plus *dust* equals *Exodusters*), these settlers were recently freed slaves from the South who took advantage of the legislation to escape the oppressive environment of the post–Civil War South by moving west. They arrived in the West after the end of Reconstruction, the majority of them settling in Kansas in the late 1870s and early 1880s— principally because Texas banned black settlement and Oklahoma, then Indian Territory, was unstable at the time. The new arrivals built small all-black communities, including Nicodemus, Kansas, which survives today. Like other settlers, the Exodusters took up farming, opened small business such as dry goods stores, and set themselves up in other occupations and professions in order to make a livelihood and keep their families going.

Before the Civil War, free blacks and escaped slaves stayed away from Kansas and Nebraska. Slave traders patrolled those territories, kidnapping blacks to resell them into slavery. Other states, like Iowa, restricted black settlement. Iowa had a pass-through law, letting blacks pass through the state but requiring all blacks in the state to have on their person court-issued manumission papers (legally granting one's freedom) and a deposit of $500 to settle there. Few whites could afford that kind of money, much less most blacks. The law effectively banned black settlement. In addition to having a pass-through law, Oregon prohibited blacks from settling at all, though historians have raised questions about the enforcement of the measure. Additionally, the Oregon law punished any white who helped or harbored blacks. Though the law was spottily enforced, public opinion strongly opposed black settlement. In 1900, 90 percent of the voters shot down a proposed repeal of the law. It would take twenty-six more years before the state finally repealed it.

The Exodusters were atypical for the black communities in the West for two reasons. First, they settled in the Great Plains. The majority of the black population during the mid- to late-nineteenth century was urban,

Buffalo soldier, Pine Ridge Agency, South Dakota, 1891. African-American cavalry men, called "Buffalo Soldiers," served throughout the Great Plains and the Southwest, often in conflict with Indians. Many transferred their cowboy skills to work as cavalrymen and used the military as a way to migrate West. *C. G. Morledge, Western History/ Geneaology Department, Denver Public Library, Denver Colorado*

settling in cities where work was available. The bulk of the pre–Civil War African American population amassed along coasts and rivers, for the simple reason that most blacks got to the West by jumping ship from sea-going vessels or riverboats. Once they made it to free territory, many blacks quietly slipped away and joined the nearest African American town or neighborhood.

And despite the problems and politics of the Homestead Act, it did solve certain problems for farm families, chiefly the issue of land scarcity. In the East, as people subdivided land among children, free and viable land became increasingly harder to find. The Homestead Act came to the rescue of many a second son who would otherwise have been landless. It also distributed vast amounts of land that the federal government possessed after conquering it or extinguishing Indian title to it. And it solved the problem of how to bring American settlers to the frontier at a time when most people lacked large amounts of capital with which to buy property. Finally, it enfranchised millions of people. While probably two-thirds of the homesteaders failed or sold out to the next generation of settlers, the Act did help to settle the West—and quickly.

The success of the Homestead Act, and the money it raised for the federal government, inspired the creation of the Dawes Act, also called the General Allotment Act, in 1887. Sponsored by Senator Henry Dawes, a reforming senator from Massachusetts who actively supported missionary work to help the Indians financially and politically, the Act dramatically reshaped the geographical, social, and political landscapes of Western Indian reservations and tribal lands. Intended to "civilize" Indians through teaching them the values of farming and property ownership, it also opened hundreds of thousands of acres of land for white settlement. Mirroring the Homestead Act, the Dawes Act required the government to survey and subdivide Indian reservations and land into 160-acre parcels for each head of household, 80 acres for single persons over the age of 18, and 40 acres for children. Indians were to farm the land individually. In other words, they were not to combine it into communal plots or work it as communities, for Senator Dawes and Congress saw such practices as "uncivilized" and "backward." Double allotments were granted for grazing rights. Indians had four years to choose an allotment from within their territory. After that period, an Indian agent, appointed by the U.S.

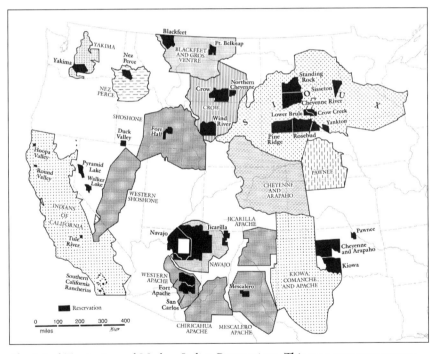

Aboriginal Territories and Modern Indian Reservations. This map represents reservations after 1946. The shaded areas represent "aboriginal territories" much of which was lost during the Dawes Act.

government and usually white, chose the land for them. The U.S. government held the land in trust for 25 years, during which time it would not tax the land. Also during that period, the "owner" could not lease, sell, or borrow against the land. This part of the Dawes Act essentially tied the hands of Indians in developing the land, as they often lacked the capital to buy equipment or seeds. After divvying up each reservation, the government sold the "surplus" lands to whites. The Five Civilized Tribes, five other tribes in Indian Territory (Oklahoma), and the Seneca in New York, thanks to prior treaties, were exempt from the Dawes Act. Any allottee who took up the "habits of civilized life" became a U.S. citizen subject to U.S. law.

Despite its good intentions, the Dawes Act proved to be ill-conceived and ultimately destructive. It reduced Indian lands from 139 million acres to 47 million acres in less than 50 years. It also disrupted, even broke up, communities, as planners purposely spread allotments across reservations to dissolve "traditional" tribal life. Many Indians fought the policy by refusing to abide by it, viewing it as voluntary, as the Homestead Act had been. When Indian agents assigned lands, they often chose parcels with poor or no access to water sources or ones that were rocky and barren, arguing that the tribe could make more money by selling off the more-fertile land. Because Indians could not lease or borrow against their land during the provisional 25 years, they lacked the funds to buy tools, seeds, and other items necessary to farm the land. Moreover, despite the provision barring sale, through squatting or chicanery much allotted land ended up in the hands of whites.

In spite of the democratic vision of individual ownership of land, the Homestead Act and the Dawes Act smacked of colonialism. Through these acts, the federal government took over a vast resource and redistributed it, largely ignoring the rights and needs of populations already occupying the land and using its resources. The acts also reflected a nationalistic belief in the superiority of American settlement.

Railroads

The Homestead Act would not have been so successful without another federal program: subsidies in land and tax breaks to privately held railroad companies. Transportation is necessary for colonization. Without a means of arriving in a place, newcomers cannot take it over. In the East, rivers and canals served this purpose. As mentioned, Lewis and Clark had hoped to find a transcontinental water route running from St. Louis to the Pacific so that the federal government might better control the recently acquired region. When they did not find such a passage, the government realized that westward expansion would remain dependent on the available roads and trails.

But traveling overland was a perilous undertaking. Dangers included poor preparation (which could entail getting lost, running out of supplies, starving, and hiring unqualified guides), insect bites, bad weather (rain, floods, unexpected snow or extreme cold, and tornadoes), and accidents (such as falling off of wagons or horses, drowning, and accidental shootings.) Although Western films, novels, and television shows abound with Indian attacks on wagon trains, recent scholars, such as Lillian Schlissel and John Unruh, suggest that far more migrants talked about seeing Indians than actually did, much less suffering attacks by them.

The dangers notwithstanding, overland travel was also expensive. The trip west from Missouri to Oregon cost around $1,000 in nineteenth-century terms: $400 for the wagon and oxen, $600 for six- to eight-months' worth of food, $70 for rifles and other weaponry. This estimate did not include the money it took to get to Missouri from parts east, more money to replace supplies that were lost or damaged along the way, and still more for food for the first winter and supplies for the farm. Few truly poor people went west to remake their lives; only people who had assets to sell could afford the trip west.

The trail west was also time consuming, taking up to eight months to get from St. Louis to Oregon along the Oregon Trail in a covered wagon pulled by horses or oxen, though some people walked or pushed their belongings in carts. Remember the order in which the states entered the Union? Coastal states achieved statehood before many of the interior states. States like California, Oregon, and Washington had access to seaports. Many Americans who went west to start anew took the harrowing journey by sea, having to brave the turbulent waters around South America's Cape Horn in order to get there. Others traveled by sea to Panama, crossed the jungle on mules or on foot, then boarded another ship to reach California or Oregon. How, then, to populate the vast Western interior in an efficient manner and then get the goods produced out there to markets? Railroads.

Although railroad technology already existed, the problem was that rail lines were inordinately expensive to build. Because of the great expanse of the West, few venture capitalists wanted to embark on a project that would take at least several years and hundreds of millions of dollars to complete and still not necessarily succeed. The federal government therefore stepped in to expedite the process. Since the American Revolution, the federal government had provided land grants and funds to private companies in order to facilitate the building of canals, roads, and schools. In the same vein, in the 1850s it began to give away public land to railroad companies in the name of internal improvements and progress.

It was a complicated process. The government did not just grant railroad companies narrow strips of land on which it might lay down tracks. Instead, it granted them large swaths of land, up to several miles, on either side of the proposed tracks. The railroad company was free to sell the excess land off to individuals or speculators for the highest price it could get, which the government approved. Buyers viewed the land as more valuable because of its proximity to the tracks. If you had any hope of having a successful business in the nineteenth-century West, you needed at least two things: water and transportation. Buying land next to a proposed railroad line satisfied at least one of those requisites.

After the Mexican-American War, pressure built to expand access to the recently acquired lands in the West. Many Americans demanded the building of a transcontinental railroad system to join the two coasts of the nation and open the interior for development. With the Pacific Railway Act of 1862, the idea moved toward fruition. Two companies sought to join their lines to create the first transcontinental railway: the Union Pacific, owned by Theodore Durant, Oakes Ames, and Oliver Ames, and the Central Pacific, owned originally by Theodore Judah, and eventually Charles Crocker, Collis Huntington, Mark Hopkins, and Leland Stanford, also known as the "Big Four." If some of these names sound familiar, they should. Huntington, Hopkins, and Stanford all became important philanthropists and have various institutions, such as libraries and universities, named after them. Believers in Manifest Destiny saw the transcontinental railroad as the last necessary step to control completely the West.

In order to build the transcontinental line, the Union Pacific laid track west from Omaha, Nebraska, while the Central Pacific built east-

"Laying the Track of the Pacific Railroad" and "On the Central Pacific Railroad." These images depict the building of western railroads. Note the presence of Indians and Chinese workers in the artwork. *Buffalo Bill Historical Center, Cody, Wyoming; RB.F.594.B78.49 and 51.51.285*

ward from Sacramento, California. The federal government subsidized the construction, not only through the land grants along the rights of way but through long-term loans. But even when government support expanded in 1864, the project languished due to a lack of capital and hindrances related to the Civil War. Ultimately, the first rail in the transcontinental line was laid on July 10, 1865; the last one, nailed down with a ceremonial golden spike, was laid on May 10, 1869, when the two lines met at Promontory Summit, Utah.

Between 1862 and 1871, the U.S. government granted 174 million acres in the West to four major railroad companies. This move suddenly made railroads the largest landowners, after the federal government, west of the Mississippi and put them in charge of selling off seemingly countless large tracts of land. So beyond transporting the settlers, the railroads now needed to recruit them as well.

While railroad companies did hold onto some land, they needed to sell a lot of it. If they laid the track to places with a few or no farmers, then there would be no crops to ship or people in need of transport. Additionally, selling the excess land handed to it by the government underwrote the cost of building the railroad. In the beginning, the railroads bent over backwards to lure farmers and keep them on the prairies. They hired recruiting companies with agents that literally traveled the world looking for people or whole communities willing to move to the West. From the 1860s through 1900, the representatives of railroad companies sought out communities in Europe and beyond who felt the need to move as a group. As previous land speculators had learned, moving as a group increased the chance that a newly transplanted community might survive—Mennonites and Jews from Russia, Germans from Poland, Czechs, and Italians were among the various groups who took the bait and moved to the American West. In addition to propaganda about the West, immigration agents also offered would-be settlers subsidies for planting crops, reduced freight costs, and other incentives.

Like every business, the railroads faced their own challenges. The building of the lines buried some companies in debt. Many of the schemes some railroad companies used to sell off the excess land (that the federal government had granted them) to pay off their debt entrapped farmers in their own circle of debt. Often offered land with very little money down and sliding rates of payment over time, many new migrants to the Great Plains found themselves in debt to the railroad companies as soon as an extended drought or crop failure limited their available cash. Unlike homesteaders, who could and often did walk away from their land before the five-year residency period expired, those who bought land from the railroads remained in debt even if they were forced to abandon the land.

While railroads seemed an excellent vehicle for promoting national interests, local communities often found the railroads antagonistic. Just the laying of the track created intense political wars between towns. Towns skipped by the railroad faced extinction as people moved their businesses closer to railroad stations where they could send and receive goods. Take a drive through Kansas. If you start at Great Bend and drive southwest to Dodge City, you will notice that most of the towns in between are built around the railroad (Dundee, Pawnee Rock, Larned, and Garfield). From a distance, you will see the large grain elevators

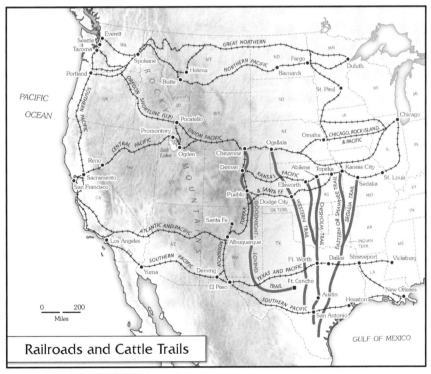

Railroads and Cattle Trails

Railroads and the Cattle Trails, 1850–1900

rising above the plains. Next to them, you will see the railroad line (and
in some cases, the state road). The railroads displaced other forms of
transportation as well. If you visit Winona, Minnesota, you will notice
that at least two rail lines still run through the town, past industrial
sites and factories. In the nineteenth century, Winona was the last stop
for barges before reaching Minneapolis/St. Paul. If you visit the Archer
Daniels Midland facility, you will see that despite being on the water,
the railroad services the plant. River barges rarely stop in Winona these
days, having been all but displaced by the railroad long ago.

Railroads shaped the physical development of the West. Being chosen as a railroad hub presented a mixed blessing to some towns. Congress
exempted the railroads from paying taxes, all the better to help them build
the massive infrastructure the nation needed to expand. For small farming
towns and counties, this took away a local tax base. When farming declined
and people could not meet their tax responsibilities, the biggest industry in
town, the railroad, did not bear any tax responsibilities. Such tax agreements
severely limited the growth and development of many small towns on the
Great Plains, effectively keeping many parts of the West as a hinterland,
even as an Eastern metropolis continued to grow on the resources they provided—the crops they grew and the ores they mined.

As time went by, the railroads rescinded the programs that reduced
the costs of shipping. They quickly raised prices, squeezing farmers even
more. They began charging higher rates for service to the more-remote
locations, again limiting business and driving farmers living on what
could be termed the *railroad frontier* out of business. As some railroad
lines terminated in farming regions expressly to bring goods to market,
the railroads owned a monopoly that the farmers, as individuals or as
groups, found difficult to fight.

While building railroads did open up the West, it also colonized it,
as the drive for economic expansion appeared to be twofold. The railroad
expanded the market for Eastern goods while enabling raw materials to
come from the West. Pricing schemes and control of the distribution of
what had been public land combined with the railroad's tax exemption to
make the West more of a colony than a region. In other words, the railroads reinforced the economic basis of the metropolis. While the railroads
snubbed many small Western towns, they helped big cities like Kansas
City and Chicago solidify as centers.

Mythmaking

Who wants to play railroad tycoon and sodbuster? How about low-paid miner and timber baron? No one? Well, how about Cowboys and Indians? Sure, everyone wants to be a cowboy, ride the range on a horse, and wear bandanas, big hats, wide belt buckles, and chaps. Who doesn't dream of singing cowboy songs around the campfire, sleeping under the stars, drinking coffee in the morning and eating chili in the evening and bravely fighting off Indians and other rustlers? While cowboys made up a small but significant proportion of western settlers, they and cattle culture almost wholly captured the American imagination about the nineteenth-century West.

Ironically, cowboy culture is not even a uniquely American phenomenon. Adopted from the vaquero culture of Mexico and Spain, the source of many of the tools and terms we identify as "cowboy," including rodeo,

Young Native American rancho worker or *vaquero.* **These young men were known for their horse-riding and roping skills.** *Courtesy of University of California, Davis, General Library, Department of Special Collections, Eastman's Originals Collections*

lariat, chaps, and even "buckaroo" (Anglos' pronunciation of *vaquero*), affected a relatively small number of people in a relatively small geographic area. Nonetheless, cattle culture, with its "wide-open" towns, gunslingers, prostitutes with a heart of gold, and colorful gamblers personifies the American West, not only to most Americans but to people around the world, with implications both good and bad. To Americans, the cowboy is the independent actor who led his herd to market, through rain and Indian attacks, fighting off rustlers, calling on prostitutes, but always remaining true to himself. To the rest of the world, the cowboy embodies independence, but he also has a sinister side: a man willing to kill another man to protect his property, a lone wolf who does what he sees fit without regard to the law, one who lives without a family and the ensuing family values, one who bullies native peoples and exploits the land. Though idealized as loners, cowboys and cowboy culture actually stem from a large and powerful frontier commercial enterprise: ranching.

Ranching in the American West, shaped by global markets and distant institutions, grew into a big business during the mid-nineteenth century. The first cattle arrived with the Spanish, who deposited small herds of them in the Southwest during their early entradas and returned to discover that the animals had flourished and gone feral. Once Spain figured out that the Southwest lacked the means for successful farms and mines, the Crown granted colonists rancherias, for the sole purpose of raising cattle. Eventually, Spanish colonists rounded up the wild stock and learned how to control the herds and breed more gentle animals. In Texas, Arizona, New Mexico, and California, the Spanish and later Mexican rancheros built up herds as large as 40,000 head of cattle and began to make long trail drives from Louisiana and Texas into northern Mexico. In the American colonies and then the United States, ranching and cattle roundups go back to the seventeenth and eighteenth centuries, especially in the mid-Atlantic and southern colonies. Cattle turned loose interbred, producing hybrid and often feral offspring, though farmers worked to breed cattle to improve the quality of milk. Good grazing land could be found from North Carolina to Texas, often in mountainous regions like the Cumberland and the Ozarks. By 1800, cattle existed in Louisiana and Arkansas. As farmers filled in land with cash crops, they pushed cattle out, as would happen in part of the West too. When Americans began taking over the Southwest in the 1840s, they encountered an already vibrant

Cowboys from the Pitchfork Ranch in Wyoming singing around the chuckwagon in the 1920s. *Buffalo Bill Historical Center, Cody, Wyoming; Gift of Mr. & Mrs. Charles Beldon, PN.67.95*

cattle industry, one in which cattle sometimes functioned as currency. At this point, some Americans picked up the technology and know-how of ranching on the open range. So while a nascent cattle industry existed in the British colonies and first American states, it was not until it was combined with the cattle culture and traditions of the Spanish that the familiar figure of the American cowboy was born.

The western American cattle industry began before the Civil War, as Texans sold cattle to the army, but the ranching industry and cowboy life of American legend took off afterwards. During the war, Confederate forces cut off cattle drives to the North, leading to the growth of herds of wild cattle as large as 5 million animals. After the war, Texans and other Southerners facing a devastated economy found they could make money by rounding up cattle and selling them for as much as $50 a head in eastern markets; in much better shape financially, the people of the industrializing North had developed a huge appetite for beef. Thus ensued the 1,200-mile-long cattle drives of yore, with the average drive comprising a herd of 3,000 cattle and 10 cowboys. At the end of the trail, the cowboys sold their herd and settled into so-called cattle towns like Abilene, Kansas, for a few days of carousing before making the long ride home to round up another herd. The cattle towns on the Great Plains, the terminuses of rail lines heading east to beef-processing centers like Kansas City and Chicago, attracted merchants, gamblers, and prostitutes who did their best to separate the cowboys, most of whom were young men eager to have a good time, from their recently garnered pay. On the trail and while awaiting shipment east, unclaimed public lands provided free grass and water for the cattle, especially as the U.S. Army pushed more and more Indian groups off the Plains and onto reservations in the 1860s and 1870s. Into the 1880s, the long cattle drives north to cattle towns with railroad service dominated the cattle industry. Several trails led north from Texas, the most famous of which were the Chisholm Trail, from San Antonio to Abilene, Kansas; the Eastern trail, which started near Waco, then ran up through Fort Worth and on to Abilene; and the Western trail, running from San Antonio to Dodge City, Kansas. In the Northwest, the Oregon Trail ran from Oregon to Montana, and the Northern Trail went from Idaho to Wyoming. By the turn of the twentieth century, the railroads had reached down into Texas and were funneling cattle directly to big cities like St Louis and especially Chicago, the gateways to and from the West, with massive stockyards and meat-processing slaughterhouses.

While romanticized in popular culture, driving cattle long distance was grueling and dangerous work. In reality, cowboys lived a hard and mostly solitary life. Many of them were white Southerners who had migrated west immediately after the Civil War. Close to half of them were African American, Hispanic, or Indian. Few men lasted longer than seven years as a cowboy, thanks to being overworked, underfed, underpaid, and sleep deprived. Few owned their own horse. The average age of a cowboy was about twenty years old. They typically worked fourteen-hour days, including a night watch, which limited their sleep. Couple this with the other dangers inherent in the job: falling off or being kicked by a horse, being trampled by stampeding cattle, bitten by a rattlesnake, struck by lightening, or drowned in a river crossing. Paid between $30 and $45 a month, many cowboys hit the trail but few of them stayed on it for long, most of them drifting off to become farmers or manual laborers in the West.

After a major economic depression in 1873, the cattle industry changed. Now the drive ended in the northern Plains, where ranchers and their cowboy employees could still graze their herds on free grass. Like the homesteaders and the railroads, ranchers needed free land. Public land without fences or crops served their needs best. When those lands dried up or disappeared in the southern Plains, ranchers and their herds had no choice but to head farther north. Many cowboys and cattle owners saw free-range grazing (these were the so-called free-rangers) as their God-given right, just as homesteaders saw their claim to their own parcel of land as part of God's plan for developing the West. As the era of the long cattle drives came to an end in the 1880s, many Americans bemoaned the loss of individuality and the rise of government power in limiting the grazing of cattle. True, much of the land had become settled by farmers who frowned on cattle tromping their winter wheat. However, the expansion of the railroads also killed off cowboy culture. As railroads built railheads in Dallas and other southwestern towns, the need to drive cattle even as far north as Kansas disappeared. So, roughly, a mere twenty-year period influenced the formation of much of the enduring mythology of the West.

Between 1865 and 1890, Texas alone produced about 10 million head of cattle, but the ranching industry could not last in its original form. The peak period was the early 1880s. Some local men like Grandville Stuart in Montana or John Iliff in Colorado and Wyoming made it big; but investors had the largest operations, as financiers from the East and even Great Britain bought huge operations in the West. Big-time ranchers began to squeeze out small operations, sometimes violently, as in the legendary gun battle in 1881 in Tombstone, Arizona, in which Wyatt Earp and his allies fought on the side of the big-time ranchers. Former rustlers on occasion became cattle barons, but once becoming respectable these same men insisted on the enforcement of law and order. The growing number of cattle also outran the supply of grass and water on the open range, forcing ranchers to seek out marginal land and protect fiercely any good land in their possession. Many turned to barbed-wire fencing, which they had once opposed, to assert control over good grassland and water sources. Toward the end of the century, brutal winters devastated herds as far south as North Texas. In 1886–87, an abnormally harsh winter featured blizzards and extreme cold that killed tens of thousands of cattle, some of which froze to death where they stood; other carcasses were found piled high against fences and snow breaks, where the desperate animals had tried to seek shelter. The devastation was so bad that it put many men out of the ranching business for good. Western ranchers also had to compete in global markets, with cattle from Argentina to Alberta. And in parts of the West, wheat farmers and sheep herders competed with cattle ranchers for access to public lands. In the years after the great "die-up" of 1886–87, the industry changed. The spread of railroads made long trail drives obsolete, and competition for land (grass and water) required whole-scale fencing. Ranchers also began to provide hay and other food for their cattle, rather than relying wholly on wild grasses. They also turned to breeding cattle, producing hardy animals that had more meat on them than did the wild longhorns. If cattle ranching started as a "found" resource, in literally rounding up wild cattle, by the 1890s ranching had become an industry that "produced" cattle.

For the cowboy of legend, the change in the cattle industry meant the end of a way of life. The romantic vision of the cowboy on the long trail drive had lured west thousands of white and black Southerners looking for work, but it also attracted thousands of young men from the Northeast, Canada, and as far away as Great Britain, looking for adventure. Dime novels, rodeos, and Wild West shows run by flamboyant figures like Buffalo Bill Cody made the cowboy life seem one of freedom and independence on the open range. By the turn of the century, and into the 1920s, aging cowboys like Teddy "Blue" Abbott, an English immigrant, wrote memoirs that chronicled life and work during the heyday of the cowboy, liberally mixing up facts and tall tales. But, as mentioned, in reality the cowboy was a poorly-paid, working-class wage laborer who rarely owned the horse on which he rode. He suffered from a less-than-balanced diet of coffee, beef, and beans, could easily break a limb or his neck falling from a horse, or lose a finger caught in a lariat, and was prone to hernias and chronic back problems from long hours in the saddle. On top of all this, on the job the cowboy faced the dangers of working in rain and lightening, intense heat, and brutal cold, especially on the northern Plains (and in the Canadian West). Except for a few ranch hands employed the year round, the work was seasonal. In short, except in legend, to be a cowboy was not to escape modern industrial life, but to be a pawn in it. That said, dangerous, hard work on a horse in the great outdoors certainly sounded better to many working Americans than did toiling in a factory, plowing a field behind a mule, mining coal in a deep, dark shaft, or cutting timber all day long in a mill.

Cowboy rescuing a calf. C. Jack Rhodes Sr. carries a Hereford calf in his saddle as he pushes his horse uphill through a winter storm on Pitchfork Ranch. Blizzards and snowstorms often threatened cattle herds, and cowboys needed to save the future of the herd–the calves. *Buffalo Bill Historical Center, Cody, Wyoming; PN.67.5*

At this point, you may well ask: you've told us a lot about the cowboys, but where are the Indians? Part of the answer is that many Indians *were* cowboys, some of them even owned their own herds of cattle and ranches. The United States government tried to wean some Indian groups off hunting buffalo by encouraging them to raise cattle. There were some conflicts between certain cowboys and Indian groups, in particular in Texas, where the Apache, who had recently agreed to live on a reservation, rustled cattle when the U.S. government provided them only sickly or diseased cattle to eat. Overall, however, the game of cowboy and Indian and the conflicts portrayed on TV and movie screens morphed from the conflicts between the U.S. Army and the Indians and the glorious Wild West shows pioneered by the likes of Buffalo Bill Cody.

Buffalo Bill and the Mythic West

William F. Cody, also known as Buffalo Bill, epitomizes the real as well as the imagined West. Born in 1846 on the farming frontier in Iowa, Cody and his family moved to Kansas when Bill was seven. Like many early residents of the West, the Codys had moved farther west to chase new opportunities. As an adult, Cody managed to ride wave after wave of image-making events. First he worked as a rider for the Pony Express, or so he claimed, the epitome of bravery and speed. He then turned to stealing horses for a living, an illegal and highly dangerous job. During the Civil War, he served in the Seventh Kansas Voluntary Calvary. After the war, he worked in a hotel in Salt Creek Valley, Kansas. After that failed, he served as a scout and guide for the U.S. Army, hunting down "rogue" Indians. He also supplied buffalo meat to the frontier forts, hence the nickname "Buffalo Bill."

On July 4, 1883, Buffalo Bill Cody reinvented himself yet again and created a new image of the American West. Asked by the people of North Platte, Nebraska, to organize a program to celebrate the Fourth, he developed what became known as a Wild West show. At first he paid cowboys to show off their considerable riding skills. Later he got more creative, hiring Indians and staging mounted battles, with guns "a blazin'" and the cowboys coming to the rescue of the Indians' kidnapped hostages. One of his most famous scenes was the settler rescue, where Indians attacked a settler cabin and cowboys rode to the rescue. Historian David Hamilton Murdoch claims that Buffalo Bill almost single-handedly rehabilitated the image of the cowboy. Prior to Cody's Wild West shows, most people viewed cowboys in one of two ways. On the one hand, they were drunken and violent single young men who added to the danger and instability of the West and the frontier. On the other hand, they were simply young men who took advantage of greenhorns from the East and pushed the rules to see what they could get away with. With the birth of the Wild West show and its many imitators, cowboys in the American popular mind became heroes and the epitome of the individualistic spirit of the West. Now cowboys did more than herd cattle; they saved women and children from outlaws and Indians and always had a story and a smile for everyone they met.

The Wild West show spread this image of the cowboy across the nation and the world. Cody and his troupe played to enthusiastic (and paying) audiences in Europe as well as North America. Queen Victoria herself attended one of his shows. But Buffalo Bill's shows did more than just create and promote the hero image of the cowboy. Buffalo Bill painted a diverse picture of the West and the image of the frontier. From 1885 to 1901, Annie Oakley toured with the Wild West Show as "Little Sure Shot," so named by the famous Hunkpapa Sioux war chief Sitting Bull, an old friend of hers. In addition to Annie Oakley, Buffalo Bill hired Indians, including Chief Sitting Bull (who along with the Ogallala Sioux Crazy Horse had dealt the U.S. Army one of its greatest defeats in the so-called Plains Indian Wars) to travel for a time with the show. Although some historians feel Cody exploited the Indian actors, he offered them one of the only paying jobs available to Indians at the time, as well as exposure to the world beyond the grim reality of the reservation. As the show grew and expanded, Buffalo Bill also included heroic peoples from European and colonial frontiers: Cossacks from Russia, Bedouins from Morocco, Zulus from South Africa, Filipinos, and others.

So there are at least two Wests that historians routinely discuss. There is the historic West, which includes the wide variety of peoples who have lived in the region, and then there is the mythic West, or the West of the popular imagination. The latter is the West as people around the United States and world tend to imagine it: cowboys fighting Indians, gunslingers squaring off in the main street through town, and brave pioneers driving their "Prairie Schooners" (covered wagons) into the sunset. It is this West that often draws students to classes on Western history and readers to books about the frontier. But as you and others have found out, there is much more to the West than these images imply.

The West as an American Colony

So we've come full circle back to the question posed at the start of this chapter: Was the American West a United States colony? In the nineteenth century, and through Turner's eyes, it appears to have been. To understand this viewpoint, one must think of the West from a colonial perspective. From the time the Spanish first marched north from Mexico and the French paddled west from the St. Lawrence River valley, Europeans viewed the land west of the Mississippi River as undeveloped. The intruders viewed the various Indian nations who resided in the West as natural resources, either as would-be slaves, fellow settlers, military allies, or trading partners. Because the Europeans did not approve of the way the Indians "used" the land, they considered all of it free for the taking. Each invading group came up with their own way in which to define Indian land as free. The Spanish granted land rights to certain Indian nations, officially freeing up other traditionally held lands for settlement. The English considered land as free if its residents could not produce a title to it. The French, whose methods represent a departure from the other two, placed several of their colonies, including those on the St. Lawrence, on the land the Indians specifically stated they did not care about.

For his part, Turner defined free land by what the census listed as untaxed land. Turner's argument posited that the West groaned under the weight of underdeveloped resources waiting for industrious Europeans or Americans to capitalize on them: gold, silver, and other minerals, timber, pelts, and rich ranch and farmland. As Euro-Americans discovered each new resource the West held, the idea that someone should exploit it swiftly followed. The gold and silver rushes of the nineteenth century opened areas up for settlement by whites with little regard for those who already lived there, be they white, Indian, or Hispanic. Behind these resource rushes came the merchants, persons hoping to profit on the needs of the newcomers, be they individual prospectors in need of pans and pick axes or commercial enterprises in need of heavy machinery to expand their markets. Land speculators, mercantile store owners, and others followed the prospectors, miners, and farmers west to try to make their own fortunes. And as the gold- and silver-rush areas became declared U.S. territories, the federal government extended territorial law over the settlers in these regions but not representation in government or the full rights of U.S. citizenship.

Deadwood, South Dakota, provides a good example of this phenomenon. Located in the Black Hills, Deadwood became a mining community that triggered political, legal and military battles. In 1868, the U.S. government gave the Black Hills, called *Paha Sapa* by the Sioux, to the Sioux in perpetuity, including the right to evict squatters, which they did until 1874—the year in which the Black Hills gold rush began and the Sioux found themselves overrun with whites. Still, they succeeded in chasing the majority of them out. Now the U.S. government sent in an army reconnaissance team to find out whether miners were being threatened. This action violated the treaty of 1868 that stated no white man could enter the territory without Sioux permission. To appease the Sioux, the U.S. Army informed the miners that (wink wink, nudge nudge) they were violating a treaty and should leave. The army did not, however, escort the miners out or otherwise enforce the treaty. In 1875, entrepreneurs and miners founded the town of Deadwood, in the heart of the Black Hills, hoping to capitalize on the gold rush. Officially, Deadwood was an illegal community. The Black Hills were not organized as a U.S. territory or even considered under U.S. law. As Deadwood and the gold rush continued to grow, Congress decided to buy the Black Hills from the Sioux. When the Sioux pointed to the treaty and refused to sell, Congress "bought" the Black Hills without Sioux approval or signatures. When the Sioux protested the action, the U.S. government deemed them *hostile,* a term that allowed them to send in the army in to "pacify" the region. The Sioux and the Cheyenne, frustrated with these actions, arranged to meet other groups in the Little Bighorn Valley in 1876 to try to negotiate with the U.S. government. As you will see, no negotiations occurred there.

The Southwest presents another case for discussion. Nationalism roared into the picture with the start of the Mexican-American War in 1846. Though the territory being contested lay far outside U.S. borders, the federal government and prominent politicians argued that it was in the national interest and the national purpose to take control of it, demonizing the Mexican leaders like Santa Anna for their "barbaric" and "uncivilized" behavior (which differed little from the behavior of U.S. military leaders in the field). The United States felt a compulsion, even a moral duty, to expand, one that only increased throughout the last half of the nineteenth century. Once the Civil War ended, the United States plowed headlong into colonizing the West and countries beyond, as if the reuniting of the United States had somehow granted them special powers and the right to dominate the world.

The West also provided a safety valve of sorts for some rural families facing land shortages and for some Southerners, white and black, after the Civil War; but as the example of the cowboy suggests, the myths of the West hide the fact that the West was no escape from industrial society. It is important to note that the stream of settlers to the West did not decrease at all during the Civil War. Twenty-five thousand families a *year* during the conflict plodded west to claim land and seek fortunes. The large migration west also created new rules and ideas, as Turner pointed out, to help restructure the United States. The Homestead Act and other pieces of legislation emerged in response to the problems and issues unique to the settlement of the vast region.

Unlike European colonies, though, territories in the American West ended up becoming states in the Union. And with statehood came the rights and privileges of participating in the national political system. States gained representation in Congress and votes in the Electoral College. But for all the years prior to the population boom of the twentieth century, when western states had populations dwarfed by their Eastern and Southern counterparts, Western senators and representatives lacked the power to shape federal policies, even those directly regulating the West. Additionally, many of the economic interests in the West belonged to people in the East: mining, timber, oil, and railroad companies. The owners and lobbyists of the people that owned these businesses operating in the West helped shaped legislation to aid their industries, even if those same policies were not in the best interest of the residents of the states that hosted their enterprises. In addition, achieving statehood for the territory in which they lived did little to change Westerners' own access to the resources the land held or access to markets.

Just because western territories became states did not necessarily mean they were no longer treated as colonies by the commercial enterprises based east of the Mississippi River and their cronies in the federal government. In addition, two factors hampered the independent growth of the West: transportation and land policy. The area of land from the Mississippi west to the Pacific Coast is vast. All the resources the region held were of no use to big business unless there was some way to move them out to markets. The Mississippi and Missouri rivers served as waterway conduits, but navigation was tricky and limited by water levels. The Pacific Coast offered unsurpassed natural harbors, but goods and resources from the interior of the continent still needed a way to reach those ports. Individual states could not afford to build roads and railroads by themselves; they needed the help of the federal government.

In addition, the federal government still controlled, except in the case of Texas, all the land that remained unclaimed. Once a territory became a state, any free land reverted to federal control, which also meant control of the resources on or under the land. True, the federal government sold much of the public land to individuals through the Homestead Act and similar legislation, but it also granted a great deal of land to privately-held railroads and other industries. By the end of the nineteenth century, the federal government also had fenced off large tracks of public land to create national parks and forests, while negotiating grazing and mineral rights to these lands. To this day, the federal government remains the biggest landowner in the West, a fact that reduces greatly the tax revenue of the individual western states.

Ꮹ Suggested Readings Ꮾ

Careless, J. M. S. "Frontierism, Metropolitanism, and Canadian History." *Canadian Historical Review* 35, No. 1 (March 1954): 1–21.

Hobson, J. A. *Imperialism: A Study.* Ann Arbor: University of Michigan Press, 1965.

Iverson, Peter. *When Indians Became Cowboys: Native Peoples and Cattle Ranching in The American West.* Norman: University of Oklahoma Press, 1997.

Moses, L. G. *Wild West Shows and the Images of American Indians, 1883–1933.* Albuquerque: University of New Mexico Press, 1999.

Murdoch, David Hamilton. *The American West: The Invention of a Myth.* Reno: University of Nevada Press, 2001.

Painter, Nell Irvin. *The Exodusters: Black Migration to Kansas after Reconstruction.* Boston: W. W. Norton, 1992.

Renehan, Edward J. *The Transcontinental Railroad: The Gateway to the West.* Chelsea House Publications, 2007.

Schumpeter, Joseph. *Imperialism and Social Classes.* New York: A. M. Kelly, 1951.

Slatta, Richard W. *Cowboys of the Americas.* New Haven: Yale University Press, 1990.

Starrs, Paul. *Let the Cowboy Ride: Cattle Ranching in the American West.* Baltimore: Johns Hopkins University Press, 2000.

Takaki, Ronald. *Iron Cages: Race and Culture in Nineteenth-Century America.* New York: Oxford University Press, 2000.

CHAPTER EIGHT

This Land is Our Land?

By the 1850s, it became clear to the United States government that the policy of removing the Indians from New England and the Southeast to the Great American Desert in the center of the nation would not work. Certain Indian groups, including the free-roaming and greatly feared Comanche, refused to be confined on a reservation in present-day Oklahoma, at that time Indian Territory. The Comanche expressed their disgust with the reservation by raiding Texas on a regular basis throughout the 1860s and 1870s. By the time of the Civil War, settlers had discovered the rich, black soil lying beneath the prairie grasses. These two factors led to a major change in Indian policy.

Two groups drove Indian policy between the 1850s and 1870s: the federal government and reformers, including missionaries, philanthropists, and congressmen. A third group played a powerful role in Indian policy but had no say in its formation: the U.S. Army. As for the Indians, they had little say in Indian policy as designed by the United States government and enforced by the military. They believed otherwise, however, as they signed treaties, expecting the United States to abide by the terms it signed and respect their sovereignty, including their right to defend their land from intruders. For example, the Fort Laramie Treaty of 1868 gave the Black Hills of South Dakota to the Sioux in perpetuity and deemed that white men needed permission to enter the area. This was a revision and extension of the Fort Laramie Treaty of 1851, which essentially turned the Northern Great Plains into one large reservation for the Sioux, Cheyenne, Arapaho, Crow, Arikara, Assinboine, Mandan, Gros Ventre, and Blackfeet. All of these Indian nations saw the United States as a foreign nation. As such, they expected to be able to negotiate in good faith with its government. In reality and with hindsight, the United States government designed its Indian policies around the needs and desires of United States citizens, with little regard for the needs and desires of the Indians, those persons with the most at stake in the matter.

Basic Indian Policy

In 1850, few Indians nations remained east of the Mississippi River. Indian Territory contained the Five Civilized Tribes plus the Kiowa, Comanche, Apache, Wichita, Caddo, Iowa, Sac and Fox, Pottawatomie, Shawnee, and several others. Between the Rockies and the Mississippi River, relatively few American whites had settled. Instead, most American settlers had rushed to the Pacific Coast in California, Oregon, and Washington. This pattern of settlement created new pressures on the United States government to alter its Indian policy. Though many territorial governments simply advocated killing off the Indians or letting diseases slowly lower the population levels, the United States government realized it could no longer hope to remove all the remaining western Indian nations to Indian Territory—there were just too many of them. In California, the Gold Rush of 1848 wreaked havoc on the Indian population. In 1848, about 14,000 people lived in California territory, half of which were Spanish-speaking, non-Indian inhabitants. By 1849, there were 100,000 non-Indians in California. By 1860, the number stood at 380,000. Between claim jumpers, federal bounties placed on Indians, and rising disease rates among Indians caused by the influx of new immigrants, the Gold Rush dramatically reduced the Indian population in California, essentially wiping out whole communities. By the 1850s, the federal government began to search for new solutions to the old "Indian Problem."

Indian policy, whether articulated by the government or reformers, revolved around three concepts: assimilation, agrarianism, and extermination. These concepts were not new ones. Various governments and reformers had tried them before, including during the British period, but by the 1850s the stakes had changed and now these ideas became official policy. Settlers were pouring into territories controlled by Indian nations who had never before had their homeland invaded. In 1850, the Bureau of Ethnology estimated the Indian population west of the Mississippi to be between 350,000 and 500,000. In 1860, the white population west of the Mississippi was 1.4 million. By 1890, it had grown to 8.5 million. The Indians of the Great Plains and Northwest Coast may have traded with Europeans for centuries, but now the Euro-Americans were overtaking them. The Indians, at first, did not see the settlers as permanent residents; they saw themselves as superior and able to repel this threat to their land. The United States government saw things the opposite way. A clash was inevitable.

The first such conflict came over the rights of the Indians. The U.S. Constitution grants the federal government the sole right to regulate and deal with the Indians. It also says that the Indians cannot be taxed. Both of these statements led legal scholars to argue that the founding fathers saw the Indians as separate sovereign nations, not as people of the United States. After the American Revolution, the federal government made treaties with Indian groups. Like most other national governments, the U.S. Congress only signs treaties with other nation-states, not with individuals or individual groups of people. By signing treaties with the Indian nations, the United States appeared to recognize them as nation-states. Nonetheless, the United States government continually violated the terms of those treaties, actions that demonstrate two things: the United States government knew the Indian nations did not possess the political or military power to demand the enforcement of the treaties; and the United States government had little to no regard for the Indian peoples as individuals. Even though it executed treaties with Indians, it never respected, or even saw, Indian tribes as true nations.

In general, the United States government borrowed much of its early Indian policy from the British. During their reign, the British had pursued treaties with various Indian groups and occasionally had attempted to assimilate the Indians through setting up schools and religious communities for them. At first, the Americans followed suit. Perhaps most important, the United States government followed the British policy that basically gave the Indians a clear choice: assimilate or get out of the way. Within the United States government, the Bureau of Indian Affairs (BIA)—modeled on the British Office of Indian affairs and founded in

1824—was charged with pursuing a similar policy, and it proceeded to negotiate treaties with Indians, which were typically delivered and signed by officers of the U.S. Army in the field. By the 1850s, the government tasked the BIA with clearing the Indians from any lands desired by settlers, as if the Indians were not people but timber or buffalo. Officially, the government referred to this policy of undisguised ethnic cleansing as "extinguishing Indian land title."

Another policy that demonstrated the low regard held by the United States government, and even many so-called reformers, against Indians was the movement that demanded that the Indians assimilate to the mainstream (read white) American culture. Completely ignoring the unique cultures of the various Indian nations, both the federal government and reformers thought it best if the Indians started to act like other Americans. Then, the argument continued, the Indians would renounce their tribal affiliations, abandon "the chase," and settle down permanently on individual farms. Policymakers continually blamed the Indians' need to hunt for their control of vast amounts of land. They hoped that by making Indians more American, meaning farmers, they would free up large tracts of land for use by white settlers and commercial enterprises.

But what did it mean to be American? For early-nineteenth-century white Americans, the answer was farming and property ownership. This idea brings us to the second policy the BIA pursed: agrarianism. Throughout the nineteenth century, policymakers and reformers argued that simply making the Indians into small farmers would transform them into Americans. Unwilling to grant the Indians citizenship until they became American-like, the government continually raised the bar for citizenship for Indians. Remember, under the Dawes Act, if the Indians accepted "civilized habits," then they could claim citizenship. Those habits covered everything from changing religion, language, family structure, names, and means of survival. Think for a moment about Turner's thesis. Whom does he credit with finally securing and closing the frontier? The farmer. Farming was the "proper" use land, and it tied populations to it, invested them in a community. The United States figured that teaching Indians to farm, and giving individuals plots of 180 to 300 acres to work, would free up millions of acres of land for white settlement. In this light, the government was attempting to give the Indians, too, a role to play in the closing of the frontier.

As mentioned, the United States government had never recognized traditional Indian agriculture as farming. For one thing, it was not farming if women oversaw and conducted it. For another, planting crops, leaving them to fend for themselves, then coming back to harvest what they had naturally produced did not constitute farming either. When the BIA instituted its agrarian policies, it ignored tribal and environmental differences and encouraged, even forced, some groups to become farmers, whether they lived in the middle of a desert, on the Pacific Coast, or on the Great Plains. Beginning in the 1850s, treaties between the federal government and Indians nations included stipulations for "farming instructors" and farming tools. These stipulations used some of the money put in trust as payment for the land the Indians had rescinded to the government to pay for the tools and instructors. In other words, the money promised to the Indians in exchange for their land got redirected to pay for farming instructors, missionaries, and schools—not necessarily things the Indians wanted. Sometimes these instructors actually showed up in Indian country and provided the people with practical and useful information. Other times these so-called instructors arrived in Indian country

Blackfoot on horse-drawn plow, 1920. As the U.S. government emphasized "farming," its instructors and Indian agents often passed down antiquated farm equipment, like that shown here, to Indians. *Buffalo Bill Historical Center, Cody, Wyoming; PN.165.3.9*

and simply became local squatters who cultivated Indian land and then claimed it as their own.

Other factors that designated one as American were education and the ability to speak English. So beginning in the 1850s, treaties began to include stipulations for the funding and building of schools for Indian children so that missionaries and reformers could teach the Indian children English and other attributes of the mainstream American culture. Again, the funding for these came out of the money to be paid by the government to the Indians for their land. Schools for Indians were not a new idea. The British and then the Puritans had founded schools for Indians. As you'll remember, the Puritans had created praying villages. Early colonial governments started schools for Indians in Virginia and in New Hampshire. These previous efforts failed, as Indians either viewed the schools with suspicion or saw them as inferior to their own systems of learning. Though some Indian leaders sent their children, mainly boys, to be schooled in the ways of the "white man," many feared sending their children off into the hands of their enemies. The Five Civilized Tribes actually invited missionaries into their territory in the South so that their people could get schooling. Whites often misinterpreted Indians who attended white schools as wanting to become just like them. Ethnohistorians will tell you that these efforts usually represented Indian leaders' attempts to raise bicultural children who would be better equipped to deal with a culture very different from their own. Think of it as a study abroad program for future Indian leaders. Indian leaders wanted their sons to speak English fluently enough so that they did not have to rely on translators to understand the mores of American society and its trading customs. They hoped the younger generation might one day beat the Americans at their own game. These efforts should have paid off. When the Cherokee sued Georgia in 1832, the delegation they sent to Washington looked, dressed, and acted like everyone else in the capital. They even hired one of the most famous constitutional lawyers of the time. Yet the Cherokee still lost their case. This fact notwithstanding, mid-nineteenth-century reformers and the United States government continued to ply education and assimilation as the surest way to solve the "Indian Problem."

Policymakers, reformers, and journalists continued to use the term "Indian Problem" to refer to the conundrum of the United States government: Now that we own the West, how do we clear it for settlement?

Tipis in front of a mission school. This picture of the U.S. School for Indians in Pine Ridge, North Dakota, was taken in 1891, shortly before Turner declared the frontier closing. *Buffalo Bill Historical Center, Cody, Wyoming; P.35.17.2*

The Americans faced the same issues that the Spanish and British had. Religious groups wanted to "help" the Indians improve and reach their potential through conversion to Christianity, but the government had to balance this ideal with practicality: the amount of time it would take to clear the region. In other words: How do you save the Indian while gaining his land? Several issues shaped proposed solutions to the Indian Problem in its nineteenth-century form. Some believed, based on observations by Lewis and Clark and other explorers, the Indians were dying off and would soon vacate the land anyway. Those who espoused the racially-based "science" of the day took this as evidence that the Indians were an inferior race—for, in any region, only the "fittest" were meant to survive. When coupled with the idea of Manifest Destiny, the misplaced notion of natural selection seemed to justify any actions—including wholesale annihilation—that might speed up the process of the Indians dying off or otherwise clearing the land for use by whites.

Those who preferred to conquer the Indians through assimilation held on to their solutions of education and conversion to Christianity. One could not be American, they believed, without being a Christian. This belief opened the door for missionaries and other Christian reformers to become involved in Indian policy. Though the missionaries had maintained a relationship with the federal government as far back as the

Whitman period, it became stronger now. Just as they began to write treaties with stipulations that the Indians agree to take up farming, policymakers also begin to write in clauses about the maintenance of missions in Indian territories.

Missionaries, both Protestant and Catholic, became important players in Indian policy and reform. Most of the missionaries altruistically and honestly embraced Indians as their "brethren," but the corollary to this sentiment was that they wanted Indians to act more like their brothers and sisters. Missionary societies marshaled financial resources to provide books, teachers, and farming instructors to help Indians become assimilated. Missionaries came to believe that one of the factors that held Indians back was the corrupted version of Euro-American culture they had long experienced through contact with Mountain Men (traders and trappers) and other less-than-savory whites. Missionaries blamed swearing, alcoholism, premarital sex, gambling, and other "un-Christian" aspects of Indian cultures on the early contact with "heathenish whites."

As early as the 1830s, missionaries began to posit that the way to help civilize the Indians was to end their dealings with unscrupulous whites. Evoking the praying villages from the English period, nineteenth-century missionaries in the United States (and other parts of the world as well) suggested setting up a similar system: separate each tribe from the rest of society, quarantine the Indians in one place where they could be exposed to proper Christian models, taught English, so they could read the Bible, and taught how to farm. It was this kind of thinking that, after the Civil War, led to the creation of the reservation system.

Extermination and the United States Army

In addition to reformers and the BIA, the United States Army played a critical role in Indian policy after 1850. The Bureau of Indian Affairs, under the War Department during this period, negotiated treaties and settlements, approved missionaries, built schools, gave out money and food, and established Indian policy. The BIA also created Indian agencies, lead by Indian agents of its appointment. These agents were usually white civilians, though some wore two hats, as missionaries or traders as well. Agents dealt with the day-to-day applications of policy: regulating trade, distributing annuity payments, and negotiating treaties and other agreements.

Annuities were the annual payments of interest on the balance owed by the federal government to the Indians for land ceded to it. During this period, as we shall see, few annuity payments went directly to the Indians, often ending up in the hands of traders and missionaries. Additionally, the BIA tasked western military commanders with establishing relations with Indians and trying to keep the peace between Indians and white settlers on the remains of the frontier. One of the major problems with playing this role is that United States Army personnel were never trained to function as a peacekeepers or negotiators of treaties. The conflicting roles led to bloody clashes on many western battlefields.

When the Civil War, or the War Between the States, erupted, it affected the West differently than it did the North and the South. Since only five out of the thirty-three states that existed before 1861 were Western, the "War Between the States" seems more accurate. The rest of the West was territories. The states that did exist west of the Mississippi (Texas, Iowa, California, Minnesota, and Oregon) all had different reasons to side with the Confederacy or the Union—or to try to ignore the conflict altogether.

Perhaps more important, during this time the Western army lost many of its best commanders to the unfolding conflict in the East. The West quickly became a dumping ground for soldiers and commanding officers who had failed in the eastern campaigns but could be trusted, the generals figured, with protecting the gold routes from California to the Union. Rather than court-martial the incompetent or impetuous officers, it was far easier and cheaper to reassign them to the West. In other instances, poorly trained and sometimes anti-Indian territorial volunteers took over for regular army officers who had been sent east. Soldiers in the West during the Civil War often suffered under poor direction from the government. Were they supposed to protect the gold routes from Confederates or from Indians? How, exactly, were they supposed to deal with the Indians they encountered? Many of the previous military commanders in the West, including Kit Carson, had begun their careers by living and trading with Indians; they spoke local languages and understood local customs. The new commanders from the East had been trained to fight traditional wars and traditional enemies. West Point had not trained its graduates to negotiate treaties and maintain a peaceful frontier. As the Civil War erupted in the East, so did tensions between western Indians and the

Military men in front of buildings. Note the tipi behind the men and in front of the buildings. *Buffalo Bill Historical Center, Cody, Wyoming; P.35.201*

"On the Canadian" by Cheyenne artist Bear's Heart. Whereas the military might have seen white settlers as a stabilizing force, this drawing demonstrates how the Indians viewed those same settlers as disruptive. *Courtesy, National Museum of the American Indian, Smithsonian Institution (206321.000)*

troops and settlers in the West. Two cases demonstrate the tensions that bubbled to the surface: Navajo Resistance and the Sioux Uprising.

By the beginning of the Civil War in 1861, the Navajo had witnessed considerable changes in their territory. After the War with Mexico, the Navajo suddenly found themselves under the jurisdiction of the United States. They watched, mystified, as the other residents of their territory, whom they called "Mexicans," gained citizenship and protection from the American forces, the same ones who were making the Navajo feel increasingly hemmed in and oppressed. After the Navajo signed treaties with the United States, the Army assigned them an Indian agent and built Fort Defiance within the boundaries of their territory. The soldiers stationed at the new fort grazed their horses in Navajo pastures, killed their livestock as they pleased, and punished the Navajo when they raided the "Mexican" population to recoup livestock the latter had stolen from them. At various points before 1860, tensions rose then fell again into peace. The Civil War brought a change, specifically in 1862, when General James Carleton rode into Fort Defiance as the new commander. Sent west to protect the frontier from the Confederacy, Carleton began to focus on the Navajo and the Mescalero Apaches when no Confederates appeared. He immediately recognized the commercial value of the land in New Mexico and Arizona, calling it "a princely realm, a magnificent pastoral and mineral country." With white settlement and development in mind, the general announced that there would no longer be negotiations with Indian groups: they were to be killed or captured and removed to Fort Sumner at Bosque Redondo on the Pecos River, 300 miles from Navajo and Apache territory.

Carleton's new policies represented a sudden and frightening change for the Navajo. As far as the United States government was concerned, Carleton simply appeared to be pursuing the old policy of removal. The Navajo, however, were facing the possible end of life as they knew it. Prior to Carleton, Kit Carson had dealt with the Navajo as a colonel in the 1st New Mexico Volunteer Infantry. He negotiated treaties with them, or as Manuelito, Chief of the Navajo, stated, "They wrote down the promises, so that we would always remember them." Having lived with the Navajo, Carson had tried to respect their wishes and their culture. Carleton did no such thing, simply seeing the Navajo as an obstacle to progress in need of removal.

Carleton had taken it upon himself to reinvent the process. First, he cornered and forced the Mescalero Apache to remove to Bosque

Redondo, using the tactics of starvation and threats. Second, he flatly informed the Navajo that he had no faith in their promises of peace. Then he reiterated that he would not negotiate with them. Next, he ordered his men to hunt down any remaining Navajo and force them to leave their land and relocate to and stay at Bosque Redondo. Unfortunately, he went beyond even that, telling the troops to undertake a scorched-earth campaign: kill livestock, burn crops and houses, and force the Navajo to starve so they would have no choice but to acquiesce to his wishes. Some Navajo surrendered and moved to the reservation. Others, though, waited to see how the first group was treated. By the spring of 1863, Carleton announced that any Navajo in the area after July 20, the day on which they had been ordered to congregate and start heading toward Bosque Redondo, would be considered "hostiles" and given no quarter. In military parlance, the term *hostile* means threatening, and then, as now, the U.S. Army met threats with all due force. The army declared that it could justifiably kill any Navajo who remained "loose" after the deadline. Carleton defended these violent actions by invoking Manifest Destiny: "Providence has indeed blessed us . . . the gold lies here at our feet to be had by the mere picking of it up." To speed things along, Carleton offered a reward for every head of Navajo livestock killed or brought to the fort. In short, the general had signed the Navajo's death sentence. For almost a year, while the Navajo starved and froze, Carleton and his forces hunted the remaining Indians down, killing them on the spot or escorting them at the point of a gun to Bosque Redondo. By 1865, those Navajo who survived were on the reservation at Bosque Redondo, barely surviving. The soil there was too poor to grow crops, and in the close quarters disease ran rampant. Very little of the available water was potable because of a high alkaline content. Bosque Redondo was not really or officially a reservation; it was more like a death camp. Meanwhile, miners and other whites flowed into the Navajo homeland to seek their fortunes or start their lives anew.

At the end of the Civil War, Indian policy, once again, shifted abruptly. The United States government sent inspectors to Bosque Redondo, who reported the deplorable conditions at the site and predicted only more death and disease for the Navajo if the government did not do something immediately. Two issues primarily concerned the inspectors. Some had gone to the area because they were truly concerned for the Navajo; others had arrived with orders to find ways to reduce government expense. In the first two years after the Civil War, the War Department's expenses skyrocketed as it tried to deal with various Indian groups and Indian wars. The American public, who during the Civil War—for the first time in the nation's history—had been taxed directly by the federal government, revolted, demanding that costs, especially those related to the Indians, be reduced. In the end, a strange combination of compassion and thrift led to the United States government to move the Navajo back onto their traditional lands, after making them sign yet another treaty. In short, the government agents had realized that it would be less expensive to let the Navajo farm and herd for themselves on their own land than to try to feed and care for so many sick and dying Indians at the expense of the U.S. government. Still, the government allowed whites to squat on Navajo land.

The experience of the Navajo illustrates the rapidly shifting attitudes toward Indian policy, among the public and within the federal government. Over the course of the 1850s and 1860s, the United States government and the military began to see the Indians not just as hindrances but as enemies. For the Navajo, who long had lived among Mexicans and mestizos on a colonial frontier, the arrival of the Americans signaled a sea-change. They thought they understood the rules, but the rules were suddenly in flux. Carleton's push to simply remove the Indians from their rich land and warehouse them on poor land represents this shift. As the United States had recently endured a Civil War that had proved to be far longer, far more costly, and far more brutal than either side had ever imagined, white America's charity towards the Indian had all but ceased to exist. In addition, the victorious Union Army had resorted during the conflict to a scorched-earth policy that had included killing and causing the suffering of civilians, including women and children, in the South. Now the government had dispatched the same battle-hardened force to the West to deal with "hostile" Indians. After the Civil War, as the rate of violent incidents between Indians and white ranchers, miners, and settlers rose, so did the costs of trying to maintain a semblance of peace on the frontier, those who wished to reform radically Indian policy gained ground.

The Sioux (Mdewakanton, Wahpekute, Sisseton, Wahpeton) in southern Minnesota also faced increasing settlement pressure that led to disaster. Between 1850 and 1860, almost 150,000 settlers, many of them

Execution of the Sioux in Minnesota. *Buffalo Bill Historical Center, Cody, Wyoming; Vincent Mercaldo Collection, VM0012*

from Germany, flooded into the Sioux's territory between the Mississippi and Minnesota rivers. The Sioux signed several treaties in the 1850s, negotiated by Indian agents and missionaries that effectively gave away the majority of their land, reducing them to a thin strip of land along the Minnesota River from present-day New Ulm to Big Stone Lake in southwestern Minnesota. In exchange, the United States government promised to give the Indians annuities. The government hoped this money would help support the Sioux on their greatly constricted land base, which was not yet called a reservation. The annuities were supposed to pay for supplemental food, farming supplies, and other necessities. However, before the annuities could even reach the Sioux, traders and other merchants requested repayment for debts they claimed the Sioux owed them. In other words, private companies and individuals requested the federal government garnish the Sioux's annuity payments. By the time the third parties had finished making their claims, the Sioux received almost no money. By 1862, the smaller land base, the lack of money, the increased rate of settlement, and the hostility of the Indian agents combined to create an air of extreme frustration for the Sioux.

Remember the Pueblo Revolt and how the Indians in the Southwest felt caught between the government, the Catholic Church, the settlers, and their own needs? In 1862, the Sioux felt caught between the wants of the U.S. government, the settlers, and their own needs. Their reservation lacked game to hunt, and their crops had failed two years in a row, leading them to rely on the agency for food. When they searched for game and food off the reservation, they were seen as trespassers by the whites, who shot at them. When they tried to buy food at the agency, the traders charged them inflated prices and garnished their annuity payments, forcing them into debt. Called to the agency in the summer of 1862 to receive their annuity payments, several hundred Sioux ended up cooling their heels for weeks as they waited for the money, missing both the summer buffalo hunt and the prime planting season. Rumors swirled around the agency that the government had spent their annuities on the Civil War. Knowing their families were starving, the leader of the Sioux, Little Crow, demanded that the Indian agent, Andrew Myrick, open the warehouse and give them food on credit. The agent balked at the idea, saying he could not distribute food without annuity payments. Luckily, another agent overrode him and issued pork and flour to the Sioux. Surrounding the agency by this time were settlements of German immigrants, who viewed the Indians as less than human and a threat to their security and prosperity. Over the course of the summer, tensions erupted constantly between the settlers and the Sioux, especially among the younger Sioux men, who felt constricted and harassed by the military and the settlers. The settlers viewed a large group of Indians camping on their doorstep as a threat. The Indians saw the Germans and other settlers as interlopers, to whom the U.S. government appeared to grant special treatment. As the Germans became more prosperous the Indians continued to starve, and both groups claimed the land as their own, disaster loomed.

In August, a group of young Sioux men raided a farm for food. They were hungry, tired of being told what to do, and clearly acting out. The Indians tried to steal some eggs. Some members of the Sioux party considered it fair payment for the land the settlers had stolen. Others saw it as theft. When challenged by the local settler, the Indians fired their guns. Though the historical record differs, in the end five whites lay dead. The incident sparked an internal struggle within the Sioux: some wanted all-out war with the whites; others felt they should do whatever was necessary to keep peace. But, as historian Dee Brown states eloquently, "Ten years of abuse by the white men—the broken treaties, the lost hunting grounds, the unkept promises, the undelivered annuities, their hunger for food while the agency warehouses overflowed . . . all rose up to put the murders of the white settlers into the background." After a council with Little Crow, the next morning, August 18, Sioux warriors attacked the agency, raiding the buildings, killing several whites, and taking food from the warehouse. As the revolt spread, and the Indians targeted other settlements, the governor of Minnesota dispatched state militia to the area. Now the Sioux attacked the local fort, Fort Ridgely, which they saw as a symbol of the white occupation of their homeland. As far as the Sioux were concerned, little difference existed between the settlers, the Indian agents, the state government, and the military. Quickly, attacks spread to New Ulm, Faribault, and other small settlements throughout the Minnesota River valley.

Calling in the militia failed to quell the uprising. As was typical of this time, the head of the Sixth Minnesota Regiment, Henry H. Sibley, was one of the people who had garnished the Sioux's annuities for his trading company. He used the proceeds to build a spectacular mansion in Minneapolis. He arrived on the scene with 1,600 troops. It took him more than a month to quell the uprising, during which time close to 500 whites and 60 Indians died. The conflict finally ended on September 26. Trials for the Indians began two days later.

By the end of the uprising, with hundreds of people dead, Indian agents and ministers had convinced the Sioux warriors that if they surrendered the government would treat them as prisoners of war. After hundreds of Sioux surrendered, Sibley promptly broke his promise and convened a military court. Deciding as many as forty cases a day, Sibley quickly sentenced 303 Santee Sioux to death. The governor's bravery evaporated, however, when it came time to sign the execution order. He kicked this decision upstairs, to the War Department, which eventually kicked it all the way up to President Lincoln. Unwillingly to sentence that many people to death, Lincoln ordered two lawyers to investigate and verify the charges. In the end, the president signed an order for thirty-nine of the convicted to hang. A few hours after the mass execution, Minnesota government officials admitted that they had hung at least two of the executed Indians by mistake.

Whose Side Are You On?

Meanwhile, the Five Civilized Tribes in Indian Territory faced a different set of dilemmas. In 1861, representatives of the Confederacy came to them and asked them to join the South's fight for freedom. Offered some of their traditional lands back should the South prevail, the Indians had a tough choice to make: side with the North, meaning the same federal government that had cheated and removed them from their homelands; or side with the South, the same people who had called for their removal in the first place. Members of all the Five Civilized Tribes maintained important ties to the South. Many of them had intermarried with the white southerners and still had family, both white and Indian, living in the region. In addition, many of these Indians were slave owners who did not wish to lose even more of their "property." Finally, many of them

"A group of Creek Indians, post–Civil War." This portrait shows the racial diversity of Creek Indians and how much they had acculturated to American society, at least in clothing and mannerism. Left to right: Lochar Harjo, unidentified man, John McGilvry, Ho-tul-ko-mi-ko (Chief of the Whirlwind) also known as Silas Jefferson. *National Anthropoogical Archives #1164-B*

agreed with the states' rights argument that the Confederacy espoused. They were, after all, the victims of a powerful, centralized federal government, and it had been only slightly more than a generation since the State of Georgia and the U.S. government had removed their peoples. Ultimately, the decision over whether to join the Confederate States of America (C.S.A.) was not simple a one, and it almost split many of the nations, including the Cherokee, in two. As John Ross, first elected chief of the Cherokee, pointed out, if the Cherokee joined the Confederacy and the C.S.A. lost the war, the federal government would punish them severely. Conversely, if his people joined the Confederacy and the C.S.A. won, there was no guarantee that the new federal government would honor its pledges—whites had lied to the Cherokee before. In the end, the Five Civilized Tribes joined the Confederacy.

When the Civil War ended and the dust had settled, Ross proved to have been prescient. The victorious U.S. government did indeed punish the Five Civilized Tribes, by putting them on some of the first reservations in the American West. And the terms of peace the federal government demanded from the Five Civilized Tribes made for a much more difficult "Reconstruction" for them than for the defeated white Southerners, who managed to revive the antebellum political and racial status quo in the South remarkably soon after the war. The federal government sued for peace separately with the Five Civilized Tribes because it still saw them as separate, defeated, belligerent nations, not as a former part of the Confederacy or of the United States.

In order to reach a peace with the United States, the Five Civilized Tribes had to accept the following conditions, which resulted in the United States government confining groups thereafter to small reservations in what became Oklahoma. First, they had to surrender their western lands, reducing the size of their holdings considerably. During the removal process, the federal government had promised some of the Cherokee land in perpetuity in present-day western Oklahoma. The Civil War proved a convenient premise for the United States to revoke this promise. Second, the Indians had to abolish slavery within their territories, which had to be spelled out because the Emancipation Proclamation only applied to the United States, and their territories fell outside of that jurisdiction. Finally, the government required the Five Civilized Tribes to allow railroad rights-of-way through their lands, a stipulation that effectively opened their territory to white settlers. Remember the old joke, "April showers brings May flowers. What do Mayflowers bring? Pilgrims." Guess what railroads bring? Squatters and other land-grabbing whites.

The last two requirements forcefully created reservations, making the members of the Five Civilized Tribes citizens neither of their own nation nor of the United States. On top of that, the federal government established military posts within Indian Territory, establishing a military occupation of the land. Finally, the United States created a territorial government in Oklahoma, ending the Indians' own forms of government and beginning the process for statehood. Sadly, the settlement of the Five Civilized Tribes became the prototype for reservations for the rest of the western tribes.

Grant's Peace Policy

In 1868, the Civil War hero Ulysses S. Grant ran for president of the United States. When asked how he, as president, might solve the "Indian Problem," the former Union general suggested extermination might be the best solution. That bellicose comment notwithstanding, soon after reaching the White House, Grant, as one of his first official acts, created the so-called Peace Policy, one intended to civilize the Indians through education and acculturation. Over the long-term, Grant sought to create Indians who could become American citizens and, as such, renounce their ties to their traditional lands. He also attempted to hand the formation of Indian policy over to its biggest critics: the reformers and missionaries who constantly complained about the how the military and the Bureau of Indian Affairs handled the Plains and other western Indians. Under the Peace Policy, the Quakers effectively took over the administration of the BIA. Grant charged them with parceling out lands for reservations and assigning missionaries to the various Indian groups. The Peace Policy required those missionaries, in turn, to develop and institute programs of civilization, which included education and Christianization, whether the Indians wanted it or not. The founders of the program hoped to create a less bureaucratic and less corrupt Indian policy. (Many Indian agents were renowned for their ability to skim money off the annuities owed to the Indians.) Ultimately, by the 1890s the reservations were to be disbanded as these newly "civilized" Indians became part of the United States population. Or, as General Richard Henry Pratt, creator of the residential school system declared, "Kill the Indian; save the man."

Pratt created the residential school system after the Civil War in the late 1860s. Visiting Seminole captives in Florida, he theorized that rather than leaving the Indians in jail, the government should use that time to civilize them. He began a pilot program that introduced Seminole men to Christianity and white schooling. When they excelled, probably because they had no other choice and nothing else to do, Pratt enthusiastically requested money to expand the program. Pratt believed firmly that isolation from Indian culture helped with the process. Eventually, he opened the Carlisle Indian School (in Pennsylvania), which focused on training Indians to be good citizens. Other schools opened across the country, away from reservations, to help transform Indian youth into Americans. Though historians still debate the success or failure of residential schools, they remained an important part of the final push by the U.S. government to assimilate the Indians in the nineteenth century.

The Peace Policy revolved around three ideas. First, Grant appointed Ely Parker to head the BIA. Half-Seneca and half-white, Parker had been acculturated through education at Yates Academy in New York. He first met Grant when Parker served as a lieutenant colonel and military secretary to Grant during the Civil War. The choice of Parker represented the heights to which Indians could hope to ascend through education and acculturation and the idea that Indians would finally have more say in Indian policy. Next, the BIA released most of the current Indian agents and asked the various missionary and church organizations to appoint new agents for each of the reservation-bound tribes. The purpose herein lay in breaking up the patronage system that long had plagued the BIA. Every politician who got elected in the last half of the nineteenth century needed to pay back donors and envelope stuffers. Inevitably, the least competent (and greediest) of these political cronies were appointed to the BIA, where, as mentioned, there was money to be made by unscrupulous agents.

Perhaps the most significant and long-lasting change invoked by Grant was the abandonment of the treaty process. He instructed the BIA simply to offer "agreements" to the Indians. While this seems like a subtle shift in semantics, legally and politically it constituted a major change.

Native woman using treadle machine in Montana. Schools taught women the "domestic arts" such as sewing and lace-making. *Buffalo Bill Historical Center, Cody, Wyoming; Dr. William and Anna Petzoldt Collection, Gift of Genevieve Petzoldt Fitzgerald, Rev. W. A. Petzoldt, D. D., photographer. LS.95.132*

"In the supper-room – Indian pupils at prayer." Students at the schools were expected to convert to Christianity and adopt white dress and behavior. *Buffalo Bill Historical Center, Cody, Wyoming; Vincent Mercaldo Collection, VM0010*

Early-twentieth-century church service with Indians in Lodge Grass, Montana. Note the large American flag that dominates the room. *Buffalo Bill Historical Center, Cody, Wyoming; Dr. William and Anna Petzoldt Collection, Gift of Genevieve Petzoldt Fitzgerald, Rev. W. A. Petzoldt, D. D., photographer, LS.95.134*

Grey Bull and Wolf Lies Down with Dr. E. E. Chivers of the American Baptist Missionary Society near a river in Montana. Dr. Chivers ran a mission in Montana. *Buffalo Bill Historical Center, Cody, Wyoming; Dr. William and Anna Petzoldt Collection, Gift of Genevieve Petzoldt Fitzgerald, Rev. W. A. Petzoldt, D. D., photographer, LS.95.103*

Teachers and employees of Ogallala Indian School—Pine Ridge Agency South
Dakota, 1891. Note that the majority of teachers and staff are white and the students
are Indian. *C. G. Morledge, Western History/Geneaology Department, Denver Public
Library, Denver Colorado*

Chiricahua Apache Students, 1862. A typical "after" picture, depicting them in
"modern" dress. *Buffalo Bill Historical Center, Cody, Wyoming; Vincent Mercaldo
Collection, P.71.1862*

The United States government only treats with "foreign nations," but it can make "agreements," which are not necessarily binding, with anyone. Therefore, Grant temporarily ended the debate about the status of Indians. The indigenous groups were no longer "sovereign nations" or "domestic dependent nations." The only problem was that no one actually told the various Indian groups still living off reservations that they were no longer sovereign nations.

Now the BIA was to solicit information from the Indians themselves to find out what policies might serve them best. Grant wanted to see more interaction between the Indians and the government. He wanted to co-opt them into serving a role in the solution to the "Indian Problem."

While one could argue that Grant's heart may have been in the right place, his Peace Policy failed miserably and spectacularly. The idea of the churches nominating more altruistic and trustworthy Indian agents fell apart. From the start the various denominations fought over who would be able to appoint which agents to what stations, a situation that turned into both a political and an economic row. The more missions and reservations a group controlled, the more power it wielded over policy and conversion. Equally important, since most treaties by this time earmarked money for education, the more missions and reservations a denomination controlled, the more federal money it received. The fight over control of reservations became personal and negative, souring the public's interest in the seemingly endless debate over helping the Indians. As the fight for control raged, many Indian agencies hung in limbo, as their old agents had already been told to pack their bags but their replacements had yet to appear. Eventually, the BIA rehired almost all the original Indian agents, simply perpetuating the problems of fraud and corruption in reservation administration.

Parker and the Quakers in charge of the BIA also made some significant missteps in Washington, D.C. They created the Board of Indian Commissioners (BIC) within the BIA to provide guidance on policy formation and implementation. Organized much like missionary boards, the BIC comprised missionaries and businessmen, but no politicians. Relying on political patrons to push through its recommended policy changes, the BIC found its suggestions continually turned back by Congress, which either rejected the proposed changes outright or refused to fund them. By 1876, the BIA had changed course but still had not pacified the western frontier. The Peace Policy had wrought few significant changes and left the frontier in turmoil

Although it may strike one as contradictory, the U.S. Army figured prominently in the Peace Policy. Remember, at various points during the nineteenth century the BIA resided under the aegis of the War Department. In the immediate post–Civil War period, the implementation of Indian policy fell to the army. But, as mentioned, the army was not trained as a peace-keeping or policy-making force. The soldiers of the U.S. Army had been trained to wage war, and they had just succeeded in a particularly brutal one. The Indian Wars of the late nineteenth century, however, proved even more intractable than had past conflicts with the Indians, like the Sioux Uprising. Throughout the duration of the Peace Policy, the army was never fully clear as to its role in it. In short, it had been instructed by the federal government to deal with the "hostile Indians," which begs the question: What qualifies Indians as hostile? The BIA defined things in simple terms: the army could consider any Indians off a reservation as hostile and therefore wage conventional war on them. While these instructions may seem clear, they were oversimplified. Three major nations (Blackfeet, Teton Sioux, and Ute) had not even ceded the majority of their land by 1876, much less moved to reservations. Declaring as hostiles any Indians outside the boundaries of a reservation made all the members of any group not yet assigned to a reservation—and there were still many such groups at the time—enemy combatants. This designation even included groups physically in transition to reservations, as well as those who were still in negotiations with the United States. Indian groups from California to the Great Plains found themselves under attack, even while they thought they had the guaranteed protection of the U.S. government. Attacks on women and children, whom the government deemed as hostiles as well, particularly upset Western Indians, who failed to understand the "necessity" of such acts. The Cheyenne, Arapaho, Modoc, Santee Sioux, and other groups suffered mightily from the execution of the Peace Policy. The U.S. Army and state militias waged conventional war on these peoples, leading to a number of spectacular massacres—including some, such as the Fetterman Massacre in 1866, in which the Indians turned the tables on the soldiers, slaughtering 81 of them and mutilating their corpses—that horrified the American public, spelling the end to the so-called Peace Policy and ushering in a new one: extermination.

Little Big Horn: Victory Has Its Price

Now the process to remove forcibly all "free" Western Indians onto reservations and annihilate those who offered resistance began in earnest. By the time of Frederick Jackson Turner's groundbreaking presentation in 1893, the United States government, through the army, had completed the task. In the intervening years, 1868 to 1892, the process became standardized and bloody, as exemplified by the legendary Battle of the Little Big Horn.

Early in the summer of 1876, allied Cheyenne and more than a half dozen bands of Sioux and a few Arapahoe met at the Little Big Horn River, an area the Indians called "the Valley of the Greasy Grass," to hold a conference. Constantly harassed by cavalry units of the United States and distressed by the number of settlers and miners pouring into their

"Custer and his Scouts" *Buffalo Bill Historical Center, Cody, Wyoming; Vincent Mercaldo Collection, VM0014*

countries, the allies hoped to come up with a plan to thwart further problems and, somehow, find a way to preserve their traditional lifeways. As
they discussed the potential of asking the United States government for
Montana Territory as a permanent homeland in exchange for agreeing to
lay down their arms and cease any further raids against settlers, the arrival
of General George Armstrong Custer at the head of the Seventh Cavalry
abruptly interrupted them. The famous clash on June 25 forever changed
Indian policy and Indian-white relations.

The bands of Indians gathered at the Little Big Horn River represented
the last of the free-roaming western Plains Indians, peoples residing on
the western edges of the Great Plains and the eastern slope of the Rocky
Mountains. Having been pushed increasingly farther west over the course
of the 1860s and 1870s, they had already experienced serious displacement caused by the settlement of the Great Plains. Now, as a mining
frontier began to open up in what is now Wyoming and Montana, these
same Indians, who had just agreed to move farther west into the area, saw
the same thing—white settlers and miners running amok and squatting
on their land—happening again. Remember Deadwood? So did the Indians. Additionally, both groups were aware of what was happening to other
groups of western Plains Indians. Already, the Hunkpapa Sioux had experienced contact and conflict with the United States Cavalry and Custer
in particular. A member of General Stanley's expedition in 1873 that
explored the Yellowstone River, Custer had gleefully informed people at
home that the land brimmed with gold. Recently guaranteed sovereignty
of the Black Hills of South Dakota by the Fort Laramie Treaty in 1868,
the Hunkpapa Sioux responded with force when miners invaded their
territory, near present-day Deadwood, South Dakota, in the early 1870s.
Instead of seeing the act as the Sioux's right to defend their territory from
intruders—a right the United States had always taken for granted when it
came to its territory—the U.S. government saw the Indians' attack on the
miners as a violation of the treaty and responded by ordering the military
to launch a campaign against the Indians, who now qualified as "hostile."
This response triggered a series of battles between the Plains Indians and
the U.S. Army that climaxed near the Little Big Horn River in what is
now eastern Montana.

On the evening of June 24, Custer's Crow Indian scouts—the Crow
and Shoshoni had long been enemies of the fearsome Sioux, and, unable

to defeat them, were more than happy to ally themselves with the powerful forces of the U.S. Army in order to try to defeat their common foe—informed the general that a large encampment of Indians lay fifteen miles almost directly west. Upon hearing this, Custer rousted his tired men and made the cavalry undertake a night march, halting at daybreak on the morning of June 25. Early that afternoon, Custer stood on a high ridge, overlooking a Sioux encampment (it must, Custer guessed correctly, be the camp of Sitting Bull) and a group of Cheyenne that formed a long line near the river. Without waiting for more reconnaissance or reinforcements—and with no idea that warriors hidden in the undulating terrain had been watching the advance of the Seventh Cavalry for days—Custer impetuously decided to attack. Splitting his force into three detachments, and probably expecting an easy victory like the one he and the Seventh Cavalry had enjoyed in 1868 in their destruction of a Cheyenne village on the Washita River (in present-day Oklahoma), Custer gave the signal for his troops to ride downhill at the Indians.

The few survivors of General George Armstrong Custer's unit say the general had not realized how many Indians were encamped before him (historians cannot agree on the exact number, either, with estimates ranging from 5,000 to 15,000, including women and children). Indian survivors of the battle said they could not believe that "Long Hair," as they called Custer, had had the audacity to launch an attack against a clearly superior force.

Custer broke his attack into three prongs. He failed to wait, though, for his scouts to come back. In fact, some accounts say his scouts passed him as he and his prong started down the hill. Another prong went south to circle around the Indians they saw. Instead, they discovered more Indians encamped and swarming up the ridge, intent on defending the women and children in camp. Custer's attack initially caught the Indians by surprise, leading to the deaths of many Indian women and children. Infuriated, the warriors mounted their horses and rode off to protect their families from an unjustified attack, soon surrounding and overtaking their hapless enemies. By the end of the battle, Custer and 225 of his men lay dead. However, the Indians, especially leaders like the Hunkpapa Sioux chief Sitting Bull and the renowned Ogallala warrior Crazy Horse, already realized that their victory over Custer had spelled the end of any further hope of negotiations with the United States. Determined but somber, the various Indian groups packed up, split up, and managed to elude their pursuers—now the U.S. Army was more determined than ever to exterminate the Plains Indians—until the winter.

Sitting Bull and Crazy Horse had been right. From that moment forward there was no turning back from a state of constant warfare with an outraged U.S. Army and (white) American public. In May 1877, Sitting Bull led his band of Sioux into Western Canada, where the Canadian government agreed they could stay as long as they kept the peace. But the government of Canada refused to provide them supplies, and when the scarcity of buffalo and other game left them starving, Sitting Bull led his people back to the United States in July 1881. They spent 20 months at Fort Randall, in South Dakota, and in 1883 went to the Standing Rock Agency Reservation, which spans the border of North and South Dakota. Sitting Bull spent several months in 1885 travelling with Buffalo Bill Cody's Wild West show. In the meantime, the U.S. Army coninued to fight, harass, and round up the few remianing Indian groups not yet penned in on reservation lands, notably Geronimo and the Apache. Geronimo led U.S. and Mexican forces on a several year chase in New Mexico, Mexico, before finally surrendering in Arizona in September 1886. He spent almost a decade in prisons and military facilities in Florida, Alabama, and Oklahoma, before becoming a celebrity in his own right, much like Sitting Bull, making appearanxces at fairs, notable the 1904 World's Fair in St. Louis and in President Theodore Roosevelt's 1905 inaugural parade.

The symbolic final battle of the Indian Wars came in 1890 at Wounded Knee in present-day South Dakota. There, on a cold winter day, the reconstituted U.S. Seventh Cavalry slaughtered more than 200 Indians (men, women, and children) encamped with the army and on their way to the Pine Ridge Indian Agency. The Indians had hoped to quell conflicts between the Sioux and the federal government over the Ghost Dance, a spiritual movement that had spread among various Indian groups in the West. The Ghost Dance vision promised the disappearnace of whites from the land, the return of dead relatives and ancestors and the buffalo, and a restoration of the world Indians had lost. The Ghost Dance was a spiritual vision and peaceful, but whites feared that it would inspire a new round of Indian wars. A force of white and Indian police killed Sitting Bull on December 15, 1890, as they tried to arrest him for supporting the Ghost Dance (though he had not participated in it himself). The Wounded Knee

Ghost Dance. This depiction of the Ghost Dance of 1890 shows a large group per-
forming a dance which they believed would protect them from soldiers' bullets and
restore the earth to its condition before the time of the white man. At least two aspects
of the Ghost Dance appeared threatening to the soldeirs: the large crows and the
syncretic message. Dancers believed a Messiah would return and restore the sweetgrass
and punish the white man, therefore appropriating a Christian millenialist belief as
their own. *Library of Congress, LC-USZ62-52423*

massacre took place two weeks later, on December 29. The violent sup-
pression of the Ghost Dance by the U.S. Army, in the process leading to
the death of Sitting Bull and the Wounded Knee massacre only confirmed
U.S. policies of cleansing the land and exterminating or assimilating Indians. They had lost their land and their freedom to practice their own
spiritual traditions, too.

The events leading up to the Battle of Little Big Horn and the actual
battle illustrate U.S. Indian policy in the West from the mid-1870s onward.
Simply put, an Indian nation signed a treaty releasing large amounts of its
land. Soon thereafter, white settlers, miners, or the U.S. military manage to
violate the terms of said treaty by trespassing on or taking over the already
delimited Indian territory. At this point, the Indians, who felt they had a
right to defend the land guaranteed them by tradition and legally granted
them by official agreement with the federal government, not to mention

the basic impulse to protect their families, responded with force to try to remove the intruders. But the United States government viewed this retaliation as a violation of the same treaty the Indians had been trying to uphold, deeming the violent Indians as "hostile," and sending in the full force of the U.S. Army to remove the group in question to a reservation or simply exterminate them. Using a scorched-earth technique (burning dwellings and crops and killing civilians and livestock), the United States army made the Indians "pay." Usually outmanned and outgunned, starved and driven out of their traditional territories, the Indians surrendered and agreed to relocate onto a reservation, where they lost all sovereignty and watch helplessly as their children were sent away to boarding schools and churches run by whites as their traditional culture withered and died.

Custer played a significant role in this process, even from beyond the grave. Historians either love or hate Custer. Those who love him contend that he represents the epitome of American individualism, the youngest general in the Civil War and a gutsy Indian fighter. Those who hate him say Custer represents the epitome of might, rash behavior, and self-centered motivation over thought—and this point of view is verified from the people who worked directly with him. Whichever way one views Custer, he did shape U.S. Indian policy. His death at Little Big Horn, deemed "Custer's Last Stand" by his supporters, occurred at an important moment in American history. Less than two weeks later, the United States would celebrate its centennial. In less than one hundred years, the United States had grown from 13 colonies clustered along the Atlantic Seaboard of North America to 45 states occupying half the continent. Providence, it seemed, had clearly smiled on the United States, until, that is, the Plains Indians smacked down Custer.

The death of Custer and his men became a rallying cry for those who wished to see the Indians exterminated or corralled on reservations. To some citizens of the United States, Little Big Horn raised the question of what sin God had used the "barbaric" Indians to punish the Christian, civilized nation of the United States. Little Big Horn implied that, perhaps, God *did not* smile exclusively on the citizens of the United States and their Manifest Destiny. Such doubts, true believers would not tolerate

The significance of "Custer's Last Stand" was by no means hurt by the fact that the general's wife, Elizabeth, outlived her husband by fifty-seven years, during which time she wrote several books extolling the heroism of her late husband (much of which his critics disputed) and tirelessly sang his praises to whatever group wanted to listen. During the rest of her long life, Elizabeth Custer succeeded in turning Custer into an icon for Western individualism and independence, though others certainly joined her. Just as with Buffalo Bill, fictionalized reality quickly trumped reality. Cody created an image of the cowboy as a defender of the frontier and a rugged individual who stood for honor and bravery; similarly, Libby Custer turned her husband into an icon for bravery and sacrifice. An early monument at the Little Big Horn battle site described the event as "a barbaric Indian massacre," conveniently forgetting who had started the fight.

⋙ Suggested Readings ⋘

Adams, David Wallace. *Education for Extinction: American Indians and the Boarding School Experience, 1875–1928.* Lawrence: University of Kansas Press, 1995.

Anderson, Gary Clayton. *Kinsmen of Another Kind: Dakota-White Relations in the Upper Mississippi Valley, 1650–1862.* St. Paul: Minnesota Historical Society Press, 1997.

Brown, Dee. *Bury My Heart at Wounded Knee: An Indian History of the American West.* New York: Holt, Rinehart & Winston, 1970.

Confer, Clarissa. *The Cherokee Nation in the Civil War.* Norman: University of Oklahoma Press, 2007.

Dippie, Brian. *Custer's Last Stand: The Anatomy of an American Myth.* Lincoln: Bison Books, 1976.

Hoxie, Frederick. *Parading Through History: The Making of the Crow Nation in America, 1805–1935.* New York: Cambridge University Press, 1995.

Lazarus, Edward. *Black Hills/White Justice: The Sioux Nation versus the United States.* New York: Harper Collins, 1991.

Reyhner, Jon, and Jeanne Eder. *American Indian Education.* Norman: University of Oklahoma Press, 2004.

Slotkin, Richard. *The Fatal Environment: The Myth of the Frontier in the Age of Industrialization, 1800–1890.* New York: Athenaeum Press, 1986.

Utley, Robert. *The Indian Frontier of the American West, 1846–1890.* Albuquerque: University of New Mexico Press, 1984.

CHAPTER NINE

Last Frontiers

The Indian Wars, and with them the frontier as a zone of interaction between intruders and indigenous peoples, drew to a close in the last three decades of the nineteenth century, but the American West continued to open new settlement frontiers to Americans and immigrants. These last great frontiers generally fell into one of two categories: farming or resource. The resource frontiers of the American West inspired world-famous gold and silver rushes, beginning with the California Gold Rush of 1848–49. They also included mundane products like coal, iron, lead, copper, zinc, timber, and eventually oil. Resource frontiers were distinct from farming frontiers in important ways. Farming frontiers drew families almost from the start and had a relative balance of women and men, and children and adults. They tended to have high birth rates and low death rates. Farmers usually went west with the intention of settling down, even if they did not end up staying in the first place they arrived. By contrast, resource frontiers drew young to middle-aged men, and few women, children, or elderly adults, especially at first. Typically, the population of a resource frontier was a transient one with a low birth rate and a high death rate.

These distinct population patterns profoundly affected the kind of society that evolved early on in frontiers settlement. Farming frontiers tended to be peaceful, as you would expect of places where people were raising families, while resource frontiers tended to be disorderly, even violent, as you might expect of any place in which a lot of young men with no familial responsibilities had gathered. Cowboys, after weeks on a cattle drive, or miners, flush with gold dust or nuggets from their claims, headed into town to seek amusement, be it a drink at a saloon, gambling, a hot bath, or the services of a prostitute. In this atmosphere, trouble often brewed in the form of drunk and disorderly violence, especially where men were armed. In some growing cow towns, respectable citizens passed gun-control laws and hired sheriffs to keep the peace. In the absence of law and order, individual acts of violence and vigilante violence were common. In gold and silver rush areas, for example, many white miners feared competition from Mexicans or Asians. They often took the law into their own hands, assaulting and sometimes killing non-white miners in individual or mob acts of violence or or in more organized vigilante actions. When large companies moved into resource frontiers—and began to employ large numbers of men as low-paid manual laborers, often in dangerous working conditions—labor violence broke out, pitting workers and their unions against employers and their hired guns.

This said, the late-nineteenth-century American West was never as violent as legends and movies would have us believe. And even if resource frontiers were rough, volatile places, in the long run the violence served an economic, social, and political function. One historian has called it a "war of incorporation," with big business and investors winning. Commonly, farming and resource regions were unpredictable places—some short-lived, many still in existence—that drew immigrants from across the United States as well as Canada, Europe, and Asia. Also in common, farming and resource regions in the American West from the 1870s to the 1890s were commercial frontiers tied to global markets shaped by distant metropolises where banks, railroad companies, investors, and corporations had their headquarters. The American West was indeed a land of opportunity, a place where a man could strike it rich in gold or a family could earn a good income on the Plains, growing wheat and spending their income on goods selected from the Sears & Roebuck mail-order catalog. But it also was a precarious place. Men could and did make and lose fortunes overnight. Overworked and poorly paid laborers could ruin their lungs in a mine or lose a hand to a saw or an axe. Hard-working farm or ranch families could struggle for years working land, only to stand by helplessly as grasshoppers, drought, hail, a brutal winter, high-interest bank loans, ruinous freight rates on the railroads, or a plunge in the price of wheat or beef ruined them financially and left them with nothing.

Farming Frontiers

In the mid to late nineteenth century, subsistence farming, wherein families produced diverse crops primarily for their own use, gave way to commercial farming, wherein they produced a cash crop to sell in order to purchase more or newer farming equipment and household staples and goods. The farmer was increasingly less Thomas Jefferson's independent yeoman, living off the land and beholden to no one, and ever more a producer of commodities beholden to eastern banks and international markets and in competition with farmers in the Canadian West, Argentina, and Russia. Western farm families now aspired to more than mere independence. They wanted to enjoy a degree of affluence, a middle-class lifestyle that would enable them to purchase the consumer goods they saw in the catalogs of mail-order companies such as Sears & Roebuck and Montgomery Ward. To this end, especially on the larger farms of the semi-arid western Plains, where less rain meant fewer bushels per acre, farmers needed to purchase increasingly larger acreages. To farm them, they needed increasingly more expensive equipment, from bigger plows and harrows (which break up large clumps in plowed fields, smoothing it and readying it for planting) to complex mechanical harvesters. In the Midwest, 160 acres typically was enough to yield a decent harvest—and therefore a descent income. On the Great Plains, a farmer needed 320 to 640 acres or more to make a good living.

The process had begun in the 1840s, when John Deere, a blacksmith from Illinois, invented a plow with a steel-tipped blade. Harrows with steel teeth and iron frames came next, followed by mechanical harvesters, first powered by horses, then by a combination of horses and steam. Fences made with barbed wire, a new technology that was much cheaper and easier to put up than fences made solely of wood (a scarce commodity on the Plains), also allowed farmers to work hundreds or even thousands of acres. By the end of the nineteenth century, a well-off, progressive-minded farmer could afford to buy a steam-driven tractor. The effect on production was astonishing. In 1800, it took forty man-hours to farm an acre; in 1880, with animal-drawn machinery, twelve hours; and, in

Oxen pulling a grain drill in the early 1900s, North Dakota. A grain drill was used for sowing cereals such as wheat. The man is having lunch with his family who are seated on a Monitor grain drill hitched to four oxen. *Library of Congress, Fred Hultstrand History in Pictures Collection, Hult.176*

A family outside their sod house near Rock Lake, North Dakota, in the early 1900s. From a twenty-first-century viewpoint these people appear poor. However, the chairs, book, clothing, and neat sod house itself were symbols of pride and encouragement. *Library of Congress, Fred Hultstrand History in Pictures Collection, Hult.046*

1900, eight hours. In the next few decades, gasoline- and diesel-powered tractors, chemical fertilizers, and irrigation equipment would add to a farmer's ability to conduct agriculture on an industrial scale; but buying these same things also threatened to sink him into insurmountable debt. Likewise, by the 1880s and 1890s, mail-order companies could, through the U.S. Mail, ship clothing, furniture, curtains, windows, stoves, sinks, and toys anywhere in the nation. Western families might aspire to buying toys and even musical instruments, as adults and children fantasized about the products in catalogues, even if they never could afford them. Farmers on the Plains imported lumber, barbed wire, and other prefabricated materials to construct homes, sheds, barns, and fences.

Put another way, the same commercial, industrial, and consumer revolution shaping the rest of the nation (and Canada and Europe) was unfolding in the West too. The way that farmers earned their money was different, perhaps, compared to working-class or middle-class families in Midwestern or Northeastern cities, though it was not so different from cotton farmers in the South. But with the rise of a commercial and consumer society, Americans increasingly shared common aspirations and experiences. Farmers on the Plains were becoming small businessmen, and farm families were becoming consumers. In the long run, the need to invest in expensive equipment, which usually entailed assuming debt, made the family farm an ever more precarious enterprise. The all too common result was multiple failed farms, bankruptcies, and efforts to start over. In the next century, and into our own time, family farms slowly would give way to "agribusinesses," as only larger investors could survive big losses in bad years, circumstances that broke small family operations. In the wake of such hard times, well-off larger farmers and big corporations would buy up the failed family farms around them.

Technology propelled much of this transition. Railroads and steamship companies, often interlinked, moved goods around the nation and internationally. Not only did they bring consumer goods from distant places into all parts of the American West, but they also brought immigrants. In the late nineteenth century, German, Swedish, Norwegian, Dutch, and other European immigrants settled in colonies in Iowa and western Minnesota, from Texas in the south to the Dakotas in the north, and all the way west to the eastern regions of Oregon and Washington. The newcomers founded towns, built churches and schools, opened businesses, and started newspapers in their native tongues. Modern transportation, the telegraph, and then telephones also made transplanting ethnic communities to the West and keeping ties to the Old World feasible. Although immigrant communities would assimilate to the American way of life, the process could take generations. As late as World War I and the 1920s, German Lutheran and Dutch Reformed churches worshipped in their native languages.

Processes like these are easy to miss when we envision the West through the lenses of folklore, film, and television. The reality of the farming frontier entailed generally peaceful communities, commercial farms with connections to distant markets and big businesses, and immigrants who long maintained ties to their Old World nation of origin or family heritage. In opposition to Turner's independent farming frontiers, farming frontiers in the late nineteenth century were "metropolitan" entities, places shaped culturally and economically not only by their geographical locations but also by distant commercial forces and corporate institutions.

Resource Frontiers: Mining and Timber

Gold and silver rushes promised eager men the opportunity to strike it rich, but individual miners almost never made a sustainable fortune in mining. Among those who managed to make a small fortune overnight, most lost it just as quickly to gambling, drink, prostitutes, or simply by paying the high inflationary prices of basic goods and services like tools, food, and laundry in gold-rush camps and towns. Only a few men who made fortunes kept them. Rather, it was lawyers, shippers and craftsmen, the owners of stores, saloons, restaurants, laundries and boarding houses, and investors and corporations with the capital and expertise for shaft or hydraulic mining who made the steady money in mining towns. The payoff for men who hoped to strike it rich usually turned out to be getting back home with their skin intact, having had an adventure to provide a lifetime of tall tales. In the long run, most men who worked in the mining industries of the West were wage laborers. The benefit for the nation and the global economy was the rapid opening of the Pacific Coast and the interior West after 1850, and the massive amounts of precious metal to feed expanding industrial economies and global trade networks hungry for investment capital. Gold and silver rushes also created instant cities like

Andy, an African American placer miner, at a sluice. *Courtesy of the Henry E. Huntington Library, San Marino, California*

Chinese Prospector, 1852, panning for gold on the American River in California. *California Historical Society, FN—04470*

San Francisco and Denver, or changed nearby ones, like Seattle, which boomed when it became the American gateway to the Klondike gold rush in Alaska and the Yukon in the 1890s.

There had been small gold rushes in the United States before, for example in Georgia in the 1830s; but the California gold rush that began in 1848 at Sutter's Mill (130 miles east of San Francisco) was the daddy of them all. It drew a quarter of a million people to northern California from across the United States, Canada, Europe, Mexico, Latin America, and China in five years. The veteran miners often came from abroad, and they showed the Americans the ropes. The fact that in this case some of the gold could be found near the surface of the ground or on the bottoms of streams and rivers determined the massive size of the "rush." To get this "placer" gold (from the Spanish, *placera,* meaning sandy) hopeful prospectors needed only basic equipment, such as pick-axes, shovels, camping gear, and prospecting pans and rockers (to swirl water and separate gold dust from sand). Some of the gold seekers went so far as to construct primitive dams, sluices, and water cannons. Even so, they needed to have some resources just to get to the gold-rush fields, including California in 1848–49, British Columbia in 1858, Pike's Peak in Colorado in 1858, Montana in 1862, the Black Hills of South Dakota in 1875, the Klondike in Alaska in 1896, and the Yukon Territory in Canada, also in 1896. Rushes for diamonds, silver, and gold also took place in South Africa, Rhodesia, and Australia in the late nineteenth century, revealing the global—as opposed to the simply "American"—nature of resource frontiers.

Basic patterns characterized American gold and silver rushes. They were multicultural, drawing native-born white Americans, Canadians, and Europeans, non-whites from Mexico, Latin America, and Asia, and African Americans. Non-whites typically got pushed out of the richest areas in a new gold or silver rush field, often violently, by organized vigilantes or impulsive mobs. They usually ended up working poorer or abandoned claims, or making a living by providing services to white miners. More than 25,000 Mexicans rushed to California to seek their fortunes in 1848–52. Whites lynched more than 160 of them between 1848 and 1860. Whites did not just assault and sometimes kill Mexican miners, they also attacked freight-haulers and other business operators whose competition threatened their businesses and anyone who threatened their racial preeminence. For

In the hands of a Vigilance Committee. In gold rush settlements and other frontier settlings where institutions of formal law and order had not been established, residents sometimes enforced rough justice, holding informal courts and enforcing judgments on those deemed guilty, including sentences such as hanging or banishment from the community. *Buffalo Bill Historical Center, Cody, Wyoming; Vincent Mercaldo Collection, VM0015*

example, in 1851 in Downieville, California, a mob lynched a Mexican woman named Josefa Segovia for killing a drunken white miner who had broken into her home and tried to rape her. At the same time that whites were pushing Mexicans away from land rich in gold, other Americans in California were squatting on the farms and ranches of well-off *Californios* (residents of Spanish descent who had become U.S. citizens in 1848) or using financial and legal pressure to take their land.

In some instances, such as California early on and in the Klondike, Indians worked gold claims or found other employment in gold-rush areas; but in most cases, vigilante miners or U.S. Army troops killed and pushed out local Indians. Most famously, gold strikes in the Black Hills in South Dakota and Wyoming in 1874–77 led to a rush that violated the Fort Laramie Treaty, signed by United States and the Sioux in 1868. This betrayal led to a series of battles that began with the defeat of Custer and his men at the Little Big Horn River in 1876 and ended with the massacre of more than a hundred Sioux at the Wounded Knee reservation in 1890.

The global nature of the American West dramatically expanded with the California gold rush, as it drew tens of thousands of Chinese miners, more than 20,000 in 1852 alone. In the 1850s, China was in the midst of civil war, with the Qing Dynasty declining and European nations (and later the United States and Japan) exercising growing control of China's economy. Such problems led millions of Chinese men to migrate to Southeast Asia, North and South America, Australia, and Hawaii to seek their fortune or find work. They came to California (calling it "Gold Mountain") and later to diverse parts of the American West and worked building railroads, in mines, or in such service industries as restaurants, laundries, and hotels. They faced constant discrimination, being isolated in "Chinatown" sections of cities, on the peripheries of towns, or in wholly separate camps. In the early 1850s the California legislature had already begun to pass measures aimed primarily at the Chinese, such as a tax foreign miners had to pay to enter the state, to discourage them from coming to California. Nationally, anti-Chinese sentiment led to the Chinese Exclusion Act of 1882 and to later legislation to try to block Asian immigrants (see Chapter Eleven). Mobs and vigilantes from San Francisco to Los Angeles also took matters into their own hands, burning Chinese homes and shops, cutting the braided queues worn by many Chinese men, and lynching, branding, scalping, and castrating them. Racism led most whites to consider the Chinese immoral, lazy, and unfit to adapt and become Americans (unlike European immigrants). At the same time, and contradictorily, white laborers viewed Chinese as threats to their jobs and wages. They refused to let Chinese men join labor unions, pushed political leaders to restrict migration from China, and sometimes attacked and killed Chinese workers in labor disputes. The West also drew hundreds of young Chinese women, many kidnapped or sold by their impoverished families into near slavery, to serve in laundries or (more often) as prostitutes.

A second pattern was the rough male culture of frontier mining camps and towns, with a population dominated by unattached men, some single, some leaving wives and children back home. The respectable women in such camps or nearby towns operated restaurants, hotels, and laundries. In larger, better-established towns one might find middle-class or even wealthy women who did not need to seek employment. Stories have miners coming from miles around just to see such women, and single women found many eager suitors. The socially marginal women in and around mining camps and towns worked in saloons and brothels, serving the men as waitresses, dancers, and prostitutes. The most marginal prostitutes worked out of "cribs"—small shacks or tents in the poorest areas of a town—or outside of town in a mining camp. Some prostitutes, who arrived in the initial phase of a rush, managed to marry and become respectable or save enough money to open their own businesses. But within a generation such opportunities faded for prostitutes, as men took control of the trade. Most of these "working" women lived hard lives, were addicted to alcohol or drugs (such as opium), and died young, physically battered and prematurely aged. Women who worked as prostitutes came from all over the world, often as forced labor and very young, as in the case of Chinese women.

A third common pattern was the shift from placer mining of gold near the surface, which required little special skill or equipment, to mining deeper veins of gold. The shift to hydraulic and lode mining required investors and businesses with the capital and engineering expertise to exploit the resource. Hydraulic mining was first developed in California. It involved building a reservoir above the mining area, running water down ditches, into progressively thinner pipes, and finally shooting it out of a water cannon that blasted soil and gravel from the side of a hill, gully, or riverbank. Men operating sluices and rockers then separated the gold from the dirt and gravel or excavated an exposed vein. Hydraulic mining was a variation on low-tech placer mining, but industrialized on a mass scale. It devastated the environment, leaving pock-mocked expanses that resembled moonscapes.

Lode mining, the method of exploiting rich veins of gold deep underground or far into a mountainside, required digging deep shafts, reinforcing them with wood, and often using pumps to keep water from filling the shafts. Miners then used explosives, pick-axes, and shovels to break off large chunks of rock, which they brought out of the mine using small carts on rails. Once outside the mineshaft, the men crushed the rocks and rubble with mechanical devices, sometimes steam-powered ones, then separated the gold from the waste rock. Mining operations also used toxic chemicals to separate gold from dross. Whatever the actual techniques employed, lode mining, like hydraulic mining, often left devastated landscapes in its wake, sometimes with poisonous chemicals laying in pits or seeping into nearby lakes and rivers. American companies quickly developed hydraulic and mechanical ore-crushing equipment, but they were slower to learn metallurgy (the chemistry of mining) and underground shaft-mining techniques. For this, American companies in California imported engineers and miners from Germany and Great Britain.

In the second half of the nineteenth century, Americans began seeking training abroad as engineers and specialists in geology, surveying, and prospecting. American universities quickly responded by offering their own agricultural and mechanical institutes. As a result, mining in the West became increasingly professionalized and corporate, replete with investor owners, technical experts, managers, and masses of low-paid, low-skilled laborers. Dominance by corporations and big-time investors had been the case from the start for the mining of coal and nonprecious metals such as copper, iron, and lead. Extracting large amounts of ore from deep underground and processing it necessitated sophisticated equipment and expertise. Generally, then, mining became an industry that required large amounts of capital and technical know-how. Fabulously rich families like the Rockefellers (based in New York) owned numerous mining operations in the West. Individuals might make a living by finding an area rich in a metal or coal, laying a claim to it, and then selling the mining rights to an investor or corporation. Over time, however, prospecting also became more professionalized, dominated by geologists who worked for big businesses and investors. The same general pattern was true of agriculture, as we have seen, and of manufacturing, where the work of skilled individual artisans gave way to factories. In farming, the growing pressure on small family operations resulted in numerous failed farms; in mining and manufacturing, the process resulted in most men working for a wage rather than as entrepreneurs. The mythic promise of the frontier had always been freedom and independence from wage labor and the opportunity for ordinary men to find riches, regardless of their past lives or background. For most men who went into mining, the real West offered opportunities for low-wage jobs much like those they found in the Midwest, the East, or Europe.

The evolution of the lumber industry in the West followed a similar pattern. The lumber industry, one of the oldest in the United States, dates back to colonial times. Though it was locally oriented and scattered, because of the cost of shipping fresh timber and finished lumber, farmers and loggers had removed or harvested many Eastern forests by the 1770s, making even firewood scarce in some areas. In the 1840s, 1850s, and 1860s, the lumber industry moved steadily west to forests in Pennsylvania, Michigan, Wisconsin, and Minnesota, where the Great Lakes, rivers, and canals made transporting timber relatively easy and inexpensive. Lumber camps provided work for American lumberjacks and migrants from French Canada and Scandinavia. When Americans took control of the Far West from Mexico and Britain in the 1840s, they found that a good deal of timber already had been cleared by Mexicans in California and the Hudson's Bay Company in the Northwest, mostly for local use, though some for export on the Pacific Coast. The California Gold Rush, later gold and silver rushes, nonprecious metal and coal-mining operations, the

Tractor Logging, in Stabler, Washington, in the early twentieth century. *American Environmental Photographs Collection, [AEP-WAS158], Department of Special Collections, University of Chicago Library*

transcontinental railroads, ranching, and farming—in short, the opening of the frontier in the West—created vast new markets for lumber companies. A few companies developed locally in specific forestlands, but most small operations did not grow large or last long. Transplanted companies from New England and the Midwest, with experience cutting timber and moving it on water, soon dominated the lumber industry on the Pacific Coast, from California to British Columbia. By the turn of the century, the Great Lakes region was increasingly logged-out. That left the South as the single largest regional source of lumber in the United States, but the Pacific Northwest was catching up, and quickly.

Logging became increasingly mechanized in the late nineteenth century, requiring capital investment and technical expertise. Like mining, it soon was dominated by midsize and larger companies, though small family operations continued to have a place, reflecting the scattered nature of the resource, local markets, and the limited benefits of constructing massive mills. Nevertheless, mill operations shifted from handsaws, usually operated by two men, to water and steam-powered equipment. Mills became even more efficient when they turned from powered saws that moved up and down to circular saws and then massive band saws. Each new advance in technology required more financial investment, and companies that failed to embrace the new technology usually went out of business. Transportation technology changed as well, to railroads in the nineteenth century and to trucks in the twentieth century, as the lumber industry moved away from convenient waterways and into the interior of states such as Washington and Oregon. Companies also turned to "vertical integration," cutting out the middle man and controlling every step of the process, from cutting the timber to milling it, shipping it, and even retailing finished lumber and other wood products (sawdust, pulp and paper) to the customer. For example, in the Northwest the Weyerhaeuser Timber Company held shares in more than two dozen other timber companies by 1910, and the Weyerhaeuser family had investments in forty more. The company had been founded by Frederick Weyerhaeuser, a German immigrant to the United States, who took a job in a Rock Island, Illinois, lumber mill in 1856 and bought it in 1860. At the turn of the century, with most Midwestern forests exhausted, he moved his operations west. In the mid-twentieth century the company expanded into Canada, and in the 1990s into South America and Asia. The West was one stop in a process of global expansion.

For the laborers at the bottom of the corporate pyramid, logging proved to be low-waged, dangerous work—both for native-born and immigrant men, as in the mining industry. Timber companies recruited immigrants with experience in logging, but they also took on men with no experience at all. Getting hit by a falling tree, accidentally cut by axes or saws, slipping between rolling logs, or drowning under a huge mat of logs floating down a river or lake maimed or killed many lumberjacks and mill workers. Lumberjacks usually were strong, tough men who avoided risks but also embraced a boastful, work-hard, play-harder masculinity. They lived transient lives, working seasonally in isolated logging camps, cutting timber during the winter and floating it downriver in the spring. Like cowboys after a long trail drive, or sailors in port after a long stint at sea, lumberjacks often indulged themselves in nearby towns at the end of the season, when they got paid. Consequently, middle-class townspeople tended to judge lumberjacks with suspicion, viewing them as disreputable roustabouts at best and hobos and bums at worst, rather than as hard-working migrant men living hard lives. Mill workers who held steadier jobs in towns also did dangerous, low-waged work, but they were more often able to settle into family life and become members of a stable community.

Because they did low-paying and dangerous jobs, many loggers and mill workers, both native-born and immigrant, found labor unions attractive, much to the horror of business owners and executives and establishment political leaders, who worked hard, even resorting to violence, to keep unions out of their operations and towns. When the unions fought back, labor unrest and violence ensued. Labor conflicts in the West, between lumberjacks, mill workers, and miners, and their employers, suggests that the frontier was less of an escape from class conflict and more of a breeding ground for it.

Immigration and Labor

The West was filled with astonishing resources that attracted eager investors, but it was short on laborers. Mexican Americans provided potential labor in the Southwest and California, as did American Indians in other regions. But the racial prejudices of white Americans prompted them to view Indians as unsuited for industrial work or as unwanted in jobs that properly should go to white workers of a "white" republic. To fill the need for laborers, which could not be met by native-born Americans, companies turned to European and Asian immigrants, especially in low-paying, dangerous jobs on the railroads and in the mining and timber industries.

The ethnic variety of Western labor at the turn of the century is reflected by the case of Bingham Canyon, a mining area southwest of Salt Lake City run by the Utah Copper Company. In 1911, Bingham was home to 1,210 Greeks, 639 Italians, 564 Croats, 254 Japanese, 217 Finns, 161 English, 60 Bulgarians, 59 Swedes, 52 Irish, and 23 Germans, out of a total population of almost 10,000. Employers encouraged chain migration, using immigrants in the United States to recruit people from their families and home towns. Companies often used a *padrone* ("boss," in Italian), paying an immigrant boss to recruit workers from his home region. Padrones took a cut of the worker's pay and policed the workers for the company, in an effort to keep unions out of the picture. Leonidas Skliris was the Greek labor contractor in Bingham. He had arrived in New York City in 1898, where he sold flowers on Wall Street. By 1901, he spoke English and worked for the Baltimore & Ohio Railroad as a foreman. He moved to Bingham in 1902 at the suggestion of a childhood friend, William Caravelis, a labor agent. By 1911, Skliris was recruiting Greeks from Crete (rather than his home town in mainland Greece). He owned a grocery store in Bingham and required his Greek workers to shop there, threatening to get them fired if they did not. Frustrated by his control over their lives, the Greek workers sent a letter to the governor of Utah, complaining about Skliris and asking him to abolish the padrone system run by men like him. Skliris and the company denied the charges, but within a week he had left Bingham, reportedly to become partial owner of a mine in Mexico. The company soon brought in a new boss.

Besides working in mining cities and towns like Bingham, or lumber and mill towns like Raymond, Cosmopolis, and Aberdeen, in Grays Harbor County, Washington, immigrants in the West ran small construction companies, bakeries, saloons, and groceries. By 1900, immigrant communities existed in many urban areas. Where their numbers were large enough, they started newspapers in their own language and organized parish churches, insurance societies, beer halls, and other ethnic institutions. For example, more than 3,000 Italians lived in Nevada by 1910. Most of them had come from northern Italy. Some worked as "truck farmers," growing vegetables and selling them door-to-door or to local groceries. There were "Little Italys" in towns across the West, including in Reno, Los Angeles, San Francisco, and Portland. Some of these migrants had come to the United States with the intention of staying permanently. Many others were "birds of passage," migrant laborers who intended to work in the United States seasonally or for a few years, save up some money, and then return home to the old country, where they hoped to use the money to buy their own land, start a business, or simply retire.

This was true not only in the West and the United States more generally, but in many parts of Europe and the Americas. Many Italians, for example, migrated from southern to northern Italy, to other parts of Europe, and to Canada, Brazil, and Argentina (in addition to the United States) in order to find work. The same was true of Chinese migrants who worked on the railroads and in the mines in the American West. At the same time, Chinese workers also could be found in the Canadian West, Australia, and Southeast Asia. Migration to the American West was only one destination among many in a global system. By the late nineteenth century, railroads and steamships had made transoceanic and transcontinental passage cheap enough for laborers to migrate long distances as birds of passage. The dream of many immigrant laborers in the West thus was not an "American" dream but one of a farm or business on a hillside or in a little town back in the Old World.

In common, laborers in the West faced low wages, dangerous work, and control of their lives off the job by their employers. This was especially so in company-run towns in which the employer also owned the homes and boarding houses in which workers lived, the grocery and general goods stores in which they shopped, and the saloons where they spent their leisure time. Some employers paid their workers in company script, "money" that could be redeemed only in company-owned stores; others deducted rent and other costs directly off the top of their workers' pay. Despite common experiences like these, racial-ethnic divisions and tensions between native-born American and immigrant workers typically made it difficult for them to organize together in unions, a pattern that employers were eager to try to exploit, as the history of labor organizing and violence between workers and their employers in the American West reveals.

In general, early labor unions organized only skilled workers, such as those in the building trades and printing. In San Francisco in 1850, printers organized a craft union. Skilled laborers in other crafts soon organized as well. San Francisco remained the most significant center of labor organizing in the West into the 1870s, when Denis Kearney and the Workingmen's Party attracted many labor voters by agitating against Chinese workers. The second area in which unions appeared was the mining industry, the first union being formed in Virginia City, Nevada, in 1863, with others soon following in Butte, Montana, and in mining towns in South Dakota, Arizona, and Colorado.

As in San Francisco in the 1870s, anti-Chinese sentiment defined the labor movement in the larger West in the 1870s and 1880s. California remained a center of anti-Chinese movements in politics and labor, but politicians in other states and territories fostered the same racial prejudice to curry labor support. Violence against Chinese also took place outside California, notably in Rock Springs, Wyoming, in 1885. The Union Pacific Coal Department's policy of paying Chinese miners less than white miners sparked the incident. White, mostly immigrant, miners killed twenty-eight Chinese men, wounded fifteen more, burned dozens of Chinese homes, and caused $150,000 in property damage. Most of the white miners belonged to a local chapter of the Knights of Labor, a radical labor union that sought to organize miners from all industries, both skilled and unskilled, and across ethnic lines. The Knights' leadership criticized anti-Chinese agitation for dividing workers; and the Chinese Exclusion Act of 1882, which made it more difficult for Chinese to enter the United States, muted fear of the "yellow peril." But virulent racism and the fear that nonwhites inevitably dragged wages down continued to prevent white laborers from organizing with Asians, African Americans, and Mexican Americans.

Labor conflict on the railroads marked the West and much of the nation from the 1870s to the 1890s. Railroad strikes took place across the nation in 1877, spreading from the Midwest to Omaha, Nebraska, and San Francisco. Major waves of strikes followed in 1886 and again in 1893–94, with the founding of the American Railway Union. The 1886 strikes started when the Texas and Pacific Railroad fired a worker in Marshall, Texas, for doing Knights of Labor organizing while on the job. Soon, more than 200,000 workers struck in Illinois, Kansas, Arkansas, Missouri,

"Massacre of the Chinese at Rock Springs, Wyoming," from *Harper's Weekly*, Vol. 29.
The Bancroft Library, University of California, Berkeley, Call Number: MTP/HW: Vol. 29: 637

and Texas in what became known as the Great Southwest Railroad Strike. That year, nationally, more than 600,000 workers struck in over 1,500 actions. Although the incident in Marshall had sparked the initial strike, low wages, long hours, and hazardous working conditions motivated most strikers. Skilled workers in the Brotherhood of Engineers refused to honor the strike, however, dividing the workers. A divide between skilled and unskilled workers hindered labor organizing in most industries during the nineteenth century. In the Great Southwest Railroad Strike of 1886, Jay Gould, the owner of the Texas and Pacific Railroad, brought in strike-breakers and vowed that he would use one half of the working class to destroy the other. (Gould also owned the powerful Union Pacific Railroad, as well as approximately 15 percent of railroads nationally.) Gould also brought in the Pinkerton Detective Agency, employing operatives to break up or spy on union meetings, attack union leaders and sympathizers, and commit acts of violence. When the strikers fought back, Gould blamed the outbreaks on the Knights of Labor. He also convinced governors in several states to use state militia and police to protect railroad property and help break the strike. The governor of Texas, for example, sent Texas Rangers to Fort Worth to help break up the strike. Incidents in Fort Worth and East St. Louis, in Illinois, led to the deaths of several workers and bystanders. In response, strikers sabotaged railroad tracks, engines, and machine shops. As acts of sabotage spread, public sentiment around the nation turned against the strikers, especially among the middle classes, who typically viewed labor agitators as foreign radicals and feared the effect of a strike on their lives. The strike petered out by the end of the summer of 1886, and most of the workers returned to their jobs. This incident was emblematic of the era, it highlighted the divisions between skilled and unskilled workers, the use of strikebreakers, the recourse to violence and sabotage, the support of employers by government, police officers, and the military, and the association in the public opinion of all strikers and labor unions with radicals, "subversives," and foreigners.

The Coeur d'Alene War in Idaho in 1892 is another example. This incident pitted silver miners against the Mine Owners Protective Association, a fraternal organization of local mine owners, who had hired Pinkerton agents to infiltrate the local union and spy on the real members. The mine owners also had the support of the state and federal governments. The trouble began in 1892 when five mine guards shot to death five striking workers who had intended to sabotage a mine. Other strikers forcibly marched the guards and more than 100 strikebreakers out of town. In response, the governor of Idaho asked President Benjamin Harrison to send in U.S. Army troops. Harrison dispatched General J. M. Schofield to the scene. He declared martial law in the region and held more than 600 striking miners in a stockade without formal charges. The mine owners then fired all of the workers associated with the strike. The bitterness left by the failed strike led workers to organize the Western Federation of Miners (WFM) in 1893, with Idaho mine, mill, and smelter workers joining workers from Montana, Colorado, and South Dakota. The WFM was a radical labor organization known for incidents of sabotage and violence. In 1905 WFM leaders helped to found the Industrial Workers of the World (IWW; known informally as the "Wobblies"), another radical organization that sought to organize workers from all industries across the United States. It was especially active among miners and loggers in the West. (The IWW also was active the Canadian West, where it was known as the One Big Union.) Like most labor unions, the IWW attracted workers by promoting practical goals such as shorter hours and better wages, but it also promoted a revolutionary anarchist vision in which workers would take direct control of industries.

A strike in Bingham, Utah, in 1912 provides a final example of the relationship between radical labor politics, conflict between workers and employers, and racial divisions. Anti-immigrant sentiment had grown steadily in Bingham between 1900 and 1912, as immigrants from Southern and Eastern Europe and Asia became increasingly common. Racial prejudice kept the WFM from recruiting recent immigrants from Eastern Europe and Asia, who got the lowest pay and did the dirtiest and most dangerous jobs in the mines. Immigrants did organize, but along ethnic lines and informally. In 1908, for example, the Utah Copper Company gave in to the demands of its Greek workers that it restore their wage to $1.75 a day, this after the company had cut their pay during a recession. The company met the workers' demand because it wanted to prevent them from affiliating with the WFM. In 1912, however, the Greeks took over the local chapter of the WFM and hired a strike organizer. Regional WFM leaders opposed a strike led by Greeks or other recent immigrants, in part because the WFM was almost bankrupt, but also because it wanted to prevent the implicit challenge to the authority of its American-born leadership, with its headquarters in Denver. The Greek workers struck anyway. Middle-class Greeks in Bingham (such as Skliris) opposed the strike, and the Greek workers condemned them as well. WFM organizers moved in to try to take control of the strike, but they cooperated with the immigrants. Whites continued to exclude Japanese workers from the WFM, however, as unions generally did with non-whites during this period, even during strikes. This exclusionary policy weakened the WFM's position, though its leaders were able to keep the peace between American and European members of the union and convince other local unions to support the strike. The Utah Copper Company eventually broke the strike by dividing workers along ethnic lines, fostering divisions in the Greek community, and bringing in strikebreakers. As noted earlier, Skliris resigned as the company's labor agent when workers protested the padrone system to the governor of Utah; but another Greek contractor soon took his place and began to recruit strikebreakers. Many Greek supporters of the strike left Bingham, some of the more militant ones going on to work for other labor organizations in the West. In Bingham, the weakened WFM local survived for only a few years after the strike. The failure of the strike also undermined local support for radical political organizations. The Socialist Party, which won 20 percent of the vote locally in the congressional election of 1912, got only 3 percent in 1914.

This kind of labor conflict, with regular violence, has been described by historians as a "war of incorporation" pitting workers against employers. Industrial conflict and violence was part of a larger "war" to impose order on the West. It included suppressing the Mexican American population, conquering Indian peoples and forcing them onto reservations, keeping Asian and African American minorities in "their place" socially and economically, and victories of big-time ranchers over small ranchers and rustlers. While the whole phenomenon, writ large, was by no means an orchestrated conspiracy—it was too public to be a conspiracy—it clearly represented a victory for middle- and upper-class white Westerners. Furthermore, it had the one-sided support of the respective state governments and the federal government, all of which used military forces (state militias, the U.S. Army) and police to uphold the interests of individual white Westerners and big commercial interests doing business in the West.

Hired Guns

The history of violence between employers and workers in the West points to the basic images in Western mythology: gunfighters and shootouts. Dime novels, films, and TV shows are filled with (or based on) historical characters like Jesse James and Wild Bill Hickock. They replay events such as the standoff at the OK Corral in Tombstone, Arizona, in 1881, in which Wyatt Earp, his brothers, and Doc Holiday defeated the Clanton gang. Images of John Wayne, Clint Eastwood, or Kevin Costner portraying cowboys, lawmen, soldiers, or outlaws are familiar to movie-goers around the nation and the world, and generations of kids have grown up acting out gunfights and army battles with toy guns. But the reality behind the mythology of the American West is complex and more about politics and economics than honor and machismo. The shootout at the OK Corral, for example, is often remembered as a blood feud between two clans. This is partly true, but it also was a conflict between well-off, socially respectable, Republican-voting ranchers who represented the business-class establishment in Tombstone (the Earps), and Democratic-voting,

Wyatt Earp and the Dodge City Peace Commission, 1883. Earp is seated in the front row, second from the left; Bat Masterson is in the back row on the far right. *Courtesy, National Archives, Department of Defense, ARC ID: 530707*

rural, socially marginal, small-time rancher-cowboys with a reputation as rustlers (the Clantons). In the long run, and in its impact on Western society, gun fighting was more about who would control society in the West than about manliness, family, and honor.

The tragedy at Mussel Slough, in the San Joaquin Valley in central California, illustrates this point. It was a conflict between farmers and the Southern Pacific Railroad. The farmers had settled the land in the 1870s, with promises from the railroad to sell it to them at a low rate in the future. Assuming that the railroad would keep its word, the farmers improved the land, installing an irrigation system that turned a virtual desert into productive farmland. However, the Southern Pacific repeatedly delayed conveying the land titles to the farmers and began to discuss evicting the farmers or selling them the land at substantially higher prices based on the improvements that the farmers themselves had made. The farmers refused. When the local sheriff and men allied with the Southern Pacific tried to evict some of the farmers in May 1880, they armed themselves and offered resistance. In a gun battle on May 11, the farmers killed one railroad man, but a pro-railroad farmer-gunfighter named Walter Crow killed five of the resisters. Later that same day a band of farmers shot Crow in the back, killing him in revenge. Backed by the courts, the Southern Pacific eventually had five of the settlers imprisoned for eight months. In the end, most of the settlers purchased their land from the railroad at a slightly reduced price.

Generally, gunfighters were hired guns. The significant question is: Who employed them and to what end? As the stories of industrial violence suggest, it was the forces of incorporation who hired gunfighters to protect their commercial enterprises. Mining companies bought the services of the Pinkerton National Detective Agency and similar outfits. Big-time ranchers paid gunmen to fight off cattle rustlers, though some of the ranchers had themselves done some rustling and had been none too respectable when they started out. Sometimes wealthy ranchers used gunfighters to intimidate smaller ranchers and farmers competing for the same public land or access to water. Even so-called respectable citizens in cattle towns hired gunfighters as sheriffs to keep social order when cowboys at the end of the cattle drive celebrated in a drunk and disorderly fashion in the streets and saloons. Of course, businessmen in town made money by selling the cowboys booze, baths, clothes, and the company of prostitutes, but middle-class townsfolk wanted to keep that part of the economy out of sight. On occasion, labor unions, small-time ranchers and farmers, and other "little guys" hired gunfighters. But they rarely had the money to do so and usually had to fight their own battles.

In addition to the economics of violence, other factors that shaped gun fighting included politics and the Civil War. Most hired guns in the West worked for investors from the North who voted Republican (pro-business advocates of a strong federal government). The men they fought typically had come to the West from the South and voted Democratic (virulently anti–African American and pro-states' rights). In addition, the sheer number of men toting guns in the West after 1870—whether gunslingers, rustlers, bandits, or merely farmers, ranchers, or business- men—reflects the legacy of the Civil War. The devastated economy of the post–Civil War South forced many indigent young men to go west in search of work. Many of these men had spent their teens and young adulthood in Confederate armies and did not easily adapt to civilian, peacetime life. For example, Jesse James and his gang had fought a guerilla war against the North in Missouri during the Civil War, and they contin- ued to lead violent lives as outlaws after the war, often targeting trains and banks in the North. Even the ready availability of cheap hand guns and rifles was a legacy of the Civil War and the technological advances that had come out of it.

The violence of the frontier West thus must be understood in relation to larger forces, most especially the economics of who hired the gunmen, but also party politics and the legacy of the Civil War. Industrial violence in mining towns and gunfights between farmers and corporate investors may not be the stuff of romance and honor, but it is the larger context of our myths about gunfighters and shootouts. Like the Plains Indian Wars, the gunslinger phenomenon was a product of the struggle over which social groups would control the West.

Western Cities

As the stories of violent labor strikes and hired guns suggest, even the "frontier" West was a region of towns and cities. This runs counter to Frederick Jackson Turner's story of the evolution of frontiers from moun- tain men and fur traders to settler farmers who eventually built towns and cities. Some parts of the West did evolve in the way that Turner described, but before the end of the nineteenth century the West already was the second-most urban region in the nation, trailing only the Northeast. As early as 1880, the population of the West was more urban than rural. By one count, 30 percent of people in the Mountain West and Pacific Coast lived in cities, compared to 28 percent nationally. This trend continued in the next decade and into the twentieth century, and after 1890 the West was increasingly more urban than the national average.

Three major Western urban sites were "instant cities" created by unusual circumstances. The gold rush transformed San Francisco from a town of 900 in 1848, when Mexico lost California to the United States, into a city of 10,000 in 1849, 36,000 in 1852, 56,000 in 1860, 149,000 in 1870, and 299,000 in 1890. Tens of thousands more people, many of whom had arrived to seek gold, lived in the surrounding region. The dramatic rise in population between 1860 and 1870 was part of the transition of the Bay Area into a center of finance, trade, and shipping, both nationally and globally, as it benefited from later booms, such as the discovery of silver in western Nevada in 1859. The completion of the transcontinental railroad in 1869 dramatically extended the city's influence in the region (and nationally), as bulk goods and people could move efficiently and cheaply across the nation and by sea to Asia. By the 1870s, San Francisco had passed from its early boomtown phase, marked by vigilante violence, into a metropolis with banks, theaters, hotels, factories, and stores that sold the latest European fashions. It attracted immigrants from China to Europe and was not just an American city but a global city.

Salt Lake City also got a fast start, but for very different reasons, as Mormons fleeing persecution in Illinois arrived in the Salt Lake Valley in 1847. Unlike San Francisco, which grew unplanned out of gold-rush chaos, leaders in the Church Jesus Christ of Latter Day Saints (LDS) wanted Salt Lake City to be a new "Zion," a New Jerusalem, and constructed it following plans laid down by Joseph Smith in the 1830s. The city had 8,000 residents in 1860, 13,000 in 1870, 44,000 in 1890, and more than 50,000 in 1900. Salt Lake City residents suffered from hunger in the early years, but the start of the California Gold Rush saw tens of thousands of miners pass through the region every year on their way to northern California. Mormons began making money hand over fist as eager non-Mormon "gentiles" bought food and other supplies on their way through the Salt Lake Valley. Salt Lake City became the capital of the Utah Territory in 1856 and flourished as a center of trade. The arrival of the railroad in 1869 only enhanced its role as a regional entrepôt, as did the development of mining in Utah. Nonetheless, Mormon relations with federal officials remained tense into the late nineteenth century. In the second half of century, Mormon leaders recognized that their community could not remain separate from the larger nation and sought compromises that would allow Utah to enter the union as a state. The Mormon leader Brigham Young had long since given up direct political rule of Utah in 1857 in the wake of the Utah War. In "The Manifesto" in 1890, the LDS

Salt Lake City. The LDS quickly built Salt Lake City as represented by this engraving. Brigham Young wanted streets large enough to turn a wagon around in. From *Scribner's Magazine,* Volume 3, Issue 4, February 1872, p. 402. *Buffalo Bill Historical Center, Cody, Wyoming; Vincent Mercaldo Collection VM0008*

forswore polygamy and Utah soon became a full-fledged state (1896). With prosperity and change came worries, however. Would the LDS Zion remain a saintly city dominated by the faithful, or would gentiles undermine its religious foundations? Though the city remains the global capital of the LDS faith today, non-Mormons have grown much more influential. When the Winter Olympics came to Salt Lake City in 2002, it, as a "dry" city, had to put special measures in place to allow athletes and other visitors to readily enjoy beer and other forms of alcohol.

Like San Francisco, a gold rush created Denver. Miners had found small quantities of gold in Colorado as early as 1849 while en route to California. In 1858, a prospector from Georgia named William Greeneberry Russell, who was married to a Cherokee woman, found a deposit of placer gold at the confluence of the South Platte River and Cherry Creek—the home territory of the Cheyenne and Arapaho Indians. The rush started in 1859, and the new settlement quickly attracted town promoters, bankers, and merchants to serve those streaming to the gold-mining camps. The Civil War and attacks by Indians angry about having so many intruders on their land slowed Denver's growth, as did a devastating fire and a flood in the 1860s. In 1870 Denver was home to less than 5,000 residents, about the same population it had in 1860. But in the next three decades its population grew dramatically—to 36,000 in 1880, 106,000 in 1890, and 134,000 in 1900. Colorado became a territory in 1861 and Denver its capital in 1865. The arrival of the railroad in 1870 and the defeat and pacification of most of the Indians in the area spurred economic development and settlement. Investors soon made Denver a center of banking, smelting, merchandizing, ranching, and small-scale manufacturing for the Mountain West.

More generally, towns and cities grew to serve frontier settlements and economic development of various sorts, especially where the railroads and ports made them local and regional centers of trade and commerce for mining, ranching, lumber, or agriculture. In 1890, the only large cities in the West other than Denver, Salt Lake City, and those in California were Seattle (43,000), Tacoma (36,000), and Portland (46,000). Other cities, such as Butte, Montana, Sioux Falls, South Dakota, and San Antonio and El Paso, in Texas, remained smaller, with residents numbering in the thousands or tens of thousands. Gateway cities on the edge of the West—especially Chicago, but also Omaha, St. Louis, and the Kansas City area on the border of Missouri and Kansas—connected the region to the Midwest and the East. These Midwestern entrepôts served as metropolitan centers for the region, managing its economy and providing passage in and out of the region for migrants, products from the West, and manufactured goods imported into the region from the East.

Populism

For farmers on the Great Plains, the evolution of the Western economy held both promise and peril—the promise of commercial success and the peril of being inextricably linked to global markets and the corporations that dominated them. In the larger scheme of things the economic position of farmers was a precarious one at best. Natural disasters visited farm families regularly in the last three decades of the nineteenth century, in the form of drought, grasshoppers, wheat rust, and hail, each of which could devastate an entire crop. But economic problems hurt farmers even worse, although the latter might, they hoped, be addressed politically. Farmers argued that several business institutions and government policies oppressed them. The banks charged them immorally high rates of interest for the money they needed to buy equipment, fertilizer, seed, and other necessary items for their farms and homes. Grain elevator companies sometimes cheated them by grading their wheat as low in quality and then selling it at a higher grade, or by fixing prices to keep them universally low. The railroads, which typically had monopolies in isolated regions of the Plains, charged farmers ruinously high freight rates, compared to lower rates in areas of the nation where individual railroads faced competition. Farmers in the Midwest, South, and West also argued that U.S. monetary policy was unfair to them. The U.S. dollar was based on the gold standard, so the amount of gold in the national treasury literally limited the amount of money in circulation. In the rapidly growing economy of the late nineteenth century, these circumstances created a state of deflation, which meant that the price of goods and products (including farm products) stayed low while interest rates on loans stayed high. Hoping to remedy the situation, farmers began to advocate basing the money supply on gold *and* silver, which would increase the amount of money in the economy, leading to inflation, which would simultaneously raise the price of products like wheat and bring interest rates down. But the big banks and mainstream politicians opposed such a change, reflecting their financial self-interest (benefiting from high interest rates) and a fear of financial chaos. Finally, competition with wheat farmers in Canada, Russia, and South America meant that even when American farmers produced bumper crops, a glut of wheat on the global markets could leave prices for a bushel of grain lower than the cost of producing it.

These complaints all pointed to real problems, but the sheer unpredictability of the weather, bank and railroad rates, and global prices for agricultural products bedeviled farmers, as did their geographic isolation. Many lived in out-of-the-way rural areas or near small towns, far from the centers of economic and political influence, where mainstream (Democratic and Republican) politicians and economic boosters lived. Some historians have argued that the disgruntled farmers—most of them Protestant and Anglo—also felt alienated by the changing character of the nation, as immigrants to the United States increasingly came from Southern and Eastern Europe and were Roman Catholic or Jewish, and as the nation grew more urban and industrial. Jeffersonian ideology had put the yeoman farmer at the center of American life, but in the late nineteenth century America seemed to be leaving them behind in favor of outsiders. Such resentment may have been common, but it is easily overplayed, as Western farmers wanted to enjoy the benefits of commercial farming and prosperity and likely were no more anti-Catholic or anti-Semitic than socially and economically prominent Anglo-Protestants in Eastern towns and cities. What farmers resented most was not having a political voice or a way of influencing the new economic institutions and markets that controlled their fate.

Wheat farmers in the West (and cotton farmers in the South, who had similar problems) began organizing in the 1860s. In 1867, farmers organized the Grange—the official name was the Patrons of Husbandry—which attracted 1.5 million members by the 1870s. At first, the Grange created a "movement culture," rather than a political party. This movement involved education programs and lectures about scientific farming, community events such as picnics, and stump speeches extolling the evils of railroads, banks, and the Gold Standard and celebrating the importance to the nation of the family farm. Grange activists also ran cooperative stores and grain elevators in an attempt take the exploitative "middle men" out of the economic system.

When these kinds of activities failed to solve their problems, farmers turned to political lobbying and organizing. In the 1880s, they organized regional farmers' alliances, the Southern Alliance, the Colored Farmers National Alliance, and the Northwestern Alliance (in the West and Midwest), together comprising several million members. There also was a National Women's Alliance, known for fiery speakers such as Mary E. Lease, who told farmers to raise less corn and more hell. The policies advocated by farmers and alliance leaders were forward-looking in important ways, including calls for state and federal regulation of the railroads, banks, and other big businesses to prevent monopolies and price fixing. But their vision was tradition-laden (Jeffersonian) in seeing "producers" as the foundation of American society and morality. Men who produced tangible goods—farmers, ranchers, craftsmen, laborers—created the wealth enjoyed by all Americans. Merchants and bankers might be necessary for the economy, but their practices were parasitical in nature. The fervor behind this ideal of the independent American producer often was expressed in moral and religious terms, as farm alliance leaders took old-time Protestant hymns and wrote new words for them, calling on Almighty God to hear the cries of farm families "who labor and toil." As these examples suggest, farmer activists appealed to long-held American values and drew on the Anglo-Protestant cultural and religious traditions. But one cannot dismiss the Grangers as backward looking, nostalgic, and resistant to change. They wanted to protect their independence and way of life, and they also wanted to prosper in a commercial economy and proposed innovative policies that reformers of all stripes would pursue in subsequent decades. Furthermore, American farmers were not alone, as similar farm movements and political organizing took place in Western Canada in the early twentieth century.

In the 1880s, American farmers began to elect politicians to state government who supported their goals. But since their economic problems were national and international, local-and state-level solutions would not suffice. Farmers also found that working through the Democratic and Republican parties got them nowhere. So, in 1892, Southern and Western farmers created the People's Party of the United States, commonly known as the Populist Party, the name "populist" reflecting the movement and party's emphasis on defending the common people of the nation. In the 1892 presidential election the Populists nominated James B. Weaver, a former Union general, for president, and balanced the ticket with a Southerner and former Confederate, James Field. Although the Populist ticket lost badly that year, it garnered more than 1 million votes, or 8.5 percent of the total vote. The two major parties took notice. In 1896, the Populists "fused" with the Democratic Party, nominating William Jennings Bryan as their standard bearer. Bryan's presidential campaign was as much a moral crusade as political one. In a famous speech at the Democratic National Convention in July 1896, he thundered: "Burn down your cities and leave our farms, and your cities will spring up as if by magic; but destroy our farms and the grass will grow in the streets of every city in the country." In addition to Western and Southern farmers, Bryan attracted some support from silver miners and companies, who hoped that a Bryan presidential administration would begin to "coin" silver, as the Populist farmers had long wanted (thus increasing the amount of money in circulation and lowering interest rates). In this case, farmers' needs and the interests of silver-mining companies overlapped.

But Bryan and his farmers' crusade failed to attract immigrant or urban voters, who were suspicious of the Protestant religiosity and fervor of his campaign, which sounded suspiciously like anti-Catholic, anti-immigrant

Railroad lines with grain elevators. *Buffalo Bill Historical Center, Cody, Wyoming; Vincent Mercaldo Collection VM0018*

"Gift for the Grangers" The image reflects Thomas Jefferson's ideal of the yeoman farmer; independent, productive, and the basis of American democracy. The reality of farmers' lives aside, the political appeal of this myth was powerful. *Library of Congress, LC-DIG-ppmsca-02956*

sentiment to them. Bryan ran twice more as a Democrat, losing presidential elections in 1900 and 1908. The Populist movement foundered after 1900, having failed to change the circumstances of farmers in a major way. In the early twentieth century, the Progressive movement would take up and begin to implement some of the policy goals of the Populists (see Chapter Ten). Bryan never won the presidency, but he later served as the secretary of state in the first Woodrow Wilson administration. Though Bryan would resign his cabinet post in 1915, in opposition to Wilson's increasingly aggressive foreign policy, he did support U.S. intervention in Mexico in 1914, when Mexico's brutal civil war spilled over the border into the United States.

Where Does the "West" End?: Overseas Expansion and Investment

By 1853 the United States had accumulated all of the territory we know today as the "lower 48" states through wars and treaties with Indian nations, Mexico, and Great Britain and treaties with France. In the 1860s and 1870s, the United States fought the last major Indian wars, asserting effective control of the interior of the West. During the same years, successive presidential administrations continued the process of expanding American territory—this time overseas. In 1867, at the behest of Secretary of State William Seward, the United States purchased Alaska from Russia for $7 million. Called "Seward's folly" by some at the time, the purchase soon proved to be a bargain with the discovery in Alaska of gold, oil, and other natural resources. In addition to financial considerations, what many people to this day call "America's last frontier" ended up being important in the twentieth century as a base for American forces in the Arctic.

In 1867, the United States also formally claimed possession of the Midway Islands, halfway around the globe in the North Pacific—the first of many overseas annexations. Missionaries and businessmen from the United States had begun arriving in Hawaii in the 1830s. They took control of the islands in 1887 by forcing the Hawaiian king, Kalākaua, to sign a constitution. It limited the rights of Asian residents and gave property-holding Americans, Europeans, and native Hawaiians the right to vote (though the requirements largely restricted the franchise to wealthy Americans). Critics called it the "Bayonet Constitution," reflecting the threat of military force used to persuade Kalākaua to sign it. His sister and successor, Queen Liliuokalani, announced plans in 1893 to throw out the Bayonet Constitution and create a new one that would restore power to the monarchy. A committee of local American and European investors responded by seizing control of the government and asking the U.S. diplomatic representative, John L. Stevens, to protect the safety of American citizens. Stevens did so, ostensibly remaining neutral, by ordering a company of U.S. Marines aboard a ship in the harbor to enforce order. In 1898, the United States formally annexed Hawaii as an American territory. The islands proved valuable for their agricultural products, such as sugar, but especially as a base for the U.S. Navy's Pacific Fleet in the twentieth century.

In 1898, the United States went to war with Spain, ostensibly out of demands by the American public that Spain stop oppressing the Cuban people and give them their independence. By the end of the brief war, however, the United States had taken effective possession of Cuba (which greatly pleased American sugar magnates and other Americans doing business there), the Philippines, Puerto Rico, and Guam, paying Spain $20 million for the Philippines in the treaty it signed at the conclusion of the Spanish-American War. The war ignited a vigorous debate between those who thought the United States should become an imperial power like France and Great Britain and others who feared this new form of imperialism was incompatible with the nation's revolutionary heritage and democratic ideals. Filipino rebels, led by their "George Washington," Emilio Aguinaldo, had all but defeated the Spanish by 1898 and now had to watch as American soldiers took control of the major towns, cities, and harbors of the islands. Despite the efforts of the anti-imperialists in Congress, and an offer by industrialist Andrew Carnegie to pay the U.S. government $20 million to give the Filipinos independence, the voices of American imperialism won the day. The United States would soon have to fight a vicious war against Filipino guerillas, who turned from fighting Spain to fighting the United States for independence (see Chapter Ten). The United States also took control of the Panama Canal Zone in 1903. The Philippines were touted by investors as a gateway for American trade with China and the rest of Asia. Along with the Panama Canal, and Pacific islands like Hawaii, Guam, and Midway, the Philippines became a base for projecting American naval and commercial power in the Pacific.

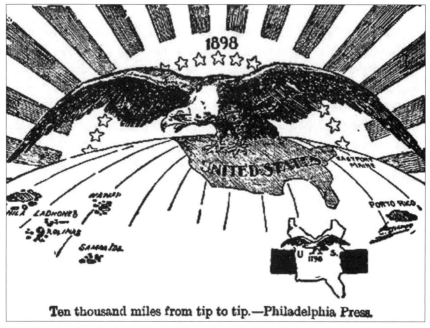

"Ten Thousand Miles from Tip to Tip" *Editorial cartoon from the* Philadelphia Press *celebrating the American empire (1898).*

More generally, the United States followed European powers like Britain and France in using military force, or the threat of it, to shape trade relations with Asian societies such as China and Japan. In the 1850s, the U.S. government sent successive naval flotillas to Japan, forcing it to sign what were known as "unequal" treaties and open its borders to American merchants and diplomats—but refusing to allow the Japanese government legal power over Americans who had committed crimes in Japan. Ironically, the humiliation imposed on Japan led to a revolution and dramatic reforms in Japanese politics and industry, which by the dawn of the twentieth century saw Japan remake itself into an imperialist power in the Pacific Ocean in its own right. In the early 1900s, Japan won a war with Russia, took control of Korea, and imposed unequal treaties of its own on China. And the rivalry between Japan and the United States for control in the Pacific would eventually lead to the Japanese invasion of China in the 1930s and its attack on the United States in 1941 (at the Pearl Harbor naval base in Hawaii). Along with several European nations, the United States sent more than 3,000 troops to China during the Boxer Rebellion (1899–1901) to protect American investments and merchants there. In 1901, the foreign powers forced China to sign the "Boxer Protocol," which reinforced older unequal treaties that the United States, Britain, and other European imperialist powers had imposed on China starting in the 1840s. This humiliation contributed to the collapse of China's Qing Dynasty in 1912 and to decades of revolution and civil war that ultimately ended with a victory by Chinese communist forces in 1949.

In the interest of protecting American investments, the United States intervened militarily and politically on a regular basis in Mexico and Central and South America in the nineteenth and twentieth centuries. It justified such intervention with the Monroe Doctrine of 1823, proclaimed by President James Monroe, which announced that European nations no longer could interfere with nations of the Americas that had recently won their independence in revolutionary wars against such powers as Spain and France. In the 1850s, American leaders began to use the Monroe Doctrine to legitimize American intervention in the Caribbean, Mexico, and Latin America more widely, typically to protect American investments. The mining industry in particular connects this imperialist history to expansion in the American West. American mining companies regularly moved from the American West over the border into Mexico, beginning in the 1870s. In the 1910s and 1920s, they began investing farther afield, in places like Chile. Most notably, the Anaconda Copper Mining Company added to it original holdings in Butte, Montana, by acquiring copper mines in Chuquicamata, Chile. Such investment reinforces the point that expansion in the West was part and parcel of globalization.

For many Americans more was at stake than trade and strategic power. The views of Theodore Roosevelt exemplify the belief of many Americans at the turn of the century that the nation's vitality depended on frontier conquests. A New Yorker by birth from an influential, wealthy family, the young "Teddy" Roosevelt built himself up from a sickly, frail child into a powerful adult, working as a cowboy on the ranch that he bought in North Dakota in the 1880s. While there he met the famous sheriff of Deadwood, South Dakota, Seth Bullock (a character in the recent HBO TV series *Deadwood*), later calling Bullock a "true Westerner" and "the finest type of frontiersmen." Roosevelt wrote influential histories of the frontier West and its conquest. In 1898, he organized the "Rough Riders,"

Teddy Roosevelt dressed in his U.S. volunteer forces "Rough Rider" uniform, 1898. *Buffalo Bill Historical Center, Cody, Wyoming; MS6.6A.2.4.2.28*

a militia made up of cowboys and other friends, among them Bullock, which he led on the highly publicized, somewhat fictionalized "charge up San Juan Hill" during the Spanish-American War. (They actually played a secondary role in the battle and went up Kettle Hill.) San Juan Hill made Roosevelt a legend. He was elected vice-president in 1900 and became president in 1901, after the assignation of President William McKinley. This led Mark Hanna, one of his Roosevelt's critics in his own Republican Party, to groan, "Now look, that damned cowboy is president." As president Roosevelt believed in a strong foreign policy, one that would spread the nation's political and economic power, and in the obligation of the United States to bring civilization to "backward" parts of the world, such as the Philippines. He also believed that wars and conquests—from the Indian wars of the American West, to the war with Spain, and the defeat of Filipino guerillas afterwards—were essential to the vitality and health of the American race, men in particular. Without such frontiers and battles to prove their courage against lesser races, American men would become accustomed to indolence and grow weak, both morally and physically. His ideas also reflected the ongoing, respectable influence of racial thought and frontier mythology that date back to the late colonial era.

Conclusion

Some have described the frontier West as a safety valve for American society. This argument claims that the young United States did not experience the rise of socialist political parties, radical labor unions, poverty, or violence, as had the nations of Europe and other Old World societies. The frontier was the basis of American freedom, prosperity, and peace, which made United States a unique society historically. But labor violence, the hard, low-paying work done by miners and loggers, and the travails of farmers in the American West in the late nineteenth century all suggest something quite different. The West was indeed a land of opportunity, but it was no haven from the social, economic, and political problems of the modern world. It was a spawning ground of labor-union organizing, violence, and even socialist politics. The American West was perhaps unique in drawing so many workers, farmers, and investors in such a short time, and perhaps unique in the vastness of its resources and the opportunities they promised. Even in this regard, however, one must compare the American West to similar frontiers in Brazil, Argentina, Western Canada, South Africa, New Zealand, and Australia. The American West and the larger American nation also shared basic patterns of economic development and territorial expansion with the imperialist nations in Europe such as Great Britain and France.

A sign of the imperialist aspect of the frontier was the seamless transition from American expansion in the West to Alaska, Hawaii, and other imperialist ventures overseas. By the late nineteenth century and into the 1920s, American politicians and pundits worried aloud about the end of the frontier. What, they asked, would happen to freedom, opportunity, and the American spirit with no new frontiers to conquer and settle? Americans today tend to think of the frontier and the West in terms of "expansion" and "settlement," not as a series of imperialist conquests comparable to those undertaken by the overseas empires of Spain, France, and Great Britain. But the relationship between continental conquest in the American West and American conquests overseas suggests otherwise. This point also would not have been lost on American Indians, Mexicans, and

Mexican Americans. For them, the story of the American frontier had been one of conquest all along.

Many Americans recognized this connection at the time. As we have seen, Roosevelt celebrated American conquests on the frontier and overseas as necessary to the vitality of the "American race." His language seems strange, even offensive today—what we might associate with outwardly racist groups such as the Ku Klux Klan. But such ideas were respectable and mainstream in the United States a century ago. This legacy of bellicose imperialism is important not only for understanding some contemporary problems in the American West, but more widely suspicion of U.S. foreign policy in Vietnam and Iraq in the second half of the twentieth century. While Americans have been quick to forget their nation's imperialist history, people overseas remember it all too well.

℞ Suggested Readings ₹

Barth, Gunther. *Instant Cities: Urbanization and the Rise of San Francisco and Denver.* New York: Oxford University Press, 1975.

Brown, Richard Maxwell. *No Duty to Retreat: Violence and Values in American History and Society.* New York: Oxford University Press, 1991.

Brown, Ronald C. *Hard-Rock Miners: The Inter-Mountain West, 1860–1920.* College Station: Texas A&M University Press, 1979.

Cronon, William. *Nature's Metropolis: Chicago and the Great West.* New York: Norton, 1992.

Fite, Gilbert C. *The Farmer's Frontier, 1865–1900.* New York: Holt, Rinehart, & Winston, 1966.

Goodwyn, Lawrence. *The Populist Moment: A Short History of the Agrarian Revolt in America.* New York: Oxford University Press, 1978.

Jameson, Elizabeth, and Susan Armitage. *Writing the Range: Race, Class, and Culture in the Women's West.* Norman: University of Oklahoma Press, 1997.

Larsen, Lawrence H. *The Urban West at the End of the Frontier.* Lawrence: Regents Press of Kansas, 1978.

Luebke, Frederick C., ed. *European Immigrants in the American West: Community Histories.* Albuquerque: University of New Mexico Press, 1998.

Maffly-Kipp, Laurie F. *Religion and Society in Frontier California.* New Haven: Yale University Press, 1994.

Nugent, Walter. *Habits of Empire: A History of American Expansion.* New York: Knopf, 2008.

Paul, Rodman. *The Far West and the Great Plains in Transition, 1859–1900.* Norman: University of Oklahoma Press, 1998.

Peck, Gunther. *Reinventing Free Labor: Padrones and Immigrant Workers in the North American West, 1880–1930.* New York: Cambridge University Press, 2000.

Petrik, Paula. *No Step Backward: Women and Family on the Rocky Mountain Mining Frontier, 1865–1900.* Helena: Montana Historical Society, 1987.

Schlissel, Lillian, Vicki L. Ruiz, and Janice Monk, eds. *Western Women: Their Land, Their Lives.* Albuquerque: University of New Mexico Press, 1988.

Schwantes, Carlos Arnaldo. *Hard Traveling: A Portrait of Work Life in the New Northwest.* Lincoln: University of Nebraska Press, 1999.

Takaki, Ronald. *Strangers from a Different Shore: A History of Asian Americans.* Boston: Little, Brown, 1989.

West, Elliot. *The Contested Plains: Indians, Goldseekers, and the Rush to Colorado.* Lawrence: University Press of Kansas, 1998.

Wrobel, David M. *The End of American Exceptionalism: Frontier Anxiety from the Old West to the New Deal.* Lawrence: University Press of Kansas, 1993.

CHAPTER TEN

The "Progressive" Era

In some places, the American West of the early twentieth century still resembled the mythic American ideal of pioneer farmers making new lives for themselves on the frontier, but the region was becoming increasingly modern and urban. The promise of land of their own continued to lure farm families to the West, more than ever before in terms of raw numbers between 1900 and 1920. In that sense, Americans who worried about the end of the frontier and feared how the nation was changing were wrong. But when one looks at the West as a whole, farm families do seem like old news. By 1920 cities like Los Angeles were enjoying boom times, and cowboys and Indians working in Hollywood can tell us as much about the West as could ranchers and farmers working the land. This, most Western Americans believed, was progress, even if they worried about labor strife, problems in the region's rapidly growing cities, and the masses of European and Asian immigrants coming into the region in search of employment and new homes.

Progress was a word on the lips of many Westerners during the era; naturally, the term meant different things to different people. Progress for bankers, railroad executives, and city fathers was not necessarily progress for white-collar professionals, farm families, and urban laborers. Progress for white Americans generally relegated American Indians, Mexican, Asian, and African Americans to subordinate status. Debates over the meaning of progress went to the core of the Progressive movement. For some Westerners, "Progressive" reform implied more orderly cities and conservation-minded economic growth. Others called for radical changes that would fulfill the promise of the West for the working people of the region. The demand for radical change could take strange turns. In 1914, Oklahoma had the largest number of dues-paying members of any state in the Socialist Party, more than 12,000. Most of them were farmers, either tenant farmers unable to make ends meet or small farmers deeply in debt to local banks and businesses, trying to hold onto their land and way of life. In 1914, Oklahomans elected six Socialist members to the state legislature and more than 100 local officials. This unusual relationship did not last long. Socialists could not easily fit devoutly religious, property-owning farmers into their vision of a classless society, and conservative patriotism during World War I and the postwar, anti-communist "Red Scare" pushed radical labor unions and political parties to the margins of American politics. But the example of radicalized farmers signals the depth of ordinary people's discontent and the potential for economic conflict in the American West to lead not just industrial laborers but even farmers in radical directions.

For most Progressives and most Westerners, progress required harnessing the power of government, locally and in state capitals, but also in Washington, D.C. Westerners were not so different from other Americans in this regard. But the question remained: for whom and to what ends should the power of government be harnessed? The Progressive movement and the messy and often violent conflicts associated with the evolution of modern society in the American West transformed communities in the West and around the world during the first two decades of the twentieth century.

Urbanization

The immediate context for the Progressive Movement in the West was the rapid growth of cities: metropolises like Los Angeles and San Francisco, regional centers like Houston, Salt Lake City, Seattle, Portland, Denver, Tulsa, Omaha, Billings, and Des Moines, and dozens of smaller cities and towns. By 1920, the majority of Americans lived in urban areas, and, as mentioned earlier, the West had been a region of cities from the start of the American era, more so than any part of the nation except for the

San Francisco earthquake of 1906. This photograph shows Sacramento Street and the approaching fire. *Library of Congress, Arnold Genthe Collection, LC-USZ62-128020*

Displaced San Francisco residents wait in a bread line, April, 1906. *Courtesy, National Archives, NWDNS-92-ER-15*

Northeast. Keen observers of the West like Theodore Roosevelt had noted this reality back in the 1890s.

With a population of almost 680,000 in the larger Bay Area, San Francisco was the preeminent city in the West. Its large banks and busy port (one of the world's finest natural harbors) made it the financial and trading center of the region. San Francisco had grand hotels and colorful residents—including flamboyant millionaires, starving artists, and a poly-glot European and Asian immigrant population (in its famous Chinatown especially, but also in its vibrant Italian community). All of this gave it an aura that few cities in the world at the time could match. The city's stature survived the earthquake that devastated it in April 1906. Indeed, its legend grew. The quake and the four days of citywide fires that fol-lowed killed 700 people and leveled 28,000 buildings, leaving more than a quarter of a million people homeless. In the next decade San Franciscans rebuilt their city, and it spread out into small towns in the larger Bay Area. Among the most influential men in the city was Amadeo Peter Giannini, the son of an immigrant grocer family that sold fruit and vegetables. He became a banker when he was in his thirties, and his bank was the first to reopen after the 1906 quake. It played a key role in financing the rebuild-ing of the city. His Bank of America (renamed that in 1930) also created new forms of consumer services by lending money to ordinary people and opening "branches" in ethnic neighborhoods. With the terrible fires of 1906 in mind, the city in the 1910s would look 190 miles east to Yosemite National Park for a more secure source of water, both as a basic resource and to better fight fires, sparking a major conflict within the early conser-vation movement in the West.

The city's quick revival reflected its wealth and vitality and its links to national and global economies. The opening of the American-controlled Panama Canal in 1914, combined with the older transcontinental rail-road lines, would only increase the value of the port of San Francisco. The Panama-Pacific International Exposition held in San Francisco in 1915 symbolized and celebrated the revival. The city was more ready than ever to host a world fair, with luxurious new hotels built on Nob Hill, where mansions destroyed in the 1906 earthquake had once sat. Little remains of the grandiose buildings put up for the fair itself, as the fair's chief architect designed them to be temporary. Only the Palace of Fine Arts survived, and it had to be rebuilt in the 1960s. Today it is the Exploratorium, an interactive science museum. The Palace and its fate perhaps symbolize the impermanence implied by American mythology—that it is a New World frontier, unlike the Old World of Europe with its millennia old monuments, cities, cathedrals, and art. The economic strength of San Francisco would stand more solid, however, growing in the 1910s and 1920s. Indeed, when the Great Depression hit in 1929, San Francisco's banks survived the crisis.

Despite San Francisco's power and prestige, by 1920 Los Angeles had leapfrogged it and become the West's largest and most economically dynamic city. More than that, LA's sprawling scale and surreal character heralded the future of the West in important ways. Most notably, LA and the American West would be marked by a creative and stubborn defiance (foolish and ultimately unsustainable its critics would say) of the ecological and resource limitations of nature in the twentieth century.

As early as 1900, Los Angles had already begun to defy nature. It had been a cattle town in the Mexican era. Angelinos saw the cattle trade all but die out in the years after the American conquest of California. By the 1880s, Hispanics made up less than 20 percent of the city's population. The arrival of the railroad and thousands of migrants from the Midwest and Europe transformed the city. There was nothing *natural* about this process, however, for San Diego, less than one hundred miles south of LA, had a better natural harbor but by no means experienced a similar growth pattern. It was the civic and business leaders of LA who, by their efforts and sheer will, made their city the center of southern California. They subsidized railroads in the 1860s and 1870s and in the 1890s successfully schemed to get the U.S. Congress (with taxes paid by all Americans) to build a major port, essentially a man-made harbor, for the city.

A similar refusal to accept environmental limits continued to determine the growth of Los Angeles after the turn of the twentieth century. With little other than the pleasant weather to attract migrants and investors to the city, boosters built LA up through marketing and real estate campaigns that made southern California sound to the rest of America like Eden. From the start of the century, LA itself and surrounding towns in Los Angeles County grew out rather than up, spreading out widely from their urban cores, as new arrivals from the Midwest preferred to live in single-family homes rather than apartment buildings. Inter-urban and electric street railways linked the satellite towns and connected downtown

LA to farms, orchards, the ocean, and the mountains. Soon, the newly invented automobile redefined the city, as Angelinos made the horseless carriage not only a symbol of their lifestyle but a practical source of their mobility. There were more than 400,000 cars in the Los Angles County by 1923. Indeed, building homes, roads, railways, and highways provided jobs for many people who had moved to southern California from other parts of the nation. The irony of being "tied down" by the car in horrendous LA traffic would come only in later years. Migrants also found work drilling for oil and in the service sector. The dreamworld of LA came into its own in the 1910s, when film producers like D. W. Griffith set up shop, first in downtown LA and then in a little village just outside the city called Hollywood. One of the first films made there was Griffith's *In Old California* (1910), set in Mexican California of the 1800s. But even before Hollywood became "Hollywood," cowboy films stood out as a dominant genre in motion pictures. By World War I, Hollywood was already becoming the film capital of the world, and by 1920 Los Angeles had more than 575,000 residents.

All of this growth demanded water, much more water than the narrow Los Angeles River could provide. Confronted with this dilemma, civic leaders realized that they would have to bring water to Los Angeles from another part of the state, and they set their sights two hundred miles north, on the Owens Valley. Former Los Angeles mayor Frederick Eaton and other civic and business leaders quietly bought up water rights in the Owens Valley in the early 1900s (later selling them to the city at a profit, on the tab of city taxpayers). They secretly planned to take the water from the valley and bring it to a growing, thirsty LA. Then, between 1905 and 1913, William Mulholland, the self-taught superintendent of the Los Angeles Department of Water and Power, planned and supervised the construction of the 223-mile-long Los Angeles Aqueduct between the valley and LA. J .J. Lippincott, the superintending engineer of the federal government's Reclamation Service (see below), worked with Eaton, who supported the project, leading Owens Valley residents to believe that the aqueduct was an irrigation project that would benefit them. Meanwhile, Eaton and his cronies bought huge tracts of cheap land in the dry San Fernando Valley, northwest of LA, and had the city annex it. These wheeler-dealers secretly intended to use most of the water meant for LA—and paid for through local taxes and fees by the residents of LA—to make the dry

San Fernando Valley bloom, and thereby increase their fortunes through orange groves, wheat fields, and eventually another real estate boom. After superintendent Mulholland opened the aqueduct in November 1913 and began diverting water from the Owens River to LA, the city continued to buy up land and water rights in the valley and take more water. By 1924, Owens Lake had gone dry and the valley with it, destroying the way of life of Owens Valley residents. Vigilantes in the valley blew up part of the Aqueduct in 1924 and continued sabotaging it until 1927. Heavily armed police from LA imposed martial law on the valley—without clear legal authority to do so—but failed to stop the sabotage. The "water war" ended only when two of the leaders behind the resistance in the valley, the brothers Wilfred W. and Mark Quayle Watterson, were indicted for fraud and embezzlement in their banking business. The "water war" illustrates the power of urban areas over rural ones, common in the West, and the close relationship between business boosters and local politicians in the development of the region—crony capitalism and outright corruption, according to their critics.

Like Los Angeles, Seattle and Portland grew dramatically during the first two decades of the twentieth century. Each city had a good harbor, railroad lines, and well-established trade ties to the interior, notably rivers that linked the cities to timber and agricultural lands. Seattle, which started the century smaller than Portland, had important connections to Asia and Alaska, serving as the key transport and supply point for Americans heading to the great Klondike Gold Rush. It also became a shipbuilding center in the early twentieth century. This economic growth and the efforts of city boosters (as in LA) caused Seattle's population to shoot up from 81,000 in 1900 to 315,000 in 1920, while Portland was almost as impressive, going from 90,000 to 258,000.

Urban centers on the Plains did not grow as spectacularly, but they did grow steadily. Cities like Omaha and Kansas City served the agriculture and ranching economies of the Plains, but also were commercial and railroad hubs. Their growth slowed in the 1920s, as settlement on the Plains slowed and the wheat boom of World War I ended, but some Plains cities did begin to develop manufacturing. Likewise, cities on the southern Plains and in the Southwest—such as Wichita, Tulsa, Oklahoma City, Dallas, Houston, and San Antonio—enjoyed rising populations and diversifying economies, as commercial centers and in manufacturing, especially after 1920. In Texas and Oklahoma, oil booms led to rapid growth. For example, Houston grew from 45,000 to 138,000, after the discovery of oil under Spindletop Hill (a salt dome) in nearby Beaumont in 1901. Similarly, Tulsa's population expanded rapidly after 1901 with the discovery of oil in Red Fork, southwest of the city. Tulsa went from little more than a frontier town in 1900 to a city of 72,000 in 1920. The oil continued to flow after 1920, and the city grew to 170,000 by 1930, proclaiming itself the "Oil Capital of the World." The oil boom fueled the economic and cultural growth of the local economy, as Tulsa became a center of the new aviation industry and a hotbed of jazz and blues, especially in the African American neighborhood of Greenberg.

The major cities in the mountain West—Denver and Salt Lake City—were already important regional centers in 1900 but continued to grow slowly and steadily. Denver's population increased from 134,000 to 256,000 between 1900 and 1920, and Salt Lake City's from 54,000 to 116,000. Salt Lake City was unique as a cultural center for the Mormon West, which was concentrated in Utah but had important communities in nearby states as well. The city continued to be primarily a regional trading center and did not industrialize significantly until World War II. The most notable change in the early twentieth century was the growing influence in the city of non-Mormons, known as "gentiles," economically and politically, and the increasingly secular-pluralist character of municipal government. With the end of the silver boom in the early 1890s, and the beginning of a depression, business and civic leaders in Denver began promoting economic diversity in such sectors as brewing, baking, meat packing, food processing, tourism, manufacturing (ranching and farming equipment and supplies), and service industries. The discovery of gold in nearby Cripple Creek in the 1890s—and the demand for metal during World War I—also helped to restore the economic vitality of Denver during the early twentieth century. In both cities, then, the early twentieth century was not a time of dramatic change, but one of gradual political and economic diversity and maturation.

As in the case of Los Angeles, the rapid growth of cities in the West entailed close and sometimes corrupt ties between business and civic leaders. It also regularly sparked heated labor conflict and violence and interethnic and racial clashes. The labor violence typically was worst in smaller cities and towns and isolated rural areas, but it also sometimes took place in larger cities. In smaller urban areas and isolated rural areas, companies more thoroughly dominated local economies, often owning the stores, homes, saloons, and other business frequented by the working men they employed. Their control over local communities, and with it often control of local politics and police, fostered exploitation of laborers and sharp responses by laborers and unions. In Cripple Creek, Colorado, for example, regular strikes and violence between workers and their employers lasted for a decade, from 1893 to 1904. The fight was over the eight-hour workday, which had been passed in a state amendment by Colorado voters but had not been finalized by the state legislature and governor, who, under pressure from the mining companies, let it drop. The violence culminated in 1904, after the Western Federation of Miners (WFM) called for a sympathy strike to force business owners to recognize the unions in smelter mills of nearby Colorado City. By October of that year, mill workers and gold miners were on strike, and the mine owners brought in scab labor to break it. In June 1904, Harry Orchard, a WFM supporter, blew up the Independence, Colorado, railway station, killing thirteen strike-breakers. The mining companies brought in hired muscle and began to round up strikers, driving many of them to the Kansas border and leaving others stranded on isolated stretches of the Plains. The governor of Colorado eventually felt compelled to intervene, sending in the National Guard to restore order and end the strike on behalf of the companies. This decision earned him strong criticism from President Theodore Roosevelt, who argued that he should have followed the will of the people rather than bow to the mining companies.

Instances of violence between strikers and their radical labor unions and employers and their gunmen continued to take place across the West. In 1905, radicals associated with the WFM, including Harry Orchard, assassinated Frank Stuenenberg, the former governor of Idaho, in revenge for his role in the Coeur d'Alene War of the 1890s. In Los Angeles in 1910, labor-union conspirators blew up the *LA Times* building, killing more than twenty people. The backlash, engineered by *Times* owner Harrison Gray Otis, weakened the labor movement in southern California. In Washington state, between 1911 and 1917, timber barons fought striking workers and the Industrial Workers of the World, culminating in November 1916 in Everett, when 200 vigilantes deputized by the local sheriff attacked 300 IWW supporters arriving on two boats for a demonstration. The two sides exchanged gun fire, leading to several deaths on each side. In the wake of the violence, the governor of Washington, Ernest Lister, sent in the state militia to restore order.

Undoubtedly the most infamous case of anti-labor violence was the "Ludlow Massacre" and related bloodshed in and around Ludlow, Colorado, in 1914. The strike began in September 1913 and lasted through the spring of 1914, with many of the workers living in tents in the hills, having been evicted from their company-owned homes. The massacre occurred in April 1914 when thirteen women and children hiding in a pit burned to death at the hands of the Colorado National Guard and hired guns employed by the Rockefeller-owned Colorado Fuel & Iron Company, who had attacked a tent colony of striking workers and their families. The massacre became a national and international sensation. The strikers in Ludlow sabotaged mines in response, sometimes killing guards, and burned company buildings. President Woodrow Wilson sent in federal troops to restore order and disarm both sides. The strike finally ended in December, when the strikers and the union ran out of money. Dozens, perhaps hundreds, of people had been killed. The only man convicted of murder, a striker, was eventually pardoned by the Colorado Supreme Court. No one employed by the Rockefeller company, none of its hired guns, nor any of the National Guardsmen involved in the massacre was convicted. Lynchings, bombings, and vigilante action against strikers continued in places such as San Francisco in 1916, Bisbee, Arizona, in 1917, and Butte, Montana, in 1917. In the aftermath of the Ludlow strike, the federal government held a Commission on Industrial Relations, which looked into the events in Ludlow and recommended such reforms as the eight-hour workday and tighter labor regulations.

Fears among native-born, middle-class Anglo-Americans about strikers, violence, and corruption, and virulent prejudice against African Americans, immigrants, Catholics, Jews, and Asians, led to the rise of the Ku Klux Klan (KKK) in Denver in the 1920s. The growth of the KKK was also an indicator of how deep the fear of foreign subversion went after World War I. But internal divisions and excesses in the KKK, along with the courage of a few local critics, led to the undoing of the Klan in Denver within a few years of its formation there. This is just one example. Other regions where the KKK rose to influence in the West in

"The Death Special." An armored car used by the Baldwin-Felts Detective Agency against strikers in Ludlow, Colorado. The car was reinforced with steel and mounted with a machine gun. *Denver Public Library, Western History Collection, X-60380*

the 1920s include Oregon, west Texas, southern California, and Utah (and parts of the Canadian West, where similar anti-immigrant, anti-radical, and anti-Catholic sentiment flourished). The rise of the Klan, and its influence among respectable citizens and in local and state politics, suggest that it was not clear to many citizens whether the growth of urban areas in the West would lead to progress or anarchy. These kinds of fears and violent conflicts sometimes inspired reactionary politics, but they also stimulated civic boosters, worried moralists, and level-headed social workers and engineers to look for practical solutions. Like the city of Los Angeles, other cities in the West and around the modern world might become heaven on earth or pits of hell.

The Progressive Movement

In common, the progressives saw the turmoil, violence, corruption, suffering, and exploitation that came with rapid economic growth and believed that humanity had the potential to engineer solutions to such problems and achieve what they considered human progress. Little else united them, however. People who identified themselves as progressive included socially-conscious businessmen, journalists, intellectuals, social workers, suffragists, clergy, prohibitionists, socialists, union organizers, conservationists, and even crackpots who claimed to have silver-bullet solutions that would solve all the problems of the early-twentieth-century West. The progressive impulse included a desire to clean up corrupt politics, restrain corporate power by busting monopolies and cartels, use government bureaucracy both to regulate the economy and enforce morality, provide solutions to social ills such as alcohol use and poor hygiene, and expand democratic participation by ordinary citizens. Broadly speaking, progressives came in two types: moderates, advocates of order from the managerial class, who hoped to make corporate capitalism and mass democracy work more fairly and efficiently (and secure their place in it); and radicals, revolutionaries who rejected capitalism and wanted to build a genuinely free and equal socialist democracy.

In all of this, progressives in the American West shared much with their contemporaries in other parts of the United States and around the world. Uniquely, perhaps, the context of recent frontier conditions, vast natural resources, aridity, a huge domain of publicly owned land, and an emphasis on direct democracy shaped Western progressivism. The populist farmers of the 1890s had meant their reforms to preserve a largely Jeffersonian empire of individual freedom and prevent the emergence of a world dominated by corporations. Moderate progressives generally accepted and even embraced the reality of a society managed by large corporate and government bureaucracies, and they considered themselves its ideal public-minded managers. The radicals resembled the populists in their flamboyant style and their sometimes virulent hostility to this emerging managerial order, but they looked forward to a utopian future and a radically new kind of society.

The Progressive Movement started at the local, city level in the West, as elsewhere in the United States, and the alliances, competition, and conflicts between moderates and radicals are best examined as they unfolded in specific locales. San Francisco provides a good example. In 1909, the city voted the Union Labor Party (ULP) into power, electing the president of the local Building Trades Council, P. H. McCarthy, as mayor. The Building Trades Council was a local labor union affiliated with the American Federation of Labor (AFL), a moderate body that sought to win practical gains for workers, such as better pay, the eight-hour day, and safer working conditions. The ULP claimed to represent San Franciscans from all classes, but especially workingmen and owners of small businesses whom elites had ignored. Its fear of alienating moderate middle-class supporters kept the Union Labor Party from pursuing its strong pro-union goals once in office, however, and ultimately kept it from enacting any clear labor policies. This failure gave middle-class progressives an opening, and in the election of 1911 their candidate, James Rolph, a progressive-minded Republican, won.

In Los Angeles, one expression of radical progressivism was a silent film, *From Dawn to Dusk* (1913). The protagonist of the film is an iron-works employee who is fired for being a labor agitator. After his friend dies in an explosion at the ironworks, the jobless man runs for governor of California as the radical labor party candidate. *From Dawn to Dusk* opened at a socialist movie hall in downtown LA. With a cast of more than 10,000, it depicted dangerous workplaces, life in the slums in which industrial workers lived, and the violence used by private companies and police to discourage or undo union organizing. The film was informed by more than fantasy; a LA socialist leader and labor lawyer, Job Harriman, even had a cameo in the film. In 1900, he had run for vice-president of the United States on the Socialist Party ticket along with presidential candidate Eugene Debs. In 1910 and 1913 Harriman nearly won election as mayor of Los Angeles. He also fought for the rights of labor unions to organize, demonstrate, and exercise their right to free speech, taking on Harrison Otis, publisher of the *LA Times,* and the anti-union Merchant and Manufacturers Association.

In general in LA, moderate progressives aligned themselves with the interests of local business. Radical progressives wanted industrial democracy, in which workers and employers would share control of industries. After 1910, moderates and conservatives tarred radicals by associating them with the union activists who set off an explosion in the *LA Times* building in October of that year. The moderates focused on civil-service reform (trying to rid local government of employees who got their jobs through political patronage rather than on the basis of their abilities), cleaning up financial corruption in the city (such as the awarding of huge contracts to friends and campaign contributors), and working with business leaders to create a public utilities commission, public power proj-

Destruction by bombing of the *Los Angeles Times* **building, 1910.** *Courtesy of the Henry E. Huntington Library, San Marino, California*

ects, and a range of social welfare programs and measures. Together they promoted a long-time, reliable member of local government for mayor, George Alexander, in opposition to the radical Harriman. But factionalism among progressives led to their decline and loss of control of city government after 1913.

More effective progressive change took place at the state level in California, which voted in a moderately progressive legislature and governor in 1910. Hiram Johnson, perhaps the best-known example of a Western progressive, won the election for governor as a Republican. He first came to fame in 1908 as a district attorney in San Francisco, where he helped prosecute a local political "boss," Abe Ruef, for corruption. Ruef manipulated political and business life in San Francisco behind the scenes, bribing city officials to control local services such as trolley cars, the gas company, and the local monopoly over "prize fights" (boxing matches). Johnson took over the trial when a prospective jury member (a former prisoner at San Quentin, who may have had ties to Ruef) gunned down the chief prosecutor, Francis J. Heney, in the courtroom. Johnson won the gubernatorial election of 1910 in part on his anti-corruption reputation. He also associated himself with former president Theodore Roosevelt, who had championed greater regulation of powerful corporations and signed significant Progressive legislation into federal law, notably stronger regulation of the railroads, the Pure Food and Drug Act (1906), and the Meat Inspection Act (1906). Johnson campaigned hard against the abusive and monopolistic Southern Pacific Railroad, "the octopus" that for many years kept its long tentacles in every sector of the California economy and politics.

As governor, Johnson provided more money for public schools, strengthened the state railroad commission, and promoted conservation policies. He supported woman's suffrage and embraced populist planks such as the direct election of U.S. senators and allowing candidates to run for office as the candidates of multiple political parties (a practice known as fusion politics that allowed candidates from small, often radical, parties to also run as Republicans or Democrats). During Johnson's time in office, the California legislature passed a workman's compensation act, child labor laws, a factory inspection act, and an eight-hour day for women laborers. Policies like these won him national recognition. In 1912, Theodore Roosevelt chose Johnson to run with him as the vice-presidential candidate of the Progressive Party, in an unsuccessful bid to return to the presidency. In addition to political and economic reforms, Johnson also promoted law and order and, like many progressives, played to the prejudices of the day. For example, he supported the Alien Land Act of 1913, which prevented Asian residents of California (those who were not American-born citizens) from owning land. Johnson's ambition led him to run for the Senate in 1916, where he served for twenty years, supporting dam-building projects and conservation measures. As a sign of his moderate viewpoint, he later opposed many of the New Deal policies of the administrations of Franklin Delano Roosevelt in the 1930s and 1940s.

Examples of progressivism on the Plains further make the point of the diversity of movement in the West. On the northern Plains, South Dakota elected Coe Isaac Crawford as governor in 1907 and as a U.S. senator in 1908. Like Hiram Johnson, Crawford was a lawyer, serving as the state attorney general in the 1890s, and a Republican. He supported Teddy Roosevelt's 1912 run for the presidency as a Progressive. Progressives in

South Dakota used the referendum and initiative to promote policies such as prohibition of alcohol, tax reform, direct primary elections, and railroad regulation. This moderate agenda was designed to promote morality and social order, notably Prohibition, the teaching of good hygiene, encouraging morally uplifting, healthy leisure activities, and regulating business practices by railroads and other large corporations that exploited farmers and small businesses.

On the southern Plains, Oklahoma offers an example of progressivism and its more radical potential. A coalition of humanitarians and labor organizers centered in Oklahoma City pursued a variety of policies in the years just before and after Oklahoma became a state in 1907. This coalition was noteworthy for including not only middle-class charity workers but also the radical Farmers Union and labor organizations. Though mostly agricultural, Oklahoma had a significant union presence in the railroad and coal industries and in cities such as Tulsa and Oklahoma City, which grew rapidly during the early twentieth century. Between 1906 and 1910, the coalition successfully promoted laws and constitutional provisions that required a minimum attendance in public schools, reformed the state penal system (by prohibiting the leasing out of convict labor by the state and by forming juvenile courts), created a state office for charities, and restricted the use of child labor. In the 1910s, radical politics flourished among Oklahoma farmers, especially tenant farmers, and the Socialist Party received a quarter of the vote in some elections. In August 1917, during World War I, impoverished tenant farmers and railroad workers opposed to conscription aligned with the Socialist Party and threatened to march on Washington, D.C., in what became known as the Green Corn Rebellion. Several hundred of the farmers and railroad workers armed themselves and prepared to march. Fearful townspeople took them seriously, formed a posse to oppose to the rebels, and fought several skirmishes with them, eventually arresting several hundred of the rebels. The fighting killed a few men on each side. Courts convicted more than 150 of the Green Corn rebels, handing out sentences ranging from ten days to several years in jail. World War I and the postwar Red Scare put Socialists and other radicals in the same category as foreign subversives and Communists in the public mind, dramatically undermining support for them, fostering the spread of a conservative nationalism, and allowing the government to suppress radicals, at times forcibly, across the nation.

One can also see the diverse, sometimes conflicting, strands of progressivism in campaigns to restrict immigration and legislate the outlawing of the sale of alcohol. Radicals in organizations like the IWW scorned both restrictive immigration policies and Prohibition and sought to organize immigrant workers. But moderate progressives embraced Prohibition as a means of promoting social order and moral regeneration. Prohibition promised better health and more-stable families and communities, the argument holding that sober men would bring home pay checks rather than get drunk at taverns and come home to commit acts of domestic violence. National prohibition of alcohol also seemed practical because it backed up the temperance and social work done locally by churches, settlement houses, and social-service agencies. Such organizations believed that drugs, alcohol, and other vices exacerbated the social and economic inequities already suffered by recent immigrants, whom they worked to *Americanize,* the term the settlement-house workers employed. These social workers, many of whom were women, worked not only in settlement houses but visited poor immigrants in their homes or apartments, trying to help the urban underclass and working class by providing them food, shelters, sermons, and education in American history, English, and personal hygiene. But advocates of Prohibition from the white, Protestant middle class commonly associated societal ills with recent immigrants from the poorer nations of Europe, viewing the newcomers, many of whom were Catholic, as morally, religiously, and even racially inferior. Americanization programs, they believed, could help turn some down-and-out immigrants into good Americans, but the federal government still needed to restrict further immigration (from Europe as well as Asia) in order to maintain control, limit the danger to the order and health of American society, and give Americanization programs time to assimilate immigrants. Progressives in the West were not unique in their pursuit of these goals, but in areas where Protestants dominated numerically, as on the Plains, they often were successful at passing local and state laws that restricted or prohibited the sale of alcohol.

During the first two decades of the twentieth century, the Prohibition movement gained support, with an increasing number of "dry" candidates winning election to Congress. In January 1919, the nation outlawed the sale, manufacture, and transport of alcohol with the ratification of the Eighteenth Amendment to the U.S. Constitution. Prohibition failed in important ways. It led to organized crime selling alcohol illegally and to "speakeasies," underground bars and night clubs that paid off police and attracted both working-class and well-heeled customers. Indeed, it is hard to imagine the "Jazz Age" of the 1920s having its risqué, avant-garde reputation without Prohibition turning alcohol into "forbidden fruit." Although national Prohibition ultimately failed and was overturned in 1933, after Franklin Roosevelt came to power, the temperance movement and Prohibition did lead to a significant decline in alcohol consumption in the United States and did perhaps reduce some of the violence and health problems associated with alcohol, as both Progressive-Era advocates and later scholars of women's history have argued.

As the case of Prohibition suggests, the radical potential of the Progressive Era gave way to an orderly, reform-minded, managerial movement, with the goal of a more-regulated society. Ultimately, progressivism would serve the interests of the middle class and corporations more than those of down-and-out Americans. Another good example of managerial progressivism is the conservation movement of the early-twentieth-century West, which aimed to manage the vast natural resources of the region wisely, and to use the powers of modern technology to solve its ecological problems—especially the availability of water. Conservative powerbrokers typically resisted such changes, seeing any form of government regulation as an annoying hindrance and a morally illegitimate restraint on the free market. In the long run, however, they benefited from such government activism, which was more effective at promoting the economic welfare of investors than that of ordinary working folk.

Conservation & Preservation

The success of the Los Angeles city fathers in building a 223-mile-long aqueduct and taking water from the Owens Valley—this with the blessing of the federal government—represents the kind of political cronyism that progressive reformers targeted. But the complex engineering feat and the general goal of using modern technology to make the desert bloom and provide water for thirsty cities (sometimes at the expense of the water needs of rural areas) also points toward the goals of the turn-of-the-century "conservation" movement. The basic ideal of the movement was the "wise use" of natural resources in ways that would conserve them and guarantee economic growth for future generations. One such conservation program was the construction of massive dams that could generate electricity, create huge reservoirs for agriculture and cities, and provide beautiful lakes for boating, fishing, and other forms of recreation. National parks and forests also represent this ideal of the wise, multiple use of resources. Parks could provide grazing land for cattle, renewable sources of timber, and glorious scenic wilderness destinations for tourists. Like Prohibition, conservation programs also depended on the power of government. Conservationists argued that only dedicated government officials could protect Western public lands from rapacious businessmen whose only thought was short-term profits, and only federal money and agencies could undertake

Major John Wesley Powell. Powell, on horseback, is talking with a member of a local Paiute community near the Grand Canyon in northern Arizona, in the 1870s. In addition to being a geologist, Powell was an ethnographer who wrote significant studies of Indian peoples in the Southwest. Congress named him the first director of the Bureau of Ethnology in 1879. *SPC BAE 4605 01603507, Smithsonian Institution National Anthropological Archives*

projects such as dam construction that were too big and expensive even for big business and state governments.

An important example of such policies was the Reclamation Act of 1902. In the 1860s and 1870s, scientists on expeditions funded by Congress and the U.S. Army indentified aridity as a major problem to overcome if the West was to continue to develop agriculturally. One of the scientists, Major John Wesley Powell, authored the influential *Report on the Lands of the Arid Region* (1878), arguing that individual homesteaders and private enterprise would not be able to build the massive dams and irrigation projects needed to address the problem of aridity. He advocated cooperative projects. In 1879, Congress established the United States Geological Survey. Part of its mandate was to study the West and help develop policy to promote economic development in it. Congress also funded irrigation surveys. By the turn of the century it had become clear that local projects and even state-funded and corporate efforts did not have the resources necessary for the widespread dam building and water projects needed by cities and agricultural districts in the arid parts of the West. Only the vast resources of the federal government could handle the job. Building on Powell's vision, Nevada representative Francis G. Newlands introduced legislation in Congress to provide federal aid in designing and paying for water projects. The resulting Reclamation Act passed in 1902 with the support of President Roosevelt, who was a progressive and an avid conservationist. The act reflected the growing influence in Congress of Western politicians, but also the concern of American leaders generally that the economy continue to grow nationally, especially at a time when the frontier seemed to be ending and a crucial source of American abundance might be disappearing. The act created a new Bureau of Reclamation (in the Department of the Interior) and empowered the secretary of the interior to withdraw federal land from public sale, designate water projects, contract for them, and manage them. It required users to pay for half the cost of the water these projects delivered them and limited the freedom of users to sell their water rights to others. Its advocates recognized that creating a "hydraulic civilization," in which water was manipulated by dams, reservoirs, and concrete rivers spanning hundreds of miles, was essential to agricultural and urban development of the West.

In the long run, users typically ended up paying one-tenth or less of the cost the water. Taxpayers from all regions of the nation footed

The Buffalo Bill Dam, also known as the Shoshone Dam, was part of the larger Shoshone Project, and was designed for irrigation projects and to generate electricity. *Buffalo Bill Historical Center, Cody, Wyoming; Gift of Russell and Barbara Shefrin, P.21.167*

some of the bill, thus subsidizing agricultural and urban development in the West, but the sales of hydro-electricity generated by dams on western rivers paid the bulk of the cost of delivering water. The intent of the Reclamation Act and similar legislation was to aid family farms, but agribusiness benefited more, as only corporate farms had the resources to build large-scale irrigation systems. Corporate farms often played fast and loose with water rights, using children, kin, and employees to get around regulations that limited the amount of water rights that any one individual or business could legally own. For their part, members of Congress from the West used water projects as "pork barrel" opportunities, bringing jobs, construction contracts, and land booms to their states and districts. Finally, land speculators benefited greatly from the so-called conservation measures, as the value of land shot up from $10 an acre to $200 or more as soon as news of a water project became public.

The first big dams built via the Reclamation Act in the West were the Shoshone Dam in Wyoming (1910) and the Roosevelt Dam near Phoenix, Arizona (1911). The Shoshone Dam, near Buffalo Bill Cody's home in Cody (also known as the Buffalo Bill Dam), is 325 feet high, 200 feet across, and required 82,900 cubic yards of concrete at a cost of $1 million. Projects like these drew engineering talent, and the dams earned praise as technological wonders. But they often ran vastly over estimated costs, and they became increasingly geared to agribusiness and cities, whose leaders had cozy political connections with the Bureau of Reclamation, rather than to small farmers and other people with no such connections. By the 1920s, embarrassment at this fact and penny-pinching instincts led presidents such as Herbert Hoover to scale back dam projects. Only the employment needs of the Great Depression and the industrial needs of World War II would turn the financial spigots of the federal government back on and revive the dam-building spirit (see Chapter Twelve).

Like dams, national parks served an economic purpose, though they also appealed to a wider variety of moral and sentimental values. The idea of national parks goes back to the 1830s, when George Catlin, the artist famous for his paintings of Western American Indians, first proposed creating one. He feared that westward expansion was destroying the Indian way of life, so he advocated creating "a nation's park, containing man and beast, in all wildness and freshness of their nature's beauty!" In 1864, Congress set aside the first national public lands, in the Yosemite Grant, which preserved the land for public use. President Ulysses S. Grant signed the act of Congress that created the first national park—Yellowstone, in parts of Wyoming, Idaho, and Montana—in 1872. The idea behind the creation of national parks and national forests and monuments (the last created using presidential powers, not by Congress) was the Romantic belief that the spectacular natural wonders of the United States, especially those in the West, provided the American people with their great monuments, rather than the age-old, man-made cathedrals, artworks, and other cultural trappings of Europe, which a young America could not hope to imitate. The desire for such monuments, for "wild" and "natural" spaces, also grew out of a fear that an increasingly urban, industrial America was losing the very wilderness frontier that had defined its greatness and uniqueness. Parks like Yellowstone and Yosemite were America's heritage—some of the gigantic sequoias of California had been living for 2,000 years, as old as the ruins of ancient Rome.

Congress created Yellowstone in 1872, turned Yosemite into a national park in 1890, and in the years that followed presidents and Con-

Mammoth Hotel, Yellowstone National Park, 1886. The Wakefield stage line's stagecoach "Bighorn," which was held up and robbed by William James and Charlie Higgenbotham in July 1887, is shown in front of the Mammoth Hotel. *Buffalo Bill Historical Center, Cody, Wyoming; P.21.39*

gress steadily created more national parks and monuments, under Teddy Roosevelt especially. States and cities also began setting aside parklands during this era. In 1916, Congress went further, creating the National Park Service (NPS) to manage the parks, monuments, and other natural and historical properties. It gave the NPS a mandate "to conserve the scenery and the natural and historic objects and the wild life therein and to provide for the enjoyment of the same in such manner and by such means as will leave them unimpaired for the enjoyment of future generations." Though the general public supported these projects, local officials, hunters, ranchers, developers, and some remaining American Indian groups (still tied to fishing and hunting in the West) sometimes opposed the creation or the boundaries of specific parks. For example, in the 1920s John D. Rockefeller purchased more than 30,000 acres near Jackson Hole, Wyoming, and persuaded President Calvin Coolidge to add four times more acreage to that holding and create Grand Teton National Park. Congress created the park in 1928, but because of local opposition the NPS refused to accept the land from Rockefeller. President Franklin D. Roosevelt created the Jackson Hole National Monument in 1943, after a frustrated

Rockefeller threatened to sell his land. But local opponents continued to prevent the government from accepting Rockefeller's land. They also tried to get Congress to abolish the monument, claiming that its creation interfered with states' rights and was against the interests of local economic development. In 1949, the opposing parties reached a compromise, and the Rockefeller land was incorporated into the monument. A year later, in 1950, Congress made most of the monument part of the Grand Teton National Park, but it also passed an act that limited the powers of future presidents to create national monuments in Wyoming.

At the same time that the federal government was creating the NPS under the Department of the Interior, it also was organizing the National Forest Service (NFS) under the Department of Agriculture (USDA). Congress passed and President Benjamin Harrison signed the Forest Reserve Act in 1891. The mandate of national forests, and that of the national grasslands, was one of multiple use. The national forests eventually were divided up into "ranger districts," with forest rangers charged with maintaining trails and roads, running campgrounds, regulating grazing, logging, and mining by private individuals or companies in the forests, and protecting fish and game. Predictably, the Forest Service's work has always been controversial. Various interest groups, both locally and nationally, have fought to influence NFS regulations and decisions in their favor.

The work of Gifford Pinchot exemplifies the tensions built into the mandate of the NFS. In 1896, President Grover Cleveland appointed Pinchot to the National Forest Commission, a special commission with a mandate to report on public timberlands in the West. In 1898, he became the head of the Division of Forestry, the precursor of the NFS. It was Pinchot, a progressive who had a strong faith in technocratic efficiency, who popularized the term *conservation.* He was a master of both bureaucratic procedure and publicity campaigns. Early on, he worked with the famous writer and naturalist John Muir to sell the idea of national parks and forests to Congress and the public. Muir, who helped found the Sierra Club in 1892 and served as its first president, had originally proposed the creation of Yosemite National Park. But Muir and the Sierra Club parted company with Pinchot in 1897, when Pinchot came out in support of sheep grazing in national forests. Muir saw public lands as a wilderness heritage to be staunchly defended and preserved, and he feared that so-called conservation policies would sacrifice wilderness in the name of economic development.

The potential for controversy between advocates of *conservation* and advocates of *preservation* became reality with the damming of the Hetch Hetchy Valley, some 190 miles west of San Francisco, inside the borders of Yosemite National park. San Francisco, still recovering from the earthquake and fires of 1906, saw the valley's high canyon walls as an ideal site for a dam and reservoir to meet the water demands of its growing population. Damming the valley would provide water for the entire Bay Area and offer boating, swimming, and fishing in the reservoir. Dam supporters argued that land had little value as a wilderness and claimed that it would provide an economic boon for future generations and be more beautiful if turned into a lake by building the dam. Preservationists like Muir wanted to keep the valley as a pristine wilderness area. They flatly opposed the damming of the valley and morally objected to viewing nature as an economic commodity. It was holy ground and valuable in and of itself. Muir, the Sierra Club, the Audubon Society, and preservationists across the nation rejected the logic of the conservationists, saying: "Dam Hetch Hetchy! As well dam for water-tanks the people's cathedrals and churches, for no holier temple has ever been consecrated by the heart of man." The federal government issued a permit for the construction of the dam in 1908, but Congress blocked the permit a year later, after a letter-writing campaign led by Muir and the Sierra Club. Finally, in 1913, after extensive debate over the merits of scenery versus economic development, Congress and the progressive Democratic president Woodrow Wilson approved the dam, passing the Raker Act, which "decommissioned" part of Yosemite. Dam supporters like Wilson decided that the dam offered the most practical source of water for San Francisco and hoped to protect the valley and the park from further private development. The O'Shaughnessy Dam (the official name of the dam on the Hetch Hetchy) took two decades to build and cost $100 million, twice the original estimate. The debate over the dam had been a national one, with a much of the opposition coming from the East. Some observers wondered why Easterners had been so concerned to preserve a Western valley.

The ideal of preservation and the steadily growing interest in wilderness tourism tells us something about the needs of an increasingly urban America. In the East, where the economy was mature, most of the land

President Theodore
Roosevelt and John Muir
at Glacier Point, Yosemite
Valley, California, 1906.
*Library of Congress, LC-
USZ62-107389 DLC*

was settled or developed and the scarcity of open land, or "nature," was obvious. In this context, preservation had a strong appeal. Wilderness itself was the scarce resource, and idealist visions of wildness spoke to people living settled, urban lives. In the West, where economic development was newer and more limited, conservation and laissez-faire ideals regarding land use spoke to people's needs. In general, the Hetch Hetchy debate was significant for having occurred at all. A century earlier, proposals to dam a river would not have incurred any opposition or public protest. Traditional American values about undeveloped wilderness space had been neither to preserve nor conserve, but to exploit in the name of civilization, progress, prosperity, and religious calling. By 1900, a more "developed" America, one that was "over-civilized" and wasteful its critics said, was noticing the costs of industrial progress. Conflicts over preservation and development, and between local Westerners and national institutions and sentiments, would recur again and again in the second half of the twentieth century. Eventually, however, the urban and suburban majority in the West would become sympathetic to the preservationist impulse.

As the examples of the Los Angeles Aqueduct, Reclamation Act, and Hetch Hetchy dam suggest, conservation was both progressive and conservative. It was progressive in regulating economic development and using the power of government to conserve resources, protect the nation's wilderness heritage, and promote expensive infrastructure development. And it was conservative in promoting the power and interests of middle-class managers and corporate economic development. Conservation practices also left important conflicts to be decided in the future. To whom did the public land of the West ultimately belong? To local people in the region (especially entrepreneurs), to the nation as a whole, or to the federal government? Resources such as water, national parks, and the animals that live in them often crossed state and even international borders. What was the relationship between state, federal, and international agencies, in the United States, Canada, and Mexico? These questions point to the power of the federal government in the West. That power would expand during World War I, and even more during the Great Depression and World War II. These issues also serve as a good reminder that one cannot separate the history of the American West from that of the larger nation or wider world.

World War I

America's New World mythology implied that the nation's ties to the Old World had become increasingly thin over time, but World War I revealed just how closely the United States remained tied to Europe, both economically and in sentiment. Some Americans with German or Central European roots were sympathetic to Germany and its allies, while Anglo-Americans typically supported Great Britain and its allies. After the United States entered the war in 1917, many native-born Americans feared that recent immigrants from Germany and Central Europe might not remain loyal to their new nation and its ideals and end up actively supporting Germany in its aggression and militarism. Western American men served in the military in significant numbers, of course. But the most obvious effect of the war was on the economy and politics of the West, which revealed once again the influence of national and global forces on the region.

That said, America's entry into the war was peculiarly regional. In 1911, Mexican rebels ousted from power the Mexican dictator Porfirio Díaz, setting off a long and brutal civil war. The revolution and fighting eventually spilled over into the American Southwest. In 1914, the United States first intervened in the revolution, when President Wilson sent in troops to take control of the Mexican port city of Veracruz and prevent a German ship from violating an American embargo against importing armaments into Mexico. In January 1916, "Pancho" Villa, a populist general in Northern Mexico, attacked the town of Columbus, New Mexico, in response to American support for the conservative Mexican government of President Venustiano Carranza Garza (which included allowing Carranza to use American trains to transport his troops). In March, President Wilson sent U.S. Army general John Pershing into Mexico to capture Villa. The Mexican government demanded that the United States withdraw its troops from its soil, but Wilson did so only after letting the army chase Villa for almost a year. Despite the American use of airplanes in combat for the first time, the Mexican Expedition failed to catch Villa and returned to the United States in February 1917. Meanwhile, the interception of the "Zimmerman telegram" by the British government in January 1917 exposed German promises of support for a Mexican invasion of the American Southwest, to reclaim land lost in the Mexican-American War of the 1840s, should the United States enter World War I against Germany. The uncovering of the telegram, along with Germany's unrestricted submarine attacks on American shipping in the North Atlantic, led Wilson to declare war on Germany in 1917. For a time, it looked like the United States might go to war with both Germany and Mexico. But Wilson went no further than sending troops to watch the Mexican-American border in the Southwest.

Even before the United States declared war on Germany, however, the fighting in Europe provided an economic boon to the nation in general and the West in particular. Europe's wartime food needs increased demands for wheat and corn grown on the Plains, prolonging the general prosperity of the early twentieth century, when 1 million people applied for quarter-section family farms. For a measure of this homesteading "Indian Summer," compare the 1 million new farms from 1900 to 1913 to the 1.4 million from 1862 to 1899. This era also saw the increasing mechanization of High Plains wheat farming, with tractors, and the risky debt that came with it. When the wheat boom ended with the close of World War I in 1918, and was followed by a new cycle of drought, many Western farmers succumbed to indebtedness and lost their land to foreclosure. Enticed by the wartime boom and shameless bonanza advertising, which promised easy money on ecologically marginal land, many farmers had gambled on risky markets and the arid environment and lost. The end of World War I thus foreshadowed the end of the homesteading era, which would close decisively during the 1930s. Wartime demands also meant a boom for Western oil and mining products (aided in some instances by government subsidies) as well as in lumbering, smelters, food processing, and canneries. It also meant the expansion of existing military bases and the building of new ones, along with highly lucrative government contracts for shipyards and airplane manufacturers on the West Coast. Even Hollywood got into the action. Studios feared that the powerful War Industries Board would restrict the film industry by rationing chemicals used to make and process film and setting them aside for the manufacture of explosives and weapons. But the studios convinced the federal government that they could play a key role in the propaganda effort by churning out patriotic films that would build support at home and abroad for the American and allied war effort against the German enemy. The financial and political success of these wartime films, coupled with the postwar Red Scare, proved that patriotic films were good for both wartime governments and the increasingly vibrant film industry. If World War I did not dramatically transform the economy of the American West, as World War II would do, it nonetheless was good for business.

World War I also had a significant impact on the social evolution of the West. Wartime circumstances cut off immigration from Europe to major cities in the East and West, homesteads on the Plains, mining towns, and logging camps in the Mountain West. The sudden end to mass immigration resulted from millions of European men volunteering for or being conscripted into their nations' armies, and the dangers of crossing the Atlantic while German submarine "wolf-packs" waged warfare on military and civilian ships alike. But this change in the inflow of immigrants also was a consequence of U.S. immigration policy, fueled by a growing hostility towards immigrants by anti-German, native-born Americans. To be sure, some German immigrants did support Germany and its allies and oppose U.S. entry into the war on behalf of Great Britain, France, and their allies (as did many Irish Americans). While most immigrant Germans and German American citizens posed no actual threat to the war effort, their communities endured threats, intimidation, and actual violence by government officials, citizens groups, and vigilantes, who sometimes forced them to buy war bonds, barred them from joining organizations such as the Red Cross, banned the use of foreign languages in public places (in Nebraska), and even assaulted them. Some German families, such as that of the future president Dwight D. Eisenhower, changed their names to make the spelling seem more American. The xenophobic atmosphere also spilled over onto other immigrant groups, for example, in the burning of several Dutch Reformed churches in Iowa (the angry vigilantes having mistaken them for German-Lutheran ones). In the Red Scare that followed the war, fears of ethnic disloyalty turned into unfounded, even hysterical, fears of political subversion by immigrant radicals and led to new legislation that would severely restrict immigration to the United States from both Europe and Asia.

Beginning in 1917, hundreds of thousands of men volunteered for the American Expeditionary Force (Army) and other branches of the armed services. Eventually, the federal government conscripted about 4 million more men, sending tens of thousands a day across the Atlantic in 1918 (ultimately over 2 million that year). About 1.5 million soldiers from Western states served during World War I, about one-third of the total.

The practical consequences of this situation for laborers in the West were twofold: the resulting scarcity of laborers meant new opportunities for workers and unions to demand and win higher wages and better working conditions; on the downside, chauvinistic patriotism and wartime restrictions on free speech and other politics rights were devastating for radical political organizations. The high wartime profits of business owners led workers to demand better wages, so much so that the conservative American Federation of Labor (AFL) joined with the radical IWW in organizing strikes in the timber industries of the Northwest in 1917. Political pressure led the AFL to abandon the strike, but the IWW continued to support the strikers and oppose the war. Federal officials responded by raiding IWW offices, then arresting and quickly trying IWW leaders under the Espionage Act of 1917, which forbade interfering with the operation or success of the American armed forces. For their part, the striking workers engaged in sabotage and all but shut down the timber industry. Eventually, the federal government sent in 25,000 U.S. soldiers to suppress the strike and cut the timber, though it also mandated an eight-hour workday and better working conditions. These actions, plus vigilante violence against the IWW and the strikers, cut the legs from under the IWW.

In addition, both federal and state governments, with powers created in the Sedition Act of 1918 and with the support of the Supreme Court, restricted freedom of assembly and speech rights for socialists, pacifists, and other opponents of the war.

Restrictions on civil liberties and campaigns against radicals continued when a combination of events sparked a postwar Red Scare in the United States. These included the Communist Revolution in Russia late in 1917, fear about the economic chaos that might follow demobilization in 1918– 19, recent memories of labor violence and the surge in radical political groups in the 1910s, and a wave of strikes in 1918 and 1919, notably a citywide strike in Seattle. The federal government and the American public writ large would no longer tolerate militant labor unions and radical political parties, viewing them with heightened suspicion and antipathy.

The Seattle General Strike started on February 6, 1919, as workers in all sectors of the city's economy walked off the job. They formed a General Strike Committee, which functioned as a city government. The only economic activity it allowed was the delivery of food and other basic necessities needed by residents to live. The city hired 600 police, added 2,400 "special deputies" to the force, and got the support of almost 1,000 federal soldiers and sailors, at the request of the state attorney general of Washington. The threat of violence at the hands of police and the military, and pressure from moderate labor unions such as the AFL, led the General Strike Committee to end the strike on February 11. Although it had lasted only a week, the strike had led to a national panic. Congress passed legislation to close the doors to immigration tightly, to keep out foreign radicals. The General Intelligence Division of the Justice Department rounded up "radicals" already in the nation. This initiative was led by a young J. Edgar Hoover, future director of the FBI and a notorious anti-communist who hounded persons he deemed radical for much of the twentieth century. The federal government deported some of the radicals and jailed others, while some, such as Big Bill Haywood, the leader of the IWW, fled to the Soviet Union. This era also saw the creation of the Bureau of Investigation, which later became the FBI.

The result of all the postwar measures was the destruction of the small but vibrant movement of left-wing labor unions and political parties that had been active in the American West in the 1910s. The economic boom of the mid-1920s would confirm the wisdom of this destruction in the eyes of most Americans, even if this new wave of "good times" largely bypassed most farmers and industrial laborers. But this result had not been inevitable. In Western Canada in May–June 1919, the Winnipeg General Strike lasted several weeks and ended only when the military and Northwest Mounted Police (today the Royal Canadian Mounted Police) intervened. While the failed strike led to the decline of labor unions in the region, left-wing political movements continued to exist well thereafter. In 1921, one of the strike's leaders, J. S. Woodsworth, was among the first radicals elected to the House of Commons in Canada, as a member of the Independent Labor Party. He later helped found the Cooperative Commonwealth Federation, a democratic socialist party with roots in the Western Canadian labor and populist movements.

The West and Empire

By 1920, then, the American West was becoming more mature and complex economically, culturally, and politically. As a result, its role as a region of the United States was evolving too. It no longer could be described as a "colony" of the larger nation but neither did it lie at the metropolitan center of the rising American empire. The West's grow-ing economic clout and its growing population signaled its potential influence on the nation, but national and global trends continued to exercise a defining influence on it. Somewhere between a "periphery" and a "metropolitan" heartland, the American West might at the time be compared to the place of "dominions" such as Canada in the British Empire, rather than to a true colony like India. The West was defined by the culture and institutions of the "Old World" (the Eastern United States) but also had been shaped in unique ways by its distinct environ-ment, ethnic and racial diversity, and historical experience. It was all but equal in status to the "mother country," but not yet recognized or treated as such, or powerful enough to dictate the terms of the relation-ship. Westerners sometimes were resentful of these facts, and yet they were optimistic that the twentieth century would belong to them. Early in the twentieth century, as the historian Richard White has argued, the West became a "proving ground" for the powers of the federal govern-ment. The most obvious examples of federal experiments in this period were dam building and the creation of the national parks and forests.

American soldiers during the Philippine Insurrection, 1899. *Library of Congress, LC-USZ61-957*

Insurgent dead, just as they fell in a trench near Santa Ana, Philippines, February 5, 1899. The trench was circular and the image shows only a small portion of the dead. *Courtesy, National Archives, ARC Identifier 524389*

Developments like these, along with the wartime experiments of the War Industries Board, would continue on a larger scale in the 1930s and 1940s, with the onset of the Great Depression and World War II. The result would be the economic and political transformation of the West into an American heartland and a center of metropolitan power in its own right. For the moment, though, in the 1920s, Westerners might well resent the power that the center continued to have over the region, as well as feel frustrated with their inability to direct the course of the nation.

That said, for American Indians especially but also for African, Asian, and Mexican Americans, the mainstream, white-dominated West still seemed like an empire, with them at its periphery. For American Indians, not much had changed in the first two decades of the twentieth century in terms of government policies, the assimilationist pressures of churches, residential schools, and other cultural institutions, or basic social and economic patterns and problems on reservations. Occasional violence between Indians who challenged reservation boundaries and local officials who tried to contain them led to the deaths of Indians and reminded people on both sides of the Indian Wars and the fact of conquest. And yet, the emergence of a community of Indian entertainment and sports figures, college-educated professionals and intellectuals—clergy, writers, doctors, and lawyers—signaled the evolution of Indians as both Natives and Americans. In 1911, for example, a group of Indian professionals formed the Society of American Indians (SAI). The SAI declined in the 1920s, but its mere existence indicated that from now on white reformers and government officials would have a harder time ignoring Indian voices.

In short, Indians began to show up in "unexpected places" in the 1910s, doing things that challenged the common white assumption that Indians by nature did not fit modern American culture and could not adapt to it. For example, Vine Deloria, Sr., an Oglala Lakota Sioux, was a heroic football player at St. Stephens College in New York in the 1920s (now Bard College) and later an Episcopal clergyman who served parishes in South Dakota and directed the Episcopal Church's Indian missions program from New York City. In Hollywood in the 1910s, Princess Red Wing and James Young Deer starred in and produced films for Bison, a subsidiary of the New York Motion Picture Company. Their films chal-

"A famous photograph of Geronimo in a Cadillac," 1904 or 1905. Geronimo is at the wheel of an automobile, probably a Locomobile Model C, with three other men. The photo was taken near Oklahoma City at the 101 Ranch, founded by Colonel George W. Miller in 1893. The ranch put on Wild West shows and loaned workers and equipment to the Bison 101 Film Company. Buffalo Bill Cody's show combined with the 101 show in 1916. The ranch, now an Oklahoma Historical Site, failed during the Great Depression and was sold off in parcels. *Courtesy, National Archives, Department of the Interior, Office of Indian Affairs, ARC Identifier 518935*

lenged notions of natural white dominance, and in romances and failed romances explored relationships that defied the boundaries between white and Indian characters. Indian actors and their countercultural films did not long retain the place they held in the early years of the film industry, but their very existence in the 1910s showed that Indians could become modern, and on their own terms. Those facts, along with the end of Indian population decline and the beginning of a demographic renaissance, foreshadowed the resurgence of Indian politics and autonomy in the second half of the twentieth century.

The ongoing story of American empire could be seen most clearly in the Philippines in the early 1900s. Between 1899 and 1902, the United States fought a vicious guerilla war there against nationalist rebels, with more than 4,000 American soldiers and 15,000 Filipino rebels killed, and 200,000 Filipino civilians dying, most of them from a cholera epidemic and starvation; nonetheless, thousands of civilians, including women and children, were slaughtered by American soldiers in retaliation for guerilla attacks on American units. This was, perhaps, the Plains Indian Wars taken overseas. Indeed, some of the American troops in the Philippines had served in the American West and they typically viewed Filipinos as savages akin to the Indians, using the racist epithet *gook* to describe them—a term that Americans soldiers would use again in Vietnam in the 1960s. Sporadic fighting in the Philippines continued for a few years after 1902, as the United States pacified and took control of its new gateway to China and then began to consider how to exercise what the poet Rudyard Kipling called the "white man's burden," a task of bringing civilization to people it deemed benighted.

These examples of conquest and their complex legacies must be kept in mind because it is easy to forget people at the margins of society in a chapter that is focused on the social and economic evolution of the West as a whole. The West as a whole was becoming more "mature" and less of a "colony," in part because mainstream whites had successfully pushed nonwhites (along with economically marginal whites and political radicals) to the margins. But if the history of the region is a story of success and triumph for some, it is one of tragedy, irony, and ambiguity for others.

A famous photograph of the Apache leader Geronimo in a "Cadillac" exemplifies these complexities. Its strangeness and seeming comic quality is a reminder of how marginal the status was of even so famous an Indian in 1904, when the picture was taken. The automobile was a symbol of American progress and freedom, especially in cities like Los Angeles and in the vast spaces of the West. It represented progress for Geronimo, too. He was a legendary man, having fought against whites tenaciously in the Southwest and then traveled the nation and the world in Wild West shows and educational expos. Geronimo had opportunities most whites did not at the time, and he owned a fancy car that was the envy of most Americans, whites included. Someday an ordinary American might afford a car. In 1904, however, the automobile was still a toy that only a few men with money could enjoy. Even more for Geronimo, perhaps—as a man whose people suffered confinement on reservations that whites did not know—the car symbolized power and autonomy. So the photograph is strange, yes, but not so funny, and it is telling.

෬ Suggested Readings ෨

Deloria, Philip. *Indians in Unexpected Places.* Lawrence: University Press of Kansas, 2004.

Derickson, Alan. *Workers' Health, Workers' Democracy: The Western Miners' Struggle, 1891–1925.* Ithaca, NY: Cornell University Press, 1988.

Deverell, William, and Greg Hise, eds. *Land of Sunshine: An Environmental History of Metropolitan Los Angeles.* Pittsburgh: University of Pittsburgh Press, 2006.

Deverell, William, and Tom Sitton, eds. *California Progressivism Revisited.* Berkeley: University of California Press, 1994.

Fradkin, Philip L. *The Great Earthquake and Firestorms of 1906: How San Francisco Nearly Destroyed Itself.* Berkeley: University of California Press, 2005.

Hoxie, Frederick E. *A Final Promise: The Campaign to Assimilate the Indians, 1880–1920.* Lincoln: University of Nebraska Press, 1984.

Jameson, Elizabeth. *All That Glitters: Class, Conflict, and Community in Cripple Creek.* Urbana and Chicago: University of Illinois Press, 1998.

Krainz, Thomas A. *Delivering Aid: Implementing Progressive Era Welfare in the American West.* Albuquerque: University of New Mexico Press, 2005.

Lukas, J. Anthony. *Big Trouble: A Murder in a Small Western Town Sets off a Struggle for the Soul of America.* New York: Simon & Schuster, 1998.

McGerr, Michael. *A Fierce Discontent: The Rise and Fall of the Progressive Movement in America, 1870–1920.* New York: Free Press, 2003.

Nash, Roderick. *Wilderness and the American Mind,* Fourth Edition. New Haven: Yale University Press, 2001.

Sellers, Richard West. *Preserving Nature in the National Parks: A History.* New Haven: Yale University Press, 1997.

Silbey, David J. *A War of Frontier and Empire: The Philippine-American War, 1899–1902.* New York: Hill & Wang, 2007.

Smith, Andrew Brodie. *Shooting Cowboys and Indians: Silent Western Films, American Culture, and the Birth of Hollywood.* Boulder: University Press of Colorado, 2003.

Starr, Kevin. *Inventing the Dream: California through the Progressive Era.* New York: Oxford University Press, 1985.

Nuys, Frank Van. *Americanizing the West: Race, Immigrants, and Citizenship, 1890–1930.* Lawrence: University Press of Kansas, 2002.

Watts, Sarah. *Rough Rider in the White House: Theodore Roosevelt and the Politics of Desire.* Chicago: University of Chicago Press, 2003.

Worster, Donald. *A Passion for Nature: The Life of John Muir.* New York: Oxford University Press, 2008.

Worster, Donald. *Rivers of Empire: Water, Aridity, and the Growth of the American West.* New York: Oxford University Press, 1992.

CHAPTER ELEVEN

From Boom to Bust

In most United States history texts the 1920s herald the onset of "modern times." The phrase points to technologies and lifestyles that would define the twentieth century—movies, radio, cars, airplanes, air conditioning, sexual freedom, and new forms of popular music such as jazz. It also points to conflicts between people who embraced individualism and the emerging consumer culture and those who resisted many aspects of the new lifestyles, such as fundamentalists, regionalists, prohibitionists, and the KKK. But in many histories of the American West, the 1920s fall through the cracks. Sandwiched between the dramas of the Progressive Era and the Great Depression, the 1920s seem to have no distinguishing features. The stories of two people in particular speak to the very real ways in which the decade redefined and reshaped the American West: Benjamin Franklin McCardle and Aimee Semple McPherson.

McCardle was not a famous man. Born in Virginia in 1862, he arrived in the Dakota Territory in 1888. Two years late he married Mary Alguire, (also born in 1862), who had been raised by a foster family in New York State and the Dakota Territory. In 1892, McCardle made a timber-culture homesteading claim, which meant that he could get an additional 160 acres if he planted 40 acres of trees on his land. Over the years McCardle purchased animals and machinery, often struggling to pay off the loans he had been forced to take out. Nonetheless, he also enjoyed occasional windfall years in which good crops and high prices in agricultural commodities markets made him good money. By 1920, the values of McCardle's property holdings totaled $30,000–$40,000. Soon thereafter the cattle and wheat markets began to bottom out and unpaid taxes and debts began to catch up with him. In 1923 he began to sign his land over to his children, including his daughter Mary and son-in-law Clyde Fite. This land was no gift, as it came with mortgages and unpaid interest. Like many farmers on the Plains, the Fites and McCardles lost their land in the 1930s, as government officials foreclosed on unpaid loans and taxes, a process that went on until 1942. Their story symbolizes the end of the farm frontier and the decline of the family farm, for hundreds of thousands of Western farmers lost their land in the 1920s and 1930s. But their story is not one of failure, or not wholly so. True, the McCardles had endured hard work, unpredictable weather, and fluctuating markets, but during their decades as farmers they also had enjoyed a decent standard of living and the freedom to live life as they wanted. They had paid taxes that helped build roads and schools, had helped to build communities and social institutions in South Dakota, and had raised three children, all of whom went on to better lives. Their grandson, Gilbert Fite, would become a prominent historian of agriculture and the American West.

In stark contrast to McCardle, McPherson was perhaps the most famous woman in America in the 1920s. Born in rural southern Ontario, Canada, in 1890, young Aimee Kennedy married Robert Semple, an American revival preacher, in 1908 and accompanied him as a missionary in China, where he died. In 1911 Aimee returned to the United States, married Harold McPherson, left him, and became a revival preacher in her own right. She toured the East Coast, spreading the gospel of salvation, and then crisscrossed the West. In 1923, she settled down in Los Angeles, where she built her famous Angelus Temple, the site of highly theatrical religious meetings—she famously used a police motorcycle as a prop on stage—and became one of the nation's first great radio preachers. In 1926 McPherson disappeared, reappearing weeks later claiming she had been kidnapped. Reporters soon began spreading stories that "Sister Aimee" had been having an affair. The scandal nearly ruined her, but when she died in 1944 from an overdose of sleeping pills, she was exploring the new medium of television. "Sister Aimee" represents the many migrants who came to the West from other parts of North America and the world to seek their fortune. She also represents 1920s-era Hollywood celebrity and notoriety at its finest and—at the same time—the many pockets of conservatism that would end up shaping religion and politics in the West for the rest of the twentieth century.

As these stories reveal, the "Old West" collided with the "modern West" in the 1920s, an era that may seem like the least distinct in the history of the region but perhaps is the most telling. The 1920s was a dynamic era of farm foreclosures, Hollywood glamour, and a growing tourist industry. The West was moving toward a postindustrial economy without having become fully industrialized—the economy was developed, in that it was becoming more diverse, but one that remained heavily dependent on the East, with its industrial economy and much larger and wealthier financial institutions. It also was a time when writers and artists began to define regional cultures in the West, and when maturing communities and subregions came into their own as communities. Finally, if the growing American Indian, Mexican, Asian, and African American communities in

Aimee Semple McPherson with delegates to the nineteenth annual Four Square Gospel Church Convention, early 1940s. Some participants have fainted during the spiritual ecstasy of prayer. *Los Angeles Examiner* photo. *Courtesy of The Bancroft Library, University of California, Berkeley*

the region continued to find themselves pushed to the margins of society in these years, it was also during this time that they began to find their voices and develop the means to resist their second-class citizenship.

Speculation

The post–World War I Red Scare, which severely undermined the labor union movement in the West, had been based in part on fear of political subversion, but it also reflected widespread apprehension about the post-war economy. Would the transition from wartime to peacetime lead to falling production and prices and large-scale unemployment, as millions of soldiers returned home from Europe to farms or looking for work? Or would things go back to normal? For people living in the Mountain West or on the Plains, who were dependent on timber, agriculture, ranching, mining, and oil for their livelihood, the 1920s spun them through cycles of boom and bust. These sectors of the economy began to transform themselves, with machinery replacing animal and human power (putting unskilled laborers out of work) and "agribusinesses" replacing family farms and ranches. For Californians, the 1920s generally proved to be a time of prosperity. Finally, some parts of the West began to take advantage of the new tourist industry, as the ever more pervasive automobile made it easier for wealthy and even some middle-class Americans to visit national parks and pursue new forms of recreation like skiing.

One can clearly see the boom-and-bust cycle and frenzied economic speculation of the 1920s by looking at the oil industry. In 1900, companies operating in Ohio, West Virginia, and Pennsylvania dominated the oil industry. By 1911, the West produced 72 percent of American oil, most of it coming from California, Oklahoma, Louisiana, and Texas. Much of this newfound oil was high in gasoline content and ideal for the automotive industries that took off in the 1910s and 1920s. The shift of American oil production to the West led to a decline in the market dominance of the Standard Oil Trust, as the old company could no longer expect to buy up and exploit all of the many new oilfields being discovered in the West. Nonetheless, Standard Oil was quick to get a share of the action in California, where it purchased the Pacific Coast Oil Company, renamed it the Standard Oil Company, and soon acted

Oil well drilling rigs on Signal Hill in Los Angeles County, 1923. *Library of Congress, Call Number: PAN US GEOG - California no. 1 (F size) [P&P]*

as a major player in the state. Competitors emerged along the Texas Gulf Coast, such as Texaco, Gulf Oil, and Sun Oil. The quasi-colonial character of the Western economy continued with the new oil boom, as the skilled laborers and the moneyed families that dominated it—the Mellons, Pews, Gates, and Laphams—initially came from the East and Midwest, as in the case of the Rockefellers of Standard Oil. In the 1910s, Royal Dutch Shell, Standard Oil's biggest global competitor, also began to invest in California fields.

The oil boom was a boon for big business, but it also fueled unregulated speculation among small-time investors and con artists. A good example is that of C. C. Julian, a Canadian who had been a land speculator in Western Canada and had worked in the oil industry. In 1922 Julian borrowed money and began purchasing land and drilling in parts of Los Angeles already subdivided into lots for housing. He was highly talented when it came to exploiting the greed and anxiety of small-time investors. He sold them "common law trusts" as an alternative to conventional oil stocks, using newspaper ads that told folksy stories and played on people's fears of big business and monopolies. Julian admitted to his "investors"—"suckers" was more like it—that his venture was risky, but he sold himself as an honest man and got hundreds of people, rich and poor, to invest in his schemes. When one of his wells started gushing oil, he incorporated the Julian Petroleum Company and began selling stock in it at $50 a share.

Julian began to run into trouble when Edward "Mike" Daugherty, the state's Corporation Commissioner, began investigating him, shutting down the company and indicting him. (He was never convicted.) Julian posted bail and through some financial wrangling was able to turn his company over to a Texas businessman named S. C. Lewis. Julian continued to present himself as a champion of the underdog against big business executives and government bureaucrats. He later started a mining scheme in Death Valley, even luring the famous director Cecil B. DeMille into putting money into the company. Meanwhile, Lewis kept Julian Petroleum going by creating "investment pools" that collected millions of dollars from prominent Southern California bankers and movie moguls such as Louis B. Mayer. Eventually, under pressure from both banks and state regulators, the bubble of investments collapsed. Julian Petroleum fell apart when the Los Angeles Stock Exchange shut down trading on the company in May 1927. The debacle sullied the reputations of some local businessmen, ruined many small investors and a few local financial institutions, and it led to the murders of a banker, a gangster, and a newspaper editor. Some local politicians, and Lewis, briefly went to jail. All told, the fraud had exceeded $150 million.

Before his schemes caught up with him, Julian had been the toast of LA. He was famous for his fancy cars and flashy clothes, the bejeweled women on his arms, and a knock-down fight with the actor Charlie Chaplin at a nightclub (won handily by Chaplin). The fantastic promise of his schemes and his luxurious, Jazz-Age lifestyle proved too much even for wary politicians and otherwise cautious businessmen. Like the gold rush of the 1850s and the dotcom frenzy of the 1990s, the oil boom of the 1920s in California inspired greed and corruption on a grand scale, cloaked in the name of progress. In 1934 in his final act, hiding from investigators seeking to extradite him and indict him for mail fraud, Julian committed suicide in a Shanghai hotel.

Alongside the oil boom and its associated scandals, the California economy grew steadily during the 1920s. New technology in irrigation turned the otherwise dry Central Valley into one of the leading fruit- and vegetable-producing regions in the nation. Manufacturing increased steadily. And the entertainment and film industries in Hollywood came into their own, especially with the emergence of "talkies" (films with sound). Not surprisingly, the population of the Golden State almost doubled in the 1920s, reaching nearly 6 six million by 1930.

Western Culture

The logic of capitalism leads ever toward accumulation, as individual entrepreneurs give way to corporate investors and big businesses, which in turn get subsumed by even bigger businesses. This was as true of the film industry as it had been of gold mining sixty years before it. Film-making began to evolve in the 1910s, as actors, directors, and producers pooled their resources in conglomerates such as United Artists—formed in 1919 by Mary Pickford, Charlie Chaplin, D. W. Griffith, Douglas Fairbanks, and their lawyer, William Gibbs McAdoo. New technology also contributed to the transformation of the film industry, the most significant innovation coming in 1927 with the opening of *The Jazz Singer*, the first feature-length film to include sound. "Talkies" initially gave a boost to Warner Brothers, the first studio to feature them, but in 1928 and 1929 all of the major studios abandoned silent films and shifted to sound. The advent of talkies also ended the careers of silent film stars like Pickford and Fairbanks, whose voices and acting styles did not suit the new medium. Crucially, this new technology most benefited the major studios, which could afford the costs that came with implementing the new sound technology.

By 1929, two years into the sound era, the film industry was big business, employing more than 100,000 people, dominated by major studios such as Paramount, and making more money than the gold-seeking "forty-niners" had ever dreamed possible. The new "studio system" integrated the film industry "vertically," meaning from the top down, as the major studios signed actors, directors, and other creative personnel to long-term, exclusive contracts and owned their own distribution companies and theater chains, or controlled theaters through manipulative film-booking practices. Despite the Great Depression that began in late 1929—or perhaps because of it, with so many people unemployed and in need of an inexpensive diversion, a break from the hard times they were living—the 1930s and 1940s were the Golden Age of Hollywood films. Whatever the cost to individual artists and experimental films, the studio system provided stability and industry-wide integration until the late 1940s and 1950s. At that time, the movie industry faced tough new competition for people's attention from the new medium of television. A

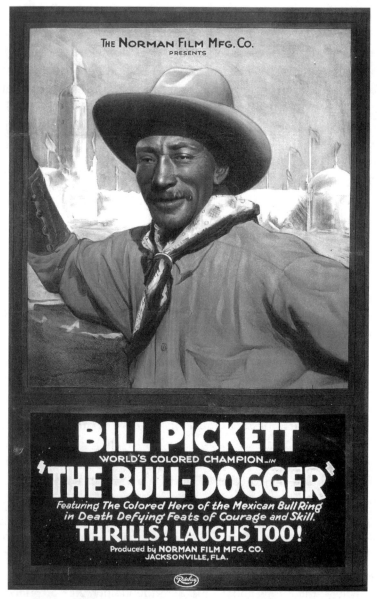

Bill Pickett. Pickett was born in Texas in 1870 or 1871 and formed a cowboy outfit with his brothers in the 1890s. He performed in bronco-busting shows at fairs and eventually joined the 101 Ranch Wild West Show in Oklahoma that, at various points, included Buffalo Bill, Will Rogers, and Tom Mix. The image is a poster from 1921 for the movie *The Bull Dogger*. *Buffalo Bill Historical Center, Cody, Wyoming; Museum Purchase, 1.69.2030*

Supreme Court decision in 1948 against "block booking" also hurt the studio system, by breaking the monopolistic relationship between the studios and the theater chains.

The domination of the film industry by the major studios also encouraged the standardization of a widely popular film genre known as the Western. The experimental Westerns made by pioneers in film such as Princess Red Wing and James Young Deer in the 1910s declined, as did Buffalo Bill's documentary style of "Wild West" shows, through which he attempted to educate audiences about the real lives of cowboys and Indians. Instead, studios churned out Westerns that appealed to mass audiences, employing sentimental conventions and formulaic depictions of outlaw violence, heroic cowboys, and savage Indians. In the process, the once-unique elements of Western films and Western music began to blur with other genres. One example of this is movies with singing cowboys such as Carl Sprague, Gene Autry, and Roy Rogers. Their musical Westerns included "country" music that had Southern and Midwestern origins. The songs of singing movie stars also were played on the radio, a sign of the new ties between the radio networks, film studios, and the parent companies that owned them. One can get an idea of how quickly the formulaic Western film took shape (and radio shows and later TV shows) by considering the career of John Wayne, who made his first appearance in a film in 1926. His first major film, *The Big Trail*, came out in 1930. Nine years later, the genre-defining *Stagecoach* (1939) influenced filmmakers around the world and made Wayne and director John Ford Hollywood icons—a status they would hold into the 1960s and 1970s.

Matinee idols and musicians like Wayne and Autry sold mass-market Western stories to Americans across the nation, but they were not the only purveyors of Western culture. Writers and artists from the diverse parts of the West began to depict what they viewed as authentic regional culture rooted in the unique physical environment and historical experience of distinct locales, in opposition to generic and highly fictionalized frontier stories. Some of the most famous and best-selling writers contributed mightily to the Western genre of cowboys, outlaws, and Indians. Zane Grey wrote dozens of novels from the 1910s to the 1930s, most famously *Riders of the Purple Sage* (1912), and countless lesser-known writers contributed to magazines such as *Western Stories*. Other writers, more often recognized for their contribution to American literature, wrote regional fiction that pointedly rejected, avoided, or subverted the formulaic Western story. They included Frank Norris, whose novel *The Octopus* (1901) was based on the Mussel Slough incident and depicted violence in rural California between small-time farmers and gunmen hired by the Southern Pacific Railroad. Another was Jack London, a one-time sailor, manual laborer, and tramp born in California in 1876. London briefly attended the University of California at Berkeley and in 1897 went to find his fortune in the Klondike gold rush in the Yukon Territory of Canada. His novels included adventure stories like *The Call of the Wild* (1903), which was set in the Klondike; *The Iron Heel* (1907), in which an oppressive capitalist oligarchy takes over the United States; and utopian fiction like *The Valley of the Moon* (1913), which critiqued urban life and the brutality of employers and envisioned a rural Eden in northern California for ordinary working men and their families. Perhaps the most significant Western writer of the era was Willa Cather. In novels such as *O Pioneers* (1913), *My Antonia* (1918), *The Professor's House* (1925), and *Death Comes for the Archbishop* (1927), Cather wrote about communities and natural environments on the Plains and in the Southwest. Compared to formulaic Westerns, her stories depicted the ambiguity and complexity of specific places, family life, women, and conflicts between ethnic groups that shaped communities. Such regional writing often expressed a wary sense of loss in response to the encroaching modern world.

One can see similar trends in the visual arts. Artists like Frederic Remington and Charles M. Russell contributed greatly to still-familiar images of cowboys, violence, and the tragic nobility of the disappearing Indian. Remington's paintings and statues, especially, influenced the staging of Western films. In addition, artists such as Mary Hallock Foote, Georgia O'Keeffe, and Victor Higgins produced work that depicted Mexican Americans, women, and the historic continuity of landscapes and communities. O'Keeffe brought Western painting into the twentieth century by exploring the same modernist trends then shaping the medium in cultural capitals like New York and Paris. Higgins and the Taos Society of Artists (founded in New Mexico in 1915) started an enduring tradition of artist colonies in the Southwest. More than regional writers, visual artists, including sculptors, demonstrated that art and culture could be specific to the West and still be a part of international currents. Many of these works were not popular at the

Skiers in Jackson Hole, Wyoming, 1930. Photograph by Charles J. Beldon. *Buffalo Bill Historical Center, Cody, Wyoming; Gift of Mr. & Mrs. Charles Beldon, PN.67.436a*

Cowboys teach a tourist "dude" to rope in a corral at the Pitchfork Ranch, near Meeteetse, Wyoming, in the 1920s or 1930s. Photograph by Charles J. Beldon. *Buffalo Bill Historical Center, Cody, Wyoming; Gift of Mr. & Mrs. Charles Beldon, PN.67.797b*

time of their creation, or even recognized as "Western," because they defied or ignored stereotypical "Western" genre conventions. But the techniques and images developed by O'Keeffe especially have become the stuff of calendars and coffee-table books in recent years, joining those of Remington and Russell, and shaping the vision of American deserts and ancient peoples that most of us have today, blending Western myth with modernist sensibilities.

As much as writers and artists, the tourist industries of the region sold the West and its natural wonders to the nation and the world. The railroads had been the first big business interest to sell the region as a tourist destination. But it was the automobile that made it possible for the masses, or at least the well-off and middle classes, to make summer trips to national parks a new family ritual. By the 1920s, dude ranches and artist colonies in the Southwest and mining towns in the Mountain West attracted tourists. The national parks in the region drew 199,000 visitors in 1910, 920,000 in 1920, and an amazing 2.75 million in 1930. The popularity of camp grounds, tourist cabins, and motels, which were cheaper than traditional hotels, reflected the fact that the rise of the personal automobile, together with the growth of the middle class, made travel to the West an industry in its own right. In the 1930s, resort communities began to attract winter-only residents and retirees. At this point, the great irony of Western tourism became impossible to ignore. The mythic appeal of the West had always been the chance to escape from the modern world (cities and commercialism) by leaving the conventions of city and suburban life behind and seeing natural wonders and experiencing something of the life of cowboys, Indians, and settlers on the frontier. But tourism had already become big business and a crucial part of many local Western economies. Every tourist dollar—and every new motel, campground, highway, rest stop, restaurant, and gas station that popped up to take more of them in—made the West a bit more modern and a bit less distinct from other regions of the nation. For long-time residents of the West, tourist dollars and well-off tourists wandering about their towns were a welcome necessity, but nonetheless a clear sign of how changing times often meant unwanted changes to Westerners' ways of life.

The contradictions of modern change, in the West as in other parts of the nation, defined the 1920s. Prohibition is a good example. The Eighteenth Amendment had made the production and sale of alcohol illegal in 1919, and its passage reflected both Protestant moralism and a progressive desire for social order and health. But Prohibition also gave the Jazz Age its subversive edge. Would the music and dance and libertine sexuality of the "Roaring Twenties" have been so deliciously and scandalously modern if it had not been forced undercover into speakeasies rather than conventional pubs, bars, saloons, and taverns, all of which had been forced to shut down?

In this context, "Sister Aimee" McPherson stands as a curiously representative figure of the time. She was indeed a Los Angeles celebrity, but she was also a moral conservative who railed in her sermons against the evils of drink and sexual immorality. In addition, she appealed to religious folk in Southern California who sought economic opportunity but feared what the new consumer culture was doing to sexual morality, the family, and traditional roles of men and women. As a small-town girl from rural Canada, she understood firsthand the anxieties and the moral outrage of traditional rural folk from the Midwest and South who, like her, had migrated to the West early in the twentieth century. Still, like most religious revivalists, McPherson embraced modern technology. She used glamour and celebrity to promote the "old time" gospel, which she sold like a consumer item, promising her listeners that faith in Jesus would make them happy. Like other Hollywood celebrities, her antics, especially her disappearance and alleged affair, inspired gossip and drove sales of tabloid newspapers.

Put together, these examples suggest that even as Hollywood and the tourist industry sold the myths of the Old West and the region's natural wonders to consumers across the nation and around the world, the West itself was becoming a complex, modern place of mass culture and cities, as well as of farms, ranches, mining towns, Indian reservations, and deserts, forests, and mountains. Los Angeles, like cities, towns, and rural areas throughout the larger West, was home both to conservative preachers and politicians and decadent hucksters and bon vivants. Americans today generally think of the religious right as a recent phenomenon. But its roots, too, go back to the West of the 1920s (among other places).

The Southern West

During the 1920s, more than 250,000 western Southerners—people from Arkansas, Missouri, Texas, and Oklahoma—migrated to Southern California. Soil erosion, drought, and the failure to move from tenancy to farm ownership pushed them out of the cotton fields. The promise of a better life drew them to the greater Los Angeles region in search of jobs in manufacturing and the oil fields. These migrants can best be described as lower middle class. A few made their fortune in LA, but most of them aspired to a decent job and home ownership. These migrants brought with them hard-scrabble values, notably a frontier ethic that embraced entrepreneurial opportunity and economic progress, a fierce defense of property rights, a conservative desire to maintain the social order, an aggressive religious fundamentalism, and a dedication to Southern ways, racial segregation among them. Their folkways included strict Biblicist doctrine, revivalist piety, and musical entertainment that had evolved over the decades from banjos and hillbilly music into guitar-driven country-western music. Compared to the "Okies" and "Arkies" who would flee to California to escape the "Dust Bowl" in the 1930s, those who migrated to California in the 1920s were modestly upwardly mobile. By the time a third wave of migrants from the South arrived on the West Coast during and after World War II, there were familiar social, religious, and political institutions already in place to welcome them. In the 1960s, 1970s, and 1980s, their descendents, centered in Southern California, would overwhelmingly vote for Republicans like Richard Nixon and Ronald Reagan and provide strong grass-roots support for the rise of the political and religious right. This social group is not part of the common image that most people have of LA, California, and the "left coast," but it is as old as Hollywood.

The jobs that migrants from the western South sought in Southern California were mostly blue-collar ones, but paid enough to permit the newcomers to aspire to home ownership and a middle-class lifestyle. In the oil industry, the migrants worked as both roughnecks and engineers. In towns like Downey, northeast of LA, companies such as EMSCO Aircraft Corp, founded by E. M. Smith in 1929, provided both white-collar positions for engineers and technicians and semi-skilled assembly jobs. In addition to aerospace, industrial plants in the greater LA region in the 1920s included oil refineries, steel mills, shipyards, food-processing, textiles, and railroad yards. Some blue-collar communities in greater LA were company towns, with corporations choosing to locate their plants in suburban areas that could be kept racially pure (i.e., all-white) and effectively closed to trade unions, reflecting common values among Southern migrants.

One can describe the values of Southern (along with many Midwestern) migrants to the region as "plain-folk Americanism." Their reaction to life in the 1920s in Southern California—with its large Asian, Hispanic, and African American populations, progressive-left political movements, and entertainment-consumer culture of Jazz Age Hollywood—helped to harden their brand of conservatism. Hostility to New Deal government activism in the 1930s, fighting World War II, especially against Japan, and anti-Communist fears inspired by the Cold War further sharpened and intensified their religious, social, and political outlook. When they arrived in Southern California, migrants from the western South built their own Baptist churches. Their religious communities became a crucial base for grassroots political organizing against the New Deal, against the spread of communism, and for the Republican Party during the 1930s and 1940s.

In maintaining their religious traditions, the new arrivals built on a network of conservative Protestant churches and other religious institutions that already existed in the region. Pentecostalism got its start at the Azusa Street revivals in LA between 1906 and 1909; and between 1909 and 1917 two oil tycoons from Pennsylvania, Milton and Lyman Stewart, paid for the publication of *The Fundamentals,* a series of pamphlets that inspired the term *fundamentalist.* The Stewarts, who moved to LA in the 1880s, helped found the Bible Institute of Los Angeles (today Biola University).

If the mainstream expression of these conservative religious and political migrants can be seen in churches and local political organizing, its violent edge showed itself in the rise of the Ku Klux Klan and other extremist and white-supremacist organizations. In some parts of the West, notably on the Plains, the Klan and more respectable like-minded groups such as the Independent Voters Association, continued activities begun in the 1910s, organizing communities against the IWW, socialists (in Oklahoma), progressive organizations (such as the Nonpartisan League in North Dakota), and Germans, Jews, and other "suspect" ethnic groups. In Los Angeles, the Klan terrorized labor organizers (raiding union halls, kidnapping labor activists, tarring and feathering opponents) and fought to keep white towns and suburbs racially segregated. It took over the Anaheim city council in 1924 before quickly being ousted. In Oregon, notably Portland, the KKK intimidated African Americans with cross burnings, parades, near-lynchings, and possibly murder, as an unsolved homicide suggests. They also worked to maintain supremacy over Catholics, Jews,

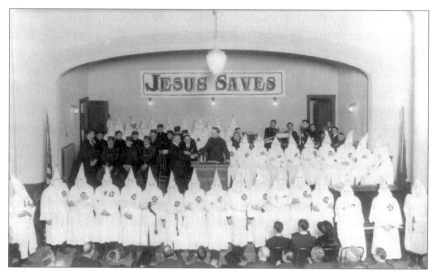

KKK meeting in Portland, Oregon, early 1920s. The KKK members share the stage with members of the Royal Riders of the Red Robe, a Klan auxiliary for foreign-born white Protestants. *Oregon Historical Society Research Library, Oregon History Project, OrHi 51017*

and people whom they deemed sexually immoral, such as homosexuals. In the 1930s, many of these reactionary groups would oppose the New Deal, promote fascism, express support for Nazi Germany, and resist the entry of the United States into World War II. At the extreme, William Dudley Pelley's Silver Legion of America mixed American nationalism and fundamentalist Christianity, modeling itself on the "brown shirt" paramilitary corps that helped bring Adolf Hitler to power. The Silver Legion had about 15,000 members nationally in 1934, with offices and hundreds of members in Los Angeles and San Diego. In 1936, in the State of Washington, Pelley founded the Christian Party, a fascist group, and ran for the presidency. His movement and other extremist right-wing movements like it collapsed in the wake of Japan's attack on Pearl Harbor in December 1941, when the United States entered the war.

Groups like these were significant for their sheer numbers, in the hundreds and tens of thousands in some locales, and millions nationally, but also for their extreme, extralegal expression of what many other white Americans pursued in mainstream politics. Migrants from older white Protestant communities in the South, the western South, and the Midwest brought both the mainstream and extremist versions of their values to the Plains, Mountain West, and California in the late nineteenth and early twentieth centuries. In the West, these militant groups pointed backward to the vigilante traditions of the nineteenth century and forward to extremist groups that would shape Western politics in the late twentieth and early twenty-first centuries.

Race Relations in the West

Extremist, sometimes violent groups like the KKK might have operated on the margins of American society, but their goals and even their membership and influence overlapped with mainstream political organizations. A sign of this was the transformation of U.S. immigration policy by Congress into one defined by restriction. In 1924, the National Origins Act created quotas for racial-ethnic groups that favored Northwestern Europeans and discriminated against Southern and Eastern Europeans. The Asian Exclusion Act of 1924 banned immigration from China, Japan, and other parts of Southern and Eastern Asia. These policies reflected the commonplace racial thinking of the day, which divided whites from non-whites and also put Europeans into preferred and nonpreferred racial categories. The National Origins Act codified the ever more restrictive policies that had been passed from the 1880s to 1920s, for Asians especially. It did not set limits on immigration from Latin America, Mexico, or Canada, but this did not mean that white Americans welcomed Mexican immigrants or treated Mexican Americans as equals, simply that they were not necessarily defined as an immigration problem.

For Asian Americans, notably the long-standing Chinese American community and the newer Japanese community, the new restrictions meant that families divided between the United States and the old country would remain separated. It also meant that many male members of ethnic communities with a significant surplus of men, who had come alone to the United States seeking work, would remain single throughout their lives. As a result, their communities would have an even more difficult time achieving social stability or finding a secure, let alone welcome, place in American society.

This was especially true of Chinese Americans. Large Chinese American communities sprang up along the Pacific Coast and smaller ones dotted the Mountain West, where mining companies and the railroads had recruited Chinese men as inexpensive (even expendable, in the minds of managers) laborers in the nineteenth century. By 1882, when Congress passed the first Chinese Exclusion Act, about 100,000 Chinese men (and 5,000 women) lived in the United States. The new restrictions on immigration made it difficult for Chinese men to send for their families back in China. It also meant that the Chinese American population did not grow, and even shrank for a time because restrictive immigration policies greatly slowed the flow of immigrants from China. The number of Chinese in the United States had fallen to about 62,000 in 1920. In 1930, because of modest natural increase, and more accurate counting methods, the census counted it at 75,000. In the 1920s, most Chinese lived in cities. They made clothing, cigars, and shoes in small shops, grew and sold fruit and vegetables for local markets, worked in service industries such as laundries and restaurants, and operated groceries and other small businesses in the big-city "Chinatowns," the growth of which were fostered by discrimination (and later by tourism, as curious whites flocked to see such exotic urban locales). Where large enough, especially in the famous Chinatowns in places like San Francisco, Chinese Americans forged family associations, guilds, secret societies, and mutual aid societies that reflected their origins in different parts of China. Ironically, and cruelly, while white racism fostered and exaggerated these "exotic" patterns, most Anglo-Americans viewed them as evidence that the Chinese could never assimilate, that they were dangerous, immoral, lazy, and stuck in their own strange world.

The Japanese faced the opposite problem—whites deemed them a threat for being too successful, mostly in fishing, truck farming, and small businesses. In 1900 the number of Japanese stood at 10,000 in California, and 61,000 in Hawaii. By 1920, the total number of Japanese and Japanese Americans in the United States was 110,000, mostly in California and Hawaii, but with large numbers in Washington and smaller numbers in Oregon, Utah, Wyoming, Montana, and Idaho. About a quarter of Japanese in the United States worked in agriculture, forestry, and animal husbandry. Others worked in service-industry jobs—in restaurants and hotels, and as launderers, janitors, and barbers. Some *Issei* (first-generation) immigrants, had economic success running "truck farms" (growing and selling vegetables), despite being barred from becoming U.S. citizens and having limited property rights. Their children, the American-born *Nisei* (second generation), were U.S. citizens but also faced discrimination in land owning. They often went into business, took clerical jobs, or became professionals. A substantial minority of them went to Japan for childhood visits or some schooling, but only a small number of the Nisei identified with the old country. In 1941, when Japan attacked Pearl Harbor and the United States entered World War II, nearly 130,000 Japanese lived in the American West, mostly on the coast, and another 160,000 in Hawaii. Compared to the Chinese, the Japanese often had migrated as families, usually a man first but soon followed by a bride. Anglo-Americans typically viewed the Japanese as moral, civilized, and hard working, and consequently a threat to the American middle class rather than to the moral and social order, as they perceived Chinese Americans. However, Anglo-Americans still viewed the Japanese, like the Chinese, as culturally and racially inassimilable.

Filipinos began migrating to the United States in 1906, in the wake of the American conquest and colonization of the Philippines. They worked in Washington lumber camps and Alaskan fish canneries and on Hawaiian plantations and California farms. By the 1930s, there were tens of thousands of them living in the mainland United States, mostly on the West Coast, migrating seasonally between cities and rural areas for work. Their growing presence already had begun to spark fears of a new wave of "yellow peril." In the 1920s, Filipino labor leaders began to organize to promote Filipino rights and better working and living conditions. Still, their status in the United States remained uncertain. Western states began passing laws to restrict Filipino immigration and limit their rights. California passed a law against Filipinos marrying whites (in this case Latinos also were classified as white), and Washington forbade Filipinos to own property (a law nullified in 1941 by the Washington State Supreme Court). Tellingly, the Tydings-McDuffie Act of 1934, which promised independence to the Philippines in 1946, also stripped Filipinos of their status as American nationals and made it easier to bar their entry into the mainland United States. In 1943, in his semi-autobiographical novel *America is in the Heart*, the Filipino writer Carlos Bulosan described his experiences in the American-occupied Philippines and later as a migrant laborer in the rural West. He had arrived in Seattle from the Philippines in 1930 and worked in hotels, as a migrant agricultural laborer, and in canneries in Alaska and

Washington. In the 1950s, during the anti-communist hysteria fostered by the Cold War, the FBI hounded Bulosan, preventing him from getting jobs in journalism. His life and writing showed how the racial inequality and economic exploitation suffered by non-whites in the American West were similar to the experiences of conquered peoples in European and American colonies in Asia, Africa, and the Pacific.

By 1910, most people of Mexican descent in the United States were native-born, living in increasingly assimilated, economically mature (if still white-dominated) communities. The anti-radical, anti-labor, and anti-immigrant political currents of the 1910s and 1920s coincided with a rapid influx of Mexican immigrants, which incited nativist fears among white Americans in the Southwest, and unsettled the cultural evolution of the existing Mexican American population. In 1910, the Mexican-born population in the United States was 222,000; by 1920 it was 486,000, and ten years later 648,000. Most people who left Mexico for "El Norte" went to Texas, and to a lesser extent California and Arizona, but some went to mountain states such as Colorado and Montana and the Plains and the Midwest. A few of these migrants had fled political persecution during Mexico's civil wars and hoped to carry on the Mexican revolution from the United States, but most of them went north to find work, hoping to rebuild lives destroyed by revolution and civil strife in Mexico. When there was an obvious economic need for inexpensive labor, Anglo-Americans tolerated and even welcomed the arrival of Mexicans looking for work. But in bad economic times, nativist bigotry quickly flared, and anti-immigrant groups began calling for mass deportation and more effective measures to secure the border. In short, Mexicans provided white Westerners with a convenient, flexible labor force, one to be recruited and sent home at will. In Mexican American communities—known as *barrios* in urban areas—a small, usually native-born middle class and elite emerged during the 1920s. However, the majority of Mexicans in the United States lived on the margins of society, economically and geographically—in barrios, colonias and migrant-worker camps in Western cities, towns, and rural areas.

African Americans faced similar sorts of discrimination. Tens of thousands of blacks had settled on the frontier in the late nineteenth century, notably in Oklahoma in the 1890s. Over the years, thousands more African Americans had migrated to California and the Northwest, with 10,000 living in Los Angeles in 1910, 5,200 in the Bay Area, and 6,000 in Washington. After 1910, the flow from the South to the Far West continued modestly. Once in the West, African Americans hoped to own homes, run small businesses, or get decent blue-collar jobs in Western cities. In most cities where a substantial African American community existed, a small middle class and business class took root because of segregation—black customers being pressured to avoid white businesses, and black professionals, artisans, and small business owners serving a primarily black clientele. Black laborers often faced job discrimination, and they found it difficult to land skilled blue-collar jobs. In addition, they had to compete with the growing Asian, especially Japanese, population in the West for jobs traditionally given to African Americans. Japanese Americans generally faced less-virulent discrimination, and by 1930 Japanese businesses outnumbered black ones by four to one, especially because the Japanese business owners were more likely to serve a racially mixed clientele than the more highly segregated black businesses. The result of segregation and job discrimination was poverty and the birth of all-black ghettos and slums in cities such as Los Angeles and Oakland. Africans Americans did not accept these trends passively, however. By 1915, they had organized six chapters of the National Association for the Advancement of Colored People (NAACP) in California,

Migrant mother and baby wait for help with a broken-down truck containing all the family's possessions. Photographer, Dorothea Lange. *Library of Congress, LC-USZ-16453*

Washington, and Oregon, and several local chapters of the National Negro Business League in California.

Patterns of racial discrimination in West in the 1920s reflected white prejudices common nationally, but the West was unique for the complexity of its race relations, with a large Mexican and Mexican American population and large, diverse Asian communities. This racial mix, which included African Americans and Indians, might be seen as a result of American empire building—the conquering of "foreign" peoples on the frontier and then recruiting them as inexpensive and expendable laborers. But white Americans clearly remained ambivalent about the consequences of their empire building and the cultural and racial diversity that it had fostered. In any event, by the 1930s, an increasingly modern America was struggling with how its diverse groups would coexist in a postfrontier democratic society.

The Great Depression

In 1929 Herbert Hoover became the nation's first "Western" president. Born in 1874 in Iowa, and raised there as a boy, he moved to Oregon to live with an uncle in 1885, after his parents died. He attended Stanford University, became an engineer, and worked in the Sierra Nevada range for the United States Geological Service. During World War I, Hoover won fame as a humanitarian, heading the Committee for Relief in Belgium. After the war, he ran the American Relief Administration, organizing food shipments to Europe, including to the defeated Germany. Hoover served in the Republican administration of Warren Harding in the 1920s and stayed active in relief work, notably in 1927 in response to the Mississippi River flooding. In 1928, he parlayed his "wonder boy" image to the White House, but his timing was bad. The Great Depression began with the stock market crash of October 1929. Seemingly overnight, Hoover's celebrated know-how crashed head-on into the reality of a deepening economic crisis and the limitations of his traditionally American, small-government ideology.

For some Westerners, the start of the Great Depression in 1929 and 1930 was hardly noticeable. In the Mountain West, towns dependent on mining or timber already had experienced severe market swings in prices, along with the low wages and unemployment that resulted in the 1920s.

On the Plains, farmers like the McCardles and Fites had for years suffered drought, low prices for their crops and animals, and crushing debt loads, and already had begun to leave the land they once owned. But the long years of the Great Depression, its national and global impact, and the terrible "Dust Bowl" drought that accompanied it on the Plains, soon proved that this crisis went deeper than previous downturns in the American economy. The dramatic slowdown of manufacturing in the East and the weak markets overseas hit the American West especially hard because its economy remained so dependent on natural resources. California continued to be seen as a land of milk and honey, where a man still could find a job; and Hollywood seemed almost immune to the Depression, with theater attendance staying reliable. (Cheap double features provided a sorely needed escape from the realities of unemployment and hardship.) But even the film industry lost money in some years during the 1930s. In general, the Depression also hurt Californians. The oil industry, vegetable and fruit farmers, and manufacturers all saw prices fall, cut production, and laid off workers. By 1934, nearly 20 percent of the state's population was on relief. Still, as a measure of how bad things were in the region, California remained a destination for migrants from other parts of the West—300,000 from the western South alone.

Images of the Dust Bowl and the migration of desperate Okie and Arkie farm families to places like California—depicted most famously in the novel and subsequent film *The Grapes of Wrath*—have often symbolized the Great Depression for the entire West. In the 1910s and early 1920s, farmers, bamboozled by unusually high prices and the promotions of land speculators, had extended wheat farming to the drought-prone Western plains, from Texas and Oklahoma to the Dakotas and the Canadian prairies. The farmers ploughed under the native grasses that had evolved to hold the soil down in times of drought. Record-breaking years of drought and terrible wind storms combined with these environmentally harmful farming practices to create an ecological crisis that began in 1931. Severe wind storms carried dust from the Plains all the way to the Atlantic Ocean. The drought, together with the collapse of wheat markets nationally and abroad, forced hundreds of thousands of farm families to abandon their land and leave their old homes for good. People from nearby towns on the Plains, suffering from the collapse of the wheat economy, left too. In addition to going to California, to find work in cities like LA or on farms and

Motion picture still from Darryl F. Zanuck's successful production of *The Grapes of Wrath*, based on the novel by John Steinbeck. Pictured here is Henry Fonda (center) and the cast as migrants in camp scene. *Courtesy of the Museum of Modern Art, Film Stills Archive*

orchards in the Central Valley, Dust Bowl families and single men went to Washington, Oregon, New Mexico, and Arizona, packing up their jalopies and trucks, or illegally "riding the rails" in freight cars.

With hundreds of thousands of desperate people on the move, Western cities often posted signs and instructed police officers to warn migrants that there was no work in town and to keep on moving. Okies and other poor white migrants endured prejudice similar to that experienced by migrant Mexican workers, as morally benighted, dim-witted, and listless. Police and vigilantes often raided their camps, especially when they feared that migrant families might be organizing to better their living and working conditions on California farms and orchards. And when the migrants could find work, harvesting fruit or vegetables, farmers sometimes exploited them terribly, paying them less for a day's work than they needed to buy a day's worth of food.

President Hoover and state and local officials urged Americans to hold on, claiming that the economy was basically sound and that it would right itself. The government might help large corporations, Hoover reasoned, but charities and churches could better serve the poor. The problem was that charities and churches, along with local and state governments, had limited resources. Aimee Semple McPherson's Angelus Temple in LA had begun to hand out meals to the indigent back in the 1920s. During the 1930s, it used a donated building and volunteers to distribute more than 1.5 million meals, run free medical-dental clinics, and provide lunches for schoolchildren. In some cities, people started cooperatives as a form of practical and radical self-help. The Seattle Unemployed Citizens League organized bartering and cooperative labor programs, and it lobbied the city council to start public works projects, unemployment insurance, and direct relief. Some state governments, with farmers defaulting on taxes and loans, could ill afford relief work. Most refused to raise taxes, or had economies so weak that there was little revenue to tax. Families also adapted, with women trying to find "women's" jobs as launderers, nurses, maids, and secretaries when their men could not find work. The stress that resulted on families, and especially on men's sense of pride as failed breadwinners, was more severe at the lower end of the social order. Some urban families, though ill-equipped in basic tools or skills, considered going to the rural areas, where they hoped to feed themselves. All told, such efforts were not nearly enough to deal with the region's problems.

In this context, a few members of Congress, such as Colorado senator Edward Costigan, urged President Hoover to create federal relief programs. Hoover refused initially, but eventually he signed the Emergency Relief and Construction Act of 1932, which created the Reconstruction Finance Corporation (RFC). Rather than provide direct relief, the RFC gave aid to businesses that might hire the unemployed (3 million in the West alone that year). But it only provided $30 million in loans, not the $300 million authorized by Congress. Under Hoover's Mexican Repatriation campaign, the Immigration and Naturalization Service began to deport Mexican migrant workers (some 1.5 to 2 million), the sweeps sometimes exiling American citizens along with the "illegals." President Franklin Roosevelt ended the program when he took office in 1933, but some local and state governments continued to deport Mexicans.

Evidence of a systemic crisis in American political and economic institutions began to mount. Western veterans took part in the 25,000-

man "Bonus Army" of World War I veterans who marched on the White House in 1932, to claim bonuses promised to them after the war but not yet paid. The bonuses were certificates that would mature like bonds, but not until 1945. Desperate veterans insisted that they needed the money now and that the government had an obligation to help them. The marchers set up a camp for themselves and their families on the Anacostia Flats, a vacant area across the Anacostia River near the center of Washington, D.C. In June, with the Senate deadlocked over legislation that would disburse the bonus, President Hoover dispatched the U.S. Army to drive them out. Under the command of General Douglas MacArthur, and other future leading generals in World War II—George Patton and Dwight D. Eisenhower—soldiers armed with tear gas, rifles, and bayonets cleared the Bonus Army out of the Anacostia Flats, leading to hundreds of injuries, several deaths, and the miscarriage of a baby among the veterans and their families. The Bonus Army had failed, but the brutal federal response undermined Hoover's image, making him seem cold and callout.

In the West and Midwest, farmers organized demonstrations and turned to vigilante tactics to save their farms. An Iowa farmer and ordained minister named Milo Reno organized the Farmer's Holiday Association, in effect a strike, the idea being that preventing food from going to market might drive up prices for farm products. In some areas, vigilantes threatened violence against court officials and prospective buyers of foreclosed farms put up for sale. In one case in Iowa they dragged a judge of out his courtroom and threatened to hang him if he did not stop foreclosing on farms. Farmers also burned crops and blockaded roads, using telephone poles, hay bales, and rifles, leading to at least one death, to prevent crops from going to market. The protests failed, as police cleared the blockades and arrested some of the strikers, but the events signaled the depth of the crisis and the willingness of some Western Americans to consider extreme measures. Into this regional and national crisis stepped Franklin Delano Roosevelt, the patrician candidate of the Democratic Party in the presidential election of 1932. His New Deal programs, designed to help Americans weather the economic storm, would, in effect, try to reconcile Western ideals of rugged individualism with the long history of federal activism and subsidies in the region. Some parts of the New Deal also would begin to transform the West economically and socially.

The New Deal

In the presidential election of 1932 Roosevelt won every state in the West, and on his coattails the Democrats would dominate elections in the West until 1946. In contrast to Hoover, FDR provided Americans with direct relief. He set out the first phase of the New Deal—his program to address the Depression—in short order in the winter of 1933. It included the creation of the Federal Emergency Relief Administration (FERA), Public Works Administration, and Civilian Conservation Corps (CCC). Agencies like these often worked with state and local governments, providing relief and jobs for unemployed men and women and their families. All told in the 1930s, the West got more aid per capita than did any other region of the nation, and ideals of rugged individualism did not prevent most regional leaders and citizens from demanding more, even if grudgingly. Nonetheless, local governments sometimes refused to spend money to match federal funds, as required by FERA programs. When FERA administrators cut off funds to Colorado for this reason, residents of Denver rioted, forcing the city to come up with matching funds. As in the South, local officials running New Deal programs in the West often discriminated against American Indians, African Americans, and Mexican Americans, with an eye toward keeping them in their place.

Despite his willingness to use direct relief, Roosevelt was never entirely comfortable with it. Public works programs that gave people jobs in exchange for federal dollars suited American ideals much better, providing economic relief but also promoting responsibility and a sense of self-worth. The CCC exemplified this ideal. It employed in excess of 2.5 million men between 1933 and 1942, including an Indian division more than 80,000 strong. CCC workers planted trees, built roads, trails, and campgrounds in national forests and parks, and constructed ranger stations and even interpretive centers. The impact of the CCC was greater in the West than in other regions because its projects focused primarily on public lands, the majority of which are in the West. If they did not fundamentally transform the West, the CCC projects did provide work for millions of men and contributed in the long run to the development of the Western tourism industry. Indeed, visitors to parks in the West today still use facilities first built by the CCC in the 1930s.

The New Deal response to the exodus from the Dust Bowl fundamentally transformed the Western economy and society in some areas,
by bringing conservation policies to bear on the agricultural economy of
the Plains. The Taylor Grazing Act of 1934 ended the homestead era and
shifted economic development on the Plains from wheat to stock raising. Okies, Arkies, and other migrants leaving the Plains had effectively
already ended the homesteading era, but the Taylor Act wrote the change
into law, withdrawing remaining public lands from homesteading, a policy that had defined the West for 150 years. The Taylor Act also created
new regulations for grazing, recognizing overgrazing as an environmental
problem in its own right. The new Grazing Service (since 1946 part of the
Bureau of Land Management) created districts to lease grazing rights on
public land to ranchers and regulate the number of animals on it. Local
officials and stockmen worked with federal bureaucrats to set fees, apportion leases, and enforce the animal-number limits. Alongside the Taylor
Act, the Agricultural Adjustment Administration (AAA) of 1933 empowered the U.S. Department of Agriculture (USDA) to revitalize farming on
the Plains and in the Midwest. The AAA paid farmers to keep land out
of production and slaughter animals. It hoped these measures would slow
soil erosion and raise farm incomes by eliminating the surpluses of crops
and livestock that kept the prices of agricultural products so low that small
farmers could never hope to break even. The associated Soil Conservation
Service, created in 1935, helped farmers build shelterbelts of trees to blunt
the force of wind storms. The federal programs also provided loans to stabilize farm debt and thereby help farming communities. The Resettlement
Administration (1935) and Farm Security Administration (FSA) helped
farmers on land devastated by drought and soil erosion to move to new
land better suited for agriculture, and it provided other forms of relief and
aid to tenant farmers. The FSA also employed photographers and writers
to document life on the Plains during the Depression. A few years later,
the Rural Electrification Program (1936) brought electricity to rural areas
of the West (and elsewhere in the nation) that had never before had it. The
result of these diverse programs was both the documentation of a way of
life near collapse and an effort to transform it by helping farmers adjust to
the vagaries of a modern industrial economy.

This first phase of the New Deal ended in 1935–36 when the
United States Supreme Court declared several major pieces of its legisla-

tion unconstitutional, notably the National Recovery Administration (created in June 1933), which worked with leaders in industry to set voluntary schedules of wages and prices and get corporations to recognize unions, and the AAA. In the West, as in the rest of the nation, court decisions raised the question of the nature and extent of federal powers. But important enduring pieces of New Deal legislation remained, most notably the Social Security Act of 1935. Across the nation in decades to come, its provisions for senior citizens would dramatically decrease the poverty level among the elderly and also be a major boon for younger and middle aged adults, as they would be relieved of much of the cost of caring for aging parents. And FDR soon would try to quell the Supreme Court, threatening to add a new judge to its roster, one who supported his programs, whenever a current judge reached the age of seventy and did not retire in six months. The so-called court-packing plan produced a storm of political opposition, even among many FDR supporters, so the president quickly abandoned it. But thereafter the high court seemed to soften its opposition to New Deal programs and the Roosevelt administration redefined some of its most controversial legislation and programs to mollify judicial critics.

The Indian New Deal

Like the Taylor Grazing Act, the Indian Reorganization Act (IRA) of 1934 transformed a major federal policy in the West. The new policy acknowledged the failures of assimilation policies, encouraged Native communities to revitalize their traditions and institutions, and intended to give them more freedom to determine how to adapt to modern American life on their own terms. The IRA did not specifically declare an end to official policies of assimilation that dated back to the Dawes Act of 1887, but it pointed in that direction. Other New Deal programs also targeted problems in Indian communities. The CCC and Indian Emergency Conservation Work (a program run by the Bureau of Indian Affairs) provided jobs, while other agencies provided relief and programs for public health and housing. Still, the long habit of white government officials, reformers, and missionaries telling Indians what to do, even coercing them when "necessary," continued. The Indian New Deal thus did not fully embrace ideals of Indian self-determination.

The roots of the IRA go back to the 1920s. Indians had not died out, as opponents and defenders from George Custer to Charlie Russell had imagined. Nor had they fully assimilated or stayed put on reservations, though they certainly had changed and adapted, whether living on reservations or moving to towns and cities. In the 1920s, a series of reports by government agencies and private foundations revealed low levels of education, substandard housing, and high levels of unemployment, poverty, and poor health among Indian peoples. The Merriam Report of 1928, sponsored by the Institute for Government Research, emphasized that government policies and neglect had played an important role in the problems Indians faced. In addition, the intellectual landscape had begun to change, as anthropologists and biologists challenged assimilationist ideals and scientific racism, and instead began to promote pluralist ways of thinking that valued diversity and insisted on the necessity of understanding Indian cultures on their own terms.

The new Indian commissioner, appointed when the Democrats took power in 1933, had participated in these reformist efforts. John Collier was trained as a social worker and had been part of settlement house and public school social reform efforts in cities during the 1910s. In the 1920s he became interested in the Indians of the Southwest, and he determined to try to preserve the ideals of community that Indian peoples still embraced, perceiving their values and ways of life as an antidote to the problems of modern capitalist civilization. Collier organized the Indian Defense Association to defend Pueblo land and mining rights, promote Indian self-governance, and reverse restrictions on the rights of Indians to practice traditional ways of life and religious rituals. His position as Indian commissioner and the passage of the IRA gave him an opportunity to enact these changes. The act empowered reservation communities to develop constitutions and institutions of limited self-government, elect officials, and start businesses. It created a credit fund to aid tribes in developing their economies, enacted educational and medical programs, and helped tribes purchase land and water rights. It also gave Indians greater religious freedom and sought to revitalize their cultural heritages, which included the production of traditional craftwork and art. Collier also made sure that other New Deal agencies did not discriminate against but helped Indians and their communities.

Woody Guthrie, 1943. The
sticker on his guitar reads,
"This Machine Kills Fascists."
Library of Congress,
LC-USZ62-130859

These positive effects notwithstanding, Collier remained a typical reformer. While he consulted Indians and sometimes listened to their suggestions, he and other BIA officials at times imposed unwanted policies on them. For example, Collier forced Navajo entrepreneurs who had taken up sheep ranching to reduce their stock in order to conserve their rangeland. His idealized vision of Native communities clashed with the views of Indians who had embraced individual capitalist enterprise. Indeed, some Indians who favored assimilation accused him of communist subversion and attacked him for undermining Indian progress. Collier's stubbornness, resistance by BIA bureaucrats, and opposition by whites who wanted access to Indian land weakened his authority as Indian commissioner. So too did complaints by various progressive and traditionalist Indian groups and the decline in New Deal funding in the late 1930s and during World War II. Indian opposition to some of the programs he designed to "help" them also highlighted the diversity within Native communities and signaled their growing ability to make their voices heard and determine their own destiny.

Nonetheless, Collier's policies signaled a significant change in government policy. It was not just more well-meaning reform imposed by white outsiders, but an opening for the small but growing class of Indian leaders—educated professionals, artists, and small businesspersons—to defend traditions and promote changes defined by native peoples themselves for their own communities, and on their own terms. That promise would not truly begin to be fulfilled until the 1960s and 1970s, but already in the 1930s and 1940s Indians had constructed the institutional basis for future change, notably the National Congress of American Indians (created in 1944), which continued the efforts begun in the 1910s by the Society of American Indians. From now on, they would be both Indians and modern Americans.

Conclusion

If Aimee Semple McPherson and Frank McCardle symbolized the 1920s West, perhaps the folksinger Woody Guthrie symbolizes the 1930s. An Okie-Texan migrant who fled to California to escape the Dust Bowl, Guthrie rode the rails and eventually became a radio performer, labor activist, and sometime writer for the *Daily Worker,* a communist newspaper. He toured camps where migrant Okies who worked in the fields and orchards of California fought to keep body and soul together. His most famous song, "This Land is Your Land," is at once patriotic and radical. It is patriotic in its images of land from "California to the New York Island" and "the redwood forest to the Gulf Stream waters," and of wandering "endless skyways." And it is radical in insisting that "this land was made for you and me." Some verses of the song—not those usually sung around Boy Scout camp fires—mention the hungry people Guthrie saw in his wanderings and the "no trespassing" signs that barred many Americans from land that he considered their rightful heritage. In the 1930s, the question of to whom "this land" (the vast stretches of the American West) belonged, was more poignant than ever. Not just Indians and other Americans of color, but tens of millions of farmers and blue-collar and white-collar workers wondered the same thing. The next phase of the New Deal and the coming world war would provide some answers to this question.

In the process, the West as a whole would be transformed. The region had always been what political economists call dependent, in that its economy was powerfully shaped by political and economic powers in great cities outside the region—New York, Chicago, Washington, D.C., and before that Mexico City, London, Paris, and Madrid. In the past four decades, the economy of the West and its cities and culture had become more fully developed and modern. Hollywood films and the election of the first Westerner as president in 1928 perhaps symbolized the region's growing influence. But the West remained dependent in crucial ways. In the next two decades, the great metropolises of the West—such as LA, San Francisco, Seattle, Dallas–Fort Worth—if not the region as a whole, would become a political and economic power in their own right.

✂ Suggested Readings ❧

Cray, Ed. *Ramblin' Man: The Life and Times of Woody Guthrie.* New York: W. W. Norton & Co., 2004.

Deloria, Philip J. *Indians in Unexpected Places.* Lawrence: University Press of Kansas, 2004.

Etulain, Richard W. *Re-Imagining the Modern American West: A Century of Fiction, History, and Art.* Tucson: University of Arizona Press, 1996.

Fite, Gilbert C. "Failure on the Last Frontier: A Family Chronicle." *Western Historical Quarterly 18* (1987): 5–14.

Friday, Chris. *Organizing Asian American Labor: The Pacific Coast Canned-Salmon Industry, 1870–1942.* Philadelphia: Temple University Press, 1994.

Gregory, James N. *American Exodus: The Dust Bowl Migration and Okie Culture in California.* New York: Oxford University Press, 1991.

Lay, Shawn. *The Invisible Empire in the West: Toward a New Historical Appraisal of the Ku Klux Klan of the 1920s.* Urbana and Chicago: University of Illinois Press, 2004.

Lowitt, Michael. *The New Deal and the West.* Bloomington: University of Indiana Press, 1984.

Philp, Kenneth R. . *John Collier's Crusade for Indian Reform, 1920–1954.* Tucson: University of Arizona Press, 1977.

Rothman, Hal K. *Devil's Bargains: Tourism in the Twentieth-Century American West.* Lawrence: University Press of Kansas, 1998.

Sánchez, George J. *Becoming Mexican-American: Ethnicity, Culture and Identity in Chicano Los Angeles, 1900-1945.* New York: Oxford University Press, 1995.

Sutton, Matthew Avery. *Aimee Semple McPherson and the Resurrection of Christian America.* Cambridge, MA: Harvard University Press, 2007.

Szasz, Ferenc Morton. *Religion in the Modern American West.* Tucson: University of Arizona Press, 2000.

Taylor, Quintard. *In Search of the Racial Frontier: African Americans in the West, 1528–1990.* New York: Norton, 1999.

Tygiel, Jules. *The Great Los Angeles Swindle: Oil, Stocks, and Scandal during the Roaring Twenties.* Berkeley: University of California Press, 1996.

CHAPTER TWELVE

Depression to Cold War

The New Deal and World War II transformed the West, altering its political, economic, and social trajectory. New Deal programs resettled families that had lost their farms to drought or debt and provided jobs building dams, roads, schools, and other public infrastructure that would help to lay the basis for economic growth during the war and postwar years. Fighting World War II required the federal government to build military bases around the West and provide billions of dollars in loans and contracts to businesses that retooled factories or built new ones to supply America and its allies with weapons and other war materiel. The government's active role in the economy continued in the decades after the war, as the United States and its democratic-capitalist allies fought the Cold War against communist powers like the Soviet Union and China. In the process, as the federal government industrialized the region, millions of migrants headed west, seeking work in wartime industries and new lives in its rapidly growing cities and suburbs. These trends increased the political clout of the region, as the weight of the American population and economy shifted to the West, giving it proportionally more voters and financial power.

Behind the story of these broad economic, social, and political transformations lie the personal stories of millions of individuals and families who took advantage of the opportunities created by an activist government in the New Deal and World War II. They included Mexicans and Canadians, Westerners from the drought-devastated Great Plains, and African

Americans from the South. But not all the migration was voluntary or uplifting. For example, wartime fears that Japanese American immigrants and citizens would sabotage the American war effort, combined with long-held racist attitudes, inspired the government to seize their property, force them to abandon their homes on the Pacific coast, and move them to relocation camps in the interior West. Only in the decades after the war would race relations in the region begin to change in fundamental ways.

These events are a reminder of the contingency of history. If not for the Great Depression, the rise of Hitler, and the Japanese attack on Pearl Harbor, the West and the nation might look quite different today. The industrial sector of the Western economy likely would have continued to grow along with tourism, as in the 1910s and 1920s, but not with the same stunning speed and transformative effect. Frederick Jackson Turner died in 1932. He and many other Americans in his life-time had worried about the future of a United States without a frontier. What, they asked, would ensure American wealth and freedom, inspire brave endeavors, and make people into true Americans? The onset of the Great Depression seemed to confirm their fears, yet the demands of a world war and the Cold War seemed to provide the answer: an activist federal government, new industries, and high-tech military and civilian products. As previous chapters have shown, the federal government had always played a major role in conquering, settling, and developing the West, from building the transcontinental railroads to the first great dam building projects in the early twentieth century. Federal influence sim-ply became more decisive during the war and thereafter. In fact, Turner's successors two generations later, the New Western Historians, would make the role of the federal government in the region a central theme in their work—one of them, Richard White, calling the West a "proving ground" for federal programs.

The New Deal Transforms the West

New Deal relief programs may have secured a powerful Democratic vot-ing coalition for FDR, but they did not leave a permanent mark on the West; that was the legacy of other aspects of the New Deal, namely the public works projects of the Works Progress Administration (WPA) and other federal agencies. As noted in Chapter Eleven, the West received a dis-

Construction of the Boulder Dam (now, Hoover Dam), 1934 or 1935, east of Las Vegas, on the Nevada-Arizona border. *Library of Congress, LC-DIG-hec-14559*

proportionate share of assistance between 1933 and 1939, partly because its residents were hit so badly by the Great Depression. States with the lowest personal income levels received more relief aid. Nevada, Montana, Wyoming, Arizona and ten other Western states led the nation in the amount of federal dollars taken in. In North Dakota, two out of three residents received federal help, through farm support programs, business loans, and direct relief. In addition to basic economic need—for jobs to keep body and soul together—much of the West lay in need of basic public infrastructure, just the job for public works programs. The biggest projects that New Deal agencies undertook were dams, but projects included everything from building schools, courthouses, water-treatment plants, rural electrical grids, bridges, and culverts, to swimming pools, golf courses, and lodges at national parks. Some of the projects laid the basis for an expanded postwar tourist industry in the West. In general, they underlay industrial development during World War II and the Cold War. Even if one sees them as an extension of the kind of projects started by the federal government in the 1910s and 1920s, such work expanded exponentially in the 1930s and 1940s.

Dam building provides the most obvious example of this stepped-up pace of construction. The construction of the Boulder Dam (now called the Hoover Dam) was authorized in 1928, but it became a Depression-era project. The dam was built by the Bureau of Reclamation on the Colorado River in Black Canyon, near Las Vegas. The Six Companies, Inc., that did the work included firms from five cities and four states. The dam took six years to construct (1931–36) at a cost of $49 million in era currency, and it required the building of a nearby town (Boulder City) in which the workers (5,100 in 1934) and their families could live. The dam was an architectural wonder—in its elegant design and as the largest dam in the world (surpassed by the Grand Coulee Dam in Washington in 1942). Men called "high-scalers" descended on ropes and used dynamite and jackhammers to clear the canyon walls of loose rock and prepare them for the placement of the dam. One hundred and ten workers died building the dam, some from the intense summer heat, up to 140 degrees Fahrenheit. The resulting dam was 726 feet high, 1,244 feet wide, and had required 6.6 million tons of concrete poured over two years, between June 1933 and March 1935. The workers, the tourists that the dam soon drew, and the water and electricity that it supplied would help to turn Las Vegas, then a struggling mining and railroad town, into a worldwide gambling and tourism destination in subsequent decades.

The construction of more major dams followed. The Public Works Administration paid for the building of the Fort Peck Dam on the Missouri River in northeast Montana and the Army Corps of Engineers built it, along with a planned town, Fort Peck City, which had 280 units for families and barracks with space for 3,200 single men. The town also attracted and employed barkeepers, barbers, doctors, prostitutes, and other sorts of service providers. On the Columbia River alone, federal agencies eventually built fourteen dams, including the Grand Coulee, Chief Joseph, Bonneville, McNary, Hungry Horse, and Libby dams. The dams functioned together as a hydraulic system, regulating the flow of water and storing it in reservoirs to generate electricity, reliably deliver water to the cities and industrial-scale farms of the region, and prevent flooding caused by spring snow melt and periods of heavy rain. Similar systems of dams followed for the Colorado and the other major rivers in the region.

The frenzy of federally sponsored dam building continued through World War II and the 1950s, not slowing down until the 1960s and 1970s.

The dams created a "hydraulic civilization" in the West, a way of life engineered by physically transforming the environment and moving resources on a planet-altering scale. (Globally, dams have subtly altered the earth's rotational speed and axis by moving water further from the equator than normal flow would allow.) Dams have provided water for cities such as Las Vegas, LA, and Phoenix, irrigation for agribusiness in California and other parts of the West, and electrical power for homes and businesses in the region. Smaller dams helped control soil erosion and springtime flooding. Local, state, interstate, and international commissions (where rivers and watersheds cross into Mexico or Canada) have met regularly over the years to decide where the water and electrical power will be used and to monitor the environmental impact of the dams on local ecosystems.

The building of these dams not only provided work for tens thousands of Westerners during the Depression—and for many more who provided services, food, consumer goods, and housing for the workers—but the dams themselves provided a crucial infrastructural basis for wartime industries during World War II. The electrical power that the Grand Coulee Dam generated, for example, would power electricity-hungry aluminum and plutonium plants in Oregon and Washington. In addition, through the building of dams entrepreneurs such as Henry J. Kaiser gained experience in handling large projects and cultivating relationships with federal bureaucrats, national and local politicians, and military officials. Kaiser started building roads for the federal government in the 1920s. During the Great Depression, his companies participated in building the Boulder (Hoover), Grand Coulee, Bonneville, and Shasta dams. They also constructed natural-gas pipelines in the Southwest, levees in Mississippi, and the underwater foundations for the San Francisco–Oakland Bay Bridge.

In addition to employing blue-collar workers in public works projects, agencies such as the Works Progress Administration, Federal Writers Project, and Farm Security Administration put artists, photographers, writers, and scholars to work. Culture workers like these recorded the experiences of people during the Depression, but they also studied and preserved the ways of life of diverse groups. In some cases this work was used as propaganda for the New Deal, FDR, and the Democratic Party, and some of it reflected paternalistic attitudes towards Indians, migrant Okies, and other marginal social groups in the West. But it also helped to preserve heritages and provided resources for both ordinary folk and scholars to use in the future. In addition, writers working for the federal government wrote guide books on every state (further laying the basis for postwar tourism), artists created works of public art, and theater groups toured isolated areas in Western states. A famous example of these projects is the photographs of migrant Okie families done by Dorothea Lange.

One can also see the progressive and conservative character of the New Deal in FDR's labor policies. Right-wing critics of the New Deal painted FDR as a socialist who had betrayed his own patrician class. While his administration did write new laws that recognized labor unions and provided new rights and protections to workers, FDR's policies were not radical or socialist. Instead, they reflected his desire to preserve capitalism. Like those of the Progressive Era, New Deal policies reinforced the political and economic authority of the managerial class.

At the center of these policies was the National Industrial Recovery Act of 1933, which for the first time guaranteed the right of American workers to organize and join labor unions. The new law did not have strong enforcement powers, but it did inspire laborers and empower their unions. For example, in 1934 the International Longshoreman's Association (ILA) went on strike, shutting down the major ports on the West Coast. As in the past, police, vigilantes, and employers tried to break the strike and violence ensued, with two strikers dying in one incident. When the governor of California declared martial law, and the Industrial Association tried to reopen the port of San Francisco, the city's unions called for a general strike and workers around the city joined the longshoremen in walking off the job. Sympathetic small business owners closed their doors too, though the strike committee ensured that food deliveries continued. The unions voted to end the strike and accept government arbitration, which later gave the ILA broad power to control hiring on the docks.

The labor policies of FDR's administration coincided with the founding of a new national labor union, the Congress of Industrial Organizations (CIO). The CIO was more radical than the older, more mainstream American Federation of Labor (AFL). The CIO sought to organize both skilled and unskilled workers on an industrywide basis rather than focus on skilled workers craft by craft, as did the AFL. The CIO also aspired to "industrial democracy," in which workers would share with their employers the management of businesses. The CIO grew quickly. In 1937, for example, the Sawmill and Timber Workers' Union (created in 1933) shifted its allegiance from the AFL to the CIO. Competition between AFL and CIO affiliates sometimes turned violent. In general, however, unions increased their membership significantly during the late 1930s and the 1940s, and through strikes they forced employers to concede gains in wages, benefits, hours, and safety for workers. Indeed, there were more strikes in 1944 than in 1937. Wartime needs and the low unemployment rate (with millions of men in the armed forces) forced employers and the government to accommodate the demands of workers. Anti-communist agitation after the war, however, would lead to a decline of radicalism in the CIO and other unions, as well as to the willingness of big business to meet some of the demands of employees, most notably better wages and benefits.

World War II and the West

The United States entered World War II in December 1941, after Japan launched a surprise aerial attack on the U.S. Pacific Fleet at port in Pearl Harbor, Hawaii. In the next year, Japan overran the Philippines and Guam. Its goal was to become the major power in the western Pacific. To do this, it needed to take control of the Pacific trade empire created by the United States in the late nineteenth and early twentieth centuries, with its key naval and economic strategic points. The Japanese plans began to fall short in June 1942 in a naval battle near the Midway Islands, home of an American naval base. American and British cryptographers had broken the radio code used by the Japanese in their communications and knew of the Japanese plans to attack the American fleet at Midway. The battle was fought largely by carrier-based planes, and in it the Japanese lost four aircraft carriers to the United States's one. The defeat devastated Japan's naval forces, and Midway continued to serve the United States as a staging point for operations. On the other side of the globe, another part of the U.S. trade empire, the Panama Canal Zone, also served as a crucial component to the war effort. The United States had occupied the territory in Panama in 1903 and then built the canal, finishing it in 1914. The canal was important for trade, as ships no longer had to sail all the way around the tip of South America in order to go between the Atlantic and Pacific oceans. But the canal also was vital to U.S. military interests, as U.S. and Allied naval ships (both warships and supply vessels) could

Men and women work on an assembly line building an A-20 attack bomber at the
Douglas Aircraft plant in Long Beach, California (just south of Los Angeles), 1943,
during World War II. *Courtesy of the Franklin D. Roosevelt Library Digital Archives*

move more efficiently between the European and Asian theaters of the
war. Indeed, the threat of German submarines forced the United States to
station protective bases around the Atlantic entrance to the canal. The war
was a defense of freedom, as American leaders claimed, but it also secured
and greatly expanded American military influence in both the Atlantic
and Pacific oceans. It also fostered an American-led globalization in the
decades afterward, notably in close links between the West Coast and Asia
(see below).

The dramatic increase in the number of military bases in the West was
primarily a matter of military necessity, but it also transformed the region.
In fighting a global war in Europe and Asia, military and government
officials thought it prudent to spread bases around the nation, building
a preponderance of new ones in the West and South, where fewer had
been built in the past, thereby decreasing the likelihood that its military
infrastructure could be crippled by a blow from a hostile power (Japan

and Germany during World War II; the Soviet Union during the Cold War, notably with the advent of atomic bombs and long-range bombers and missiles). Lobbying by local and regional politicians to spread the economic benefits of building, staffing, and maintaining military bases and airfields—and providing consumer goods and services to their personnel—also underlay the policy. Western boosters had been pushing the federal government since the 1920s to increase the number of bases in the West, and they turned up the pressure in 1940 and 1941 as FDR and his administration began preparing for a war that seemed likely to come.

The militarization of the West in the 1940s and its economic impact locally was stunning. For the military, part of the appeal of building new bases in the interior West was the vast spaces and low population density. The region had ample room to host large bases, and it enjoyed wide open spaces for training and testing in artillery, air combat, and bombing. Training bases, supply bases, reserve bases, and regular military bases boosted the economies of states, small towns and rural areas, and large cities, but in the long run they also often made such places dependent on the military. In addition to military bases of various sorts, the government also subsidized the building or retooling of factories to produce war materiel, which included everything from aluminum and C-rations to uniforms and airplanes.

Bases and manufacturing facilities often went together. The Dallas–Fort Worth area, for example, secured a naval reserve aviation base, a major army air corps base (at Tarrant Air Field), and two plants that manufactured aircraft—Vultee Aircraft (Corvair) and the North American Aviation Company, the latter alone employing a high of 43,000 people in the middle of the war. Local politicians and lobbyists landed Tinker Air Base near Oklahoma City, an aircraft manufacturing center. On the Pacific Coast, cities like Los Angeles, San Diego, San Francisco, Seattle, and Portland saw the expansion of naval facilities, from bases to shipyards. To coordinate production and provide investment capital, the federal government created the Defense Plant Corporation (DPC). The DPC and other military and government offices awarded huge contracts to the manufacturers of everything from uniforms and C-rations, as well as to shipyards that repaired navy and merchant marine ships. Where it did not subsidize private industrial plants, the DPC built its own, including ore-processing (magnesium, aluminum) and high-tech manufacturing (aircraft) facilities. The DPC practically created a steel industry in the West where none had been, notably in Utah and California. In addition, Utah alone had ten military bases by 1942, which employed 60,000 civilians and purchased some of their supplies locally. Military personnel also spent their own money locally, both staff who lived in the community for significant lengths of time and soldiers who cycled through the bases more quickly and spent cash freely during their rest and relaxation ("R&R") time.

San Diego provides another good example of the transformative affect of military bases. The city had been home to a Navy coaling station and modest Marine and Navy training centers and bases since the 1910s. But during World War II, San Diego County became one of the largest Marine-Navy centers in the nation, with a destroyer base, a repair base, a fuel depot, a navy hospital, marine rifle ranges, Navy and Marine housing centers, and more. (In the 1990s, the city would become the new home of the U.S. Pacific Fleet.) San Diego also had airplane manufacturers such as the Consolidated Aircraft Corporation, which had moved there from Buffalo, New York, in the late 1930s, attracted by the city's climate, available land, and the growing military presence. By 1944, the city's population had gone from about 200,000 residents to 500,000, many of them temporary. This dramatic expansion was a mixed blessing. Military bases and manufacturing plants became the heart of San Diego County's economy and provided direct and indirect employment for tens of thousands of local residents, but the military also appropriated vast tracts of land for bases and housing on which it paid no property taxes. The military personnel cycling through the region during the war also changed the character of the city, as a relatively quiet residential city now served an often boisterous population of single young men.

The West also was the site of the most significant new research program of the war: the Manhattan Project. The race to produce an atomic bomb began when exiled German scientists such as Albert Einstein warned of Nazi efforts and lobbied FDR to start an American nuclear program. There were laboratories in different parts of the country (and allied research and uranium mining programs in Britain and Canada). But Los Alamos, New Mexico, was the home of "the bomb." The head scientist in the project, J. Robert Oppenheimer, had gone to a boys' camp near Los Alamos, forty miles west of Santa Fe and accessible only by dirt road. He loved the New Mexico landscape and recognized that the isolated ranching area would be an ideal place to carry out a secret research project. In 1942, the federal government appropriated the Los Alamos Ranch School for Boys and built a small city for the 7,000 scientists, technicians, soldiers, and other workers who would take part in the project. They removed the name Los Alamos from the map and listed the base as a Santa Fe post office box. Scientists detonated the first atomic bomb in the New Mexico desert in July 1945. In August 1945, the United States dropped the first two atomic bombs on Japan—not Germany, which had surrendered in May 1945—and ended the war in the Pacific.

Los Alamos continued to exist as a highly controlled, though no longer secret, "federal city" until the 1950s. Desert sites in other parts of the Southwest—notably the Nevada Test Site, sixty-five miles northwest of Las Vegas—became testing grounds for atomic weaponry, with more than 1,000 bombs set off in the 1950s and early 1960s. In the 1960s, concerns about wind-blown atomic dust clouds, radiation poisoning, dead animals, and unusually high rates of cancer in towns downwind of tests, such as St. George, Utah, led to public pressure to end above-ground testing of nuclear weapons. (International nuclear arms and testing treaties also contributed to end of testing.) Wartime and Cold War exigencies had justified such risks in the minds of government and military officials. But in the 1960s, Westerners began to reject the notion that their homes should be treated as "national sacrifice zones." Nonetheless, the Manhattan Project and other high-tech weapons development programs in the West would further transform the economy of the region, not just in its general industrial development, but in the emergence of a high-tech economy oriented around research and development.

In total, the government spent $40 billion on factories, military bases, and other infrastructure improvements during the war. San Francisco, Los Angeles, Portland, Houston, Fort Worth, Wichita, Seattle, and San Diego each got more than $1 billion in war-supply contracts. The impact on such metropolitan centers can be measured in various ways. By the end of the war, for example, LA had moved from the seventh to the second largest manufacturing center in the nation, behind only Detroit. When all wartime contracts are added to the tally, the region had received $70 billion. The resulting transformation process can best be described as the creation of a "garrison state," one in which the government mobilized the entire society to fight a war. But wartime mobilization also did the work of subsidizing economic development and public welfare.

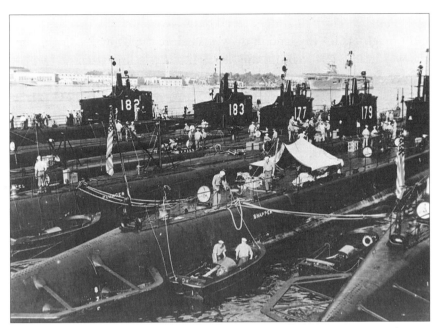

Submarines at San Diego, 1940. *Courtesy of the U.S. Naval Institute, James C. Fahey Collection, nh68479*

Liberty ship *SS Carlos Carrillo,* off the cost of San Francisco, California, in 1945 or 1946. *Courtesy of the U.S. Naval Institute, James C. Fahey Collection, nh98700*

Henry J. Kaiser provides a good example of how it worked. He had built freighters for England in the years before the United States entered the war in late 1941. Beginning in 1942, he got loans—close to $200 million in total—to expand his shipyards, build a steel mill, and start a magnesium plant. The relationship between government and private corporations such as his was tight, with the federal government providing startup capital and businesses meeting payrolls and building the products, while entrepreneurs like Kaiser worked with federal government officials to coordinate production. By 1945, Kaiser had shipyards in Richmond (California), Portland, and Vancouver (Washington), and every forty-two days his plants turned out a 440-foot "Liberty" cargo ship that could carry more than 9,000 tons of cargo, completing three a day by 1943. Kaiser's methods of manufacturing are still used for merchant and navy ships, and his steel mill just east of Los Angeles was state of the art in the 1940s and 1950s.

In addition to innovation in manufacturing, Kaiser also led in defining new employee benefits, creating Kaiser Permanente in 1945, an integrated, managed medical care organization (a forerunner of today's HMOs). Organizations like this were not wholly new, with roots in the 1910s and 1920s. Kaiser's own businesses had developed medical facilities to deal with worker's compensation obligations in the 1930s. In the 1940s, Kaiser expanded medical and insurance programs for his employees at shipyards and other plants. In 1944, he decided to keep operating his medical facilities after the war, to expand the programs, and to offer them to the general public. Kaiser had started such programs to meet union demands and maintain a stable workforce, but they eventually became potential money makers in their own right. They also reflected the new power of labor unions to win benefits and the encouragement of the federal government, which hoped to placate laborers to help maintain social order and legitimate claims about the superiority of the American way during the war and the Cold War that followed.

Kaiser was an entrepreneur: he invested his own money, took risks, and worked hard to cultivate ties to military officials and politicians; but he also benefited from massive federal subsidies and loans, and from regulatory powers that allowed government officials to set prices on goods and decide where resources would be used. Wartime needs and the interests of nation building legitimized such government intervention in the economy and did not seem subversive or a threat to capitalism in the way that the less-intrusive New Deal programs had. Put another way, wartime (and Cold War) circumstances reconciled classic frontier-Western ideals of rugged individualism and hostility toward government interference with a form of corporate welfare.

The G.I. Bill of 1944 was another case in point. It promised to pay for the education of veterans of the armed forces, provide them low-interest home loans (without a down payment), and pay disability benefits. (The bill included women and non-white veterans, but not men who had served in the merchant marine.) The result was the dramatic expansion and democratization of student bodies, a sudden increase in the size and number of colleges and universities, and a postwar suburban housing boom. All of these programs sparked a major economic boon in the short run and subsequent decades. They benefited both the individuals and institutions that received money directly and the local economies in communities where they lived. The G.I. Bill seemed legitimate to most Americans—again, in a way that past New Deal and future 1960s-era War on Poverty programs sometimes did not—because they did not perceive it as welfare but as an earned reward for soldiers who had put their lives on the line for their country. The G.I. Bill also cushioned the economic transition from a wartime economy to a peacetime one, and it reflected a desire to prevent the nation from falling back into another economic depression or intractable political conflicts and labor violence, as had happened after World War I.

This "welfare" transformed the Western economy and consequently began to transform the social landscape of the region. Not all parts of the West changed or benefited equally. States on the Pacific Coast (especially California) and in the Southwest (especially Texas) profited the most and Plains and Mountain states to a lesser degree. It also is noteworthy that the South was similarly transformed during the war. In general, this era saw a shift in industrial power in the United States from the Northeast and Midwest to the South and West. Such patterns help to explain where people migrated to and from in the West (and other parts of the nation) during the war and in subsequent decades.

The War and Racism in the West

The most notorious episode in the American prosecution of World War II was the decision by the federal government to forcibly relocate Japanese Americans (legal immigrants as well as U.S. citizens) from their homes on the Pacific Coast out of fear that they threatened the nation as "alien" agents of Japan. The U.S. government also incarcerated some men of German and Italian descent whom it suspected of specific activities, but it rounded up only Japanese Americans as a race: children, women, and men. The irony, of course, is that the legitimacy of World War II as a "just war" was based on Allied opposition to German Nazism, the Holocaust, and Japanese militarism, rape, massacres, and forced labor in Korea and China. The "good war" was, in this regard at least, an ambiguous affair. This is especially so when the World War II experiences of Indians, Mexicans, and African Americans—in military and civilian contexts—are factored in. As in other parts of the nation, in the West, African Americans faced discrimination in housing, the armed forces, and finding jobs, though to a lesser extent in the last case because of wartime employment needs. The contest between the United States and Japan to control the Pacific, along with racist wartime policies in the West, suggest that Americans continued to wrestle with the complex legacies of empire during the war, and that empire and democratic ideals continued to rest together uneasily.

FDR's decision to relocate Japanese Americans came in his Executive Order 9066 in February 1942. Politicians and ordinary citizens generally favored it, their attitudes reflecting long-held anti-Japanese sentiments—for example, by white farmers and fishermen who resented competition from the Japanese. Most administration and military officials reluctantly accepted it, but the order was controversial. A sign of this was the decision of the military governor in Hawaii not to round up its long-standing Japanese population of 160,000, but only 1,400 men suspected of specific activities against the United States. The Japanese were 35 percent of the population in Hawaii and were too important to its economy to intern. Moreover, the government had put Hawaii under martial law, which allowed it to control the population generally and thereby limit the possibility of spying and sabotage. The Japanese in Hawaii thus endured restrictions and racist suspicion during the war, but did not wholly lose their freedom and property, as did Japanese Americans on the mainland.

About 130,000 Japanese lived on the mainland in 1942—94,000 in California, and most of the rest in Oregon and Washington. Of the 112,000 interned, 41,000 were Japanese-born *Issei* "aliens" who were not eligible for citizenship, and 72,000 American-born *Nisei* citizens. The government gave Japanese Americans very little time to wrap up their affairs (e.g., try to sell the businesses and homes they had worked so hard to get and maintain) and report to transfer centers, whence they were sent to one of 10 "relocation camps" in Arizona, Idaho, Utah, California, Wyoming, Colorado, and Arkansas. The concentration camp–like facilities had spartan barracks, were surrounded by barbed-wire fences and watchtowers, and had hostile, occasionally violent guards. Many of the prisoners, the elderly and children especially, suffered from the cold, poor sanitation, dust, and meager diets that characterized living conditions in the camps. All of the prisoners in the camps experienced the indignity of being treated by their own government as criminals simply because of their racial heritage.

In a display of hypocrisy, in 1943 the U.S. Army began recruiting Nisei men. Eager to show their loyalty to their country of birth, more than 33,000 Japanese Americans joined up, notably in the 100th Infantry Battalion and the 442nd Regimental Combat Team. They served in Europe and were among the most decorated units in the war. A small number of Japanese Americans joined the secret Nisei Military Intelligence Service, which served in the Pacific.

In December 1944, the U.S. Supreme Court ruled the detainment of loyal citizens unconstitutional, and the government began allowing families to leave the camps. Most returned to their home regions—sometimes welcomed with sympathy, more often with hostility, and often to find their homes and fields damaged by neglect or even sold or taken over by white "neighbors." Some moved to other parts of the United States or back to Japan, reflecting the trauma they had experienced during the war. At the time, the only government official with the decency to apologize to the internees was Governor Ralph Lawrence Carr of Colorado, an act that cost him reelection. In 1948, Congress provided the former internees limited compensation for lost property, but this hardly covered the actual loses or made up for lives and families that had been shattered. In the 1960s, Japanese American civil rights activists and lawyers began pursuing further compensation and a formal apology. In 1980, a Congressional

Japanese American boy waiting to be transported to a War Relocation Authority Camp, Salinas, California, 1942. *Library of Congress, LC-USF34-T01-072499-D*

Below: Relocation evacuation sale at Okano Bros. five and dime store in San Francisco, 1942. *Courtesy of the Franklin D. Roosevelt Library Digital Archives*

Laborers from all over the Big Horn Basin stand in line to sign up for work to help build the barracks at the Heart Mountain Relocation Center in northwest Wyoming, 1942. *Buffalo Bill Historical Center, Cody, Wyoming; Jack Richard Collection, PN.89.111.21236.8*

View from a nearby hill of the Heart Mountain Relocation Center, northwest Wyoming, as construction workers build the barracks, 1942. *Buffalo Bill Historical Center, Cody, Wyoming; Jack Richard Collection, PN.89.111.21236.17*

A Japanese American soldier visiting his family at the Heart Mountain Relocation Center in northwest Wyoming, 1942 or 1943. *Buffalo Bill Historical Center, Cody, Wyoming; Jack Richard Collection, PN.89.111.21236.11*

Japanese American women walk through the snow to their barracks at the Heart Mountain Relocation Center, 1942. Heart Mountain can be seen in the background. *Buffalo Bill Historical Center, Cody, Wyoming; Jack Richard Collection, PN.89.111.21236.3*

commission studied the issue, and eventually in 1988 President Ronald Reagan signed The Civil Liberties Act, which awarded $20,000 to each relocation camp survivor.

Like Japanese men, thousands of American Indians volunteered for the armed forces despite the racism and discriminatory policies they faced. About 25,000 reservation Indians and 20,000 nonreservation Indians served in the military during the war, proportionally the highest of any racial-ethnic group in the nation. In some Indian communities, as many as 70 percent of men joined. Their motivations likely were diverse, from escaping unemployment or boredom to patriotic, romantic, and masculine notions of warrior honor. Navajo "code talkers," who fought in the Pacific against Japan, are the most famous Indian soldiers, their native language serving as a code that the Japanese could not break. Clarence Tinker, an Osage from Oklahoma, was the highest-ranking Native American officer during the war, as a career pilot with the rank of Major General. Joseph J. "Jocko" Clark, a Cherokee from Oklahoma, the first Indian graduate from the U.S. Naval Academy at Annapolis (in 1918) and a pilot, served in the Pacific, commanding aircraft carriers and carrier task forces as a Rear Admiral. On many reservations, as in American society in general, Indian women took on traditionally male roles during the war—"manning" fire lookouts or working as mechanics and lumberjacks. About 40,000 Indians left reservations to work in defense industries. If such experiences assimilated some Indians to national life, to a degree, it is also the case that Indian veterans, both those returning to reservations and those who lived in urban areas, would form a key cohort in the civil rights and pan-Indian movements of the 1950s and 1960s. They would refuse to accept discrimination and fight new threats to their reservation communities. Indians did not have the right to vote in six states until the 1950s, and in the same decade the federal government would adopt "termination" policies designed to abolish reservations and forcibly speed up Indian assimilation into mainstream American life.

Up to 400,000 Americans of Mexican descent served in the armed forces during the war. They too faced discrimination in their units and when on R&R. As with American Indians, the experience of sacrificing for their country (to fight racist dictators), being barred from whites-only establishments in their native United States, and seeing greater inter-racial cooperation, racial tolerance, and social interaction abroad led some Mexican American veterans to organize against discrimination at home.

Civilian Mexican Americans migrated to cities in large numbers during World War II, leaving agricultural work for wartime industries and other urban jobs that had opened up to them. By 1970, 85 percent of Mexicans Americans were residents of urban areas. The Mexican American story is doubly complex because wartime needs meant that hundreds of thousands of Mexicans crossed into the United States to meet the shortage of agricultural laborers. In 1942, the United States signed an agreement with Mexico to create a *Bracero* program, a contract labor system that let Mexicans come to the United States to work seasonally on farms. It suspended laws requiring contract laborers to pay a head tax and be literate. Between 1942 and 1964, more than 4.5 million Braceros worked in the United States on farms and in food-processing plants, especially in California, Texas, and Arizona, but also in the Northwest and Mountain West.

Navajo Code Talkers, Saipan, June 1944. *Courtesy, National Archives, Record Group 127: Records of the U.S. Marine Corps, 1775 - 9999, ARC Identifier 532526*

Under the terms of the agreement, Mexico required American employers to provide the migrant workers with round-trip fares (from their homes to the work sites) and pay them wages equal to those of local workers. But the government made little effort to enforce these obligations, and they usually went unmet. On the job many Braceros endured squalid living conditions (lacking proper bathroom facilities, for example), exploitative working conditions, and legal discrimination. Migrant workers as well as Mexican American U.S. citizens often endured violence at the hands of angry and racist white Americans, often in the West.

In June 1943, for example, racial tensions in Los Angeles led white soldiers and sailors to attack "zoot-suit" wearing Mexican American youths (known as *pachucos* in the slang of the day) whom they perceived as gang members. Zoot-suiters wore pants with high waists, baggy legs, tight cuffs at the ankles, and long coats with padded shoulders, often worn with a long decorative chain going from a belt loop to a pocket. The popularity of zoot suits reflected the outsider status of the pachucos, whose foreign look and civilian status offended the servicemen. The riots began when several white sailors fought with a group of young Mexican American men, leaving one sailor severely hurt. To retaliate, dozens of sailors, and eventually thousands of servicemen, attacked Mexican American men (and later African American men) in Downtown and East LA. The riots lasted several days before the police restored order, with the help of volunteer "Vengeance Squads" that resembled the vigilantes of the Gold Rush Era. Vigilantes "arrested" and beat young Mexican American men for "harassing" sailors. The police eventually arrested several hundred Mexican American men but only a few sailors, leaving most of the servicemen for the military to deal with. In the wake of the riots, the military restricted the access of servicemen to the city. The local press generally praised the white rioters and vigilantes, crediting them with cleaning up a juvenile delinquent and criminal menace.

Despite such experiences, and despite the unique resurgence of anti-Japanese racism after the attack on Pearl Harbor, World War II did lead to policy changes. However slowly, these changes would contribute to the civil rights movements that marginalized groups of Americans organized in the 1950s and 1960s. In 1948, President Harry Truman (who had taken office in 1944 after FDR's death) desegregated the armed forces with Executive Order 9981, though not until a 1963 order from Defense

Secretary Robert McNamara did all segregation in the armed forces end. Likewise, the G.I. Bill of 1944 applied to all veterans regardless of race, at least in theory, as discrimination often continued to prevent nonwhites (even those with money or low-interest loans available to them) from buying homes in the suburbs that sprang up across the West after the war.

People on the Move

One can sum up national population trends during World War II and the subsequent Cold War era quite simply: the population shifted West and South. In the West itself, people moved from rural areas and small towns to metropolises. In urban areas, people moved from city centers out to suburbs, whites especially. A new trend was African Americans moving in large numbers from the South (especially the western South) to the West. In California the black population went from 125,000 in 1940 to more than 600,000 in 1950, most of it in LA and the Bay Area. As unions desegregated in the late 1930s and 1940s, African Americans sought industrial jobs in the West now open to them. More than a million whites moved from the Midwest to the West in the 1940s, and another 800,000 from the South. In this instance, the war had accelerated well-established trends.

The millions of whites who migrated to the West in the 1940s and 1950s assumed that segregated housing patterns would continue, and a home in a white neighborhood remained at the core of their dreams. Whether in Detroit or LA, blacks continued to find that real estate agents would not even show them homes in certain neighborhoods; neighborhood covenants barred African Americans from many areas, while threats, intimidation, and actual violence remained a last resort for white homeowners in neighborhoods in which a black family managed to buy a home. When factories and good jobs moved with white families to the suburbs in the 1950s, African American and other nonwhite families typically remained stuck in inner cities—this despite the service of millions of minority men during the war and the mortgages that the G.I. Bill promised them. Such segregationist realities ensured that migration to the West, migration within the West, and the region's growing population meant different things to whites and persons of color.

If the West as a whole grew, the long-term shift of the population from rural areas and small towns to big cities accelerated. Rural areas on the Plains saw their population decline, though Plains cities grew modestly, especially where they had military bases. Established centers like Denver, Dallas–Fort Worth, LA, and Seattle continued to grow, and some small cities in the Southwest became major metropolitan centers by the 1950s—the population of Phoenix jumping from 65,000 in 1940 to 439,000 in 1960, and that of Albuquerque from 35,000 to 201,000. Such trends were national, but Western cities grew faster than those in other parts of the nation. The percentage of the U.S. population in the Mountain and Pacific states alone went from 10.5 percent in 1940 to 15 percent in 1960 and 18.5 percent in 1980. More than that, in the 1950s and 1960s metropolitan areas in the West led the nation in terms of the highest proportion of high school graduates and white-collar workers, average number of years of schooling, and median income. They also led the nation in the geographic sprawl that would characterize suburban America. In short, World War II not only changed where Americans lived, but how they lived.

American households also changed during the war, as many working-class and middle-class women moved into factory jobs that had long been the dominion of men. With millions of men serving overseas, and wartime industries running day and night, necessity required women to take jobs traditionally barred to them by employers, unions, and social mores. Necessity even demanded that employers like Kaiser build daycare facilities for the children of their employees. Wartime need benefited minority men, too, as necessity trumped prejudice. Women working in wartime industries were celebrated in publicity campaigns and popular songs, such as "Rosie the Riveter" from 1943. But many songs, posters, and magazine stories about women like Rosie suggest that Americans saw the mass movement of women into the industrial workplace as something revolutionary and dangerous, however necessary. They feared for a generation of children raised without mothers during their early years. After the war, when white servicemen returned home, they generally found their jobs waiting for them, and nonwhite men and women had to move back to lower-paying jobs or the home. In the suburbs of the West, as in other parts of the nation, many women had enjoyed their wartime jobs, had earned a college education, or launched dreams of careers of their own. Those who found domestic life or the suburbs stifling would look for work or explore the new women's movement in steadily growing numbers. In short, wartime changes and experiences would continue to foster social and political changes in the decades to come.

The Cold War

In the years after World War II, fears of a postwar economic depression seemed to be coming true in the West, as government spending dropped by $90 billion and orders for war materiel declined. In Washington State, for example, Boeing Corporation's orders dropped from $600 million in 1944 to $14 million in 1946. California suffered similarly, with military orders falling and unemployment rising. A true crisis never came, however, in part because of the G.I. Bill and a postwar housing and consumer boom, and in part because of the Cold War.

The postwar boom reflected the impact of the G.I. Bill—on education and housing—and programs run by the Social Security and Federal Housing administrations. It also was based on the savings accumulated by wartime workers and their families, as wages had risen but consumer goods had remained scarce, with natural resources and manufacturing directed to wartime needs. Housing was in short supply across the country in the 1930s, but young families were eager to purchase homes after the war. When William J. Levitt, a wartime engineer in the Pacific, and his father's company, Levitt & Sons, developed ways to mass-produce affordable standardized houses, first in Long Island and Pennsylvania, a postwar boom began for the lower middle class. Now, blue-collar and low-level white-collar employees could aspire to own a home. The boom soon followed on the Pacific Coast and then in the Mountain West and Southwest, where the population had been rising steadily during the 1930s and 1940s. The rate of home ownership in the United States rose from 44 percent in 1934 to 63 percent in 1972. The economy was further aided by the federal government through its funding of the construction of new airports and the new interstate highway system, the West consistently getting a share of national funding proportionally larger than its population—for example, 35 percent of airport construction aid and 42 percent of the cost of the construction of interstate highway mileage between 1946 and 1972. Democratic and Republican politicians from the West also made sure that companies in their districts got federal dollars to help convert their plants to produce civilian products. In short, American citizens, especially West-

Construction of the underground combat operations center known as NORAD in the heart of Cheyenne Mountain, near Colorado Springs, Colorado, 1961 or 1962. *Special Collections Department, Stewart Library, Weber State University*

erners, returned to normal lives in the postwar years, but they continued to benefit from the federal intervention in the economy that had begun during the Great Depression and World War II.

In addition, the Cold War between the United States and its allies and the communist bloc in Eastern Europe and Asia (led by the Soviet Union and China) meant that "peacetime" military spending would remain high. In this era of heightened tension, the West and the South benefited especially. Cold War spending remained astronomical for four decades, not just during the war years in Korea (1950–53) and Vietnam (1964–73). The federal government expanded military bases, supply depots, training bases, shipyards, and aircraft maintenance facilities. It upgraded railroad, communication, and highway systems to serve them. It also developed new facilities and technologies such as the Distant Early Warning radar system it built in Alaska and northern Canada, the Strategic Air Command in Nebraska, new Air Force training centers, an Air Force Academy and North American Air Defense Command in Colorado, bases for long-range B-52 bombers that carried atomic bombs, and eventually nuclear missile bases, many of the bomber and missile bases located in northern-tier states such as North Dakota, Wyoming, and Montana. All of the new technology required extensive research, development, testing, and manufacturing facilities.

One can measure the economic significance of this military spending in various ways. The U.S. Navy alone was responsible for adding 215,000 people to the San Diego area by 1957. Into the mid-1950s, as much as 98 percent of Boeing's production was to fulfill orders for military contracts. Orders for passenger jetliners, starting in the 1960s, would change that, but much civilian technology—everything from radar to jet airliners to microwave technology and the Internet—was first developed for the military and thus effectively subsidized by tax-payer dollars. Finally, in the 1950s, out-of-state income related to the military ranged as high as 25 percent or more for California, Washington, Hawaii, Utah, and Colorado, and 15 to 24 percent for Nevada, Arizona, New Mexico, Kansas, Oklahoma, and Texas. States such as North Dakota would lobby for more nuclear-missile facilities towards the end of the Cold War, so dependent had their economies become on military spending, as family incomes in traditional agricultural, ranching, and natural resource industries steadily declined.

Cold War military expansion also highlights the relationship between the West and American expansion overseas. To contain communism, project American military power and political influence globally, support trade overseas, and fight wars in Korea and Vietnam, the U.S. military built and expanded bases in the Philippines, Okinawa and Japan, Korea, Vietnam, the Middle East, and the Indian Ocean, and on central Pacific islands such as Guam. All of this was in addition to the permanent American presence in Western Europe and Canada. The social and cultural impact of this Cold War empire on the West and the rest of the nation can be observed in numerous ways. Some military personnel stationed in Korea, Japan, the Philippines, Vietnam, and other parts of Asia returned home with Asian brides. Others brought home a love of the martial arts or a familiarity with Asian foods and other elements of Asian culture. Refugees and immigrants followed, especially in the wake of the Vietnam War, and especially as U.S immigration policy opened back up to nonwhite parts of the world in the 1960s. Immigrants to the United States increasingly would come from "West" to "East," from Asia, and through airports such as LAX (in Los Angeles), rather than from Europe and the through port of New York, as in the past.

The American West became part of an increasingly integrated and globally influential Pacific Rim transoceanic region. This transoceanic nexus was by fostered by military alliances, economic ties, cultural exchange, and migration. It resulted in politicians, business leaders, lobbyists, and citizen groups from the American West playing a larger role in shaping U.S. policy, not simply being shaped by it. As noted earlier, Herbert Hoover was the first president from the West. In the second half of the twentieth century, the West could make claims on eight more: Harry Truman (Missouri), Dwight D. Eisenhower (Kansas), Richard M. Nixon (California), Lyndon Baines Johnson (Texas), George H. W. Bush (many years as an oil man in Texas and having served the House of Representatives from Texas), Ronald Reagan (California), Bill Clinton (Arkansas), and George W. Bush (Texas). Along with such presidents, Western delegates to Congress exercised growing influence in Washington. In 2008, Barack Obama, a native son of Hawaii, won election as the nation's 44th president.

The Turning Point: From Periphery to Metropolis

The region we call the American West once was colonial territory in the overseas empires of Spain, France, and Great Britain. When recounting the history of the West, scholars tend to stop thinking of it as a colony and begin to describe it as a commercial and settlement frontier every time the United States takes possession of another part of it from a European power, Mexico, or an Indian people—by war, purchase, annexation, and diplomacy. In function, however, the West remained something like a colony and its Indian and Mexican inhabitants subject peoples. Even as unorganized lands became formally organized territories and then states—with equal constitutional status in the Union—the West remained colony-like in its relationship to the older parts of the nation. Politicians in Washington, D.C. and businesspersons in cities such as New York and

Chicago continued to shape the fate of the region and its peoples. In the Canadian frontier thesis, developed by the historians H. A. Innis and J. M. S. Careless, this sort of relationship is described in terms of metropolitan centers and peripheral regions (see Chapter One). In global terms, in world systems theory, this relationship is described as one between core areas and peripheries. Like India, Rhodesia, Algeria, and Vietnam in relation to Britain and France, the West once was a periphery of the eastern United States. No longer.

By the early twentieth century, the West had evolved into a semi-periphery, with a somewhat developed, modern economy that included some manufacturing. The region remained dependent, however, in that banks, corporations, and investors from the Midwest and East still had a prevailing influence over its development, and business executives and politicians from the West still had limited influence in the nation's capital and financial centers in other regions. That the United States had moved on to conquest and colonization overseas—in the Philippines, the Panama Canal Zone, Puerto Rico, and Hawaii—was a sign of the changing status of the West. Perhaps most important, the West itself and the new American possessions in the Pacific Ocean served as a gateway to the markets of Asia and Latin America.

Whatever might have happened had World War II and the Cold War not taken place, it was these events that turned the United States into a global superpower—the sole superpower economically—and transformed the American West from a semi-periphery into a core region in its own right, with its own metropolitan centers to rival those in the East and around the world. LA in particular became a peer of New York, Chicago, London, and Paris—as the second leading manufacturing center in the country at the end of World War II, a major financial center, and the symbolic global capital of the entertainment industry and mass culture. LA and other Western metropolitan centers such as Seattle, Denver, Dallas–Fort Worth, and the San Francisco Bay Area and powerful Western states like Texas and California began to exercise influence in the nation's capital and around the world. The key point here is to recognize the transformation of the West and its major urban centers into a core American region and a core region globally. Its rise has been central to the evolution of the Pacific Rim, the most rapidly growing international economic region in the world since World War II. Indeed, if California separated from the United States, it alone would have one of the ten largest national economies in the world. By contrast, Western Canada was not transformed in the same fundamental way by World War II and the Cold War. It benefitted from military bases and rising prices in agricultural and resource commodities during the war and since the war has enjoyed growing economic importance with the rise of the Pacific Rim. But it did not undergo rapid industrialization comparable to that of the American West. Industrial growth remained primarily in the central-Eastern Canadian provinces of Ontario and Quebec in the 1940s. Despite growth in banking, tourism, and industry since the war, including high-tech and cultural areas, the heart of Western Canada's economy remains driven by natural resources, most obviously by oil in Alberta. In this regard, its evolution perhaps compares best to that of the American West in the first three decades of the twentieth century.

Most Americans do not think of the West as once having been a "colony" of the United States; and until recently most have not considered the notion that the United States is a global empire. If the West was a unique sort of colony, compared to the overseas colonies of European nations, so too has the United States become a new sort of free-trade empire. The U.S. prefers to exercise its power indirectly, through trade and investment overseas and diplomatic pressure. Nonetheless, it has intervened militarily on a regular basis in the twentieth and early twenty-first centuries in other nations to protect its interests and promote its policies, especially in Mexico and Latin America, but also in Africa, the Middle East, and Asia. It has occupied other nations on occasion (in Iraq most recently, since 2003). And it has hundreds of military bases overseas served by hundreds of thousands of soldiers and diplomats.

The federal government played the central role in all of this. Through the Marshall Plan in Western Europe and the American occupation of postwar Japan, and efforts to rebuild their economies and promote capitalism and democracy, the United States promoted economic and cultural globalization. These policies might be described as "New Deals" for Europe and Japan, with the goal of creating flourishing societies open to American trade. Like the actual New Deal and the wartime policies that transformed the American West, these succeeded too, in the long run perhaps too well. If the unintended effect of the New Deal and wartime policy was to transform the West into a core region of the

United States, an unintended effect of American-led globalization and the free-trade empire was to produce competitors that by the end of the twentieth century would threaten America's global economic power. Likewise, globalization has begun to transform the United States itself, both culturally and demographically, most notably in the West. Westerners might grudgingly acknowledge, if not thank, the federal government for the New Deal and wartime economic growth. But they often would blame it for the unsettling effects of globalization. In this regard, at least, things did not change in the West.

An example of the connection between the rapid wartime modernization of the American West, the Cold War, and the free-trade empire created by the American superpower is Bechtel Corporation, which started building railroad lines in California at the turn of the century and worked on dam-building projects in the 1920s. Bechtel was part of the Six Companies group that built the Hoover Dam and was a major player during World War II, building shipyards, oil tankers, cargo ships, bases, the Alaska-Canadian Highway, and the CANOL oil pipeline (to bring oil from Alaska to the lower 48 states). During the Cold War, Bechtel and some of the other Six Companies firms built American bases in the Pacific, securing military contracts on a scale much larger than those of the 1940s. Bechtel became a major player in Iraq in 2003, getting no-bid contracts to build water, power, and sewage plants during the American occupation of that nation after its invasion and the ouster of the dictator Saddam Hussein. The Texas-based firm Kellogg Brown and Root (KBR) provides a second example. Today a subsidiary of Halliburton Energy Services, KBR's roots go back to Depression-era public works projects and World War II military contracts. A former Halliburton CEO from Wyoming, Richard "Dick" Cheney, became Vice-President of the United States in 2001, and KBR was given major contracts in Iraq by the administration of Texan George W. Bush. Such ties are not evidence of conspiracies or of the American political system suddenly gone awry. They are part of the long and continuing story of the American trade empire, the global economy it fostered, and what President Eisenhower in 1961 warned of as the "military-industrial complex" that had began to transform the American West in the 1940s.

Terms such as *colony* and *empire* are loaded ones, with strong political resonances for most Americans. Their use here is not meant to damn or praise, but to shed light on the evolution of the West and the larger nation. They can help us to see these stories in comparison to other parts of the world and in unfamiliar ways. If they make our own history seem a little strange, as a result, they also can help us to see it more fully.

Conclusion

The controversy over the proposed Echo Park Dam in the 1950s exemplifies how the West had changed. By then, most Westerners lived in cities and suburbs. Like people in the East, they too looked forward to vacations in national parks and other wilderness spaces. The region had developed economically to the point that that they too began to fear that nature was under threat and in need of preservation. Having achieved material success, they began to count the costs of "progress." No longer simply a battle between Eastern preservationists and Western developers, such conflicts increasingly were between Westerners with conflicting interests.

The proposed dam, at the juncture of the Green and Yampa rivers, was part of a larger Colorado River Storage Project, a system of dams designed to control water flow, provide water for farms and cities, and generate electricity. The controversy began in 1950 when the Bureau of Reclamation decided to build a dam in a hidden canyon called Echo Park in the Dinosaur National Monument near the Utah-Colorado border. In the 1940s, preservationists and the National Park Service (NPS) had begun to work together to oppose building more dams on NPS lands. Ever since the Hetch Hetchy battles of the 1910s, the Bureau itself had been careful about building in national parks and monuments. By the 1950s, however, Reclamation bureaucrats had become arrogant in the power they wielded, and miscalculated. The Sierra Club, at the time led by John Brower, played a key role in organizing the opposition to the Echo Park dam, as it had in the case of Hetch Hetchy under the leadership of John Muir. Along with the Wilderness Society, Brower and the Sierra Club started a publicity campaign that forced the Bureau to back down. Stories and advertisements in newspapers and magazines asked, "Shall We Let Them Ruin Our National Parks?" The popular historian Bernard DeVoto explained and pleaded for the historical and ecological significance of Echo Park. When Congress passed the Colorado River Storage Project in 1956 it included a provision forbidding the building of dams in national parks.

Lake Powell, Arizona (May 2007). Note the prominent "bathtub ring" made visible by low water, a sign of a long period of drought. *Photo: PRA*

This was hardly the last battle between preservationists and the advocates of "progress," and Brower and his allies soon regretted that in the negotiations over Echo Park they had agreed not to oppose the construction of a dam in Glen Canyon, upstream from the Grand Canyon. The Glen Canyon Dam ended up destroying a unique and beautiful canyon that now sits under a giant reservoir (Lake Powell) busy with houseboaters and water-skiers. Glen Canyon had contained beautiful rock formations, including many sheltered sites under cliffs where Indian peoples had once lived. These rare archeological sites featured rock and cave paintings done by Indians that dated back hundreds, even thousands of years. Even some proponents of the Glen Canyon Dam, such as Arizona Senator Barry Goldwater, later said they had made a mistake. Then, in the 1960s, the Bureau of Reclamation proposed two dams that would have flooded part of the Grand Canyon. Again, a public campaign and bureaucratic maneuvering stymied the Bureau, and in 1968 Congress approved a smaller version of the larger Central Arizona Project that did not call for the two dams. The key point here is that the tide had turned, beginning in the

1950s and more definitively in the 1960s and 1970s, as many Westerners agreed with critics who depicted dam-building projects as environmentally damaging, unnecessary, and merely corrupt "pork barrel" projects for members of Congress and local developers. Put another way, Westerners, too, began to question the conservation ideal and had come to value the preservation of wilderness spaces, especially those in national parks and monuments. These Westerners, like other Americans, were defining and embracing what people began to call "environmental" values.

As these examples suggest, Western problems and patterns increasingly mirrored those of the rest of the nation. The West had not lost all of its distinctiveness. More than in any other region, aridity and water resources remained a problem. The federal government remained by far the region's biggest land owner. And many people still thought of the West as different, as a frontier of sorts, and definitely as a place to escape for a few days or weeks every year, to fly-fish, kayak, ski or snowboard, mountain climb, hike, camp, or simply kick back and take in the beauty of the land and its many and varied natural settings. On the other hand, modern technologies (such as air conditioning, dams, cookie-cutter suburbs, strip malls, the car, mass culture) and the social and environmental costs associated with them meant that how Westerners lived, and the buildings and man-made landscapes in which they worked, worshipped, studied, and played, differed increasingly less from the rest of the country.

ℭ℥ Suggested Readings ℵ℧

Abbott, Carl. *The Metropolitan Frontier: Cities in the Modern American West.* Tucson: University of Arizona Press, 1995.

Anderson, Karen. *Wartime Women: Sex Roles, Family Relations, and the Status of Women during World War II.* Westport, CT: Greenwood Press, 1981.

Bernstein, Alison R. *American Indians and World War II: Toward a New Era in Indian Affairs.* Norman: University of Oklahoma Press, 1999.

Billington, David P., and Donald C. Jackson. *Big Dams of the New Deal Era: A Confluence of Engineering and Politics.* Norman: University of Oklahoma Press, 2006.

Clayton, James. "The Impact of the Cold War on the Economies of California and Utah, 1946–1965." *Pacific Historical Review* 36 (1967): 449–453.

Daniels, Roger. *Prisoners without Trial: Japanese Americans in World War II.* New York: Hill & Wang, 1993.

Davis, Mike. *City of Quartz: Excavating the Future in Los Angeles.* New York: Vintage, 1992.

Ferlund, Kevin J., ed. *The Cold War American West, 1945–1989.* Albuquerque: University of New Mexico Press, 1998.

Leonard, Kevin Allen. *The Battle for Los Angeles: Racial Ideology and World War II.* Albuquerque: University of New Mexico Press, 2006.

Lotchin, Roger. *Fortress California, 1910–1961: From Warfare to Welfare.* Champaign: University of Illinois Press, 2002.

Lotchin, Roger, ed. *The Martial Metropolis: U.S. Cities in War and Peace.* New York: Praeger, 1984.

Nash, Gerald. *The American West Transformed: The Impact of the Second World War.* Bloomington: Indiana University Press, 1985.

Rivas-Rodriguez, Maggie. *Mexican Americans and World War II.* Austin: University of Texas Press, 2005.

Taylor, Quintard. *In Search of the Racial Frontier: African Americans in the West, 1528–1990.* New York: Norton, 1998.

Wolf, Donald E. *Big Dams and Other Dreams: The Six Companies Story.* Norman: University of Oklahoma Press, 1996.

Wrobel, David M. *The End of American Exceptionalism: Frontier Anxiety from the Old West to the New Deal.* Lawrence: University Press of Kansas, 1993.

CHAPTER THIRTEEN

The Metropolitan West to the 1980s

In the 1970s, what did it mean to be a "Westerner"? The frontier West never had been a uniform region in terms of race, geography, climate, or local economies, and it had settlements ranging from farming communities of white families to male-dominated, racially mixed mining camps. It had, however, enjoyed the collective mythic aura of long having been a frontier, and thus distinct from more-established regions of the nation. Now the frontier was long gone, the West had arrived, and, for better or worse, it was largely a suburban "frontier"—just like the rest of the country. What made the metropolitan West distinct, especially in terms of how Westerners lived?

Many signs point to the confusion that accompanied the arrival of the metropolitan West. In 1992, a poll of Western scholars, writers, and journalists found that they could not even agree on the boundaries of the West or what defined them. Does the West begin at the Mississippi River or the 100th meridian, where the arid Plains begin? Is California part of the West, or is it unique? Do the U.S. borders in the West make sense, or, in terms of economy, demography, and culture does the region stretch into northern Mexico and western Canada? Another sign of the confusion was the frustration of longtime residents in different parts of the West with the rush of newcomers, whether immigrants from Asia, tourists from around the nation and the world, or city slickers who bought ranches so they could play at being cowboys in their free time. In the eyes of many longtime residents the newcomers were not "real" Westerners, and their growing presence seemed to threaten people's livelihoods and ways of life. How could such regional parochialism be reconciled with frontier ideals of innovation and progress? Were longtime Westerners getting settled in their ways? Were they willing to take the money tourists shelled out but unhappy about hosting the visitors and dealing with the changes they wrought? Ironically, in this aspect unhappy Westerners distantly echoed the feelings of Indians and Mexicans when Americans had begun coming west in large numbers in the nineteenth century.

It stretches the idea to the breaking point, perhaps, but this situation points back to the frontier as a zone of interpenetration where intruders and indigenous peoples meet, interact, and struggle for control. Now the conquerors felt like the victims of an invasion. Asians had been there all along during the American era in the West, and Indians and Mexicans long before that. But having built an empire by conquering Indians and Mexicans and taming nature itself, white Americans in the region now encountered unexpected consequences brought about by their very success. Most did not appreciate the irony. Suddenly what was theirs—and they felt like it always had been theirs—had come under threat. Frontier myth has it that the West is a place where the past does not matter, where people are free to become whatever they want. But what Patricia Limerick has called the legacies of conquest began to trouble the region in the 1960s, 1970s, and 1980s. Now residents and scholars began to ask, yet again: Who, exactly, was a Westerner, and whose West was it?

To address these questions, this chapter looks at broad social trends that emerged in the 1960s and 1970s and continued into the 1980s and 1990s. It also considers political changes from the 1960s to the 1980s, such as the civil rights and environmental movements, as well as conservative reactions like the "Sagebrush" Rebellion.

A Consumer Society

Numbers tell an important part of the story of suburbs from the 1950s to the 1980s. Cities like Dallas, Phoenix, San Diego, Oklahoma City, and San Antonio gobbled up territory by annexing land around their city

"Mall Sprawl. Los Cerritos Shopping Mall in a Los Angeles area suburb, 2006. *Copyright, Xavier Marchant/Dreamstime.com*

centers, absorbing existing suburbs and creating new ones. San Antonio, for example, grew by 264 square miles between 1950 and 1990, while Oklahoma City added 557 square miles and Phoenix 402. The many levels of local government complicated bringing water, other utilities, social services, and schools to the new suburbs, but real estate speculation and a fever of growth pushed the resolution of such problems into the future. By the 1970s and 1980s, moreover, a new urban pattern was emerging, that of "edge cities." Traditional urban areas had concentric rings, or "collars," of suburbs around inner cities, to which suburban people commuted to work. Edge cities lie outside traditional urban areas, in what recently had been a suburb or semi-rural area. They do not rely economically on the center of a nearby city, and they have no city center of their own. They include city-like areas such as office complexes, industrial parks, and shopping-entertainment centers, as well as nearby "bedroom communities" (suburbs and exurbs) where people live, go to school, worship and play. Examples of metropolitan areas shaped by edge cities are Phoenix, Houston, Orange County (in Southern California), and the San Francisco Bay Area. By 1990, the West had six of the nation's ten largest cities. It also had four of the top seven metropolitan areas (LA, the Bay Area, Dallas–Fort Worth, and Houston), each one a sprawled-out region with large suburbs and semi-independent exurbs and edge cities. Put another way, in 1950, less than 60 percent of Westerners lived in metropolitan areas; in 1990, more than 80 percent did. The distribution, however, was not even. On the Plains and in the northern Mountain states, the rural population continued to range from one-third to one-half of the population, and state populations had stagnated. In short, suburbs and edge cities grew, while inner cities and rural areas stagnated or declined.

There is more to the story of suburbs than numbers, of course. Growth and stagnation tell us something about changing ways of life and the health of local economies. In the 1950s and 1960s, some suburban-ites fled what they saw as dangerous inner cities for peaceful, prosperous areas in which to live and raise families. But suburbs themselves eventually grew crowded and expanded as a result of population growth and baby boomers moving West in search of affordable homes, good jobs, and con-venient shopping centers, churches, and parks that fit their lifestyle. Much like the millions of (mostly) white families who went to suburbs to find new homes, in the postwar era many corporations moved manufacturing, warehousing, office work, and big retail and department stores from inner cities to the suburbs, seeking inexpensive land, lower property taxes, and easy access to customers and interstate highways. Warehouse districts and factory smokestacks still shaped the look of cities, but entire sections lay idle and abandoned, no longer producing tax revenue and "blighting" cityscapes. In the 1980s and 1990s, in the name of urban redevelopment, city governments and investors would tear down some of these run-down areas and transform others into upscale housing (apartments, lofts, and condominiums) for middle- and upper-class professionals and financial elites. Such efforts tended to push out rather than help the inner city poor, who could no longer afford to live in the renovated, or "gentrified," neighborhoods.

In the meantime, people who could not escape or chose not to leave inner cities and rural areas found themselves marginalized. Housing segre-gation meant that racial minorities—African Americans especially—often remained trapped in inner cities, where high unemployment and low-wage service and retails jobs created a grinding culture of poverty and gang violence that would lead to riots in the 1960s and 1990s, most famously in LA neighborhoods such as Watts. White Americans tend to identify poverty with African Americans in inner cities, but economic life also became grim among whites in rural areas and small cities on the Plains and parts of the Mountain West. The family farm continued to decline, factories, struggling to compete with low wages overseas, often shut down, and resource industries such as logging and mining stagnated, sometimes because of overseas competition, other times because local resources had been depleted or exhausted. The result was unemployment (or employment primarily in low-wage service and retail jobs) and farm-protest movements. Tourism might have created new jobs in the Mountain West, where national parks, skiing, and gambling drew throngs of visitors, but these jobs tended to be low paying and often frustrating, as locals found themselves catering to the needs of well-off outsiders. A sign of the resulting social stress in both inner cities and rural communities was a rise in substance abuse, drug trafficking, and violence.

One thing that most suburbanites, rural folk, and city dwellers in the West shared—even if unequally, in economic terms—was an embrace of mass culture and a consumer society. Films and professional sports fran-

"Welcome to Las Vegas." The iconic sign that welcomes visitors to the "Las Vegas Strip" on Las Vegas Boulevard South. Most of the strip and the casinos associated with it lie outside the city of Las Vegas, in Paradise and Winchester counties. *Photo, KC Ferret, June 2005*

chises flourished in the second half of the twentieth century, as they had in the 1920s and 1930s. But television and new genres of pop music, such as rock 'n roll, signaled important new trends during the postwar era: the arrival of a pronounced youth culture and the increasingly uninhibited expression of sexuality by men, women, and adolescents. The West was not alone in this revolution, but the cultural, economic, and symbolic importance of Hollywood and later Las Vegas should not be underestimated. In the 1950s and early 1960s, most Americans still abided by strict gender roles and a code of "decent" behavior in public, but increasingly they began to seek out personal self-expression and pleasure in clothing, their sexual lives, and leisure activities generally. The revolution is symbolized by musical acts from the early 1960s, like the Beach Boys, from Hawthorne, in LA County, who idealized the youth culture of dating, surfing, and adolescent sexuality in their songs. The movement evolved along with groups like the Doors, also from LA, in the later 1960s, whose songs and public reputation promoted a raw sexuality and a psychedelic drug culture. In short, the revolution in behavior and values associated with TV, youth culture, rock 'n roll, and the counterculture of the 1960s and 1970s took place at the same time as the makeover of the West into a region where most people lived in cities and suburbs.

The tourist industries of the West also participated in this pleasure-oriented way of life and drew millions of visitors every year. The completion of the interstate highway system and the good wages and paid vacations enjoyed by the middle-class and many blue-collar workers saw tourism become big business. Vacations in state and national parks on the Pacific Coast, in the Mountain West, in the Southwest (the Grand Canyon, most famously), and in some Plains states (e.g., the Badlands and Mount Rushmore in South Dakota) became a summer ritual for many families, with campgrounds providing cheap places to stay. In the winter there was skiing, most notably in Utah and Colorado. For those with more money to spend, whether in ski country or ranch country, the decline of mining towns and family farms and ranches meant lots of readily available land for purchase, and many tourists ended up buying property and putting up a "cabin" with a half dozen bedrooms and three full baths. There was legal gambling in cities like Las Vegas and Reno, Nevada, and later in other parts of the nation. And there were resort towns such as Palm Springs, California, where the well-off could enjoy spas, plastic surgery, and other indulgences.

An aerial view of Disneyland in 1956. *USC Regional Historical Photo Collection*

For families that did not want to travel the wide spaces of the West to see the remarkable sights firsthand, Disneyland, which opened in Anaheim, California, in 1955, gave them virtually the whole show in one stop. The Frontierland section of the park included a scaled-down version of the Grand Canyon and a mish-mash of all things "Western," from Davey Crockett and the Alamo to a Mississippi riverboat, Indian villages, a Mexican imports store, and staged gunfights in a faux Western town. The rides, exhibits, and souvenirs offered a family-friendly version of the West—excitement and natural wonders without dirt or danger and Indians and Mexicans without wars of conquest. (Buffalo Bill would have been baffled.) In the 1960s, in response to civil rights movements, Disney removed the Indians and Mexicans, replacing them with Bear Country and Indian robot exhibits. Instead of portraying villains or victims in a heroic American story, Indians and Mexicans were virtually erased from it. Disneyland symbolizes the carefully packaged suburban West of the postwar era: though no longer a frontier, the West could still play one.

Tourism and temporary residents provided jobs in construction, the service sector, and retail, but this made locals economically dependent on keeping visitors happy. Could a Western man still consider himself a rugged individual when serving snotty suburban tourists and their children for a living? At the same time, expensive hotels, condos, and second homes for seasonal residents inflated local real estate markets. In many towns, the second or even third homes of the temporary "Westerners" were much nicer than the homes in which the locals lived, and in some places the rise in the real-estate market began to price locals out of their own communities. For example, fashion designer Ralph Lauren has a 16,000-acre ranch near Telluride, Colorado, complete with carefully chosen décor and paint colors to give it an "authentic" Western feel. Likewise, film star Dennis Quaid has a "modest" 500-acre ranch in Montana, just north of Yellowstone National Park, and he occasionally shows up in town to eat at a local restaurant or buy groceries. In addition, locals typically maintained and cleaned the homes of the wealthy visitors, watched their children, or guided them on hunting or fishing trips. In pricey tourist areas such as Jackson Hole, Wyoming, the median price of homes was $1 million by the early twenty-first century. Restaurants, hotels, and other service providers often had trouble keeping workers, for whom there was little affordable local housing and who might have no choice but to live an hour or more away. If the West as a whole and metropolitan centers in particular had a powerful presence in the national and global economies, locals stuck working in the tourist trade could easily feel colonized.

These trends suggest that despite the industrialization of some parts of the West, natural resources remained basic to the economy, but now as pretty tourist attractions rather than raw materials for factories. A good example is fish-and-game resources. The actual animals of the West in essence became products to sell to tourist hunters and fishers; and out-of-state licenses, which cost more than in-state licenses, generated large revenue for the respective state fish-and-game departments, which in turn became almost like businesses. This, too, exacerbated tensions between locals and visitors. No matter how much more out-of-state licenses might cost a tourist, some locals felt that they should cost more, for visitors ruined their traditionally good hunting and fishing by overpressuring streams and herds. Resistance to tourists and their dollars often took subtle forms. Guides, usually permanent residents, sometimes refused to take certain people fishing or hunting anymore, or kept them away from the best sites because they had been obnoxious to locals or disrespectful of nature.

Tourism in Jackson Hole, Wyoming, today includes hiking, mountain climbing, and fishing during the summer and skiing during the winter. The author, Will Katerberg, and his wife, Simona Goi, climbed Grand Teton in 2007 with Jackson Hole Mountain Guides. *Image courtesy of Will Katerberg*

The memories of the New Western Historian Patricia Nelson Limerick indicate that conflict between Westerners was not inevitable. In the 1950s, when she was a toddler, Limerick and her parents lived in Banning, California, just down the road from the resort town Palm Springs. Maids, bellboys, gardeners, and others who worked in Palm Springs, but could not afford to live there, also lived in Banning. Her father owned a date shop, selling chocolate covered dates, date shakes, and the like, making a living selling to tourists visiting Palm Springs. Young Patty's parents dressed her up in a cowgirl outfit (fringed skirt and vest, cowboy boots) and she provided cute Western ambiance in the shop. But rather than look back with regret at being commodified to help her family sell more date products to indulgent tourists, Limerick points out that her family also played tourist itself, going on annual vacations to the Grand Canyon and other iconic Western destinations. She recalls beaches in California and Indian dances in Arizona. In her college years in Santa Cruz, Limerick worked as a maid in a hotel that served tourists. Her story reminds us that those who serve tourists can themselves enjoy being tourists elsewhere.

Developments in Driggs, Idaho, near Grand Teton National Park, provide an example of conflict. The region has long attracted skiers and summertime visitors to the Grand Teton and Yellowstone national parks. Until recently, local farmers and ranchers and their families had maintained their traditional place in the community. In the 1980s, however, economic changes began to pit long-time residents against developers and the new condo crowd. When the Forest Service backed a proposal to build an Italian-style community of 880 condominiums at a ski resort near Grand Teton National Park, officials promised that the project would give a much needed boost to the local economy. Residents of Driggs could hang on to a ranching and farming past, they explained, or seek a more prosperous future in tourism. "'You can't stop the march of progress in the Teton Valley,' said James Caswell, supervisor of the 1.8 million-acre Targhee National Forest, which forms the western border of Yellowstone and Grand Teton national parks. 'It's just going to happen, no matter what we do. So let's take the opportunity to plan accordingly.'"

But farmers and ranchers opposed the project, fearing that their children would not be able to afford to live in the community and would be forced to move out of it. "The folks who live in the valley now don't live here for money," Boyd Bowles, "an alfalfa farmer who [led] a citizens' group fighting the development," told the *New York Times* in 1989. "We live here because we like it the way it is. Letting all those condos go up is going to change everything in this valley." Another unhappy local resident, Jake Kittle of nearby Wilson, Wyoming, explained, "We've been told that we're no good at farming and what we should do is get a job making beds for Mory Bergmeyer" (one of the investors behind the condo project). For his part, Bergmeyer, an architect from Boston, went from being a "savior" to a "bad developer" in two short years, as locals began to worry about how the project would impinge on their families and community. Environmentalists remained especially concerned to minimize the ecological impact of the condo development and looked carefully at the deal between the Forest Service and the developers to swap land. In recent years, the town's official website has advertised Driggs as combining "the old west with the eclectic," including "new and used bookstores, an authentic Austrian bakery, an historic soda fountain, impressive local artist galleries, cafes, pubs, grills, outdoor gear shops, and more!" Stories like this have played out countless times since the 1970s in subregions of the West where tourism is a major part of the local economy. This was one face of the New West: Old West nostalgia combined with Starbuck's convenience and amenities.

Tourism often is seen as part of a "post-industrial" economy. It became the largest sector in the Western American economy in the late twentieth century, outpacing even the information economy of computers, software, the Internet, and video games. But the dependence on outsiders and the resentment that it sometimes fostered echoed familiar regional experiences from the past for some Westerners, even as it created economic opportunities for others. And as in the past, this new sector of the economy exploited the land, now with ski slopes, campgrounds, and souvenir shops where miners and ranchers once worked.

Earth Day

From the point of view of preservation, a tourist economy seemed like an improvement on the resource-based economy of the late nineteenth and early twentieth century and the industrial economy of mid-century. Western tourism depends on delivering natural beauty, recreational spaces, and fish-and-game resources to visitors who have money to spend. Tourists and tourism industry providers had good reasons to support and even promote some environmental policies. All Americans also became more concerned about health, fitness, and exercise in the 1960s and 1970s. With this in mind, historians have shown a strong connection between the development of a consumer-oriented economy and successful environmentalist movements. Clean air and water and stunning wilderness spaces are luxuries that consumers in economically advanced, affluent societies can afford and typically demand. The West has long drawn visitors seeking the rest, relaxation, and good mental and physical health promised by its spectacular scenery, open spaces, and dry air. It is no surprise, then, that the West played a prominent role in the postwar environmental movement in the United States.

Opposition to new dam-building projects in national parks was one sign of the change by the early 1960s, but not the only one. Rachel Carson's apocalyptic book *Silent Spring* (1962)—which sold widely enough to end up on the *New York Times* best-seller list and the Book of the Month Club—depicted the impact of toxic chemicals such as DDT on wildlife and people. DDT is a pesticide used to combat disease-bearing insects such as mosquitoes. In the 1950s and 1960s, scientists found that it had become part of the food chain, as small animals and fish consumed water and plants tainted by the chemical. DDT thinned the egg shells of eagles, ospreys, hawks, and other birds that ate tainted fish and small animals, greatly decreasing the number of hatchlings and threatening the very survival of certain species. Human blood and fat-tissue samples also showed detectable levels of DDT by the early 1970s. The Montrose Chemical Corporation of California manufactured DDT and dumped tons of waste into the ocean through the Los Angeles sewage system. It defended DDT vigorously, but in the changed political climate that followed Carson's book it was forced to amend its practices. In the wake of this victory, TV news programs and a new generation of environmental activists picked up Carson's message and ran with it. A major oil spill off the coast of Santa Barbara in 1969, the infamous smog of LA and other Western cities, news of declining or extinct bird and animal species, and similar examples regionally and nationally further alerted Western Americans to the mounting problem of pollution.

The oil crisis of the 1970s also shook Americans, especially in the car culture of Southern California and other parts of the West with vast spaces and wide-open highways. The crisis began in 1973, when Arab oil-producing states threatened to refuse to sell oil to countries that supported Israel. It continued as the oil-producing countries associated with the Organization of the Petroleum Exporting Countries (OPEC) cut oil production and placed an embargo on oil shipments to Western Europe and North America. This led to a shortage in oil, dramatically higher prices for gasoline, long lines at gas stations, and a rush to produce smaller, more fuel-efficient cars, and it contributed to a global economic recession. The oil crisis, along with the steep increase in the human population globally after World War II, made people aware of the limited resources of the planet—such as water in the West.

Activists with experience in the civil rights and anti–Vietnam war movements of the 1960s, prominent consumer advocates such as Ralph Nader, and preservationist organizations like the Sierra Club and Wilderness Society joined to create what quickly became a national movement. The movement was not uniquely Western, but its "coming out" party, the first Earth Day celebration on April 22, 1970, was conceived in the West. It got its start in September 1969 when Wisconsin Senator Gaylord Nelson, an environmental activist on tour on the West Coast to promote conservation, gave a speech in Seattle in which he proposed a grass-roots event, a "National Teach-in on the Crisis of the Environment," to be held in locales around the country. Twenty million Americans participated in marches, rallies, and teach-ins at hundreds of campuses and dozens of cities that first Earth Day.

Western writers also helped shape the new environmental consciousness and ideology. Aldo Leopold articulated a new environmental ethic. Born in Iowa in 1886, he worked for the U.S. Forest Service in the 1910s in New Mexico and Arizona. From the 1920s to the 1940s his thinking evolved from older, wise-use conservation ideals to the belief that nature is a community of which human beings are merely one part and which is built on a balance of relations between all living things and the nonliving environment. This ecological consciousness led Leopold to insist that the environment has its own moral status and that human beings have an ethical obligation to respect and not harm it. His "land ethic" would influence both mainstream and radical environmental groups in the late twentieth century. Prominent Western writers such as novelist Wallace Stegner and historian Bernard DeVoto also contributed to movement, critiquing both the mythology of the frontier West and the historical exploitation of the region in the name of development. In addition, new writers like novelist Edward Abby and poet and essayist Terry Tempest Williams began promoting environmental activism and spirituality in their books in the 1970s and 1980s. Abbey's novel, *The Monkey-Wrench Gang* (1975) helped to inspire the formation of the radical, eco-terrorist organization Earth First! in the late 1970s, which uses sabotage to oppose economic development that harms the environment.

In mainstream politics, the concerns of voters led politicians to legislate change. In 1964 Congress passed the Wilderness Act, which created a 9-million-acre Wilderness Preservation System. In 1970 it created the Environmental Protection Agency (EPA), with mandates to repair damage already done to nature and establish institutions to protect the environment in the future. Congress also passed clean air and water initiatives in the 1960s and 1970s. The West, along with the rest of the nation, benefited ecologically from all of these measures. Other new legislation especially affected the West, with its vast federal public lands: the Land and Water Conservation Fund (1964), which gave the National Park Service a budget to acquire new parklands; the Wild and Scenic Rivers Act (1968), which protected rivers; the Endangered Species Act (1973), which mandated protecting endangered species such as grey wolves and grizzly bears; and, to the north, the Alaska National Interest Lands Conservation Act (1980), which recognized the need to settle Native land claims and designated more than 100 million acres of land as wilderness areas, national monuments, wildlife refuges, and preserves. All of this amounted to what some observers called an Environmental New Deal. Many state governments created their own environmental regulations and programs, especially Pacific Coast states.

Much of the new legislation was signed by presidents from the West—Lyndon Johnson (Texas) and Richard Nixon (California)—but there was no regional consensus on these policies. Ranchers and logging and mining operators found their access to national forests restricted. Ranchers no longer could freely exterminate wolves and other predators that threatened their herds. Builders, manufacturers, and even farmers had to follow new environmental regulations and zoning laws designed to protect wilderness areas or residents in metropolitan areas. The new rules increased their costs, restricted their property rights, and denied them access to public lands that they considered a birthright. More than any other change in the region or the nation since World War II, the Environmental New Deal revived deep distrust and even hatred of the federal government among some Westerners. By contrast, weekend hikers, climbers, and campers from Western cities and suburbs, tourists from outside the region, and environmentalists everywhere supported the new measures and demanded even more. Both sides claimed to love the West and be the true inheritors of the regional heritage. But which one was authentically "Western"?

Migration

Immigration to the West after 1960 raised the question of who was a real Westerner, because Asians, Mexicans, and Latinos composed the major-

Vietnamese mother and daughters, Christmas 1983. The mother and two daughters were Vietnamese refugees, "boat people" rescued by the French oil tanker "Ventose" on the South China Seas in 1979. The youngest daughter was born in Ibarakiken, Japan on August 7, 1979. *Los Angeles Public Library Photo Collection*

ity of the newcomers. By the turn of the twenty-first century, it would be clear that whites soon would be a minority in much of the region (relative to the number of nonwhites combined). White migrants from other parts of the United States and other nations also continued to move to the West in significant numbers, seeking jobs or attracted by the region's mythic environment. They included Canadians with aspirations of making it big in the movies or on TV in Hollywood and (in later years) computer engineers and entrepreneurs seeking their fortune in Seattle, Portland, and the Bay Area. "Snowbirds" from northern states and Canada bought second homes in what became known as the "Sunbelt South," stretching from Florida to Southern California. Fleeing cold winter weather, they lived part of the year in the Southwest. As well-off, often retired consumers, the "snowbirds" might be compared to both tourists and the migrant agricultural laborers who worked in various parts of the West during the year. The economic circumstances of these three groups are vastly diverse, of course, but together they point to the growing significance in recent decades of temporary migration. In the 1990s migration patterns began to change subtly, as housing prices made living in some parts of the West prohibitively expensive and less attractive for young families, notably in California. This led to a net out-migration from some areas, as many Californians chose to move to parts of the nation where they could afford to buy a decent home. But whatever subtle migration patterns played out, they all paled in significance to the obvious fact of nonwhite migration into the West.

The larger context for immigration to the United States generally and to the American West in particular was globalization, American ventures overseas in Asia, and a fundamental redefinition of U.S. immigration policy with the passage of the Immigration and Nationality Act of 1965. The new act was not the first revision to U.S. immigration policy in the postwar period, but, having been shaped by the recent civil rights movements, it fundamentally redefined American immigration policy. It ended discrimination against Asians and replaced ethnic-racial quotas with a preference system that favored family members and people with skills and training in occupations for which labor was in short supply. Though not intended as revolutionary, it had that effect. From the 1920s to the 1960s, 58 percent of immigrants to the United States had come from Europe and 19 percent from Canada. By the 1970s the change was stunning, as under the new preferences Latin America sent 40 percent of the immigrants and Asia 35 percent. "Non-preference" immigrants, such as refugees, also came primarily from Asia and Latin America. The 1965 immigration act enabled the new patterns, but globalization and the exercise of American economic and political power overseas explained them. Crucially, rather than arriving on the East Coast, as millions of Europeans had done in the previous century and a half, the bulk of the new immigrants entered from the West, especially California and other states on the Mexican–United States border, spreading into the interior of the region and nation from there.

With this in mind, it is noteworthy that Japan no longer supplied a significant number of Asian immigrants. In the 1960s Japan's economy was growing at a faster rate than the American economy, so it sent few immigrants. Instead, Asian migrants came from China (and Hong Kong and Taiwan), the Philippines, South Korea, and increasingly from Vietnam, Cambodia, and Laos, many of them refugees from the chaos caused by communist revolutions and the Cold War. Chinese immigrants tended to be well-off, educated, or students, and included both women and men. Southeast Asians often were refugees from a variety of economic and professional backgrounds, and they were an entirely new source of migrants dating from the late 1960s, one growing in number in the late 1970s and 1980s, after the end of the Vietnam War.

Mexican migrants and Latino migrants generally came to the West to find work. They came legally and illegally, especially from Mexico and Central America (often through Mexico), and many stayed only temporarily. Whether permanent or temporary, they maintained ties to their former nations, sending money back home to their families and in the process helping their homeland economies maintain a manageable trade balance with the United States. Mexican migrants, whether permanent or temporary, legal or illegal, had the largest impact on the American consciousness. From a Mexican viewpoint, the Southwest and California ("*El Norte*") was ancestral land. Moreover, the Mexican–United States border has always been a porous one, its sheer length making it impossible to police effectively. Indeed, the United States government did not make a concerted effort to patrol the border until the mid-twentieth century, a time during which it was just as concerned with bringing in Mexican laborers to meet the seasonal demand of growers in Texas and California as it was with preventing illegal immigration. In that sense, there was nothing new about recent immigration patterns. But for white Americans in the 1970s and 1980s (and ever since) Mexican migrants seemed like an invasion force that threatened their white-Anglo nation. This perceived invasion was symbolized by recent immigrants—legal or illegal—who did not learn to speak English and required the administration of public services in Spanish. Anti-immigrant movements in the past few decades have demanded stricter control of the border and campaigned to make English the official language of the United States and restrict public services to English. In turn, some Mexican American activists have cheered the likelihood that by 2050 they will be a majority in California and the Southwest and exulted that their ancestral territory will return to its rightful people—though Native Americans might dispute this claim—socially and culturally, if not politically.

The postwar era also saw migration by American Indians to cities. Government policy contributed to the trend, but most Indians who relocated chose to do so on their own, looking for work or following family members, like other migrants. By 1960, 30 percent of Indians lived in cities; by 1980 more than 50 percent did. The incomes of urban Indians were better on average than for those on reservations, but this did not guarantee a better way of life or a higher standard of living. Unfamiliar social, cultural, and economic settings and separation from extended-family and community networks proved difficult challenges for many. Some Indians responded to these challenges by creating or seeking out inter-tribal networks that helped them forge new communities, adjust to urban life, and foster a "national" sense of Indian identity.

Migration by nonwhites within and to the West, together with the changing way of life brought by consumerism and suburbanization, made some white Americans feel like strangers in their homeland. Other Americans saw progress in these changes and dreamed of creating an America where women and nonwhites would share opportunity and power equally with white men. These conflicting perceptions and aspirations came to a head in the conflicts of the 1960s and 1970s and the "culture wars" of the 1980s and 1990s (also see Chapter Fourteen). Reflecting its new standing in the nation, the American West would play a major role in these conflicts.

Countercultures

One of the cultural conflicts of the 1960s and 1970s renewed a familiar battle between Indians and mainstream America. For most Americans, Indian demands for full civil rights and the reality of new Indian power came as a shock. Most whites had long assumed that Indians had disappeared or were fast on their way. But the demographic renewal of the American Indian population in the early twentieth century and the Indian New Deal of the 1930s led to a resurgence. Led by Western members, Congress returned to trying to assimilate Indians in the decade after World War II. As in the past, a desire to control Indian lands and exploit resources on them was a key motivating factor. The new "termination" policy, defined in a resolution and a law passed by Congress in 1953, rejected the status of Indians as semi-autonomous nations in the United States. Between 1954 and 1962, Congress passed twelve bills that terminated the national status of specific Indian communities, taking away

John F. Kennedy with Edison Real Bird, 1962. Real Bird led the fight for tribal sovereignty for the Crow Nation (in Southern Montana) and was the chairman of its tribal council, 1966–72. *Courtesy, The Newberry Library*

their unique sovereign rights, privatizing land holdings, and ending federal treaty obligations and public services to them. The process began in 1954 with the Klamath tribe in Oregon. As in the past, the government paid members of the tribe to accept their new standing as United States citizens (which they already were) without special status as members of an Indian nation, giving them a choice of private land holdings or $43,000. After a burst of windfall spending, the changed status left many Klamath with no tribal assets. They had to find their way in an unfamiliar rural economy that offered them only unskilled jobs. Most fell into poverty and many became dependent on local and state resources. By the early 1960s, the fate of the Klamath and other tribes, and the determined opposition of the National Congress of American Indians and other Indian organizations, forced the government to abandon its termination policy. In later decades, the tribes won back their national status, if not their land.

The failed policy also catalyzed a national Indian movement that used courts and historic treaties to force the government to recognize Indian rights and live up to its treaty obligations. Legal efforts culminated in the 1978 Supreme Court decision *United States* vs. *Wheeler,* which required the United States to recognize Indian tribes as semi-independent nations. This decision and others in the 1960s and 1970s expanded the power of tribal governments in terms of taxing, policing, and courts. The Supreme Court also recognized the inherent conflict when the federal government acted both as a trustee for Indian peoples and in other national interests; it ruled that only tribes could dissolve themselves, not the federal government. Finally, it forced the government to address Indian land claims, pay reparations (with interest) for land taken in violation of treaties, and permit Indian religious practices and traditional hunting and fishing rights. In the future, governments and businesses would have to negotiate with Indian nations as entities with their own sovereignty. Such negotiations would reveal diversity and division among Native peoples over the wisdom of economic development and material "progress," versus traditions and environmental protection, as among Americans in general. Increasingly, however, Indians took an active role in determining their own fate. They did so as distinct Indian nations but also with a growing pan-Indian sensibility, recognizing their common cause as "Native Americans."

Other Americans opposed the resurgence of Indian power. They feared that their land might be claimed by Indians and taken from them by courts, were frustrated by what they saw as special privileges for Indians (in not paying some taxes on reservations or hunting and fishing where other Americans were barred), and irritated by having to negotiate with Indians to develop mines or drill for oil. These critics blamed the federal government as well as ordinary Americans who supported Indian rights. In turn, more radical Indians continued to push for Indian power and rights. On occasion in the 1970s, this cycle would lead to violence.

At the same time, American Indians came to prominence as writers and intellectuals. Of particular note were authors Scott Momaday and Leslie Marmon Silko, and the lawyer-scholar Vine Deloria, Jr., who wrote widely on Indian history and religion and contemporary legal and cultural issues. Momaday won the Pulitzer Prize in 1969 for his novel *House Made of Dawn*. His and Silko's novels powerfully depict the conflicted place of Native peoples and their traditions in American society. Accompanying the public recognition of the significance of Indian writers was a more general American appreciation of the countercultural value of Native lifeways and values. Critics of mainstream America in the "hippie" counterculture and the environmental movement often adopted Indian symbols and ideals to shape their own ideas, values, spirituality, and image in opposition to the mainstream of metropolitan, Cold War America.

Like Native Americans, African Americans and Mexican Americans also fought for their civil rights during the 1960s and 1970s. For African Americans, the national story started with the fight for integration in the South in the 1950s and early 1960s. It moved North and West in the mid-1960s, when Martin Luther King, Jr., and other civil rights activists began to address informal segregation in neighborhoods, housing, schools, and the job market. Frustration with such informal segregation contributed to riots in cities across the country in the mid-1960s, and it helped to inspire the "black power" movement, which rejected King's ideal of integration, seeing it as failed, accommodationist, and pandering to whites.

The necessity of civil rights battles in the West was exemplified in 1964, when white Californians voted two-to-one in favor of Proposition 14, which guaranteed property owners, real estate agents, and others the right to sell to whomever they chose. Billed as a matter of property rights, the proposition was intended to reinforce racially segregated housing markets. In 1967, the United States Supreme Court found "Prop 14" unconstitutional. This was a victory for African Americans, but actual social change—in terms of jobs and opportunity—came too slow to prevent riots in the Watts neighborhood of LA in August 1965. The rioting began on August 11, when a police officer pulled over an African American driver, Marquette Frye, on suspicion of driving while intoxicated. The ensuing argument led to a crowd forming and to the arrest of Frye, his brother, and his mother, sparking a wholesale uprising by angry, frustrated residents of Watts. The violence lasted five days, left 34 persons dead and more than 1,000 wounded, and caused as much as $200 million in property damage. Rioters, numbering more than 35,000, set buildings on fire, yelling "burn, baby, burn," looted stores (targeting those owned by white shopkeepers), taking furniture and appliances, and attacked police officers, fire fighters, and white motorists. The scale of the vandalism and violence forced the governor of California to call in the National Guard—more than 14,000 soldiers by August 15. The guardsmen enforced a curfew and restored order by August 15, and churches, government agencies, and local community groups provided aid to the residents of the beleaguered community. Most of the property damage was to businesses (more than 1,000 of them) in black neighborhoods. Likewise, while the casualties included white police officers and fire fighters, the majority were African American. In the next year, groups inspired by ideals of black power and black nationalism—not integration into "mainstream," white-dominated society—began to form in the West, notably the Black Panther Party in Oakland (see below, for more). California voters responded in 1966 by electing Ronald Reagan as governor, the conservative Republican and former cowboy actor promising to restore law and order. The Watts riot, and riots in 1966 and 1967 in cities such as Chicago, Detroit, and Newark, led the federal government to create a National Advisory Commission on Civil Disorders, which reported in 1968 that the riots reflected a growing frustration by inner-city African Americans with the economic and social consequences of de facto segregation in housing and job markets.

In important ways, the quest of Mexican Americans for their civil rights parallels that of African Americans. In the 1940s and 1950s, for example, Mexican American civil rights groups challenged segregation in schools (in California and Texas) and fought for fair electoral policies and to register Latino voters. The organizations behind these efforts included older ones, like the League of United Latin American Citizens (LULAC), an advocacy group formed in Texas in 1929, and more recent ones such as the American G.I. Forum, organized in Texas in 1948 to promote the equal rights of Mexican American veterans. In other ways, however, the story is more complex than that of African Americans because it comprises the struggle not only of Mexican Americans but also that of migrant Mexicans and other Latinos. The G.I. Forum and LULAC, for example, were composed mostly of native-born, middle-class Mexican Americans who tended to distance themselves from Mexican immigrants and aggressively pursued their rights as citizens of the United States. Some families were "mixed," however, with, say, one U.S.-born parent, one Mexican parent, and U.S.-born children. Sweeps by Immigration and Naturalization Service (INS) agents sometimes divided families when they resulted in the deportation of illegal migrants. But INS agents also sometimes ended up deporting Mexican American citizens who, like many other Americans at the time, had no proof of their U.S. citizenship. A final example of the complexity of the story comes in efforts by labor unions to secure better wages and working conditions for Mexican American laborers, who sometimes looked down on migrant Mexicans as unwanted competition who worked for even lower wages. The situation began to change in dramatic ways for people of Mexican descent in the West in the 1960s and 1970s for two reasons: the growth of the Chicano movement and the efforts of César Chávez and the United Farm Workers (UFW) to organize migrant farm workers in a labor union.

In the 1960s, Mexican American students began to claim and celebrate their *Chicano* identity, taking a term of derision and making it their own. Whites often failed to see a difference between unassimilated Mexicans and assimilated Mexican Americans from the Southwest, some of whom saw themselves as Hispanic Europeans. The student activists likewise rejected divisions of class, citizenship, and national identity. They

César Chávez breaks bread with Senator Robert F. Kennedy during a mass marking the end of Chávez's 25-day fast in March 1968. Chávez fasted to call attention to the peaceful disposition of farm workers striking against California grape growers. *Archives of Labor and Union Affairs, Wayne State University*

hoped to unite working-class Chicanos with a growing middle class of assimilated Mexican Americans and with rural migrant laborers from Mexico. Like their counterparts in the black power movement, young Chicano activists spoke of their distinct culture and community, *la raza* (the race), rejected assimilation, and called for a return as a people to Aztlán, the ancestral homeland of the Aztecs in the American Southwest. Chicano activists criticized the American "occupation" of their homeland and dreamed of the day when people of Mexican descent would once again be the dominant ethnic group.

Like the Chicano activists, Chávez sought to unite disparate groups of laborers. As a boy he had worked as a migrant laborer with his family. In 1952, he joined the Community Services Organization (CSO), which helped Mexican migrants and promoted Mexican American civil rights. He resigned from the CSO in 1962, when it refused to support his efforts to create a migrant farm workers' union. In 1963, he began organizing migrant farm laborers in a union that eventually would become known as the United Farm Workers. Chávez organized strikes, went on a hunger strike in 1968, and drew on the ideas of Gandhi, St. Paul, and Thoreau. When growers recruited workers from Mexico to break strikes, Chávez and his allies started campaigns there, talking to individual workers, coordinating with Mexican labor unions, and using radio, TV, and newspaper ads to convince potential strikebreakers to refuse to work and support the strike. His movement, which took the name *La Causa,* came to national prominence in 1968, when he promoted a national boycott of California table grapes to force the growers to improve wages and working conditions for the migrant laborers they relied on to pick the fruit. Workers earned a pittance, sometimes so little that they had to sleep in tents or cars because they could not afford to rent the shacks that farm owners provided near their fields. Farm owners sometimes refused to pay workers or demanded that they pay for the drinking water the farmers provided. Migrant children could not easily rise out of this form of poverty because they did not have regular access to an education. Chávez and his allies appealed to consumers around the nation to boycott table grapes, with activists going door to door in all parts of the country to make people aware of the terrible conditions under which the grape pickers worked and lived. This pressure forced more and more growers to sign contracts with the UFW by the early 1970s. Putting union solidarity ahead of ethnic identity, Chávez criticized the nationalism of the Chicano movement, fearing that it would divide the migrant poor (Mexicans, Filipinos, Central Americans) into competing racial-ethnic groups.

Among white Americans, the New Left, hippies, and the anti–Vietnam War movement drew inspiration from Indian, African American, and Chicano activists, both politically and culturally. White countercultural activism in the West came to national attention in October 1964 with the Free Speech movement on the Berkeley campus of the University of California. The students' goal was to force campus administrators to recognize their academic freedom and their right to organize politically on campus. After a two-month "sit-in" in a campus building, and a second wave of protests during which the university brought charges against the leaders of the sit-in, the students forced the university to recognize their rights and permit organizing and demonstrations on campus. It was major victory both for free-speech rights and student freedom in general, as universities began to end their paternalistic efforts to enforce sexual-moral codes on students and control campus politics. Soon thereafter, students at Berkeley and other Western universities, like those across the nation, shifted their attention to opposing the war in Vietnam.

Students and other activists associated with the New Left and the hippie counterculture began to criticize middle-class American life in the late 1960s and early 1970s. The New Left condemned the American empire, from its war in Vietnam to its inequitable social relations. The goal of Students for a Democratic Society (SDS) and other New Left groups was a nation that would allow all of its citizens an opportunity to realize their potential. Despite its radicalism, which combined elements of socialism and theatrical, often alienating, political tactics in angry public demonstrations, the New Left also emphasized ideals of personal, spiritual, and existential fulfillment. The hippies and larger counterculture were less overtly political and more concerned with lifestyle, in anarchist-libertarian fashion attacking middle-class manners and encouraging freedom and self-expression in art, sexuality, and community life. The symbolic center of the counterculture was San Francisco. During the "Summer of Love" in 1967, thousands of youths streamed into the city's Haight-Ashbury district to experiment with sexual freedom and drugs and experience the utopian potential of free self-expression. In the late 1960s and 1970s, utopian groups set up communes and experimental communities, many of them in northern California and the Pacific Northwest, but also other parts of the West, creatively replaying familiar American frontier myths. Such experiments generally failed, as most communes fragmented and as free sexuality and drug use often led to violence, addiction, and the spread of sexually transmitted diseases. More generally, the ideals of self-expression and personal fulfillment that shaped the New Left and the counterculture, including experimenting with sexual freedom and psychedelic drugs, mirrored the consumerism of mainstream America.

Despite the common ground, the Manson "Family" came to symbolize the logical end of the counterculture for conservatives. A quasi-religious commune controlled by Charles Manson, an ex-convict, the "family" lived on several ranches in California and prepared for "Helter Skelter," Manson's term for the apocalypse, taken from the title of a Beatles' song. Police arrested Manson and several members of his group for committing a series of murders in 1969. Manson received life imprisonment. In 1975 Lynette "Squeaky" Fromme, a former member

Ronald Reagan (right) campaigning for Barry Goldwater (left) in 1964. Goldwater won the Republican nomination that year, but lost badly to President Lyndon B. Johnson. The campaign was the starting point of Reagan's own political career, first as governor of California (1967–75) and then as president (1981–1989). *Ronald Reagan Presidential Library*

of the gang, tried to assassinate President Gerald R. Ford in Sacramento. Manson became a cult figure of sorts, over the years inspiring films, novels, and pop songs, and symbolizing for conservatives all that had gone so terribly wrong in the 1960s.

A conservative backlash against the youth counterculture—the "New Right"—was a counterculture of sorts, too, opposing political and social trends that its supporters viewed as destroying the America they loved. The New Right seemed to burst on the scene in 1964, with the presidential campaign of Senator Barry Goldwater, an Arizona Republican who ran against the incumbent Lyndon Johnson. Goldwater's small government, anti-communist militancy seemed out of the mainstream and dangerous to most voters, but his campaign built on the quiet organizing of grass-roots conservatives across the nation—in Southern California, for example, where he appealed to Christian conservatives who had migrated there from Arkansas, Texas, and Oklahoma in previous decades. Goldwater lost badly in 1964, but in 1968 Richard Nixon, a Republican from California, defeated a divided and demoralized Democratic Party by appealing to what he called "the silent majority." Nixon used the language of plain-folk Americanism. He attracted voters who believed that many postwar changes seemed socialist and un-American and threatened the roles that men and women properly should play in the home and society—whether sexual freedom, work outside the home for women, the declining public power of Christianity, government interference in society and the economy, or weak opposition to foreign threats, particularly communism. The civil rights movements of the 1950s to 1970s, suburbanization, consumerism, and the sexual revolution had transformed race relations and family life, and the conflicts of the 1960s and 1970s confirmed for New Right activists the inevitably pernicious consequences of these changes. But, like the countercultural left, the New Right also embraced essential elements of life in the metropolitan West, notably its prosperity and consumerism. Likewise, the conservative Protestant churches that grew steadily during this era embraced a spirituality that emphasized a personal relationship with Jesus and mirrored the emphasis on self-expression and personal spiritual fulfillment found in the New Left and counterculture.

The Western element of the New Right cannot be denied, as many of its leading national figures hailed from the region: Goldwater

(Arizona); Nixon (California); and Ronald Reagan (California). Reagan had once been an actor in Hollywood and a Democrat. In 1947, while he was president of the Screen Actors Guild, he testified before the communist-hunting House Un-American Activities Committee and named some of his fellow actors, thus ruining their careers. Reagan reinvented himself as a Republican in the 1950s, was elected governor of California in 1966, and opposed radicalism among the state's university students, famously sending in the California Highway Patrol to suppress unrest at the Berkeley campus of the University of California in 1969. He was elected president of the United States in 1980, propelled to office by the same grass-roots movement that had failed to elect Goldwater in 1964. The politics of "plain-folk Americanism" and Nixon's "silent majority" would become the "moral majority" in the Reagan era.

The subtle racist aspect of the New Right was most noticeable in the South, where whites moved in droves from the Democratic Party to the Republican Party in the late 1960s and 1970s, after the Democratic Party embraced civil rights for African Americans and other racial minorities. In general, however, the New Right stressed property rights, state's rights, small government, and traditional "family" values in order to restore and defend a way of life that had been defined by property-owning white families who wanted to preserve traditional gender roles. The conflicts of the era, and the fragmentation of American culture and politics, manifested itself powerfully in the West. If the countercultures of the left and right both spoke the language of consumerism—self-expression, lifestyle, and personal fulfillment—their divisions were equally as striking. To the discomfort of many whites, racial groups that they had long been able to keep at the social margins now asserted their rights and their place in the West. And the values that people once assumed that almost all Americans happily shared now came under challenge from diverse and conflicting directions, leading to what became known as the "culture wars" in the 1990s. To which groups, then, did this new West belong?

The Edge of Discontent

One can see the depth of the conflicts over the identity of the West and the nation among various extremists who, believing that America was so corrupt that its institutions were beyond redemption, advocated violence

The "Indians Welcome, Indian Land" message is partially hidden under the U.S. Penitentiary sign at the entrance to Alcatraz Island. The graffiti is a reminder of the island's 1969-71 occupation by activists emphasizing the need for American Indian self-determination. © *Alessandro Bolis/Dreamstime.com*

and revolution. These extremists shared an apocalyptic sensibility, but they also shared a Western heritage of vigilante violence and the right of persons to act on their own in the absence of the institutions of settled society and government. In this postfrontier era, the government—especially the federal government—seemed to have failed the common man, and some radicals pointed to this failure and called for violent means to rectify the situation.

On the left, extremist groups took diverse forms. African American activists frustrated with the failures of the mainstream civil rights movement to achieved real integration formed the Black Panther Party in 1966, in the wake of the Watts riots. The Black Panthers started community programs to address poverty and set up armed neighborhood patrols to watch the police—whom they considered agents of white racial oppression. Violent incidents with police lead to the deaths, all totaled, of more than a dozen police officers and thirty-four Black Panthers. Among New Left activists, a group called the Weathermen (later the Weather Underground) split from the SDS in 1969 and then went underground after the death of a Black Panther in a police raid. The Weathermen bombed government, military, and police facilities around the nation, including police stations and cars, a San Francisco Bay Area military base, and the California attorney general's office in Sacramento.

Some Native Americans also used violence. A group called Indians of All Tribes (several hundred eventually) occupied Alcatraz Island in San Francisco Bay in 1969–71, living in the abandoned federal prison there. They claimed that the Fort Laramie Treaty of 1868 had ceded out-of-use federal land to the Indian people from whom it was acquired. It proposed to build an education center on the island. After eighteen months, most of the Indians had left Alcatraz, public support for them had waned, and the government removed them from the island. The American Indian Movement (AIM) was founded in 1968 in Minneapolis to deal with police brutality locally. It modeled itself on the Black Panthers and soon became a national movement, using publicity stunts as well as violence to draw media attention. AIM briefly seized a replica of the *Mayflower* at Plymouth Rock on Thanksgiving Day in 1970; it set up a camp at Mount Rushmore in 1971 and reclaimed it for the Sioux, renaming it Mount Crazy Horse; and it occupied the offices of the Bureau of Indian Affairs in Washington, D.C., in 1972, with members barricading themselves inside the building for a week, until the government agreed to review its demands. But AIM is, perhaps, most famous for occupying the Wounded Knee massacre site on the Pine Ridge reservation in South Dakota with more than 200 members in 1973, an incident that resulted in an armed stand-off with police and the FBI that lasted for several months. The two sides traded gunfire, leaving two AIM members and two FBI agents dead and a police officer paralyzed. The FBI considered these groups serious threats to the nation's internal security, infiltrated some of them, and according to later congressional investigations sometimes acted as *agents provocateurs* by inciting violence.

Violence by leftists continued into the 1980s and 1990s in the form of "direct action" stunts and sabotage by environmentalist extremist groups such as *Earth First!*—much of it in the West. Activists sat in trees—sometimes camping out in them—to prevent loggers from cutting them down. They sometimes turned to violent means of protest, defacing, bombing, or burning development projects, and spiking trees to prevent logging—if a chainsaw hit one of these imbedded spikes it could cause serious injury or death to the logger holding it. Animal rights groups such as the Earth Liberation Front likewise sabotaged research and education facilities. No one has yet died as a result of acts of eco-sabotage, but congressional investigations and law enforcement organizations have taken them seriously as a domestic form of terrorism.

Violence and extremism have come from diverse sources on the left since the 1960s, but in the long run extremists on the right have organized on a larger scale and on a longer-term basis to prepare for the day when violent revolution becomes necessary. Extremist groups on the left have had hundreds and thousands of members, collectively. Militias and racist groups on the right have had hundreds of thousands members, and perhaps millions of supporters, in recent decades. In the minds of their membership, militias appeal to the heritage of the American Revolution and traditions of vigilante justice in the frontier West. Militia activists fear that state and federal governments, the United Nations, large corporations, and other agents of globalization threaten to take away their freedom. They have armed themselves heavily and trained for the day when, like the Minutemen of the Revolutionary Era, they will have to fight their own government. Racist groups fear similar things, but they focus their suspicions and hatreds in the defense of the purity and power of the white race—against Jews, nonwhites, feminists, and gays and lesbians. They also espouse a mix nineteenth-century racist science, Nazi politics, pseudo-Christian theology, and other mythologies. Most militia groups officially reject racist ideology, but generally their members are white, and typically they emphasize that people prefer to live with their own kind, suggesting the overlap between militias and overtly racist, white-supremacist groups.

In the 1960s, the major figure on the extreme right in the American West was William Potter Gale. He helped organize the Christian Defense League, the California Rangers, and the Minutemen. Such groups organized in small cells, stockpiled weapons, and trained to fight both leftist subversives and the federal government. Some members of these organizations committed robberies or counterfeited money to fund their efforts. Such groups in the 1960s and 1970s were part of right-wing organizing that went back to the early twentieth century and would grow in the 1980s and 1990s (see Chapter Fourteen). Their extreme militancy and willingness to use violence might seem bizarre to most Americans, but their ideas, values, and suspicions have deep roots in United States history.

In common, right-wing extremists resisted changes to the social order in the post–World War II era, notably challenges to white male authority by racial minorities and women and the growing power of government and corporations as a result of World War II, the Cold War, and globalization. As among their left-wing counterparts, the social and ideological motives of the racist right were complex. Their home in the West was an increasingly alien place. They felt like victims of changes over which they had no control, and they turned to familiar American Western ideals of revolutionary action and frontier justice as a remedy. The key point here is their growing discontent with the rise of the metropolitan West and the creation of a global American empire. The West, these people felt, was being taken from them.

The Sagebrush Rebellion

A group who called themselves the Sagebrush rebels definitely felt that the West as they knew it was being ruined by outsiders, but they focused their ire and resistance more strictly on federal environmental regulations and worked through mainstream American political institutions to try to preserve their freedoms. Their "rebellion" began in Nevada, where ranchers had grown ever more frustrated with recent government regulations designed to preserve resources and protect the environment on public lands. In the 1970s, state legislators tried to transfer control of public lands from the federal Bureau of Land Management to the state, so it could lease protected lands to ranchers. To ranchers, this federal control of public land (*their* land, rightfully, as Westerners they believed) violated their individual rights. They invoked the notion of state's rights to buttress their case. Politicians, lobbyists, and business leaders from other states in the region, such as Senator Barry Goldwater of Arizona, jumped into the fray in support. Mining and oil companies, construction companies and developers who built suburbs and exurbs, and small-government advocates also supported the Sagebrush rebels. Historical and legal precedent was on the side of the federal government, but for such Westerners the regulatory power of the federal government seemed new; indeed, the federal government had begun to regulate public lands more closely and in new ways beginning in the 1930s with the New Deal and expanding greatly with the environmental policies of the 1960s and 1970s.

The Sagebrush rebels pitched their campaign in traditional regional terms, as a conflict between local people and distant bureaucrats in Washington, D.C., but considerable opposition to the Sagebrush rebels came from other Westerners who rejected what they saw as uncontrolled, environmentally reckless development. Such critics pointed out that the Sagebrush rebels included national and multinational corporations, not just local ranchers and business owners. These critics did not trust local and state politicians and bureaucrats, whom they considered more likely to bow to influential local business leaders rather than make decisions on the basis of the long-term conservation of resources (for future generations) or preservation of wilderness spaces. They included environmentalists, tourist-industry lobbyists, consumers who looked to national parks and other public lands for leisure activities, and homeowners who did not want new developments—farms, mines, or oil fields—in their backyards.

The larger context of the Sagebrush Rebellion was the economic stagnation of the 1970s, caused in part by wartime spending in Vietnam and a sharp rise in global oil prices, but also by the end of the postwar economic boom in the North America and Western Europe. The globalization fostered by the postwar American empire that for two decades had benefited the metropolitan West was now hurting Westerners, some of them getting hit with unemployment and high inflation at the same time. The hurt also came in ironic forms. The booming housing markets in California cities saw the value of homes rise steadily in this period. In the 1970s, a growing number of middle-class homeowners found themselves unable or unwilling to pay their skyrocketing property taxes. Even when state legislators did not raise tax rates—to pay for social services that many suburbanites associated with minorities in inner cities—rising property values automatically made tax payments high enough to upset family budgets. In California in 1978, voters overwhelmingly passed Proposition 13, a "People's Initiative to Limit Property Taxation" that changed the state constitution. "Prop 13" put a cap on property tax rates and required a two-thirds majority in both houses of the state legislature for future increases in all state tax rates and in the amount of revenue collected, including state income-tax rates. Prop 13 soon forced the state to cut funding for social-service programs and education, undermining an education system that previously had been one of the most generously funded of any state in the nation.

The tax revolt in California was heard around the world and it represented a broader national shift towards small-government ideals and cutbacks in spending. States from Colorado to Michigan would write balanced-budget requirements and strict limitations on tax increases into their constitutions in the next two decades. A symbolic victory for the Sagebrush rebels came in 1980 when conservative activists, whose grass-roots organizing efforts went back to the 1964 Goldwater campaign, even to the 1930s and 1940s, helped to elect Ronald Reagan to the presidency. Reagan cheered the hearts of conservatives when he proclaimed that government was not the solution but the cause of America's problems. Though President Reagan did not trim spending—indeed, he dramatically increased spending generally and military spending in particular, and along with it the national debt—he did cut taxes and modestly reign in federal environmental regulations. Westerners continued to benefit from Cold War spending during the Reagan years as they had for the past five decades. Much of the funding for Reagan's infamous "Star Wars" missile defense program (named after the 1977 film) went to Western states, for example. Likewise, most Western homeowners, as in the rest of the nation, embraced government regulations when they suited their needs, such as zoning laws to prevent unwanted forms of economic development in their neighborhoods (e.g., publicly subsidized housing). The issue thus was less one of small government versus big government and more a matter of how government powers benefited or frustrated different groups of Westerners.

These complex and competing self-interests are another example of the historic love-hate relationship that Westerners have long had with the federal government. While their region has benefited more than any other from decades of federal funding and intervention, they have always tended to view themselves as at a great distance from Washington, D.C., as if it were an alien power. The federal government maintains a unique authority over public lands in the region, where it remains by far the largest landowner. The Sagebrush Rebellion also points back to the growing extremism and the potential for violence in the West. In thousands of incidents since the late 1980s, and in growing numbers in the 1990s, Forest Service staff, various other federal and state employees who work on

public lands, and environmental activists, particularly in the Mountain
West and Northwest, have been threatened and shot at, had their offices
bombed, or had their homes and vehicles vandalized and burglarized.

As the Sagebrush Rebellion and the tax revolt suggest, the question of
to whom the West belongs was not only a symbolic one of culture, values, and identity, but one with tangible economic costs and benefits. The
"bread and butter" economic issues were hard to separate from questions
of identity and belonging. Whose West was it? Who would control the
resources of the region? To the benefit of whom and with what individual
or civic goals in mind? Finally, just how far would people go to get what
they wanted or fight what they feared?

Conclusion

The growth of the metropolitan West and the countercultural movements that divided it in 1960s and 1970s produced an identity crisis for
the region that mirrored national divisions over what it meant to be an
American. But this crisis also was peculiarly regional. In their own ways,
the Black Panthers, the Weathermen, AIM, *Earth First!,* and white militia
groups all argued that something fundamental had gone wrong in American society. Their more moderate kin in the antiwar movement, civil rights
and women's rights groups, environmentalist organizations, the Sagebrush Rebellion, and the New Right agreed; but mainstream groups had
more faith that American institutions still worked, that conflicts could be
addressed peacefully through reform, and that revolution and violence
were not necessary.

Congress gave John Wayne, the iconic Western film hero, a special
gold medal in 1979. Wayne was 72 at the time and dying of cancer. The
actress Maureen O'Hara, who had often co-starred with Wayne, said in
her testimony about him before a congressional committee: "John Wayne
is not just an actor. John Wayne is the United States of America." When
Wayne died three months later, in July 1979, President Jimmy Carter
described him in terms Frederick Jackson Turner would have recognized
saying: "He was a symbol of many of the most basic qualities that made
America great. The ruggedness, the tough independence, the sense of personal conviction and courage—on and off the screen—reflected the best
of our national character." Wayne's death and the accolades of Congress

and the President were poignant. By the late 1970s the Western was in decline as an influential film and TV show genre, as Westerns gave way to generic "action" films. Western icon Clint Eastwood became the San Francisco cop "Dirty Harry," an amoral, vigilante rule breaker.

One can make too much of the timing, but these examples symbolize major trends from the 1960s to the 1980s. The West was becoming more generically American, and both the region and the nation became divided culturally and politically. It was harder for a Western hero to be a unifying symbol, for the region or the nation. The fruits of empire—in the social and economic transformation of the region during World War II and the Cold War, and U.S. expansion over land in the nineteenth century and overseas in the twentieth—alienated Western Americans from each other in a variety of ways during the 1960s and 1970s. The unity and prosperity of the postwar years had disappeared.

✿ Suggested Readings ✿

Cawley, R. McGregor. *Federal Land, Western Anger: The Sagebrush Rebellion and Environmental Politics.* Lawrence: University Press of Kansas, 1993.

Cohen, Lizabeth. *A Consumers' Republic: The Politics of Mass Consumption in Postwar America.* New York: Knopf, 2003.

D'Emilio, John, and Estelle B. Freedman. *Intimate Matters: A History of Sexuality in America.* Second Edition. Chicago: University of Chicago Press, 1998.

Dingemans, Dennis, and Robin Datel. "Urban Multiethnicity." *Geographical Review* 85 (1995): 458–477.

Findlay, John M. *Magic Lands: Western Cityscapes and American Culture after 1940.* Berkeley: University of California Press, 1992.

Gitlin, Todd. *The Sixties: Years of Hope, Days of Rage.* New York: Bantam, 1987.

Levitas, Daniel. *The Terrorist Next Door: The Militia Movement and the Radical Right.* New York: Thomas Dunne Books, 2002.

Patterson, James T. *Grand Expectations: The United States, 1945–1974.* New York: Oxford University Press, 1996.

McGirr, Lisa. *Suburban Warriors: The Origins of the New American Right.* Princeton: Princeton University Press, 2001.

Patterson, James T. *Restless Giant: The United States from Watergate to Bush v. Gore.* New York: Oxford University Press, 2007.

Robbins, William G. "Creating a 'New' West: Big Money Returns to the Hinterland." *Montana* 46 (1996): 66–72.

Rothman, Hal K. *The Greening of America? Environmentalism in the United States since 1945.* New York: Harcourt Brace, 1997.

Starrs, Paul F., and John B. Wright. "Great Basin Growth and the Withering of California's Pacific Idyll." *Geographical Review* 85 (1995): 417–435.

Steiner, Michael. "Frontierland as Tomorrowland: Walt Disney and the Architectural Packaging of the Mythic West." *Montana* 48 (1998): 2–17.

Wilkinson, Charles F. *Blood Struggle: The Rise of Modern Indian Nations.* New York: Norton, 2005.

Wyckoff, William. "Postindustrial Butte." *Geographical Review* 85 (1995): 478–496.

Zakin, Susan. *Coyotes and Town Dogs: Earth First! and the Environmental Movement.* Tucson: University of Arizona Press, 2002.

Zhou, Min, and J. V. Gatewood, eds. *Contemporary Asian America: A Multidisciplinary Reader.* Second Edition. New York: New York University Press, 2007.

CHAPTER FOURTEEN

From the Eighties to the New Millennium

The West as an ideal still has a powerful hold on people's imagination. Despite the conflicts that have troubled the region since the 1960s, Nevada and Arizona are the fastest growing states in the nation—especially in cities such as Las Vegas and Phoenix—places to start anew, maybe even strike it rich, and live the good life in a warm climate. Colorado is growing steadily as well, as are Washington and Oregon, if more modestly. But the costs of such growth are ever more apparent, as such a basic resource as water becomes increasingly scarce and as more and more of the Western landscape is built over with housing developments, tourist resorts, and various forms of industrial development. The mythic appeal of the West sometimes seems to be its own undoing. Furthermore, the West as a whole no longer is a place of opportunity, and some economically vibrant parts of the West are even experiencing out-migration, with some of the migrants going to the Midwest, where the cost of living, especially housing prices, is lower.

The 2000 U.S. Census revealed that the South had received the highest in-migration—meaning new residents from other parts of the United States—of any region in the previous ten years. In the federal census, Texas and Oklahoma are defined as part of the South, and had only modest net in-migration. The Northeast and the Midwest have had significant net

396

out-migration. The Mountain West and Pacific West received the second highest total of in-migration, but this was almost balanced by out-migration. States like Wyoming and the Dakotas had dramatic net outflow. Even California—still an economic powerhouse, but ever more expensive to live in—had a net outflow. Trends for immigrants to the United States followed a similar pattern in the past decade. Latin America and Asia dominate as points of origin. States such as California have received millions of immigrants, but they soon lose many of these new arrivals to other states.

In the past half-century, the larger cost of success in the West is most obvious in terms of the environmental impact, especially the dwindling water supply. As of 2007, the region had endured twelve years of drought, and it could anticipate only higher demands on regional water supplies, especially on the Colorado Plateau, in California, and in the Southwest. There, growing cities and industrial-scale agriculture continue to use water like there is no tomorrow, despite modest conservation efforts and climate change that threatens more drought in the future.

The larger global context also has changed the American West: the terrorist attacks of 9/11, the rise of the Pacific Rim as the most dynamic region of the world economically, and American-led wars in Afghanistan and Iraq. Since 2001, pundits from across the political spectrum have described the United States as a new kind of empire, some lamenting this status as a fall from democratic grace, others celebrating it as proof of the superiority of the American way of life and the nation's global mission and responsibility. China and perhaps India will catch up with the United States in economic output in the next half century, and may become serious strategic and military threats as a result. But today the United States remains the global colossus, spending more money on its military than the next ten highest-spending nations combined, and it still has the largest economy in the world.

What does all of this mean for the American West? The heyday of the region perhaps has passed. It seems to be moving from the postwar era of "metropolitan" growth, a time of rapid expansion powered by federal spending, into a new one defined less by national endeavors and more by transnational demographic, economic, and cultural contexts. These new contexts will mean very different things for people living in the various subregions of the West and will continue to undermine the distinctiveness of the West as a region, as compared to other parts of the country, making it more difficult than ever to identify what defines the region as a whole.

The End of the Cold War

The Cold War came to a sudden end between 1989 and 1992, with the collapse of the Soviet bloc in Eastern Europe in 1989–90 and the fragmentation of the Soviet Union itself in 1991 and 1992. At the same time, China and other communist nations in Southeast Asia became increasingly capitalist economically, even if they continued to call themselves communist and remained ambivalent about democratic political practices and human rights and freedoms.

The immediate effect of these changes on the West was cuts in military spending. The presidential administrations of George H. W. Bush and Bill Clinton in the 1990s oversaw the closing of some bases, shut down a number of weapons programs, and reduced the number of personnel in the services (or planned to do so). Lobbyists and local members of Congress did their best to protect spending in their own states and districts, even when it did not make sense militarily. Whether in states with a declining population like North Dakota, which had long relied on bases economically, or larger, more dynamic states like California and Texas, which benefited from research and development (R&D) money and weapons production plants, the economy of the entire West faced real cutbacks and feared potential ones. For example, in the late 1980s the aerospace industries of California, Washington, and Texas lost military contracts, and in 1993 the government dropped plans for an $8 billion Superconducting Super Collider (a particle accelerator designed to study subatomic particles) that was to be built near Dallas. Much like after World War II, many Westerners worried about what the end of the Cold War economy would mean for the region.

The late 1990s and early 2000s revealed, however, that regional concerns about potential cutbacks in military spending and their impact were exaggerated. The Gulf War of 1991, in response to the Iraqi invasion of Kuwait, the post-9/11 wars in Afghanistan and Iraq, and a potentially endless new "war on terror" provided a new sort of "Cold War" mentality and a new global mission for the U.S. military, with Muslim extremism taking the place of communism as the per-

"The Boneyard" is the 309th Aerospace Maintenance and Regeneration Group (AMA-RG) located on Davis-Monthan Air Force Base near Tucson, Arizona. The Boneyard is a storage depot for aircraft that have been "retired" from years of service or lack of use. The desert environment preserves the aircraft, which can be cannibalized for parts, junked as scrap metal, or refurbished for service if needed. *United States Department of the Air Force*

ceived threat to American freedom. Lobbyists and politicians have been good at using this "war on terror" and visions of high-tech cyber wars in the future to protect military bases from closure and win new contracts for weapons programs for their districts. For example, northern-tier Air Force bases in North Dakota and Wyoming have survived round after round of cuts (unlike many bases in the Midwest), their wide-open spaces providing useful training ground for futuristic missions. Other bases in the West still house hundreds of Inter-Continental Ballistic Missiles (ICBMs), once pointed at the Soviet empire. The U.S. military could also use such bases to launch military satellites or house missile-defense systems, particularly if nations such as North Korea and Iran develop credible ICBM programs, or if China, Pakistan, and

India expand their nuclear weapons programs. The small population of the northern-tier states also makes them attractive hosts for such programs—compared to the Southwest, where the population has grown tremendously since the days of Los Alamos and Cold War–era nuclear testing. Simply put, there are fewer people at risk in the Dakotas and Wyoming and security there is easier.

In addition to ongoing and renewed military spending, the Information Technology (IT) revolution of the 1980s and the dotcom boom of the 1990s suggest that Cold War–era military R&D had a legacy effect on the civilian economy apart from military spending. Video games, personal computers, the Internet, and digital special effects in films and on TV cannot be viewed simply as by-products of military technology. Federal spending on military R&D and weapons production provided a crucial basis from which to create certain civilian products that otherwise might have taken much longer to conceive, develop, and produce. This includes older industries such as aerospace. The Boeing Company—which long had been based in the greater Seattle-Tacoma area before moving its corporate headquarters to Chicago in 2001—in its early years depended on military contracts for much of its income, before civilian airlines provided new markets. The Internet is a more recent example. The Advanced Research Projects Agency (ARPA) of the Department of Defense originally developed a computer networking system for military use. ARPA began work on the "ARPANET" in the 1960s, with the first simple network operating in California university labs by the end of the decade. By the late 1970s, information service and delivery companies had begun to create international civilian computer networks. From these origins, computer networking spread among universities, and then in 1991 the World Wide Web was announced. Western states were at the center of the IT revolution and dotcom boom that followed, transforming the economy and culture of the United States and the world.

The New Economy

The IT revolution of the past three decades and the dot.com boom of the 1990s were not exactly "Western," but they often seem so. On the Atlantic Coast, for example, Boston is a major center of computer research and biotechnology, but no area of the nation is more synonymous with IT than the southern part of the San Francisco Bay Area, known as "Silicon Valley," originally for the large number of computer chip R&D firms and manufacturers, but more generally for high-tech research and production related to computing, video games, and other digital products and services. The Seattle area in Washington is home to the corporate software giant Microsoft, and Texas is home to many computer technology firms, notably in metropolitan Dallas–Fort Worth and Austin. While the role of entrepreneurs like Bill Gates of Microsoft cannot be discounted, a large part of the story here remains the relocation of high-tech production to the West and the South during World War II and the Cold War, and the ongoing technological and economic legacy of the resulting military-industrial complex.

The IT revolution not only has benefited large metropolitan areas on the Pacific Coast and in the Southwest, but it has some potential to revive local economies in the rural West. The fast speed of the Internet, with fiber-optic cable and satellite technology, means that geography matters less in many industries. Financial services firms, printers, publishers, and other businesses that rely on electronic documents and information can do their work as easily in Boise, Idaho, or Missoula, Montana, as in Boston, Chicago, or LA. But in Boise or Missoula, the lower cost of living and the spectacular natural setting offer a quality of life that large metropolitan centers, with high housing costs and abominable traffic, cannot match. Indeed, in metropolitan centers like the Bay Area, some companies every day bus in maintenance staff and other low-paid workers from as far away as two hours because of housing costs. Geography once drew migrants to the American West; now the hope for some parts of the region is that geography matters less.

The IT revolution has not come without a pattern familiar to the West. The curse of the dotcom boom was that it exemplified the historic boom-and-bust cycle of the Western economy. It made multimillionaires of computer programmers (many of them quite young), entrepreneurs, and financiers in the 1980s and 1990s. Then, at the turn-of-the-millennium, thousands of dotcom investors lost their fortunes and employees got laid off when the bubble suddenly burst. Specific events, such as an antimonopoly case against Microsoft, and a sudden burst of stock selling in mid-March 2000, may have triggered a collapse. But the burst of the dot.com bubble also was what economists refer to as a "market correction," as the thrill of investment in overly-optimist and often risky ventures gave way to caution, if not panic. Whether in natural resources (the great California Gold Rush comes to mind), agricultural commodities in the nineteenth and early twentieth centuries, the post–World War II economic boom that ended in the 1970s, or the dotcom boom of the 1990s, the economy of the American West has always experienced dramatic swings up and down. And as with wheat, oil, and lumber in the past, Westerners engaged in IT today face competition from companies overseas with lower operational and labor costs—for example, in India, where firms in high-tech metropolitan centers such as Bangalore can offer computing, engineering, telecom, and medical services at costs lower than can North American firms.

If geography does not matter in the way that it used to, in the IT sector especially, it still figures prominently in two other major industries in the West: tourism and real estate. The popularity in recent years of adventure tourism—mountain climbing and biking, backpacking, river running, kayaking, and the like—suggest that the mythic promise of the frontier and Western wilderness spaces remains alive, even in our Information Age. Older forms of tourism such as hunting and fly fishing, skiing weekends, family camping trips to national parks, and vacations at high-end spas and resorts in the mountains or the desert still remain strong, as do gambling and other forms of entertainment tourism in Las Vegas and other "sin cities." Tourism rises and falls somewhat with the national and global economic cycles, and it is more significant in some parts of the West than others, but it has been a core sector of the regional economy for the past half century. So too has been real estate, as people dreaming of open spaces, homes with a view of the mountains, new jobs, retiring in a warm climates, and of buying a second home drive up property sales and building contracts in states such as Colorado and Arizona, and in smaller numbers in northern-tier states such as Montana, Idaho, and Wyoming.

Growth versus Sustainability

The resulting strain on resources, especially water, and the tendency for suburbs and exurbs to eat up former ranchlands and wilderness spaces, highlights the tension between consumerism and environmentalism.

Tourists and new residents of the West love to relax, look at, and play near its natural wonders, but in many places their very presence is overwhelming those wonders, and in the long run threatens to destroy them. A sign of the larger problem is the growing effort of cities like Denver, Phoenix, and Salt Lake City to resist suburban sprawl and promote inner-city redevelopment. Long perceived as hostile to public transportation (compared to self-consciously progressive cities such as San Francisco or Portland), conservative centers like Denver, Phoenix, and Salt Lake City are also now exploring and developing rapid-transit light-rail projects, dense forms of condo and apartment housing, and natural forms of landscaping that require less water. For some residents, such developments reflect the urban lifestyle they desire, but for others the goal is more practical: to save money on public utilities and infrastructure, preserve wilderness spaces, and avoid increasingly longer commutes.

The two most obvious examples of rapid growth and sprawl are Las Vegas and Phoenix, both young cities, even if older ones like Denver face similar problems. All of the major metropolitan areas, even powerful Los Angeles, have been forced to contemplate conservation measures, as well as look for more water resources (as they always have). The courts finally have forced LA, for example, to begin returning water to the Owens Valley, by siphoning water from its aqueduct back to the Owens River, at least partially restoring the river and Owens Lake. The problem of sprawl in cities like Las Vegas and Phoenix can be measured in different ways. The city of Las Vegas had 258,000 residents in 1990, 478,000 in 2000, and about 545,000 in 2005. By 2006, the larger Las Vegas metropolitan area had almost 1.8 million residents and was about to pass Atlanta, Louisville, Nashville, and Milwaukee to become a top-twenty metropolitan area (by 2010). Las Vegas depends on water from the Colorado River storage system, taken from nearby Lake Mead, which was created by the Hoover Dam. In addition to tourism, focused on its opulent casinos, nightclubs, and restaurants, Las Vegas has worked to attract manufacturing and financial services. Its majority population is white, but it also has a growing minority population, including Latinos (about 25 percent), African Americans (10 percent), Asians (4 percent), and the largest population of native Hawaiians outside of Hawaii. Unionized jobs in the casinos and jobs in construction, landscaping, and other service jobs in the city attract migrants.

Peggy Pierce, 2009, as a Nevada
State Assemblywoman (Democratic).
Courtesy, Peggy Pierce

    Behind the popular images of gamblers, high rollers, and the surreal, magnificent hotels of the Vegas "Strip" lies a more prosaic story of families and migrants hoping to gain upward mobility. Every new resort complex needs 5,000 to 10,000 workers. Most workers are organized and get decent pay and benefits. Indeed, Las Vegas is the most unionized city in the country. (Most tourist workers in the West are not unionized, and they often have a low standard of living. It is the scale of the hotels and other Vegas businesses that makes unionizing efforts work there.) As Glen Arnodo of the Culinary Workers and Bartenders Union told *High Country News* in 1995, native-born American and immigrant workers have "been able to build good, stable jobs. If you're a maid, you might not get rich, but you're able to buy a house, send your kid to college. Our union represents the middle class of Las Vegas, and it is a microcosm of America: 25 percent Latin, 22 percent black, 7 percent Asian, and the rest Anglo." The unions tend to be good for business, too, as casinos with unionized employers have fewer problems with turnover and keep good employees. For example, in the late 1980s Peggy Pierce moved to San Francisco from Peoria, Illinois, and then to Las Vegas to become a lounge singer. She failed in that dream, but she did get a decent job as a waitress. She earned above the minimum wage, bought a home, and had health care and a pension from her employer. Her life was not glamorous, but it was stable and she had made Las Vegas home. In 2000, she went to work for the Culinary Union. In 2005 she took a job with the United Labor Agency of Nevada (ULAN), where she works as the resources coordinator. She has also been elected to the Nevada Assembly.

Population growth in Phoenix has been almost as impressive as that in Las Vegas, with a jump from 790,000 in 1980 to 1.5 million in 2006. Jobs in education, tourism, older industries such as agriculture, construction, real estate, and R&D in Phoenix's high-tech firms have attracted people to the Phoenix metropolitan area. Finally, Denver—or rather the greater "Denver-Aurora-Boulder Combined Statistical Area"—had 2.9 million people in 2006, making it the seventeenth largest metropolitan area in the

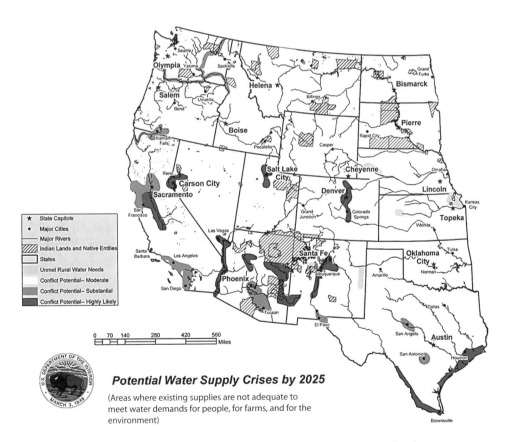

Potential Water Supply Crises by 2025

(Areas where existing supplies are not adequate to meet water demands for people, for farms, and for the environment)

Potential Water Supply Crises. *U.S. Department of the Interior, Bureau of Reclamation*

nation. The West was the one of the most highly urbanized regions in the nation in the late nineteenth century, and today it stands at the leading edge of metropolitan development.

The looming and essential question is whether, or how long, such growth is sustainable. Will the water from the region's river systems and underground aquifers run dry? Industrial-scale agriculture in California's Central and Imperial valleys, among the most productive farming regions in the world, and metropolitan development in the Southwest and Mountain West demand ever more water. Cities and farms become more efficient in using water—getting rid of grass and planting desert species in landscaping, using drip technology rather than sprinklers on farms, and raising the price of water. But the continued expansion of industrial, farm, and residential development inevitably raises overall water usage. The problem is similar to that of gasoline usage and cars. More fuel-efficient automobiles cars help conserve gasoline, but the fact of ever more cars on American roads negates better fuel efficiency. This problem is not uniquely Western, as the Southeastern states also have faced drought in the past decade, but it is distinctly Western in that the region has a much longer history of using extreme engineering measures to overcome an arid climate, cycles of drought, and limited groundwater resources. Wealthy nations like the United States have better means to adapt to waning supplies of potable water than do poor nations in Asia, Africa, and Latin America, but, nationally and globally, the competition for fresh water as well as oil will incite political conflicts, perhaps even wars. Indeed, the Bureau of Reclamation and U.S. Department of the Interior have studied the problem and begun to plan for potential conflicts over water in an initiative called *Water 2025*.

The strain on water resources is not the only problem facing the West today. The sheer number of visitors to national parks and wilderness areas—even by eco-conscious adventure tourists who take extreme measures such as bagging their feces and taking them out with them in the name of zero-impact—means more cars, buses, and recreational vehicles spewing carbon dioxide emissions, more feet trampling native plant species, trails, and river bottoms, more all-terrain vehicles (ATVs), motorboats and snowmobiles shattering the silence, and more stress on plant and animal life. All of this demand is taking place even as budget cuts make it difficult for state and national parks to keep up with basic maintenance. Some parks have begun to use volunteers as guides, garbage collectors, and maintenance workers.

Perhaps the most interesting recent trend has been a growing, if uneasy, relationship between otherwise politically conservative hunters and fishers, on the one hand, and progressive, even leftist, environmentalists, on the other. In common they have opposed industrial, mining, and residential development projects that threaten wildlife habitats. They also have fought together to limit road building and the use of motorcycles, ATVs, and snowmobiles in wilderness areas. A good example is Sportsmen for Fish and Wildlife (SFW), which got its start in Utah in 1993 and has since spread to states like New Mexico and Idaho. It sometimes works in coalition with traditional environmental organizations such as the Nature Conservancy to purchase wildlife areas or lobby government to purchase and protect them. But the SFW and other preservation-minded hunter-fisher organizations conflict with traditional environmentalists on issues such as protecting predators. Environmentalists see cougars, bears, and wolves as natural parts of healthy ecosystems, but hunters often view them as competitors for such game animals as deer, elk, and pronghorns. It is not clear how and where this ambivalent coalition of (typically) conservative hunters-fishers and progressive environmentalists will continue in regard to environmental issues themselves and in relation to other social, cultural, and political issues. Nonetheless, the tenuous partnership suggests the potential for a modest political realignment in the American West in the decades to follow, especially if environmental issues begin to replace abortion, gay rights, and foreign policy as primary motivators of voters.

Indians into the Twenty-First Century

The sympathy of many whites for Indians as victims of white "progress" waned in the 1970s and 1980s as Indians began to assert sovereignty and win land claims through court decisions, and as many tribal groups took in huge amounts of money from casinos on reservations or through the sale of natural resources such as oil. In addition, non-Indian hunters and commercial and sport fishers saw the renewal of traditional Native hunting and fishing rights, some of which focused on endangered species barred to non-Indians, as grossly unfair, even un-American, as such policies gave one race special privileges and status. This was particularly so when Indians used modern powerboats, firearms, and snowmobiles to carry out their "traditional" hunts and fishing. For their part, Indian nations saw nothing wrong with finally getting a few breaks, and they pointed to continuing problems of poverty, drug and alcohol abuse, low levels of education, and high levels of unemployment, health problems, violence, and suicide on many reservations.

Such conflicting viewpoints and experiences had many sources, old-fashioned racism among them. Whites were not accustomed to Indians exercising power and winning battles for natural resources. Another element in the conflict was diverging sensibilities about what it meant to be modern. Whites posited that if Indians used modern technology, then, by definition, they could not be undertaking "traditional" Indian pursuits. Indeed, some whites argued that in order to be authentically "Indian," Indians had to be primitive. Such notions of authenticity, and the fierce conflicts over economic and emotional issues, have often inspired racist sentiments. This new issue replays a long history of whites telling Indians what it means to be authentically Indian. Many Indians have argued that they, like all other peoples in the modern age, have found ways to incorporate new technologies into their cultures—as with the horse in the seventeenth and eighteenth centuries. Such adaptation poses no conflict with tradition, and whites have no right to tell Indians how they should honor their traditions. Other Indians sometimes have agreed that authentic Native culture ought to be defined by traditional ways and expressed wariness about the values and costs associated with the use of modern technology. In such discussions, Indians in common might assert that each group should have the right to decide for itself—rather than having to follow the dictates of federal or state governments or other Americans. But like other ethno-cultural groups in the United States, Indians were struggling with the delicate balance between maintaining traditions and adapting to change at the dawn of the new millennium.

An example of a conflict between Indians and other Americans seeking to curtail their traditional lifeways came with the annual whale hunt of the Makah on the Pacific coast of Washington. The Makah tribe returned to hunting the grey whale in the 1999 (after the federal government removed it from the endangered species list), appealing to the Treaty of Neah Bay, which they had signed in 1855. Its request to renew the whale

Makah whalers return to Neah Bay, in Washington, after practicing whale hunting techniques, November 1998. *UPI Photo/H. Ruckemann*

hunt required the United States to broker a deal through the International Whaling Commission, trading U.S. rights to bowhead whales to Russia for rights to grey whales. In order to hunt the grey whales, the Makah use a traditional canoe and harpoon to strike the mammals, but they also employed a retrofitted World War I–era antitank rifle mounted atop a nearby powerboat to pursue a wounded whale and quickly put it out of its misery. Commercial whalers and environmentalists cried foul, each for their own reasons. They claimed that the Makah hunt could not be legitimate if it used modern technology. After the 2000 hunt, in which the Makah failed to kill even one grey whale, litigation by animal-rights activists prevented them from continuing their tradition. Some environmentalists, who typically have assumed that Indians are their natural allies, felt betrayed by Indians who they saw as favoring economic development for their people over the protection of wildlife and the environment. The decision over whether the Makah can continue their traditional whale hunt has since lay in the hands of the National Oceanic and Atmospheric Administration of the U.S. Department of Commerce.

One sign of progress in Indians' rights was the greater willingness of museums to work with Native peoples to preserve their material culture and heritage. Anthropologists and museum curators have helped tribal groups find and preserve delicate historic items. They also have begun to work with certain groups to develop museum displays in ways that incorporate Native traditions and Native voices, rather than only the voices of scientists, anthropologists, historians, and other scholars, many of whom are not Indians. A good example is the National Museum of the American Indian at the Smithsonian Institution in Washington, D.C., which opened in 2004, and works with Indian nations to develop exhibits. Rather than a purely academic approach to the history and archeology of Indian peoples, which would analyze how they have changed over time, the exhibits look at the past from the viewpoint of contemporary Indian communities and emphasize continuity. They do show how Native peoples have adapted to oppression and changed over time, but also how they maintained their identity and integrity as peoples. Some museums have begun to return artifacts to Indian communities, and others have worked with them to care for the fragile relics. Likewise, at tribal colleges, Indians have a privileged voice and work with various levels of government and non-Indian education institutions. This issue is not tradition vs. modern life, but whether Indians have the power to determine how they will negotiate

Peter MacDonald (1928 –) served as Navajo tribal chairman several times in the 1970s and 1980s and a Marine Corps code talker during World War II. He is shown here at a 2008 ceremony dedicating a statue honoring code talkers outside the Arizona State Capitol in Phoenix. *Cronkite News Service Photo/Lauren Proper*

the place of their traditions and adapt to life in America and globalization in the early twenty-first century.

In addition to their growing political power and greater self-determination, the population of most Indian nations has continued to grow in the past three decades. The growing numbers reflect a greater desire by people to claim an Indian heritage (sometimes to make claims on tribal windfalls from court decisions or economic development on reservations) and have led to new conflicts over defining who is an Indian. In addition, the birthrate among Indians has been higher than that of the general population, though it fell in the 1970s and 1980s from its high in the 1960s. The Indian population was about 350,000 from the 1920s to the 1950s. It rose to 793,000 in 1970, nearly 2 million in 1990, and 2.5 million in 2000 (plus 1.6 million people who reported as part Indian). The Native presence is especially noteworthy in the American West: Oklahoma (392,000), New Mexico (173,000), Arizona (255,000), and California (628,000); and Oregon, Montana, Texas, Washington, and South Dakota each have more than 25,000. Almost 70 percent of Indians today are urban, with perhaps 100,000 living in the greater Los Angeles area alone. Still, hundreds of thousands of Indians continue to live on reservations—about 200,000 in the Southwest, for example, in the region where the states of New Mexico, Utah, and Arizona meet.

An example of diversity among Indians and the conflicts that it can foster can be seen in questions about oil drilling in environmentally sensitive areas. In 1975, Indian leaders from across the nation formed the Council of Energy Resource Tribes (CERT) to collect data, help tribes make informed decisions about resource development, and protect their rights. An early president of CERT, Peter Macdonald, a Navajo from Arizona, said that he would make CERT a native version of OPEC. Among the Navajo in the 1970s, conflicts took place over where and how the oil money would be spent. In the 1990s and the early twenty-first century in Alaska, Inupiat Inuit and Gwich'in Indians have battled over whether the Alaska National Wildlife Refuge should be opened to drilling for oil, the former wanting the money to maintain their lifestyle, which includes modern comforts, the latter seeing a threat to the caribou herds that are a cornerstone of their traditional way of life. It is also noteworthy that climate change, particularly the melting of ice flows, may fatally undermine traditional lifeways among Arctic Indians and Inuits by threatening the hunting of whales and seals and the larger ecology of the region. Native peoples, like other Americans, thus can be found on both sides of environmental issues.

This recent history suggest that Indian peoples in the American West, like indigenous peoples in other parts of the United States and the larger world, continue to struggle with the historic legacy of their conquest and coercive efforts to assimilate them. In recent years, however, they have had a stronger political voice and more economic opportunities to determine their own futures. In northern Canada, in the recently created territory of Nunavut, Native people control the territorial government. Tribal sovereignty generally has not advanced as far as that in the American West, but it suggests that the story of Native Americans is part of a larger, global story. If a frontier opens when intruders and indigenous peoples meet and closes when one group asserts hegemony over the other, then Native peoples in the West and elsewhere in the world may be reopening "frontiers" in surprising ways in the early twenty-first century.

Globalization and the Pacific Rim

The signs of globalization were everywhere in the West at the turn of the millennium. The success of Mormon missionaries in the South Pacific has drawn thousands of Polynesians to Utah, especially Salt Lake City. The two groups share traditions of strong family values, though some Polynesian adolescents in Salt Lake City have found it hard to fit in and joined gangs. In Los Angeles, Japanese and other Asian investors began to buy up and develop banks and high-priced real estate in the 1980s and have become power brokers in the local economy. In trendy shopping malls from Southern California to Arizona, affluent adolescents from the Latino middle class can buy Asian-Mexican fusion food when they're not text-messaging their friends on cell phones. Mexican immigrants, many of them illegal, make up more than half the workers in meatpacking plants in Iowa. Gas stations in Death Valley, California, have signs in German, Italian, and Spanish because Death Valley National Park draws so many European tourists. When leather-clad bikers pull up to gas pumps outside Las Vegas, they may well be French tourists following their dream of riding Harley-Davidsons across the American West. And in April 1992, following the acquittal of white cops for beating a black

Taken in Los Angeles on April 30, 1992 near the intersection of Kenmore Avenue and Beverly Boulevard. Later that day a dusk-to-dawn curfew was imposed in portions of the city. *Polaroid photo by Dana Graves.*

motorist named Rodney King, African Americans in South-Central Los Angeles vented their anger and frustration by smashing and looting corner grocery stores owned by Korean immigrants and by pulling a white trucker from his rig and beating him senseless. Together these examples suggest the complex racial-ethnic, cultural, and economic currents that globalization has been bringing to the West in past three decades. These currents are changing not only the demography and culture of the region, but also its politics and sense of community—locally, in relation to the larger nation, and in relation to Mexico, the Canadian West, and the entire Pacific Rim.

Though we tend to think of globalization as an economic phenomenon, it also involves communities and culture on the move, as the King riots in South-Central LA revealed. The riots led to 51 deaths, more than 2,300 injuries, more than 8,000 arrests, and more than $800 million in damages. But it is especially noteworthy that many of the rioters targeted Korean-owned businesses, and that members of the Korean American community banded together, even arming themselves, to protect their property during the riots. From the viewpoint of African Americans in "South-Central," the Korean Americans were outsiders who made money off of them but treated them with suspicion when they shopped and refused to employ them in their "mom 'n pop" corner grocery stores. From the Korean American point of view, they were running honest businesses that depended on the free labor of hard-working family members to make a living. In one sense, South Korean immigrants have fit in well in the United States—typically, with economic upward mobility, achievement in higher education, and as a largely Christian population. But the King riots and the charges of racism in not hiring blacks embittered many Korean Americans. The riots, of course, also revealed once again the legacy of the neighborhood covenants and quiet segregationist policies of banks and real estate brokers that kept most African Americans out of the suburbs and in the inner city during the suburban housing boom of the 1950s and 1960s. Urban redevelopment, or "gentrification," has not helped most blacks, but pushed many of them into new slums in the oldest inner ring of suburbs.

Antonio Villaraigosa gives his victory speech after defeating incumbent James Hahn, May 17, 2005. Villaraigosa became the first Latino mayor of Los Angeles since 1872. *Photo by Julio Cortez/www.JulyThePhotoGuy.com*

Compared to Asians and Latinos, the African American middle class is proportionally smaller, and African Americans also remain more socially isolated (e.g., in terms of inter-racial marriages).

It is worth noting that while a vibrant Mexican American (and more broadly Latino) middle class was growing in the cities and suburbs of Southern California and other parts of the American West, and while Latinos owned many of the businesses damaged in the riots, Latinos also participated in the King riots in significant numbers (almost half of the rioters), especially recent immigrants from Central America. The mainstream media generally portrayed the riots in familiar American terms—as a conflict between black and white—but the event was much more complex, involving people from diverse Latino and Asian backgrounds, both as participants and victims. The riots, though an extreme example, revealed the complicated quality of race relations and their intersection with economic class in the American West. Today the West, more so than the South, represents the complexity of race relations in the United States, with racial-ethnic diversity cross cut with diversity of economic class within particular groups.

This complexity is further revealed in metropolitan areas around the American West, where Latino Americans are revitalizing urban areas. Among Latinos, 50 percent describe themselves as Latino or Hispanic, 30 percent as Mexican, and the rest as Cuban, Puerto Rican, Central American, or another Latin American group. Regardless of their heritage, Latinos compose a large number of blue-collar workers in agriculture, construction, landscaping, and service industries. (Efforts to organize Latino janitors, maids, and day laborers are among the most concerted in a generally beleaguered American labor movement.) At the same time, Latinos in core areas of cities have opened small businesses. Middle-class, professional Latinos live and work in growing numbers in the suburbs and exurbs of the American West, from Phoenix to Las Vegas to Denver. They have created a growing market for Latino products, and some affluent, religiously conservative Latinos have been attracted to the Republican Party. Latinos also have run for and won elections to high office in a number of Western states—for example, Bill Richardson, as governor of New Mexico in 2002 and a presidential candidate in 2008, and Antonio Villaraigosa, as mayor of LA in 2005. As in the past, tension often exists between long-time Latino citizens and residents of the United States and recent immigrants, especially illegal migrant workers. Anti-immigrant movements, such as vigilante border-patrol groups and social conservatives in the Republican Party, tend to drive Latinos to the Democratic Party. At the same time, labor advocates in the Democratic Party, and well-established blue-collar Latinos who aspire to the middle class, sometimes fear that migrants from Mexico and Central America will hurt their image and drag down their wages. Concerns about immigrants, legal and illegal, cannot in be understood simply along left-right or white-Latino lines.

A similar general point can be made about Asian American citizens and recent Asian immigrants. These broad labels belie significant differences between diverse ethnic groups, diverse religious backgrounds, recent immigrant communities, and long-established groups (such as Chinese and Japanese Americans), and people with vastly different economic backgrounds and levels of education. The growth of immigrant and second-generation communities from South and West Asia in the past four decades has only added to the complexity. Many Iranians and Arabs ended up in the West as a result of violence in Israel, the Palestinian territories and Lebanon, the Iranian Revolution in 1979, and the Iran-Iraq war in the 1980s. In addition, high-tech firms brought in many engineers, computer programmers, doctors, and nurses from India, Pakistan, Egypt, and the Philippines. This does not mean that sweeping generalizations—such as the perception that Asians put a premium on university education—are wholly without merit. Rather, it suggests that migrant agricultural laborers from the Philippines, rural Hmong refugees from Vietnam, illegal immigrants from mainland China who work as indentured servants in sweatshops, highly educated engineers from India, wealthy investors who fled Hong Kong before Britain returned it to China in 1997, South Korean students at evangelical Protestant seminaries, and Muslims ranging from assimilated and secular to traditionalist cannot be treated as a single group with common interests. As with Europeans in the past, some Asian migrants are temporary, and thousands of tourists and students add to their presence. But even among permanent migrants, geographic mobility is common. California in particular is both a major receiver and sender of such migrants. This immigration, combined with growing networks of trade and investment among Pacific Rim nations, has dramatically increased the presence of

Asian people, cultures, and economic power in the region, especially on the Pacific Coast, but also in the interior West.

The ethnic and economic diversity of Asian and Latino communities in the American West, the geographic mobility of their residents, and evidence of a small but steady trend of racial mixing suggest how the cultural identity of the region is changing. Moreover, some observers have wondered what such trends mean for the American national identity in the long run. This question means different things in different contexts. For example, globe-trotting cosmopolitan people who work and travel comfortably live in cultural settings very different from those of recent immigrants who seek communities where they can function in their native language and feel little need to learn English. These changes are not just matters of culture, but also of regional economic self-interest. Westerners often have wondered what use politicians and bureaucrats in distant Washington are to them. This question is being raised in new ways today as a result of globalization. Many Westerners may feel a stronger kinship, economically or culturally, with people in other countries where they have family, investments, or travel for work or vacation, than with people in other parts of the United States (or across the street). Scholars call these identities "post-national," but they are "post-regional" as well. One can also look at these associations simply as pragmatic and individualist, reflecting the experience of people whose cultural identity and economic interests are fluid and mixed, and who do not define their sense of community along geographical lines.

Another variation on this theme is the impact of white Americans who have moved to rural areas and small towns in the Mountain West for lifestyle reasons, or who have purchased a second home for vacations or retirement there. In areas such as Kalispell, Montana, a twentieth-century economy based on logging and local lumber mills has fallen into decline, with global competition and tighter environmental regulations on forests in the region. Wealthy retirees and celebrities who have bought land in the area, and a steady stream of tourists, have boosted the economy of Kalispell, creating many new jobs in construction and service industries. But these new jobs do not pay as much as the ever-smaller number of union-wage logging and mill jobs. In addition, the new and even the temporary residents have driven up housing prices. They typically come from larger metropolitan areas, tend to be more liberal-progressive in their values, and often support environmental regulations that frustrate long-time residents with deep ties to hunting, individualism, and the logging-lumber mill economy. Right-wing talk radio shows and the presence of militia groups in the area have exacerbated these tensions. In the 1990s and early 2000s, unknown assailants occasionally threatened government officials, local police, and their families, sometimes taking shots at them or sabotaging their property.

A recent new resident and former police officer, Brenda Kitterman, helped organize a "Hands Against Hate" campaign in opposition to the militia groups and to encourage Kalispell residents to find nonviolent ways to deal with their differences. Threats of sexual assault and murder against her, and vandals loosening the lug nuts on the wheels of her daughter Tricia's car, led her to teach her daughters to use pepper spray and shoot hand guns. They moved from Kalispell to Oregon in 2004, not because of the violence but the rising cost of living there, but planned to move back when they could afford to do so.

In 2002, word from an informant led to an investigation and raids by the police, FBI, and Bureau of Alcohol, Tobacco, and Firearms on a militia group called Project 7, which was led by David Burgert. Two years later, the ongoing investigation led to more arrests. Officers captured a cache of weapons stored by a militia group and arrested several militia members plotting to kill local police officers, judges, prosecutors, and their families. The cache comprised more than 30,000 rounds of ammunition, machine guns, handguns, a silencer, body armor, pipe bombs, explosives, bomb-making chemicals, survivalist gear, and military rations worth hundreds of thousands of dollars. This story reveals the tension-filled connection between globalization and local changes in the economy and culture of northern Montana. In this case, the "invaders" bringing new ways that threatened older residents were largely white, native-born Americans. Nonetheless, many locals viewed them as outsiders, as aliens with values that conflicted with their own and who wished to disrupt if not ruin the local way of life, culturally and economically, making locals feel out of place in their own hometown.

If the United States created a new kind of "free trade" empire in the twentieth century, especially in years after World War II, and fostered what we have come to call globalization, it is today evolving into a more formless, postnational form of empire, with national, regional, and local identities ever-shifting, and therefore constantly changing the flavor and nature of local communities and economies. Sociologists call this phenomenon "glocalization," referring to the synergy between peculiar local dynamics and global economic processes. Glocalization is changing the United States, its relations with Mexico and Canada, the American West as a whole, and subregions therein.

Extremism

Militia and white-supremacy groups continued to organize quietly in the 1980s and early 1990s, attracting tens of thousands of active members by the mid-1990s. Their motivations are complex. A hostility toward globalization lies at the core of these movements—to the racial diversity it has fostered in the United States, the swelling power of the federal government and transnational corporations that threaten the autonomy of local communities and families, and the economic decline of family farms, ranches, and the resource economy in various parts of the Midwest, Plains states, and Mountain West. Many who support or sympathize with white supremacists and militias are also influenced by millennial Christianity and visions of violent conflicts at the end of time between the true followers of Christ and supporters of the devil. Associated with these trends, for many such supporters, are changing values about family life and sexuality, particularly a perceived decline in the place of white men in society. Indeed, many scholars who study extremist groups argue that perceived threats to male autonomy and authority motivate many of their members. This motivation also connects these groups to the mythic promise of the frontier—in the idea that the claiming and taking of land of one's own on the frontier gave a man the opportunity to be truly free, not beholden to the whims of government or employers. The socioeconomic changes associated with globalization, and with women's rights and the civil rights of American Indians, Latinos, and Asian and African Americans, have combined to threaten the status, authority, and freedom of white men in the experience and perception of the membership of militias and white-supremacy activists. They fear that Jews, liberals, people of color, homosexuals, and others are using the federal government and the United Nations in a conspiracy to subvert their rights, way of life, and freedom.

The Alfred P. Murrah Federal Building in Oklahoma City in April 1995 after the bombing. *Department of Defense*

Ironically, American white supremacists have become more influential overseas in recent years among racist groups in Europe. Their organizing and the potential threat they posed to fellow citizens and residents of the West, and to the federal government, became clear in a series of violent incidents in the 1980s and 1990s.

In the 1980s, police, the FBI, and other law enforcement agencies pursued and arrested or killed extermists who robbed banks or assassinated their enemies. For example, in 1984 a Christian Identity group called The Order, which emerged out of the American Nazi Party, killed Alan Berg, a liberal Jewish talk radio host and lawyer from Denver. Berg was infamous for his liberal views on issues such as homosexuality, gun control, and religion as well as for berating, enraging, and humiliating callers to his show. Members of the Order also committed armored-car and bank robberies and counterfeited money to purchase weapons, and blew up synagogues. In 1984, an Order member captured by the police gave them names and information, leading to the death of Order leader Robert Jay Matthews in a log cabin on Whidbey Island, Washington. Matthews refused to surrender to the FBI and in the firefight that followed the cabin burned to the ground, killing him. Militia and white supremacist websites describe Matthews as a martyr to his race. The Order was based loosely on a group described in a racist novel called *The Turner Diaries*, written by William Luther Pierce and published under the pseudonym Andrew Macdonald in 1978. It depicts a racist revolution in the United States in the 1990s and describes genocidal assaults on nonwhites around the world. It also describes an assassination similar to the one of Berg. *The Turner Diaries* is often viewed as the Bible (or perhaps *The Communist Manifesto*) of white supremacy and militia groups. When police captured militia activist Timothy McVeigh—who was convicted of bombing the Alfred P. Murrah Federal Building in Oklahoma City in April 1995, killing 168 people, including children—they found photocopies of part of *The Turner Diaries* in his car. McVeigh said he was motivated to commit the horrible crime by two recent incidents: one at Ruby Ridge in Idaho in August 1992; and the other near Waco, Texas, in April 1993.

At Ruby Ridge, federal marshals tried to arrest Randy Weaver, a Christian Identity activist, on weapons possession charges. Weaver was holed up in a cabin with his wife Vicki, two of their children, and family friend Kevin Harris. Marshals surrounded the cabin but were detected by the family dog. They began to retreat but shot the family dog when it charged them. Now Weaver, his fourteen-year-old son Sammy, and Harris rushed outside to see what was happening. What happened next remains in dispute. Nonetheless, an exchange of shots took place between Sammy and Harris and the marshals. One of the officers shot and killed Sammy, spraying him with automatic fire as he ran back toward the cabin. Harris returned fire, fatally shooting a federal marshal. The marshals then called in the FBI for help. The FBI set rules of engagement that allowed agents to use deadly force on adult men if they could do so without harming a child. In the siege that followed, the Weavers and Harris held out for eleven days. At one point during the long and tense ordeal, as the Weavers tried to get to Sammy's body in a nearby shed, an FBI agent shot at Weaver twice, hitting him once. The other bullet went through the door of the cabin and struck Vicki, killing her where she stood holding her ten-month-old daughter Elisheba. After ten more days, the FBI brought in Bo Gritz, a prominent militia supporter and later a Populist Party candidate for U.S. president, to negotiate a surrender. He mediated between the FBI and the remaining members of the Weaver family (and Harris) and convinced them to surrender to the FBI. Anger over mistakes made by the FBI in the poorly planned and executed siege generated sympathy for the Weavers that extended far beyond the membership of radical militias and the white supremacist right.

The next year, while Weaver stood trial on murder and weapons charges, the FBI laid siege to a compound near Waco, Texas. The compound housed a cultist Christian sect whose members called themselves the Branch Davidians and were led by a self-proclaimed messiah, David Koresh. At the local and federal levels, concerns about Koresh's sexual exploitation of some of the minor female children in the sect, as well as the group's extensive cache of illegally obtained weapons, led the FBI to surround the compound and demand that Koresh come out and turn himself in. After an initial firefight led to the deaths of several persons on both sides, law enforcement agents undertook a renewed siege of the compound that lasted for two months. It would end in disaster. Having finally run out of patience, and with Attorney General Janet Reno letting the FBI know that, out of concern for the children in the compound, she wanted decisive action taken, agents tried to break the stalemate. They forced a tear-gas bomb through one of the compound's windows in the hope that the smoke would flush the Branch Davidians out. Instead, the bomb ignited a raging inferno in the building. It is unclear whether or not Koresh let his people even try to escape the building, but, ultimately, the fire ended up taking the lives of all of the 79 men, women, and children inside it. In response, mainstream conservative critics accused the government of ignorance about conservative religious groups and of a liberal bias against them. Even more militia and white-supremacist groups began to form around the nation, seeing both Ruby Ridge and Waco as evidence of a Zionist-led, liberal-internationalist conspiracy that had high-jacked the federal government and aimed to take away their American rights. Indeed, two years later, McVeigh timed his bombing of the Oklahoma City Murrah Federal Building to coincide with the anniversary of the Waco tragedy.

After Ruby Ridge and Waco, the FBI improved its tactics in dealing with militia groups, white supremacy fugitives, and religious groups. In response to the Oklahoma City bombing in 1995, police, the FBI, and other agencies cracked down on radical-right groups and outside support for them, and their memberships declined. In addition, lawsuits against some groups, such as a Christian Identity community in northern Idaho, led to their property being seized and given to victims or the relatives of people they had injured or killed. In the past few years, a growing concern over illegal immigration across the Mexico–United States border has inspired a renewal of radical-right groups in the form of volunteer border-patrol militias that appeal to the Revolutionary-era tradition of the Minutemen as well as to frontier traditions of vigilante justice.

One cannot link these patrol groups directly to the older militia and white-supremacy groups, as the newer organizations often include more mainstream citizens who would reject such identification. Nonetheless, a significant ideological overlap in these groups exists. Border-patrol groups date back to the 1980s. Civilian Military Assistance (CMA) formed in Alabama in 1983 to support anti-communist groups in Central America. The CMA later decided to patrol a stretch of the Mexico–United States border not covered by federal Border Patrol agents. Its founders had roots in the U.S. military, the KKK, and the John Birch Society, an anti-communist group founded in 1958 in Indiana and named after an American missionary killed in China in 1945 by communists. CMA members were motivated by anti-communism, nativism, and, simply put, a desire for adventure. In July 1986, nineteen armed CMA members seized sixteen illegal immigrants in Arizona and handed them over to federal agents. Civil rights groups protested this action as vigilantism, and public pressure undermined the CMA's appeal to patriotic values. The federal government considered taking legal action against the CMA, but it did not go through with it. In the early 2000s, in response to 9/11 and illegal immigration across the Mexico–United States border, more than a half-dozen major groups (and many smaller ones) formed to patrol the border, apprehend illegal immigrants, and protect property. One of the most prominent of these new border-watch groups is the Minuteman Project. It was started in California in 2005 by Jim Gilchrist, an Orange County resident. California governor and former action movie star Arnold Schwarzenegger—who in several of his films played vigilante characters in search of rough "justice" and vengeance—has praised the group on an LA radio station. But the Anti-Defamation League and anti-racist watch groups like the Southern Poverty Law Center (which tracks hate crimes) have

Border fence between the United States and Mexico at the Pacific Ocean.

Mexican family enjoying the beach on the U.S. Side of the border fence.

identified the Minutemen as a nativist-extremist group with ties to neo-Nazi and other white-supremacist groups. The Minutemen also have been accused of abusing immigrants.

Some border-patrol groups clearly do have ties to militia and white supremacist groups, though most are careful to avoid the use of overtly racist language and images in their official materials. Whatever the exact relationship, those in support of such groups are strongly nativist, angered by the failure of the federal government and Republican and Democratic parties to solve the illegal immigrant problem, and approve of very public vigilante activities. The border-patrol groups use political rhetoric and imagery similar to militia groups, tend to splinter and feud like militia and white supremacist groups usually do, and express common concerns, though in more careful language. They embody the transition from the mainstream politics to extremism in their perception that American institutions are failing, perhaps even fundamentally corrupted, and in their stubborn conviction that civilian citizens must take matters into their own hands in a state of emergency. The active members of such groups number in the thousands (and tens of thousands, when combined with militia and white supremacist groups) and have the sympathy or the support of millions of Americans with similar concerns. The significance of these groups lies not only in their own numbers, but also in what their formation might tell us about recent cultural conflicts in mainstream American politics. Are they canaries in a coal mine?

Red States, Blue States?

In 2004, historian Thomas Frank published a book entitled *What's Wrong with Kansas?* In it he pondered why farmers and blue-collar workers in the Midwest and West are so conservative and tend to vote Republican when the policies of the Democratic Party better suit their social circumstances and economic needs. Voting for Republicans—who stand for tax cuts and cuts to social services, measures that primarily serve the interests of the wealthiest Americans—does not seem to make sense for ordinary folk like them. Thomas was all the more confused because a century ago farmers in these regions voted for left-leaning insurgents such as the Populists, who attacked the banks, railroads, grain merchants, and other elites that exploited them economically. Instead of voting their rational economic interests, Frank lamented, Kansas farmers and workers today vote their "values," following their conservative Christian moral convictions to oppose gay rights, legal abortion, and stem-cell research, and to promote "traditional" roles for women and men, the nuclear family, and an aggressively nationalist foreign policy. Thomas was right in many ways about the change from Populist economics to Republican fiscal conservatism, and he was right to note that the New Deal and Great Society programs had often helped people like these. But Thomas missed the continuity in religious faith and conservative social values. William Jennings Bryan, the great populist and three-time Democratic candidate for president, was a left-leaning pacifist and critic of big business, but he also was a conservative Protestant, religiously, and a moral conservative in his basic values. Thomas wrote about Kansas, but he might equally have set his story in many Plains and Mountain states, from Nebraska and Iowa to Idaho, the Dakotas, Colorado, Montana, and Utah.

The point of this story is what it tells us about the "culture wars" that increasingly have shaped American politics since 1960—between "liberals" or "progressives," on the one side, and "traditionalists" or "conservatives" on the other. People on each side accuse those on the other of hating something (hating America, or hating freedom and equality for all) and of being elitist and authoritarian (socialist and immoral, or reactionary and fascist). If the New Left, counterculture, and anti-traditional politics and social changes seemed to be ascendant in the 1960s and 1970s, in the 1980s, 1990s, and early 2000s the New Right, Moral Majority, and traditionalist political and social movements have gained greater influence. All along, many Americans have been living somewhere in the middle, with moderates and swing voters shifting right or left, in one direction or another, in the ongoing "culture wars." How do we place, for example, a suburban mom who works as a teacher, doctor, office assistant, or lawyer, is suspicious of a bellicose foreign policy that gets America into costly wars, is concerned about clean air and children in impoverished one-parent families, is active in a local church, opposed to abortion, concerned to support stable, "traditional" families, and is anxious about the possibility that terrorism might affect her family?

The culture wars have divided Westerners, as they have all Americans. If Ronald Reagan and George W. Bush symbolize the power of conservatives in the West, cities like San Francisco and Seattle signify the power of progressives. Political commentators often divide the country into "Red states" (Republican) and "Blue states" (Democratic). On the surface, this makes sense. California seems like a Blue state and Texas a Red one. But states like Oregon seem harder to pin down, with liberal cities like Portland and conservative rural areas. A better way, perhaps, to think about "Red" and "Blue" is to focus on localities, not on states. Urban areas tend to vote Democratic, while small towns and rural areas tend to go Republican. Suburbs, exurbs, and edge cities are the "swing" battlegrounds. Affluent suburbanites often have economic assets that might lead them to support Republicans, but their values on social issues, moral questions, and foreign policy range widely. They might support an aggressive foreign policy— e.g., the invasion of Iraq in 2003—but not necessarily want their children to join the armed forces and fight overseas. It is noteworthy, for example, how a state like California is divided. Cities like San Francisco and Los Angeles tend to vote Democratic, but the towns and rural areas of central California and the edge cities of greater LA (e.g., Orange County) tend to go Republican. Texas also has significant support for Democrats in cities such as Austin and Dallas–Fort Worth and among Mexican Americans. One could make a similar point about states like Colorado and Iowa. It is easy but wrong to see simple divisions, such as whites voting Republican and Latinos Democratic. Many Latinos are Christians (Roman Catholics traditionally, with more and more today attending charismatic Protestant churches) and many have conservative values about family life, women's roles, and sexuality. But other issues, such as immigration and social policies, and the nativism of some white Republicans, keep most Mexican Americans in the Democratic Party.

The culture wars in the West run deeper on some issues than others, most notably family life and sexuality. Traditional views of gender roles may reflect the enduring power of frontier ideals of masculinity—visions of men fighting to protect their families and property. But the libertarian legacy of the frontier West also can lead to "live and let live" attitudes about homosexuality and abortion. Likewise, both sides on environmental issues have appealed to the legacy of the frontier wilderness.

It is noteworthy in this regard that Barry Goldwater, the iconic Arizona conservative who served two long stints in the U.S. Senate and was the Republican presidential nominee in 1964, supported gay rights and environmental protection during the later stages of his career and life.

Barack Obama at the Democratic National Convention in Denver, Colorado, August 28, 2008. *Photo by Marc Piscotty*

In the 1990s, he criticized the military's policy of banning lesbians and gay service personnel, called abortion a matter of personal choice, and endorsed an Arizona initiative to legalize marijuana. He even endorsed Karan English, an Arizona Democrat, in her successful bid for Congress in 1992. "While I am a great believer in the free, competitive enterprise system, and all that it entails," Goldwater once said, "I am an even stronger believer in the right of our people to live in a clean and pollution-free environment." Goldwater's views might be compared to those of hunters who defend conservative positions on gun rights but have come to support some preservation policies and oppose unregulated industrial and suburban development because they want to protect wilderness areas. In particular, Goldwater opposed social conservatives, saying in 1994: "When you say 'radical right' today, I think of these moneymaking ventures by fellows like [TV preacher] Pat Robertson and others who are trying to take the Republican Party and make a religious organization out of it. If that ever happens, kiss politics goodbye." In 1960, Goldwater wrote a book entitled *The Conscience of a Conservative*, but he would not have felt at home in the Republican Party of the early twenty-first century. The

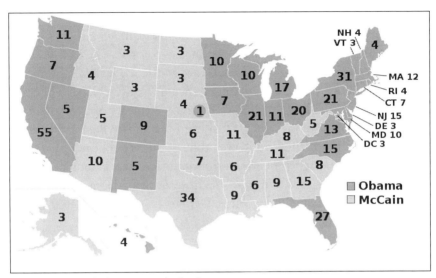

2008 Presidential Election Results by State

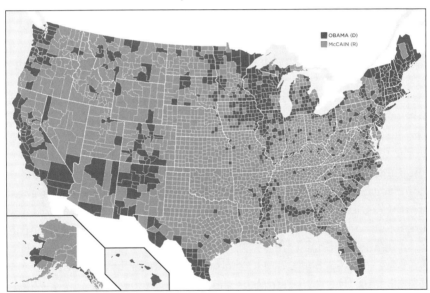

2008 United States Election Results by County

The Result by State map and most news reports suggest that the interior of the West (Mountain West and Plains) voted Republican, with the exception of Colorado, Nevada, and New Mexico, while Pacific coast states voted Democratic. The Results by County map reveals a more complex reality than "Red" versus "Blue" states. However a state as a whole voted, in all of them cities tended to be Democratic, while rural areas and small towns tended to be Republican, with suburbs split between the two parties.

legacy of the frontier West cannot easily be contained and does not follow predictable paths, be they Democratic or Republican.

This unpredictability played out in the election of 2008. Generally reliably Republican states like New Mexico, Nevada, Iowa, and Colorado—along with Western states that normally elect Democrats, such as Oregon, Washington, and California—helped vote into office the first African American president, Democratic candidate Barack Obama, a senator from Illinois. They did so even though the Republican presidential ticket included two self-proclaimed frontier mavericks, a popular senator from Arizona, John McCain, and the governor of Alaska, Sarah Palin. Obama's coattails helped carry other Democrats to office. New Mexico, Colorado, Oregon, and Alaska elected Democrats to Senate seats with Republican incumbents, and Democrats took a half dozen House seats from the Republicans. Although they favored McCain in the presidential race, voters in Montana reelected a Democratic senator and their Democratic governor. Still, the Republicans continued to dominate in Utah, Idaho, and Wyoming (along with most of the South).

Current events and national factors played into the Democratic victories in the West, but long-term trends also loomed large. Many voters blamed the Republican president George W. Bush and a decade of Republican dominance in the Senate and the House of Representatives for an increasingly unpopular war in Iraq and an economy free-falling into deep recession. Some small-government libertarians looked askance at the Republican Party of President Bush and the religious right and were disgruntled with its deficit spending, socially conservative campaigns to combat gay rights and abortion, and big-government policies that seemed to threaten civil liberties. They voted for third-party candidates, stayed home, or voted for Obama, hoping he would run a pragmatic, nonpartisan administration. Latino voters played an even larger role, especially in swing states such as Colorado and Nevada, which have growing Latino populations. The rising numbers and political influence of Latinos likely will solidify Democratic majorities in Western states such as California and may push swing states such as Colorado and New Mexico firmly into Democratic hands. Democratic strategists certainly hope that the election of 2008 heralded a realignment in American politics toward the Democratic Party and the center-left in the West and the nation as a whole. At the very least, 2008 suggested how social trends were changing the cultural and political landscape of the region. It also confirmed Patricia Limerick's argument in a *Wall Street Journal* article on the election, "How the West Will Be Won," that high levels of geographic mobility in the region historically have encouraged weak party identification. If she is right, any realignment toward the Democrats is more likely to be temporary than lasting.

Conclusion

Does it make sense today to talk about the American West as a unified region with a common identity? In *The Nine Nations of North America* (1979), journalist Joel Garreau suggested that national borders do not reflect how North America actually works culturally, economically, and ecologically. He identified "Ecotopia" as a unified region that runs from northern California, through the coastal and mountain sections of Oregon and Washington, and into British Columbia in Canada. Journalists and local leaders have referred to the same region as "Cascadia," a name that reflects the reality of shared progressive and environmentalist values, cross-border economic relations, and related types of economies (high-tech, computing, logging, agriculture, adventure tourism). The Mountain West, stretching from Utah to Alberta, Canada, is defined by oil and mining industries, libertarian economic views, conservative social values, and small-government politics. A third region includes northern Mexico, Southern California, and the Southwest. And a fourth, which Garreau called the "Breadbasket," is the American and Canadian Plains. Garreau did not wholly discount the significance of federal governments and national identities, but his point was to suggest (for example) that oil executives in Denver and Calgary (in Alberta) might well have more in common with each other than with their fellow citizens in other parts of their respective nations. In a recent essay, journalist Robert Kaplan argued that the cultural and economic mixing fostered by globalization is leading to integrated regional identities along the Pacific Rim. He speculated that in some parts of the American and Canadian Wests national identities and loyalty to the nation as a whole will weaken.

Whatever the fate of nationalism in the decades to come, relationships between locale, region, nation, and planet are becoming more fluid and unpredictable. Old mythologies of the West as a place apart are becoming increasingly less tenable. Metropolitan visions of the region, which stress the connections between centers of power and peripheral areas, seem more meaningful, even as those relationships are growing ever more global. If declining rural and small-town communities on the Plains or parts of the mountain West can be labeled peripheral, then cities like Phoenix, LA, Seattle, and Las Vegas are metropolitan centers with global influence, even as they, too, are influenced by New York and Washington, D.C., as well as by Tokyo, Hong Kong, Shanghai, and Beijing, and in the future perhaps by Mexico City and other metropolitan centers in Central and South America.

Suggested Readings

Duncan, Dayton. *Miles from Nowhere: Tales from America's Contemporary Frontier.* New York: Viking, 1993.

Glennon, Robert Jerome. *Water Follies: Groundwater Pumping and the Fate of America's Fresh Waters.* Washington, DC: Island Press, 2004.

Hunter, James Davidson, and Alan Wolfe. *Is There a Culture War? A Dialogue on Values And American Public Life.* Washington, DC: Brookings Institution Press, 2006.

Kaplan, Robert. "Travels into America's Future." *Atlantic Monthly* 282 (August 1998).

Kerstetter, Todd M. *God's Country, Uncle Sam's Land: Faith and Conflict in the American West.* Urbana and Chicago: University of Illinois Press, 2006.

Lang, Robert, Andrea Sarzynski, and Mark Muro. *Mountain Megas: America's Newest Metropolitan Places and a Federal Partnership to Help Them Prosper.* Washington, DC: Brookings Institution, 2008. www.brookings.edu/metro/intermountain_west.aspx

Launius, Roger D. "End of a 40-Year War: Demobilization in the West Coast Aerospace Industry after the Cold War." *Journal of the West* 36 (1997): 85–96.

Limerick, Patricia Nelson. "Going West and Ending Up Global." *Western Historical Quarterly* 32 (2001): 5–23.

Pellow, David, and Lisa Park. *The Silicon Valley of Dreams: Environmental Injustice, Immigrant Workers, and the High-Tech Global Economy.* New York: NYU Press, 2002.

Perlstein, Rick. *Before the Storm: Barry Goldwater and the Unmaking of the American Consensus.* New York: Hill & Wang, 2002.

Power, Thomas Michael, and Richard Barrett. *Post Cowboy Economics: Pay and Prosperity in the New American West.* Washington, DC: Island Press, 2001.

Robb, James J., ed. *Atlas of the New West: Portrait of a Changing Region.* New York: Norton, 1997.

Schlatter, Evelyn A. *Aryan Cowboys: White Supremacists and the Search for a New Frontier, 1970–2000.* Austin: University of Texas Press, 2006.

Schrag, Peter. *Paradise Lost: California's Experience, America's Future.* Berkeley: University of California Press, 1999.

Starr, Kevin. *Coast of Dreams: California on the Edge, 1990–2003.* New York: Knopf, 2004.

Travis, William R. *New Geographies of the American West: Land Use and the Changing Patterns of Place.* Washington, DC: Island Press, 2007.

Water 2025: Preventing Crises and Conflict in the American West. Washington, DC: U.S. Department of the Interior, 2005. http://www.usbr.gov/water2025/

CHAPTER FIFTEEN

Into the Future
and Back to the Past

The story told in this textbook inevitably raises moral and civic questions. Historians often shy away from such questions in the name of objectivity and professional distance, but they need not and probably should not do so. David Harlan lamented in *The Degradation of American History* that once upon a time studying the past "was one of our primary forms of moral reflection." The great historians of previous generations, he claimed, held up "a mirror to our common past." They spoke to people as fellow citizens and encouraged them to reflect on their circumstances morally as a civic community. "This is what we value and want, and don't yet have. This is how we mean to live and do not yet live." Frederick Jackson Turner was no stranger to such a vision of historical study. In an essay he published in 1890, "The Significance of History for Life," he insisted that "the historian strives to show the present to itself by revealing its origin in the past. The goal of the antiquarian is the dead past; the goal of the historian is the living present." Harlan probably overstates the moral influence of historians in the past and underplays the efforts of contemporary historians who do raise moral issues. For example, though they insisted on the need to move the study of the American West beyond Turner's frontier thesis, the New Western Historians also emphasized the need to understand the history of the West in ways that make sense of today's social, political, and envi-

cs **433** so

ronmental challenges. In addition, students and professors address moral and civic issues in the classroom on a regular basis. Many colleges and universities have made history a core liberal arts requirement as part of educating an active and informed citizenry. In short, we cannot but write history with an eye both to the "living present" and to the future that we anticipate, in hope or fear.

In such a spirit, this textbook has raised the question of the fate of the societies and empires that have shaped the region we call the American West. It opened with a comparison of the United States today to pre-Columbian societies that collapsed decades, centuries, and even millennia before Europeans arrived in North America. Will the great monuments to American progress dry up and erode like those of the Anasazi? Will the fabulous casinos of Las Vegas some day be filled only with dust and ghosts, cavernous examples of the hubris of the American empire—like the decaying statue of Ozymandias in Shelley's poem? What about LA, Denver, Seattle, Tulsa, and countless smaller cities and towns in the Mountain West and on the Plains? Will American know-how, or the know-how of people in other parts of the world, lead to new technologies that help people in the twenty-first century—us!—to conquer frontiers of scarcity or environmental degradation in the future? Implied in these questions and in the story told in this book are the responsibilities that Westerners and other Americans (from diverse backgrounds) share towards each other and the land. Will they follow such responsibilities or choose to seek advantages over one another?

Historians are taught not to draw lessons from the past to justify courses of action in the present or to speculate about the future. Certainly we should not come to easy conclusions. But students of history also are citizens who can gain wisdom and perspective by studying the past. We must make decisions today that will affect our own lives as well as those of our children and future generations. With this responsibility in mind, this book concludes by looking from the present into the future and back to the past.

Visions of global warming, waning oil resources, drought, and failing supplies of fresh water suggest the apocalyptic potential of the next half century. Yet simply concluding that the West is doomed offers no ground for action. It is too soon to confirm and date the collapse of American civilization. Moreover, from a historical point of view, we have good reasons to wonder both about apocalyptic scenarios of American decline and environmental collapse and about overly optimistic visions of technological progress fixing the ecological and social problems that Americans have created in the past century. How different are our circumstances today from those of the Anasazi so many centuries ago? How will Americans today and in the future choose to live? What will be the consequences of those choices?

In important ways, Western Americans, the nation as a whole, and humanity around the globe face challenges on a new scale. The West is now part of a truly global social and ecological system created by human activity in the past two centuries, one that has transformed the planet in ways that vary from the simply fascinating (a small shift in the planet's axis from dam building) to the potentially catastrophic (worst-case global-warming scenarios). This book has explored the place of the American West in that story of globalization. When the Anasazi civilization in the Southwest collapsed and scattered because it had extended its irrigation too far to survive a long drought, it affected only a modest regional territory and a small number of people. People then could move on as individuals and in small communities, and the land could recover over time. Today, drought in the American West and growing demand and competition for declining water resources—our "hydraulic civilization"—are part of plan-etwide patterns of global warming, sprawling cities, rising populations, environmental stress, scarce fresh water, and dying seas. News stories in recent years have described predictions by scientists that average annual temperatures in the hottest parts of the West will rise in coming decades. If such a vision seems too apocalyptic, the Dust Bowl of the 1930s, in which wind carried soil from the Great Plains all the way to the Atlantic Ocean, is a small but sobering reminder of what is possible.

Assuming for the moment that the most apocalyptic predictions bear out—and a growing number of sober scientists fear that they will in the next half century or so—it is crucial to stress that the options of Western Americans will be more limited ecologically and geographically than in the past. Science-fiction stories depict new frontiers in outer space, but that is an illusory hope. We are not like our forebears in Europe and eastern parts of North America, who could settle in large numbers on new frontiers in the Americas, Australia, New Zealand, and Africa. People today no longer can pretend to escape history, civilization, and its discontents and start over on some distant frontier. They never could, really, as "new worlds" always had indigenous peoples living in them. But "new world" frontiers often did have vast resources. Today there are no more undiscovered frontiers, no ecological safety valves. Demography makes the point. In 1750, the pre-industrial population of the planet stood at 790 million. In the industrializing era of 1900 it was 1.6 billion. In 2000 it was 6 billion. In 2050 it will be up to 9 billion according to recent projections. There were untapped resources, or at least resources to take, in the past. Reasonable scientists now project crises with oil, fresh water, agricultural land, and forests around the world. The "world" of the Anasazi collapsed in the cultural sense, yet there were still other places to go and other resources to find or take, in a way that is not true, or at least much less true, today—absent *Star Trek*–like technology and distant planets that could be settled.

This last point returns us to mythology—and science fiction. Frontier mythology often has been replayed in space, with space ships, ray guns, and aliens replacing wagon trains, six-shooters, and Indians. The popularity of science fiction points to the ongoing power of frontier mythology, both as a source of entertainment as a dream that reflects human hopes. People still dream of starting over—or at the very least they hope for some undiscovered resource that will fix their problems. Did such dreams ever make sense? Do they today? If Americans today and in the future cannot hope to escape to "new worlds," they will have to address the problems in the one in which they live. The emergence of regional identities in the American West and the diverse motives of Westerners who support the conservation and preservation of natural resources and what we call the wilderness suggest that this lesson is being learned. This would not have surprised Turner, who wrote a good deal about what he called "sectionalism" and "provincialism" later in his career—what we today would call regionalism and regional identities. But regional identities in the West are changing too, and new groups of people call the region home.

So whose home is it? In addition to environmental "challenges," if not full-blown catastrophes, the American West will experience a significant demographic, social, and cultural transformation in the next half century. The political consequences are hard to predict. Whites soon will be a minority in the region, relative to non-whites combined. Latinos of

Mexican and other Central and South American origins will be the largest ethno-cultural group in the region. What will this mean in practical terms, for economic and political relations with Mexico and Latin America? Will Spanish become, in function, a second "official" language in the region? Vigilante border-patrol groups and many other, more mainstream residents of the West have been fighting to prevent precisely such a future. It probably is too much to say that twenty-first-century migration will undo the American conquest of northern Mexico, but, like water wearing down rock, such a demographic process cannot be wholly denied.

History and contemporary trends suggest that the Mexico–United States border is not a "natural" one, environmentally or socially, but neither will the region become strictly Latino. Evidence of ethno-cultural mixing is everywhere, with Latin American, Asian, Anglo-American, African, and European mixing, literally in marriages, and culturally in entertainment, food, and the arts. Likewise, to the north, on a smaller and much less controversial scale, transborder relations and identities are evolving among residents of border states and Canadian provinces. Such regional changes, from Central America and northern Mexico to Western Canada, are combining with globalization and the emergence of a Pacific Rim economy and culture to change the American West. If the Atlantic Ocean and relations with the great societies of the Northern Hemisphere once defined American history, in the next century it may be the Pacific Ocean and the global South. Distant places like Washington, D.C., New York City, and the eastern states in general, let alone far distant Europe, may become less significant to the West than metropolitan centers in Latin America and Asia. It is hard to predict and merely informed speculation, but such a future puts the past in a different light, especially in a rethinking of the history of the American West with those of Mexico, Central and South America, China, and other parts of Asia in mind.

The story of the West, then, would be told with continuities with Mexico and China emphasized, treating them as more important to the story, equal in importance to the empires of Europe and the metropolitan centers of the eastern United States. Europe and the eastern United States would remain important to the story, of course, but they would no longer define it. Positing such a change is a reminder, again, of how easily the first residents of the West—Native Americans—were pushed to the side. What would their place be in this new telling of the story?

Tourists visiting the "Cliff Palace" in Mesa Verde National Park, Colorado, June 28, 2008. It housed a flourishing Anasazi community from the 500s to the 1200s AD and had over 150 rooms and 75 open areas. *Photographer: Massimo Catarinella, Wikipedia Commons*

Such changes—potential ones, perhaps likely ones—must be seen in relation to the environmental problems the region will face. Will competition for scarce natural resources such as water and a struggle to afford food, housing, and clean air exacerbate social and political conflicts over the cultural and ethnic identity of the region? Global warming and its effects will create refugees in many parts of the world, possibly including parts of the United States—as drought makes some areas unlivable and the flooding of coastal areas because of rising sea levels forces people to flee. Will people in some parts of the American West feel the pressure to accept refugees? Will the region serve as a refuge? Or will it contribute to the problem, if cities on the Pacific Coast flood or vast stretches of the Southwest dry up under rising temperatures and declining water resources? Will water-rich American states and Canadian provinces resist pressure to accept massive water-diversion projects to aid dry states and provinces? Will a tragic synergy between social-cultural conflicts (say, between Latinos and Anglos) and environmental factors lead to vigilante violence and even military conflict? Scholars and journalists have argued that the wars of the next century—in Asia, Latin America, and Africa—will not be fought over oil but water. Such conflicts already have taken place in countries such as Sudan in the early twenty-first century. What about the American West of the near future? (As Chapter Fourteen noted, the U.S. Department of the Interior and Bureau of Reclamation have been planning to address precisely such conflicts in the West.) If such a prospect seems far fetched, remember the battles between the city of Los Angeles and the people of the Owens Valley a century ago. That was a small conflict. Imagine much larger conflicts like it played out in the American West and around the world.

All empires fall or at least decline in power. American dominance globally will not last, and the status of its Western region will change as a result. Some parts of the region may become more powerful should Washington, D.C., and the federal government weaken. But the West also will be influenced more than ever by global trade, investment, and migration. It is too soon and too fatalistic to predict the collapse of American civilization a half-century from now, but students of history in the future may point to a transition *in* American history, or *from* American history into a new civilization akin to the transition and assimilation of portions of the Spanish, French, and British empires into the "American" West. What would such a post–American West look like? Would its residents think of themselves as citizens of a state, a region, America, the Americas, or the world? Would any such new identities be signs of decline or progress?

For all the new things prospective changes might entail, they also will invariably suggest a significant continuity with the past. The West was never an isolated frontier; it always was shaped by people on the move, interacting with each other via trade, migration, and war, even in pre-Columbian times. And it will not be an isolated region in the future. As ever, though more than ever, the West will be a part of the larger world. This point may sound like a cliché, but there is a truth in it that our experiences today drive home. This contemporary perspective can help us to illuminate the past; in turn, the past understood with such global connections in mind can help us to illuminate the complexities of the present, as Turner urged in his essay back in 1890. As students of history, we can and should look back and forth, between past and present, and with an eye to our own future and that of the next generation of global citizens in the American West.

With this in mind, we might give Turner the last word. In 1914, he gave a commencement address at the University of Washington entitled "The West and American Ideals." "In the place of old frontiers of wilderness," Turner suggested to the graduates, "there are new frontiers of unwon fields of science, fruitful for the needs of the race; there are frontiers of better social domains yet unexplored. Let us hold to our attitude of faith and courage, and creative zeal. Let us dream as our fathers dreamt and let us make our dreams come true." Turner's words sound out of time today. Certainly his assumptions about race and gender are out of date. Does his faith in science seem so too? How about his talk of faith, courage, and dreams? He was speaking to university graduates. Imagine yourself in the not-too-distant future listening to words like this. What will you think: Sentimental nonsense? A hopeful spirit? A challenge to seize? A long shot, but better than giving up?

Whose West is it? The question may seem to transcend time, but the answer never does. Nor does the sting of it. Whose West has it been? Whose West will it be? The only thing we can be sure of, history tells us, is that it will change.

Suggested Readings

Abbott, Carl. *Frontiers Past and Future: Science Fiction and the American West.* Lawrence: University Press of Kansas, 2006.

Katerberg, William. *Future West: Utopia and Apocalypse in Frontier Science Fiction.* Lawrence: University Press of Kansas, 2008.

Travis, William R., David M. Theobald, Geneva W. Mixon, and Thomas W. Dickinson. *Western Futures: A Look into the Patterns of Land Use and Future Development in the American West.* Boulder: Center of the West, University of Colorado at Boulder, 2005. http://www.centerwest.org/futures/

Index

Note: An italic page number indicates a map or photograph.

Conquests & Consequences: The American West from Frontier to Region
Developmental editor and copy editor: Andrew J. Davidson
Production editor: Linda Gaio
Indexer: Pat Rimmer
Proofreader: Claudia Siler
Cartographer: Jason Casanova, Pegleg Graphics
Typesetter: Bruce Leckie
Printer: McNaughton & Gunn

ABOUT THE AUTHORS

Carol L. Higham
University of North Carolina at Charlotte

Carol L. Higham is an independent scholar who has taught at Winona State University, Texas A&M University, Davidson College, and the University of North Carolina–Charlotte. Her first book, *Noble, Wretched and Redeemable,* examined missionary attitudes toward Indians in the Canadian and U. S. Wests. She then edited two comparative textbooks, *One West, Two Myths.* Currently, she is writing a book on myths about Indians as cannibals in Western North America.

Photo by Bill Giduz, Davidson College

William H. Katerberg
Calvin College

William H. Katerberg is an associate professor of history and director of the Dirk and JoAnn Mellema Program in Western American Studies at Calvin College in Grand Rapids, Michigan. His research focuses on national identity, religion, popular culture, and the West in North America. His published work includes *Modernity and the Dilemma of North American Anglican Identities, 1880-1950* (2001); *The Future of Hope: Christian Tradition amid Modernity and Postmodernity,* co-edited with Miroslav Volf (2004); *Future West: Utopia and Apocalypse in Frontier Science Fiction* (2008); and essays on the history and culture of the North American West in *Western American Literature* and *The American Review of Canadian Studies.* He is currently working on projects on political extremism in the United States since World War II and on violence and power in the North American West.